standard catalog of® U.S.
MILITARY VEHICLES"

David Doyle

Published by

Krause Publications, a division of F+W Media, Inc.
700 East State Street • Iola, WI 54990-0001
715-445-2214 • 888-457-2873
www.krausebooks.com

To order books or other products call toll-free 1-800-258-0929
or visit us online at www.krausebooks.com or www.Shop.Collect.com

Library of Congress Control Number: 2004273750

ISBN-13: 978-0-87349-508-0
ISBN-10: 0-87349-508-X

Edited Brian Earnest
Designed Brian Brogaard

Printed in the United States of America

To Everette and Joyce. For instilling a respect and interest in history, and understanding of mechanics, thanks Dad, and for tolerating the folly of her boys, thanks Mom.

ACKNOWLEDGEMENTS

This book would not have been possible without the generous help of the following individuals and organizations:

Candace Fuller and Charles Lemons with the Patton Museum at Fort Knox, Kentucky, spent hours answering questions and pointing me in the right direction in my never-ending quest for photographs.

Ann Bos and Randy Talbot with the U.S. Army Tank-automotive and Armaments Command History Office allowed me access to their photo files, which yielded many of the previously unpublished photographs.

My friend, John Adams-Graf, editor of *Military Vehicles Magazine*, who used his skills as a talented photographer to provide not only the color cover photos, but the interior color photos as well. But especially for his unflagging friendship and support during this project.

Tripp Jones, Max May, and Roy Coates and the rest of the staff at Memphis Equipment gave me unfettered access to their knowledge, facilities, and library.

My family, who not only endured photo-taking and archive digging excursions while on vacations, but also provided support throughout this task.

Francis Blake and Robin Markey provided photos and information regarding Harley-Davidson and Indian motorcycles, respectively. Lee Rudd spent an afternoon allowing me to photograph his beautifully restored motorcycles.

My friend, Bruce Gray, spent two hot days rolling his vehicle collection out of storage for me to photograph for this book.

Tom Loetzbeier of the Mack Truck Historical Museum provided needed production facts, specifications, and photographs of various Mack-built trucks.

Herb Muktarian of United Defense Ground Systems Division provided photos and other materials.

Thanks to Brian Earnest with Krause Publications, who guided me through the construction of my first book, and reined me in when I began to go too far astray in my research.

Craig MacNab with AM General provided extensive background information and photos of the HMMWV family of vehicles.

Fred Crismon generously provided copies of historic documents, and Richard Hunnicutt's vast collection provided several new photos.

Richard Adelman, Bryce Sunderlin, Nelson Dionne, Cecil Jones, the Diebold Safe and Lock Company, Evelyn Harless, Reg Hodgson, Don Moss, Ron Grasso, Joe Shannon, Ken Whowell, Steve Keith, Jeff Symanski with Tacticaltruck.com, Mark Dodd of Rapco, Steve Zaloga, Denise Moss, Shane G. Deemer of Military Rails Online, and Bruce Kubu all contributed photos or information without which this volume would have been badly lacking.

Larry Roberts with the United States Army Engineer School History Office, Fort Leonard Wood, Missouri, dug up several newly discovered photos for inclusion in this volume.

Also thanks to Richard Grace, Jim Davis, Gordon McMillan, Ralph Moir, and Daryl Bensinger.

My mother, Joyce Doyle, and my friend, Denise Moss, not only willingly gave untold hours proofreading this book, but also provided needed encouragement and support during its compilation.

CONTENTS

CONTENTS

SECTION THREE: TRACKLAYING VEHICLES

INTRODUCTION

While this new edition of *The Standard Catalog of U.S. Military Vehicles* is built upon the foundation laid by Tom Berndt in the first edition, it has been completely revised. Every entry in every chapter has been rewritten and expanded. While the U.S. Armed Forces have fielded quite an array of vehicles, both wheeled and tracked, it would be impossible to chronicle all of them in a single volume that one could hold in their hands. Rather, this edition covers those vehicles most often sought after or encountered by the collector. Because most vehicles of primarily civilian design are of limited interest to collectors (staff cars and certain trucks, such as the Ford F-5 1 1/2-ton 4x2 truck), they have been omitted from this edition.

ORGANIZATION

You will hopefully find the organization of this book easy to follow and user friendly. All chapters are written in a similar manner, and begin with an overview of the subject manner. Separate appendices examine weapons mountings used on an array of vehicles, as well as the paint and marking of U.S. Army vehicles from World War II through Desert Storm.

The remainder of each chapter concentrates on a specific class of vehicle, and within each chapter vehicles are grouped by series. For most wheeled vehicles, I have used the G-number assigned to each chassis type by the Standard Nomenclature list of the War Department. These series are then broken down further into specific models (as an example, the M37 cargo truck and M43 ambulance are both members of the G-740 class, and are basically the same mechanically).

DETERMINING VALUE AND RARITY

There are often seemingly infinite variations of vehicles even of the same model. Add to this factors such as condition, the relative knowledge of the buyer and the seller, the seller's desire to sell, and the buyer's desire to buy, and it is easy to see why putting together a blue book of prices is almost impossible. The pricing shown in this edition is a result of averaging the responses of several dealers and collectors in an attempt to represent a reasonable value for a given vehicle. Some vehicles are so rarely traded that it is impractical to attempt to establish a market value, either because of scarcity or current military usage. These vehicles are noted as NRS, no reported sales.

One other major factor in determining value is through vehicle material (OVM) or basic issue items (BIIL). This can range from a jack, lug wrench, and a few basic hand tools for an MB Jeep, to a list of hundreds of tools carried on contact maintenance trucks. In some cases, the value of the OVM can

exceed the value of the base vehicle. To be considered in the top grade, a vehicle must include all the BIIL equipment required to be deemed mission ready by the military.

Rarity is, of course, initially driven by production quantity and also by survivability and accessibility. Production of four-wheel-steer GP quarter-ton trucks was originally low, so they are inherently hard to find. Production of GOER vehicles was much higher, but the demilitarization standard applied to them by the Department of Defense has significantly reduced the number of survivors. Many of the Bantam Reconnaissance cars were supplied under lend-lease to Russia, and while their survivability is unknown, their accessibility is nil.

Rarity is not synonymous with value, and demand has as much influence on price as rarity. There are more MB/GPWs available than CCKW tanker trucks, but the Jeep fetches more money. Many of the vehicles in this book are rated on a rarity scale of 1 through 5, with 1 being the most common (M-37, for example), and 5 being the scarcest (M-386 rocket launcher, for example). Vehicles that existed in only prototype or extremely limited production quantities (Willys TUG for example) are omitted because they are not a significant part of the marketplace.

CONDITION

Not only does condition affect the price of a given vehicle, it also affects its collectibility. Another factor closely related is the quality of restoration. A preserved vehicle is maintained in a "state of suspended animation." All the flaws, scratches, and rust present when the vehicle is "discovered" are preserved. While this style of collecting is more popular overseas than in this country, it is commonplace in other areas of collecting, such as furniture.

The term "restoration" is often ill defined or improperly used in the military vehicle hobby. What some call a restoration is actually a representation, and sadly, is sometimes only a characterization. For a true military vehicle restoration, one must know the history of that particular vehicle. Once known, it is then important to define what time frame the vehicle is to be restored to. This could be as it appeared as it left the factory, or at any subsequent time (June 6, 1944, March 3, 1952, etc.). Because the military constantly is improving, upgrading, and modifying its vehicles, the date you wish to return to must be defined. For example, while G-742 cargo trucks were used during the Korean conflict, none of them had composite-type taillights at that time. To be restored to factory condition, a vehicle would need to have all the equipment supplied at the factory, but no more. Ambulances, for instance, didn't leave the factory outfitted with equipment and medical supplies, nor did Jeeps leave the plant with machine guns and deep-water fording pipes installed.

Many people also don't understand the difference between a restoration and a representation. A representation could mean rebuilding and painting and marking a Jeep to represent the one your grandfather drove into Paris, even though the Jeep you own never left North America. While not a true restoration, this type of representation is the most popular with collectors.

Some people think that a paint job alone qualifies as a restoration, and unfortunately that often isn't even done right (how many M-38s have you seen with invasion stars painted on them?). That is what is referred to as a characterization—it looks at a glance like something that it is not.

Some of these modifications are done from a safety standpoint, such as turn signals or safety belts. These safety-based modifications are normally overlooked by judges at shows.

Whenever possible, the vehicles illustrated in this book, if not in archival photos, are vehicles that have been restored to as-built condition. Any known discrepancies are noted in the captions

WHICH VEHICLE IS FOR YOU?

The size and weight of components relative to your facilities should obviously be considered when contemplating a purchase. Likewise, while most wheeled vehicles can be considered self-transporting, tracklaying vehicles almost always must be hauled to events for display, and have other unique problems, which are covered in the introduction to the tracked vehicles section.

Another factor to consider is what type of collection you desire to build. Do you want one of each model of Jeep vehicle built, or do you want to collect vehicles used in the Vietnam War?

Finally, when considering the purchase of a vehicle, give some thought to what grade of vehicle you wish to own. Shop and value vehicles accordingly, just as a factory-fresh appearing vehicle is probably not the best choice for a re-enactor, if you are all thumbs mechanically, a work-in-progress wouldn't be for you.

VEHICLE CONDITION SCALE

The vehicles in this book are given a value grade based on a 1-to-6 condition grading scale:

1=Excellent: Restored to maximum professional standards, or a near-perfect original.

2=Fine: Well-restored or a combination of superior restoration and excellent original parts.

3=Very Good: Complete and operable original or older restoration, or a very good amateur restoration with all presentable and serviceable parts inside and out.

4=Good: Functional or needing only minor work to be functional. Also, a deteriorated restoration or poor amateur restoration.

5=Restorable: Needs complete restoration of body, chassis, and interior. May or may not be running, but is not wrecked, weathered, or stripped to the point of being useful only for parts.

6=Parts Vehicle: Deteriorated beyond the point of restoration.

Section One:
WHEELED VEHICLES

MOTORCYCLES

G-523 Harley-Davidson WLA

The Harley-Davidson WLA is the most popular military motorcycle among collectors. However, the common name WLA is only part of the model number. There were 40-WLA, 41-WLA, 42-WLA, and other models, each slightly different. These bikes were basically a given year's civilian WL modified with the addition of military items.

The 42-WLA is what most collectors are referring to when they say "WLA." It included such military gear as a scabbard for a Thompson submachine gun on the right side of the front fork, blackout lights on the front and rear, a crankcase skid plate, and a substantial luggage rack.

The headlight was mounted on the front fender, with a small blackout light in front of it, and the electric horn was located above the headlight. Just to the driver's left of the headlight was the blackout driving light.

The spark advance was on the left handlebar, as was the front brake control, horn button, and rearview mirror. On the right handlebar was the throttle. A foot pedal on the right side of the motorcycle controlled the rear wheel brake.

The tank had two compartments — the right side holding crankcase oil, the left side gasoline. In the center of the tank were the speedometer and light switches.

The power plant was the classic 45-cid Harley-

This early 41WLA is equipped with a winter windshield. Notice the position of the headlight compared to later models, and the optional leg shields mounted just behind the crash bars. (Photo courtesy of Fran Blake collection)

Later production 41WLAs did away with the two-person buddy seat, replacing it with a solo seat. (Photo courtesy of Fran Blake collection)

The same WLA bike from another angle. The muffler used on these early bikes was the standard civilian item. Notice the long buddy saddle that was installed on early models. (Photo courtesy of Fran Blake collection)

As the war progressed, subtle changes were made in the 41WLA. The front fender was simplified, becoming little more than a curved piece of sheet metal. Harley-Davidson began to paint crankcases black, whereas previously they were unpainted. (Photo courtesy of Fran Blake collection)

MOTORCYCLES

Davidson 45-degree V-twin, which used a right side-mounted chain to drive the bike to speeds up to 70 mph.

This is a very rare 50WLA. It may be the only 50WLA ever built. Notice how the headlight has moved back to the upper position, and the taillight and muffler have been changed once again. (Photo courtesy of Fran Blake collection)

GENERAL DATA

MODEL	WLA
WEIGHT	513 lbs.
LENGTH	88 in.
WIDTH	36.25
HEIGHT	59 in.
WHEELBASE	50.75
TIRE SIZE	4.0-18
MAX SPEED	70 mph
FUEL CAPY	3 3/8 gal
RANGE	124 miles
ELECTRICAL	6 neg
TRANSMISSION	
SPEEDS	3
TURNING	
RADIUS FT	7 right 7.5 left

ENGINE DATA

ENGINE MAKE/MODEL	Harley-Davidson WLA
NUMBER OF CYLINDERS	45-degree V-2
CUBIC INCH DISPLACEMENT	45
HORSEPOWER	23 @ 4600 rpm
TORQUE	28 lbs..-ft. @ 3000 rpm
GOVERNED SPEED (rpm)	Not governed

VALUES

	6	5	4	3	2	1
WLA	2,000	5,000	10,000	13,000	17,000	20,000

SCARCITY

Scarcity 2

The box mounted on the fork of this 41WLA was used to store ammunition for the operator's submachine gun. Notice the cylindrical oil bath air cleaner just ahead of the rear wheel. (Photo courtesy of Fran Blake collection)

This overhead view of an early 41WLA shows the cut-out in the luggage rack. During tire-changing operations, the rear fender hinged upwards and the notch accepted the taillight. The upper filler on the tank is for oil, the lower for gasoline. (Photo courtesy of Fran Blake collection)

This is the machine most commonly associated with U.S. military motorcycles: the 42WLA. Notice the repositioned headlight. Also, the 42WLA had the rectangular oil bath air filter shown here instead of the somewhat fragile canister type used previously. (Photo courtesy of Fran Blake collection)

The 52WLA was the last of this classic product line. Only a few hundred of these were built, and they differed in details from the WWII production. The easiest way to distinguish the later production is their reversed shift pattern. (Photo courtesy of Fran Blake collection)

G-524 Indian 340-B

The 340-B was the big Indian, roughly equivalent to the Harley-Davidson models U and UA. In military service they were occasionally seen with their sidecar removed. These motorcycles were militarized versions of Indian's civilian Chief model. About 3,000 of these were supplied to the U.S. military, and another 5,000 had been supplied to France before that country fell.

GENERAL DATA

MODEL	340-B
WEIGHT	550 lbs..
WHEELBASE	62 in.
TIRE SIZE	4.5-18 in.
MAX SPEED	75 mph
FUEL CAPY	3.5 gal
ELECTRICAL	6 neg

ENGINE DATA

ENGINE MAKE/MODEL	Indian
NUMBER OF CYLINDERS	V-2
CUBIC-INCH DISPLACEMENT	74
HORSEPOWER	40

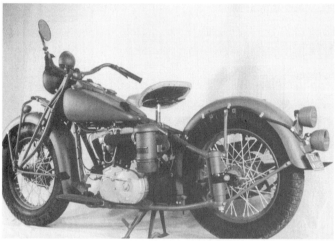

This particular 340-B was assembled by Robin Markey using essentially all NOS parts. Notice the blackout and taillights mounted on the rear fender above the vintage license plate. (Photo courtesy of Robin Markey)

Even without the sidecar, the 340-B is a big bike. In civilian form these bikes had skirts on their fenders and extensive chrome. (Photo courtesy of Robin Markey)

Here is a 340-B as delivered, with sidecar in place. The horn can be seen above the headlight. (Photo courtesy of Robin Markey)

VALUES

	6	5	4	3	2	1
340-B	5,000	10,000	16,000	25,000	30,000	35,000

Values above assume presence of sidecar.

SCARCITY

Scarcity 4

The oil-bath air cleaner and the rearview mirror can both be seen on the left-hand side of the bike in this overhead view. (Photo courtesy of Robin Markey)

G-524 Indian 640-B

The Indian model 640-B was essentially a militarized version of Indian's civilian Sport Scout. The 640-B used a 45-cid engine, and thus was considerably more powerful than the more common Model 741-B. While the 640-B was most commonly used as a single bike, a few of the 2,500 produced were equipped with sidecars.

GENERAL DATA

MODEL	640-B
WEIGHT	485 lbs.
LENGTH	58 in.
TIRE SIZE	4.00-18 in.
MAX SPEED	75 mph
FUEL CAP.	3.7 gal
ELECTRICAL	6 neg
TRANSMISSION	
SPEEDS	3

ENGINE DATA

ENGINE MAKE	Indian
NUMBER OF CYLINDERS	V-2
CUBIC-INCH DISPLACEMENT	45
HORSEPOWER	22

VALUES

	6	5	4	3	2	1
640-B	2,500	5,000	11,000	15,000	20,000	25,000

SCARCITY

Scarcity 3

This 640-B has been restored to represent a motorcycle that had a sidecar added to it by a field maintenance unit. Such modifications were not uncommon, and greatly increase the usefulness of the motorcycle to the collector. (Photo courtesy of the Robin Markey collection)

This soldier on prewar maneuvers relaxes on a break across his heavily stowed Indian 640-B. The widespread use of the Jeep greatly reduced the anticipated role of the motorcycles in the U.S. military. (Photo courtesy of the Robin Markey collection)

G-524 Indian 741-B

From 1941 to 1943 Springfield, Massachusetts-based Indian produced about 35,000 741-B motorcycles for military use. Primarily used by foreign nations, the 741-B was nevertheless the military Indian model produced in the greatest quantities.

The 741-B was powered by an Indian GDA-101 two-cylinder, 90-degree, 30.5-cid V-engine producing 15 hp, which drove the bike through a three-speed transmission. The bikes were equipped with leather saddlebags and a leather submachine gun scabbard. A metal ammunition box was attached to the left front fork. The stoplight was mounted on the rear fender, and the rear blackout marker light was mounted below it. The front blackout marker was mounted on the front fender, and the headlight was mounted above it.

GENERAL DATA

MODEL	741-B
WEIGHT	513 lbs..
LENGTH	88 in.
WIDTH	34 in.
HEIGHT	40 in.
TIRE SIZE	3.50-18 in.
MAX SPEED	65 mph
FUEL CAPY	3 gal
RANGE	90 miles
ELECTRICAL	6 neg
TRANSMISSION SPEEDS	3

ENGINE DATA

ENGINE MAKE/MODEL	Indian GDA-101
NUMBER OF CYLINDERS	V-2
CUBIC-INCH DISPLACEMENT	30.5
HORSEPOWER	15 @ 4200 rpm

VALUES

	6	5	4	3	2	1
741-B	2,000	5,000	10,000	13,000	17,000	20,000

SCARCITY

Scarcity 3

The kick-starter pedal on this 741-B is clearly visible, as is the gearshift lever. The shift lever of the 741-B could be located on either side of the tank. (Photo from the collection of Robin Markey and Bob's Indian Sales and Service)

The horn of the 741-B was mounted below the tank and just ahead of the engine. Like the early Harley-Davidson WLAs, the 741-B used a rectangular oil-bath air cleaner. (Photo from the collection of Robin Markey and Bob's Indian Sales and Service)

The leather submachine gun scabbard was mounted on the left side of the front fork, while the ammunition box was on the right side of the fork. The ammo box on this 741-B has been bar coded for the 1st Infantry Division, 26th Infantry. These barcodes were used during the Normandy invasion. (Photo from the collection of Robin Markey and Bob's Indian Sales and Service)

G-585 Harley-Davidson XA

The Harley-Davidson Model XA was a copy of the German BMW R71 military motorcycle. The advantage foreseen was the elimination of the chain and its associated maintenance, especially in a desert environment. The 1,000 XAs built all featured shaft-drive, which was unusual for American bikes at the time. The 23-hp, 45-cid engine, unlike the classic Harley V-twin design, used an opposed-piston design and featured a carburetor for each cylinder.

While the performance of the XA was adequate, critics said it unnecessarily diverted production facilities and introduced more parts into the supply chain. Production of the XA lasted from 1941 to 1943.

MOTORCYCLES

GENERAL DATA

MODEL	**XA**
WEIGHT NET	525 lbs.
WHEELBASE	59 1/2 in.
TIRE SIZES	4.00-18 in.
FUEL CAPY	4.5
ELECTRICAL	6 volt
SPEEDS	4 fwd

ENGINE DATA

ENGINE MAKE/MODEL	**Harley-Davidson**
NUMBER OF CYLINDERS	2
CUBIC-INCH DISPLACEMENT	45
HORSEPOWER	23

VALUES

	6	5	4	3	2	1
XA	2,500	5,000	11,000	15,000	20,000	30,000

SCARCITY

Scarcity 5

This Harley-Davidson XA was photographed during WWII at Ft. Knox, Kentucky. Lt. John E. Harley directed motorcycle training there in 1942. The head of the horizontally opposed engine is visible just ahead of the rider's leg. (Photo courtesy of the Patton Museum)

G-631 Indian 841

The Indian Model 841 was Indian's response to the Army's desire for a shaft-driven motorcycle similar to the BMW R71. The 45-cid Scout engine was modified with the cylinder angle spread from 45 degrees to 90 degrees and the engine rotated so that the crankshaft was to the rear. The resultant engine was much smoother running than other Indian engines.

The Model 841 featured a new four-speed foot-shift gearbox developed specially for use with shaft drive. Unfortunately, the gearbox was hard to shift and trouble prone. The 841's frame and final drive were essentially copies of the BMW R71's components, but Indian designed all new front forks made from tapered, oval cross-section tubing.

While the shaft-drive motorcycles — the Indian 841 and the Harley-Davidson XA — were developed for desert warfare, neither ever saw action. Indian manufactured just over 1,000 841 models to fulfill the prototype contract, but the sole military use of these motorcycles

Among the most sought-after Indian military motorcycles is the shaft-driven model 841. The shaft drives were developed based on the BMW R71 idea, and were intended for desert use. However, the widespread use of the Jeep precluded their deployment. Robin Markey is astride this beautifully restored example. Notice the cylinder heads protruding just ahead of his knees on either side. (Photo from the collection of Robin Markey and Bob's Indian Sales and Service)

was for testing. The vast majority of the production run was sold as surplus without ever leaving the Indian warehouse in Springfield, Massachusetts.

GENERAL DATA

MODEL	841
WEIGHT	550 lbs.
MAX SPEED	75 mph
ELECTRICAL	6 neg
TRANSMISSION	
SPEEDS	4

ENGINE DATA

ENGINE MAKE	Indian
NUMBER OF CYLINDERS	V-2, 90-degree
CUBIC-INCH DISPLACEMENT	45

VALUES

	6	5	4	3	2	1
841	2,500	5,000	11,000	15,000	20,000	30,000

SCARCITY

Scarcity 5

G-680 Harley-Davidson U&UA

The Harley-Davidson U was a civilian Harley-Davidson prewar bike powered by Harley's 74-cid flathead engine. This "Big Twin" Harley was considerably larger than the more common WLA. The additional power afforded by the larger engines allowed these motorcycles to be fitted with sidecars, and they often were. When sidecar equipped they are sometimes referred to as model US. The Navy procured some of these sidecar-equipped model U bikes and employed them with the Shore Patrol, among other things.

The Army also liked the Big Twin, and purchased some as well. These were designated model UA. Differences between the military and civilian models were limited as these machines were intended to be used

The Harley-Davidson Model U was originally designed and marketed as a civilian motorcycle. However, a limited number of these were acquired by the U.S. Navy and supplied to the Shore Patrol. Lee Rudd has restored the beautiful U shown in these photos.

The additional power of the U, compared to the WLA, was used to propel the bike and sidecar. While civilian U models were adorned with chrome, the military bikes were rather plain.

Both the U and UA carried a spare tire on the rear of the sidecar. These sidecars were not built by Harley-Davidson, but were supplied to Harley by an outside contractor.

only in rear areas. They lack the characteristic black-out lighting and large gun scabbard and ammo box of the WLA.

Sidecar-equipped examples often carried a spare tire on the rear of the sidecar. The sidecar's windshield was hinged and could be tilted forward to allow the passenger to get in and out.

Despite appearances, very few parts interchange between the U series and the WLA.

The tank had two compartments. The right side held crankcase oil, the left side gasoline. In the center of the tank were the speedometer and light switches.

GENERAL DATA

MODEL	U & UA
WEIGHT	850 lbs.
LENGTH	95
WIDTH	69
HEIGHT	42
WHEELBASE	59.5
TIRE SIZE	4.50-18
MAX SPEED	55 mph
ELECTRICAL	6 neg
TRANSMISSION	
SPEEDS	3

Overall dimensions listed in inches.

ENGINE DATA

ENGINE MAKE/MODEL Harley-Davidson U
NUMBER OF CYLINDERS   45-degree V-2
CUBIC-INCH DISPLACEMENT   74

VALUES

	6	5	4	3	2	1
UA	3,000	7,000	20,000	29,000	37,000	45,000

SCARCITY

Scarcity 4

The fuel and oil fillers, instrument panel, and mirror of the U can be seen in this view.

The canister-type oil bath air cleaner and chain drive are visible here. The U and UA models did not use saddlebags, but certain foreign sales bikes had skirted fenders.

The connection and suspension utilized by sidecar-equipped bikes is shown in this photo a model U.

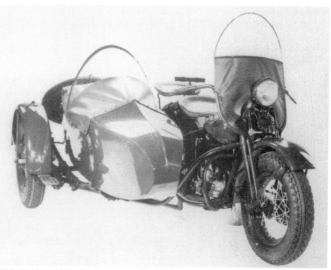

This is the builder's photo of a Harley-Davidson model UA. The particular machine was supplied to the U.S. Marine Corps. (Photo courtesy of Francis Blake collection)

This UA is set up for maximum personnel transportation, with a sidecar, operator's seat, and the tandem seat behind the operator's seat. (Photo courtesy of Francis Blake collection)

QUARTER-TON TRUCKS

Bantam BRC

While the is much debate over the origin of the term "Jeep," there is little argument among scholars that the vehicle known by that name was originated by the American Bantam Car Co. of Butler, Pennsylvania. While Karl Probst is widely credited with the design of the Jeep, more recent research indicates that Probst was a late addition to Bantam's own engineering team, which included Harold Crist, Ralph Turner, and Chet Hemphling. Crist and Hemphling were later involved in Mid-America Research Corporation's development of a later vehicle, which became the Mighty-Mite. Crist was instrumental in ensuring that the first Bantam was constructed in just 47 days, and two days later he drove it to Camp Holabird, near Baltimore.

MODEL 60

Following approval of the prototype, and after a few modifications, 69 more pre-production units were built, with eight of these being four-wheel steer models. All of these were completed by December 17, 1940. These original Bantams, known as the Bantam Model 60, had a rounded grill and fenders.

The Bantam Reconnaissance Car was placed into series production with an order for 1500 units. These vehicles were known as the BRC-40. With the appearance of the BRC-40, the Jeep had arrived.

Shown here is arguably the original Jeep, the prototype Bantam Reconnaissance Car. Notice the scalloped cutouts for crew access and the curved fenders and separate protruding headlights without brush guards. All these features that were eliminated when the first 75 pre-production units were built. The massive 4x4 beside it is a 5-ton prototype artillery tractor built by Oshkosh. (U.S. Army photo)

BRC-40

The second batch of Bantam's was an order for 1500 vehicles, which were constructed in the period March 10 through July 2, 1941. These and succeeding units built by Bantam were known as BRC-40s. Before production commenced on these vehicles the design was changed to incorporate a flat hood and grill and a two-piece windshield. All the Bantams were powered by the 48 horsepower Continental Y-4112 6-cylinder engine.

According to testimony of Francis Fenn, Bantam president, before the Truman committee, in addition to the 8 four-wheel-steer Model 60s, there were 50 four-wheel-steer BRC-40s built. Bantam's third and last order for reconnaissance cars was for only 1175 units, and work was completed on them in December 1941. Bantam produced torpedoes for the Royal Navy, and thousands of their 1/4 on T-3 trailers for use behind Jeeps, but sadly after December 1941 their days of producing the 1/4 ton reconnaissance vehicle they pioneered was done.

The underside of the floor of the earliest of the BRC-40s were made of corrugated steel, while later models used conventional flat sheet metal and hat channel construction. Other variations between early and late BRC-40s included the use of a curved shift lever on the early models, and a reinforcing fillet on the windshield hinge dogleg on the later production units.

GENERAL DATA

MODEL	BRC-40
GROSS WEIGHT	2,600 lbs.
LENGTH	126
WIDTH	54
HEIGHT TOP UP	72
TRACK	47.5
TIRE SIZE	5.50-16
MAX SPEED	55 mph
FUEL CAPY	10 gal
RANGE	165 mi
ELECTRICAL	6 neg
TRANSMISSION SPEEDS	3
TRANSFER SPEEDS	2

Overall dimensions listed in inches.

ENGINE DATA

ENGINE MAKE/MODEL	Continental BY 4112
NUMBER OF CYLINDERS	4
CUBIC-INCH DISPLACEMENT	112
HORSEPOWER	45 @ 3500 rpm

VALUES

	6	5	4	3	2	1
All models	3,500	9,000	15,000	22,000	28,000	34,000

SCARCITY

Scarcity 5

The 69 vehicles that were built on the pilot contract were known as the Bantam Model 60. This one was photographed at Aberdeen Proving Grounds in March 1941 outfitted with a machine gun. The scalloped doorway of the prototype has been replaced with a simpler opening, just as the elaborate fenders have been replaced with these simple flat versions. (Photo courtesy of the Patton Museum)

This view of the Bantam prototype at Camp Holabird clearly shows the graceful curved fenders that were soon to give way to the characteristic flat fenders. (Photo courtesy of the Patton Museum)

The Model 60 also included brush guards for the headlights. The windshield was replaced with a two-pane version on later models. (National Archives and Records Administration photo)

The rear corners of the BRC-40 bodies were all sharply squared, unlike the curving body corners of the competitive Ford and Willys products. Also notice the diminutive rear bumperettes.

The flat hood, flat fenders, and flat grille of the BRC-40 were features that were characteristic of WWII Jeeps, and all were all present on this model. (Photo courtesy of Military History Institute)

G-503 FORD

PYGMY

Ford's entry into the Army's reconnaissance car competition was the Pygmy. While the Pygmy introduced many features that were later included on the standardized Jeep, including the grille-mounted headlights, dog-legged windshield hinges, and squared-off hood, its modified tractor engine was no competition to the Willys "Go-Devil" engine installed in the Quad.

A second prototype was constructed by Ford, this time using a body supplied by Philadelphia's Budd Company. This body closely resembled the Bantam body, with its unusually shaped door openings. Only one vehicle of this design was produced.

GP

When the U.S. government ordered 1,500 reconnaissance trucks each from Bantam, Willys, and Ford, Ford delivered the GP. GP was the Ford nomenclature — G meaning government contract vehicle, and P indicating it is an 80-in.-wheelbase reconnaissance car. In addition to the 1,500 vehicles on

the initial contract, another 2,958 units were built. Four-wheel steering was fitted to 50 of these vehicles, but this setup was deemed excessively dangerous and bad for the supply channels.

GPW

Once the design of the Jeep was standardized, a production contract was awarded to Willys for its MB model. The anticipated widespread use of the Jeep led to a desire for an additional source of manufacture. Ford was licensed to build copies of the Willys design, which Ford designated GPW. Again, G meant government contract vehicle, P indicated it is an 80-in. wheelbase reconnaissance car, and the W suffix indicated it used the Willys-designed engine.

Ford built the GPW at six plants, including Ford's huge Rouge complex. Like the MB, the earliest models had the maker's name embossed in script on the rear

The now familiar "Jeep" grille was developed by Ford engineers to save labor, material, and money. It was introduced on the GPW during January of 1942. This beautifully restored GPW is owned by Charles Wilson. (Photo by Evelyn Harless)

The Pygmy was the original Ford vehicle for the Army reconnaissance car contract. Notice the dog-legged windshield hinges and squared-off hood, both features eventually incorporated into the final universal Jeep design. (Photo courtesy of Veteran's Memorial Museum/Alabama Center of Military History)

Early Ford-built Jeeps, both GP and GPW models, had the Ford name embossed in the rear panel. Tie rod ends can be seen under the rear body of this example, identifying it as one of only 50 four-wheel-steer GPs that Ford built.

During the field evaluation period, the Army ordered 1,500 vehicles of the improved GP model from Ford. These vehicles had fabricated "slat" grilles.

panel. The grille was of fabricated steel construction until January 6, 1942. At that time, Ford introduced the stamped steel grille that was later ironically registered as a trademark for Chrysler's Jeep. The script Ford name on the rear panel was discontinued in July 1942.

Ford built its own bodies at the Lincoln plant until the fall of 1943. At that time Ford began buying bodies from American Central, which was already supplying bodies to Willys. Soon, representatives of Ford, Willys, and the Ordnance Department met and created the composite body, which incorporated the best features of each maker's body. This body is what is now known as the composite body, and it was used by both Ford and Willys from January 1944 onward, although a few were used during the last months of 1943.

During the production of the 277,896 GPWs, Ford marked many of the components with the Ford "F" logo. Among these components were pintle hooks, fenders, bolts, etc. However, due to materials shortages, non-F parts were sometimes substituted on the assembly line. As a rule, the most notable difference between the MB and the GPW involves the front cross member. There is a tubular member on Willys vehicles, and an inverted U-channel on the Ford.

GENERAL DATA

MODEL	GPW	MB
GROSS WEIGHT	3,650 lbs.	3,650 lbs.
LENGTH	132.25	132.25
WIDTH	55.5	55.5
HEIGHT (TOP UP)	71.75	71.75
HEIGHT (TOP DOWN)	52	52
TRACK	49	49
TIRE SIZE	6.00-16	6.00-16
MAX SPEED	65 mph	65 mph
FUEL CAPY	15 gal	15 gal
RANGE	285 mi	285 mi
ELECTRICAL	6 neg	6 neg
TRANSMISSION		
SPEEDS	3	3
TRANSFER		
SPEEDS	2	2

Overall dimensions listed in inches.

ENGINE DATA

ENGINE MAKE/MODEL	Willys 442	Ford GPW
NUMBER OF CYLINDERS	4	4
CUBIC-IN. DISPLACEMENT	134	134
HORSEPOWER	54 @ 4000 rpm	54 @ 4000 rpm
TORQUE	105 lbs.-ft. @ 2000 rpm	105 lbs.-ft. @ 2000 rpm

VALUES

	6	5	4	3	2	1
All models	800	4,500	9,000	12,000	16,000	20,000

G-504 GPA

The GPA was developed at the request of the Quartermaster Corps by Ford Motor Company working with the National Defense Research Council. It is affectionately referred to as a "Jeep in a bathtub." Just as was the case with the DUKW, yacht builders Sparkman and Stephens Co. assisted in the design of the hull.

Mechanically, the GPA is very similar to the GPW, with the same type engine, transmission, axles, and transfer case, and only slight modifications to adapt them to the amphibious role.

Not only did the overhanging front and rear hull sections make the GPA longer than the standard Jeep, but the wheelbase itself was 4 in. longer than its non-amphibious brother. On the bow of the vehicle was a hinged splash shield. The winch was driven via pulley off

Early Jeeps, whether Ford or Willys built, did not have the rear-mounted liquid container rack. (Photo by Evelyn Harless)

The Army was not the only user of GPWs, as shown by Wayne Dowdle's restored U.S. Navy Jeep. (Photo by Evelyn Harless)

The conventional interior layout of the GPA is apparent in this period photo. The spare tire is seen stowed on the rear deck, near the fuel filler and between the protected taillights. The winch capstan is visible on the fore deck, just ahead of the surf shield, which is in the stowed position. (Photo courtesy of the Patton Museum)

The engine-cooling door has been closed in this photo, but the hood itself can just be made out ahead of the windshield. Alongside the passenger compartment is the boat hook (pike pole) that was released as standard equipment for the GPA vehicles on Dec. 27, 1942. (U.S. Army photo)

The hull of the GPA and DUKW were designed by the same firm. In this shot the surf shield has been placed in operating position, and the engine-cooling door can just be seen beyond it in the open position. (U.S. Army photo)

the front of the engine. At the rear of the vehicle were a propeller and rudder, and the standard pintle hook.

Inside, the passenger compartment was much like a standard Jeep, with two individual seats in the front and a bench-type seat in the rear. Steps were recessed into the hull sides to permit entrance and egress to the vehicle.

While Ford built the last of the 12,778 GPAs in 1943, unlicensed copies continued to be built in the Soviet Union for some time after that.

The driver's compartment of the GPA was not that different from that of a normal Jeep, as can be seen in this photo taken at the United States Army Engineer Museum, Fort Leonard Wood, Missouri.

GENERAL DATA

MODEL	GPA
WEIGHT GROSS	4,460 lbs..
LENGTH	182
WIDTH	64
HEIGHT	66.25
TRACK	49
TIRE SIZE	6.00-16
MAX SPEED	
LAND	50 mph
WATER	5.5 mph
FUEL CAPY	15 gal.
RANGE	
LAND	250 mi
WATER	35 mi
ELECTRICAL	12 neg
TRANSMISSION	
SPEEDS	3
TRANSFER	
SPEEDS	2

Overall dimensions listed in inches.

ENGINE DATA

ENGINE MAKE/MODEL	Ford GPA
NUMBER OF CYLINDERS	4
CUBIC-INCH DISPLACEMENT	134
HORSEPOWER	54 @ 4050 rpm

VALUES

	6	5	4	3	2	1
All models	4,000	14,000	20,000	25,000	32,000	38,000

On the GPA, the Danforth anchor is stowed on top of the spare tire, the rifle rack is mounted on the windshield, and the offset tunnel houses the propeller and rudder. (U.S. Army photo)

G-503 Willys

Quad

The 1940 Willys Quad was that company's offering to compete against the Bantam prototype. The Quad pushed the weight limit established for the new reconnaissance car, so much so that the original was reportedly stripped of its paint and refinished with thinner coats covering only the exposed surfaces. Two Quads were built, both powered by the Willys "Go-Devil" engine. The engine turned out to be Willys's greatest asset. None of the Quads is believed to have survived.

MA

The MA was the Willys followup to the Quad. The MA featured a flat hood, full-length front fenders with headlights mounted on them, and column shift for the transmission. The Willys name was embossed in the front of all the MA vehicles.

Willys built 1,553 of these vehicles, the bulk of which, like the Bantam BRC-40, were supplied to Russia under lend-lease arrangements. Production of the MA ran from June 5, 1941, through September 23, 1941. Today the MA is an extremely difficult vehicle to find in this country.

MB

After 1,500 units each of the Bantam BRC-40, Ford GP, and the Willys had been ordered, the road had been paved for mass production. Willys was awarded a contract for an improved MA, known as the MB. The first

25,808 of these trucks had what is now known as a "slat grille." This was a welded assembly of heavy bar stock. Vehicles produced after June 12, 1942, used the now familiar lightweight stamped-steel units originally developed by Ford for the GPW, which ironically, were later registered as a trademark for Jeep. The stamped grille was not only lighter weight, but also reportedly could be produced for about one-third the cost of the fabricated unit it replaced.

As seen on this MB, owned and restored by B.J. Smith, the bows and windshield and could be lowered to reduce the overall height of the vehicle. The stamped steel grille was developed by Ford, but was soon adopted by Willys-Overland as well. (Photo by Evelyn Harless)

The Quad, shown here, was the Willys entry into the 1/4 ton truck competition. Notice how much the designed had to evolve to become the familiar MB. (Photo courtesy of Military History Institute)

After extensive field testing of the MA, the design was improved and standardized as the MB. The first 25,808 of these featured what collectors refer to as a "slat grille." This was a welded assembly of heavy bar stock. (Photo courtesy of Reg Hodgson)

A canvas top was supplied with the MB, with two supporting bows that provided adequate headroom for passengers. The siren on the left and red light on the right front fenders were not standard equipment on MBs. (Photo courtesy of Reg Hodgson)

QUARTER-TON TRUCKS

The first 20,700 MBs used solid disk wheels. After that, combat wheels were used. Like its Willys predecessors, the MB had the "Go-Devil" engine. The early models had "Willys" embossed in the rear body panel, and are known as "script" Jeeps. This practice was discontinued in July of 1942. From March 16, 1941 through August 20, 1945, Willys-Overland bought its bodies from American Central (formerly known as Auburn Central), of Connersville, Indiana. After 65,582 vehicles had been built, the now familiar liquid container bracket began to be installed on the left-hand side of the Jeep's rear panel.

Like most of the WWII-era military vehicles, production of the MB ceased with the end of hostilities. Willys-Overland motors had built 359,489 of the vehicles when production halted. Other minor changes were made during the production run, enough so that numerous books are on the market to aid the Jeep restorer in "getting it right."

CJ-V35/U

One of the most unusual variants of the military Jeep is the CJ-V35/U. One-thousand these vehicles were ordered in February 1950 for use as communications trucks. Willys-Overland produced the CJ-V35/U from March 1950 through June 1950.

All of these vehicles were bought by the Department of the Navy, Bureau of Ships for use by the Marine Corps.

The CJ-V35/U looks very much like a civilian CJ-3A, but there were numerous detail differences. The most obvious are its use of a unique deep headlight bezel, combat rims, and a 12-volt auxiliary generator mounted between the front seats. The auxiliary generator was driven via belts of a PTO. This generator charged two 6-volt auxiliary batteries that powered the radio equipment.

Here is the production pilot for the CJ-V35/U emerging from a fording test. The Willys name is embossed in the side of the hood. While characteristic of this model, is not correct for any other model of U.S. military Jeep. (Photo courtesy of Richard Grace collection)

Although it has a waterproof electrical system and provisions for deep-water fording, it retained the 6-volt ignition system like its predecessors. A radio cabinet occupied the position normally reserved for the back seat.

GENERAL DATA

MODEL	CJ-V35/U
WEIGHT GROSS	3,500 lbs.
LENGTH	136
WIDTH	60
HEIGHT TOP UP	74
HEIGHT TOP DOWN	55
TRACK	48.25
TIRE SIZE	6.00-16
MAX SPEED	60 mph
FUEL CAPY	10.5 gal
RANGE	200 mi
ELECTRICAL	6 neg
TRANSMISSION	
SPEEDS	3 F, 1 R
TRANSFER	
SPEEDS	2

G-740 Willys MC

The Jeep that the military knew as the M38 was known by Willys as the model MC. At first glance, the M38 looks like the WWII-era Jeep, but there are several significant differences.

The vehicle was slightly larger, with more room for the driver, and there was a significant improvement in the transmission. While the fuel can rack and spare tire were mounted in the same locations as they had be previously, the fuel filler was relocated and protruded through the side of the body. The two features that most readily distinguish this from the WWII vehicles are the one-piece windshield glass (rather than two-piece glass of the MB and GPW) and the protruding headlights (they were inset on earlier Jeeps). The M38 used larger 7:00-16 tires and wheels than were used on the WWII Jeeps. Like the other postwar tactical vehicles, the M38 had a 24-volt electrical system. The 24-volt system required

Barely visible just ahead of the windshield of the M38 is the battery box cover for one battery. The other battery is under the hood. This vehicle is owned by Jane Hunt of Arkansas. (Photo courtesy of Evelyn Harless)

The postwar Willys M38 may look like its WWII brother, but closer examination reveals many differences. The protruding headlights and external fuel filler are perhaps the most obvious changes. This example is owned by Greg Stanton. (Photo courtesy of Evelyn Harless)

The pioneer tools were carried on the passenger's side of the M38, just the opposite of their position on the WWII era Jeeps. Notice the guards protecting the headlights. (Photo courtesy of Evelyn Harless)

The pioneer tools were carried on the passenger's side of the M38, just the opposite of their position on the WWII era Jeeps. (Photo courtesy of Evelyn Harless)

two batteries, one of which was mounted under the hood, the other in a special compartment in the cowling. Despite the similar appearance, very few parts are interchangeable between this truck and the WWII version.

Correspondence from Brigadier General John Christmas dated July 12, 1949, indicates that by that time the procurement process for the M38 was well advanced. From 1950 until 1952, Willys produced 45,473 of these improved Jeeps. A rare few were equipped with Ramsey PTO-driven winches.

GENERAL DATA

MODEL	M38
NET WEIGHT	2,625 lbs.
GROSS WEIGHT	3,825 lbs.
MAX TOWED LOAD	2,000 lbs.
LENGTH	133
WHEELBASE	80
WIDTH	62
HEIGHT	74
WIDTH*	41.375/57
TRACK	49 3/16
TIRE SIZE	7.00-16
MAX SPEED	60 mph
FUEL CAPY	13 gal
RANGE	220 mi
ELECTRICAL	24 neg
TRANSMISSION	
SPEEDS	3
TRANSFER	
SPEEDS	2
TURNING	
RADIUS FT	20 R, 19 L

Overall dimensions listed in inches.

*Inside/outside width at tires.

ENGINE DATA

ENGINE MAKE/MODEL	Willys MC
NUMBER OF CYLINDERS	4
CUBIC-INCH DISPLACEMENT	134
HORSEPOWER	51 @ 4000 rpm
TORQUE	97 lbs.-ft. @ 2000 rpm
GOVERNED SPEED (rpm)	Not governed

VALUES

	6	5	4	3	2	1
M38	1,000	3,000	6,000	8,500	12,000	15,000

SCARCITY

Scarcity 3

G-758 Willys MD

The M38 was a considerable improvement over the World War Two-era Jeep, but it was also heavier without a corresponding increase in horsepower. The M38A1, with its new F head "Hurricane" engine replacing the "Go Devil" L-head, increased the horsepower. What had begun as a simple revision (hence the "A1" designation) evolved into an almost totally new vehicle. MD was the Willys model designation for the M38A1.

M38A1

When production of the M38A1 began in 1952, the vehicle was being built by Willys-Overland Motors in Toledo. However, on April 28, 1953, Kaiser bought Willys-Overland and changed the name to Willys Motor

Company. It remained that way until 1963, when it became Kaiser-Jeep Corporation.

The M38A1 would be the basis for the familiar CJ-5 introduced later. In addition to the different brand names on the data plates, there were other variations

The M38A1 was the base vehicle of the recoilless rifle-armed M38A1C. Modifications included: the weapon, the split windshield, relocated spare tire, and relocated liquid container bracket to the passenger's side of the vehicle. (Photo courtesy of the Patton Museum)

The spare tire and liquid container bracket were mounted on the rear panel of the M38A1, which had no moveable tailgate. Just visible along the edges of the tarpaulin are the twist fasteners used to secure the side curtains for total enclosure of the vehicle. (U.S. Army photo)

This photo, taken at the Yuma Proving Ground in 1952, shows the recess on the right side of the vehicle that accommodated the slave receptacle. Also faintly visible in this view is the inverted V-shape panel on the hood side that was to be removed when installing the deep-water fording gear. (U.S. Army photo)

during the course of production. The early production M38A1 were built from 1952 through winter 1953. Characteristics of these early trucks include: the hinged front grille to facilitate engine and transmission removal, the cowl-mounted battery box had its cover retained by eight thumb screws, and a seam in the front fenders. The front bumper on the earliest vehicles was narrower than the 54 1/2-in. bumper that was used on subsequent trucks, but the change in bumper length preceded the other changes.

In late 1953, several minor changes were made in these vehicles, beginning at serial number MD62000. Vehicles made subsequent to this are referred to as late-production vehicles. Spotting features of these vehicles include: a single strap replacing the eight thumbscrews retaining the battery box lid, deletion of the hinged grille, seamless front fenders, and the addition of two long radiator support rods extending from the radiator support to the firewall.

Domestic production of the M38A1 ceased in 1957, by which time 80,290 vehicles had been produced for U.S. use, and an additional 21,198 units for foreign sales. M38A1 CDNs were built by Ford of Canada in the 1950s, then by Kaiser-Jeep in Windsor in the 1960s.

Beyond the basic M38A1, there were two interesting armed variants — the M38A1C, and the M38A1D.

M38A1C

The M38A1C was initially armed with the 105mm Recoilless Rifle M27 or M27A1, but that was soon replaced with the 1953 M40 106mm Recoilless Rifle. It has been reported that these vehicles were not factory built, but were converted to the armed version by the Watervliet Arsenal. There were several changes made to the vehicle to accommodate the weapons. A new windshield was installed, with a gap in it to accommodate the weapon tube. The spare tire and liquid container bracket were relocated from the rear of the vehicle to the passenger's side. The rear of the vehicle was also opened up and the rear seat removed. Ammunition racks were installed in the floor of the rear of the vehicle, and the recoilless rifle mount was suspended between the rear wheel wells.

M38A1D

The M38A1D is one of the most powerfully armed light vehicles ever built. The Davy Crockett Atomic Battle Group Weapon System was carried by several vehicles during its deployment. The M38A1D Willys MD Jeep was the first mount for the M28 launcher. The M38A1D 4x4 trucks were originally M38A1C Recoilless Rifle Carriers field modified into transporter/launchers for the Davy Crockett. Only a few M38A1Cs were converted to M38A1D standard.

Along with the more powerful F-head engine, other improvements were introduced that made the M38A1 only vaguely resemble the M38. Among the changes was a reshaped hood. (U.S. Army photo)

The M28 launchers could be demounted from their Jeeps and ground launched from their tripods by the three-man crew. The Davy Crockett Atomic Battle Group Weapon System was built around the M388 279mm Projectile. The fin-stabilized M388 was attached to a piston that was inserted into the muzzle of the 120mm M28 Launcher. The M388 projectile extended beyond the end of the launcher barrel. The propellant was placed in the rear of the recoilless rifle barrel, and when discharged fired the projectile and piston up to 1.24 miles.

The M388 projectile could be armed with either conventional explosives or a W-54 atomic fission warhead. The atomic warhead was of variable yield ranging from 10 to 250 tons of TNT. The operator selected the yield prior to firing.

The Davy Crockett system was intended to give the infantry squads the ability to combat large armored formations and infantry concentrations. Unfortunately, the blast radius from the warhead could exceed the range of the launcher.

Reportedly, the Davy Crockett system was withdrawn from service in 1971.

The M170 lower litter racks were bolted to the floor, while the upper racks hung from the top bows at the rear and were supported by a bracket on the dashboard at the front. (National Archives and Records Administration photo)

M170

The M170 was the battlefield ambulance version of the G-758 series. The M170 wheelbase was 20 in. longer than the M38A1's wheelbase and the internal layout was considerably different. The front seats were narrower and there were litter racks mounted in the rear floor. An additional litter rack hung from the bows on the passenger's side. The passenger's seat cushion was removable and could be hung from the windshield frame,

the seat back and frame pivoted forward and a cushion latched it to the floor. This provided room for a stretcher. The spare tire and fuel can were carried in a well just to the right of the passenger's seat. A droplight on a cable reel was mounted on the left rear wheel well just behind the driver's seat. Storage lockers were mounted in rear fender wells. There are many special brackets attached at various points on the body and tailgate.

While usually configured as ambulances, a few of the

This view of the M170 shows how efficiently the limited interior space was utilized. A pad on the rear of the driver's seat protects the head of on patient, while the passenger's seat cushion has been hung from the windshield to protect the head of another patient. Also visible in this view is the interior-mounted spare tire and a 5-gallon gas can. No bracket for the gas can was installed, but footmen's loops were provided to secure it. (U.S. Army photo)

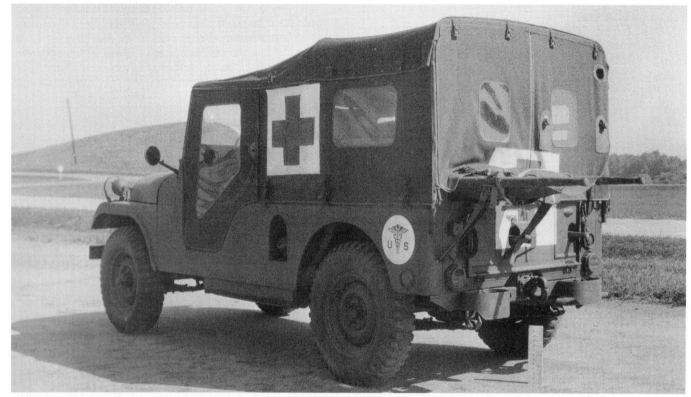

The M170 was a longer-wheelbase version of the Willys MD, and was designed for use as a field ambulance. Shown here is the XM170, photographed at Aberdeen Proving Ground in September 1953, with all canvas fitted and with three litters in place. (U.S. Army photo)

4,155 built from 1953 to 1963 were outfitted as radio trucks or airfield taxis.

The M170, or MD-A in Willys nomenclature, was the basis for the civilian CJ-6. The M170 is among the hardest military Jeeps to find.

GENERAL DATA

MODEL	M38A1	M38A1C	M170
NET WEIGHT	2,690 lbs.	2,690 lbs.	2,963 lbs.
GROSS WEIGHT	3,865 lbs.	3,865 lbs.	3,763 lbs.
MAX TOWED LOAD	2,000 lbs.	2,000 lbs.	N/A
LENGTH	138 9/16	138 9/16	155
WHEELBASE	81	81	101
WIDTH	60.625	60.625	60.5
HEIGHT	72.875	72.875	80
WIDTH*	41.875/60.625	41.875/60.625	41.875/60.625
TRACK	49.125	49.125	49.125
TIRE SIZE	7.00-16	7.00-16	7.00-16
MAX SPEED	55 mph	55 mph	55 mph
FUEL CAPY	13 gal	13 gal	13 gal
RANGE	350 mi	350 mi	300 mi
ELECTRICAL	24 neg	24 neg	24 neg
TRANSMISSION			
SPEEDS	3	3	3
TRANSFER			
SPEEDS	2	2	2
TURNING			
RADIUS FT	19.5 R, 19 L	19.5 R, 19 L	24.5 R, 24.5 L

*Overall dimensions listed in inches.

Inside/outside width at tires.

ENGINE DATA

ENGINE MAKE/MODEL	Willys MD F-head
NUMBER OF CYLINDERS	4
CUBIC-INCH DISPLACEMENT	134
HORSEPOWER	72 @4000
TORQUE	114 lbs.-ft. @ 2000
GOVERNED SPEED (rpm)	Not governed

VALUES

	6	5	4	3	2	1
M38A1	500	1,000	2,000	4,500	6,000	7,500
M170	500	1,200	2,500	6,000	8,000	12,00

SCARCITY

M38A1	2
M170	4

G-838 M151 Series

Work on the M151 MUTT (Military Utility Tactical Truck) series of vehicles began even before its predecessor, the M38A1, had been produced.

The seed of the M151 came to life in 1951, when the Ford Motor Company was contracted by the Army to start development on a new type of light utility truck that would utilize the latest features of the automotive industry at that time. Weight was (as with the MB/GPW) a major concern for the military, and Ford put together ideas for various combinations of vehicles — unibody and separate chassis versions, and both steel and aluminum bodies. Ford eventually settled on the unibody (integral chassis) version, but was also very interested in using alloy for the body. Pilot models were built in aluminum, but during testing the bodies developed severe fractures and cracks. Eventually, the steel-bodied version was selected.

It would be 1959 before the design and pilot stages evolved into a production contract.

Like its immediate predecessors, the M151 had the military standard 24-volt electrical system and selective two and four wheel drive, but there were some significant differences. The M151 used a unibody design, the suspension was all-around independent, and the transfer case was a single-speed unit. The transmission was a four-speed version, unlike the MB/GPW/M38/M38A1, which all had three-speed transmissions. The M151's first and reverse gears were low enough to negate the need for a separate low transfer range.

M151

Delivery of the vehicles of the first contract was scheduled by Ford to begin in March 1960. These vehicles were designated M151. In 1962, Willys Motors, Inc., successor firm to Willys-Overland Motors, underbid Ford and began producing 14,625 of the M151 trucks. A second contract was won in December of that year for a further 9,800 units. In 1963, Willys Motors, Inc., became the Kaiser Jeep Corporation. The contract for M151 vehicles was modified during production to specify the M151A1.

M151A1

Because of problems with the rear suspension, which buckled or collapsed, particularly when burdened with mounted weapons and cargo, the rear suspension system was redesigned. High-strength rear suspension arms, with extra bump-stops, were introduced. Vehicles

This M151 has been armed with a pedestal-mounted .30-caliber machine gun. The flat fenders and two-piece windshield are characteristics of early models. (Photo courtesy of the Patton Museum)

with this improved suspension were known as model M151A1s. Production of this new Jeep began by Willys Motors in December 1963. In January 1964, the name on the builder's plate of the M151A1s was changed to Kaiser-Jeep Corp.

In 1964, Ford regained the contract and production of the Mutt restarted in January 1965 and continued up through 1969.

Variants of the basic M151A1 design were used to carry a recoilless rifle, which was installed on the M151A1 by Watervliet Arsenal. These vehicles featured a different tailgate area, fender-mounted troop seats, and overload springs (smaller coil springs which fitted inside the main rear coil springs), and were designated M151A1C. An extended-bodied ambulance version was designated the M718.

Numerous accidents occurred after the M151 was introduced. The military invariably cited "driver error," but as the accident reports began to pile up, the Army knew that there was something inherently wrong with the handling of the vehicle.

The independent rear suspension used on both the M151 and M151A1 was the source of the problem. In fiscal 1967 the M151 was reportedly involved in 3,538 accidents that resulted in 104 deaths and 1,858 injuries. The lack of body roll when turning and a severe oversteer condition, both of which were characteristics of the rear "swing-arm" system of suspension, caused many

The M151 family did not use the traditional liquid container bracket. Instead, the spare gas can sat on the left bumperette, and was secured by a Y-shaped webbing strap. (Photo courtesy of the Patton Museum)

inattentive drivers to lose control of their vehicles. The Army introduced training courses, training films, DA circulars, and even insisted that no one drove the M151-series without a special driver permit endorsement. In spite of all these efforts, the accidents continued.

M151A2

Eventually, the U.S. military realized that it could ignore the problem no longer and the rear suspension

system was totally redesigned. The independent "A" frame used on the M151 and M151A1 was replaced with a semi-trailing arm suspension, which minimized the need for a whole range of extra supply-item parts, while retaining many of the advantages of the independent suspension.

The redesigned vehicle was designated M151A2, and its introduction heralded many other improvements, including deep-dish steering wheels, larger "composite"

The M151A2, like its predecessors, could be fitted with machine gun mount, as is the case with this example owned by Bob McFarland. This vehicle also has a radio installed.

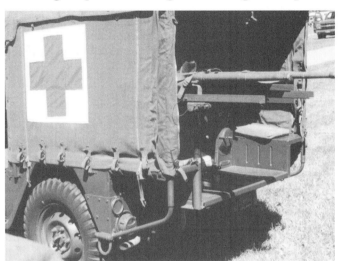

The M718 and M718A1 could each carry three litters, one in the angular lower rack, and one in each of the upper racks. The spare tire was also relocated to permit installation of the extension.

The M151A2 has scooped front fenders and a single-piece windshield. Underneath, there was a much-improved and safer suspension system. (U.S. Army photo)

type marker and tail lights, electric windshield wipers, and a mechanical (as opposed to the earlier electrical) fuel pump. The new suspension improved the "feel" of the vehicle and gave drivers a much better indication of body-tilt when turning at excessive speed.

The vehicle was now much more stable, but this brought on new risks. Because of the increased stability, a driver could become overconfident, and even this new "safe" version was involved in roll-over accidents, the results of which were just as devastating as those of the M151 and M151A1 models. This new suspension was incorporated in the recoilless rifle and ambulance versions as well, which became the M825 and M718A1, respectively.

Even though the new suspension reduced the tendency for rollovers, in 1987 a Roll Over Protection System (ROPS) was introduced that could be added to the vehicles.

Ford began producing the M151A2 in 1969, but the next contract was won in 1971 by AM General, which produced the M151A2 from 1972 through 1985, with a short production run for foreign sales in 1988. All the AM General built trucks were produced in South Bend, Indiana.

The M998 HMMWV "Humvee" replaced the Mutt for most purposes during the mid and late 1990s, but the Marine Corps continued to use the M151A2 as the basis for its Fast Attack Vehicle as late as 2000.

GENERAL DATA

MODEL	M151	M151A1C M825	M718	M718
NET WEIGHT	2,140 lbs.	—		
GROSS WEIGHT	3,340 lbs.	4,590 lbs.	3,680 lbs.	3,680 lbs.
MAX TOWED LOAD	2,000 lbs.	2,000 lbs.	—	—
LENGTH	132	143.5	143	143
WIDTH	62.25	76.5	72	71.6
HEIGHT	71	77.2	76.3	76.3
TRACK	53	53	53	53
TIRE SIZE	7.00-16	7.00-16	7.00-16	7.00-16
MAX SPEED	66 mph	50 mph	66 mph	66 mph
FUEL CAPY	17.3 gal	17.3 gal	17.3 gal	17.3 gal
RANGE	300 mi	275 mi	300 mi	300 mi
ELECTRICAL	24 neg	24 neg	24 neg	24 neg
TRANSMISSION SPEEDS	4	4	4	4
TRANSFER SPEEDS	1	1	1	1
TURNING RADIUS FT	17.9 R, 17.8 L	18.5	18.5	18.5

Overall dimensions listed in inches.

Unlike the M170, the M718 series had extensions attached to the rear of the body to accommodate litters. (Photo courtesy of Ken Whowell)

ENGINE DATA

ENGINE MAKE/MODEL	Willys MD F-head
NUMBER OF CYLINDERS	4
CUBIC-INCH DISPLACEMENT	141.5
HORSEPOWER	71 @ 3800 rpm
TORQUE	128 lbs.-ft. @ 1800 rpm

VALUES

	6	5	4	3	2	1
M151/M15A1/M151A2	1,000	2,500	3,500	5,500	7,500	11,000

SCARCITY

Scarcity 2

The M151A1 was the next generation of MUTT, and looks very similar to the M151. (Photo courtesy of the Patton Museum)

The M718 front line ambulance was based on the M151A1 vehicle, while the M718A1, shown here, was based on the M151A2 vehicle. These vehicles replaced the M38A1-based M170. (Photo courtesy of AM General)

G-843 M422

The M422 was designed for the U.S. Marine Corps to fill the requirement of a small, lightweight, low profile, highly maneuverable vehicle. What the Marines got was a vehicle that did just that, and gave incredible off-road performance as well.

The Mighty-Mite was developed at Mid-America Research Corporation by a team that included Harold Crist, Ralph Turner, Frank McMillan, and Chet Hemphling. These four men were key to the creation of the Jeep for American Bantam prior to WWII. An imported Porsche engine powered the prototypes. The search for a suitable American built power plant lead to American Motors, which perfected and produced the Mighty-Mite (before it owned Jeep) from December 1959 through December 1962. With an aluminum body, and an aluminum air-cooled 108-cid V-4 engine, the Mighty

Mite weighed just less than 1 ton.

Two versions of the Mighty Mite were built: the M422 and M422A1. There were fewer of the original M422 vehicles produce (1,250) than the later M422A1 (2,672). The most apparent differences between the two models was the 6-in. additional body length of the A1 and a different style windshield. The additional length of the A1 was between the front seat and the rear wheel well. There is an additional reinforcing embossment in this area, which aids in distinguishing the two models. The result is that the M422 has a 65-in. wheelbase, and the M422A1 has a 71-in. wheelbase. Early models used a

This beautifully restored M422 owned by Paul Harless of Adona, Arkansas, has been outfitted with the exhaust extension and snorkle for deep-water fording operations. The rear seat backrest has been folded down in this photo. (Photo courtesy of Evelyn Harless)

The original M422 windshield, as seen here, was very light weight, but also very fragile. Many M422s were retrofitted with the M422A1 windshield. It is rare to find one with the intact original style windshield seen here. (Photo courtesy of Evelyn Harless)

The initial production Mighty-Mite, the M422, was noted for its short length, tight turning radius, and minimal weight. It had an aluminum body and every component was designed with optimal weight savings in mind. (Photo courtesy of the Patton Museum)

unique, and now hard-to-find, windshield, while later models used the M38A1 Jeep windshield.

The four-speed transmission was combined with a two-speed transfer case to shorten the driveline. All Mighty-Mites had limited-slip differentials front and rear which, together with their short turning radius and light weight, gave them such superb off-road performance that they inspired a popular children's toy at the time. The limited-slip differentials, combined with the center of gravity, allow the Mighty-Mites to be operated normally with either one of the rear wheels missing. For this reason, Mighty-Mites were not originally equipped with spare tires.

ENGINE DATA

MODEL	M422	M422A1
WEIGHT NET	1,700 lbs.	1,700 lbs.
GROSS	2,700 lbs.	2,700 lbs.
MAX TOWED LOAD	1,500 lbs.	1,500 lbs.
LENGTH	107	113
WIDTH	60.625	61
WHEELBASE	65	85
HEIGHT	59.5	64.5
TRACK	52	52
TIRE SIZE	6.00-16	6.00-16
MAX SPEED	62 mph	62 mph
FUEL CAPY	13 gal	12 gal
RANGE	225 mi	225 mi
ELECTRICAL	24 neg	24 neg
TRANSMISSION		
SPEEDS	4	4
TRANSFER		
SPEEDS	1	1

Overall dimensions listed in inches.

ENGINE DATA

ENGINE MAKE/MODEL	AV-108-4
NUMBER OF CYLINDERS	4
CUBIC-INCH DISPLACEMENT	107.8
HORSEPOWER	55 @ 3600 rpm
TORQUE	90 lbs..-ft. @ 2500 rpm
GOVERNED SPEED (rpm)	3600

VALUES

	6	5	4	3	2	1
M422	1,000	2,200	3,500	5,000	6,750	9,000
M422A1	1,000	2,000	3,000	4,200	6,000	9,000
M422	4					

SCARCITY

M422A1 3

The M422A1 was longer than the original and had an M38A1-style windshield. This extra length was added between the rear wheel and the driver's seat, and can most easily be spotted by the additional embossed reinforcing rib in this area. The rear seat backrest on this example is in the upright position on this beautiful M422A1 owned and restored by Mike Riefer of Owensville, Missouri. The spare tire was a popular field addition to the original design M422. (Photo courtesy of Mike Riefer)

Even with the compact size of the air-cooled AMC AV-108 V-4 power plant, the engine compartment of the Mighty-Mite is cramped. (Photo courtesy of Daryl Bensinger)

A popular post-factory addition to the Mighty-Mite was the collapsible canvas top, as seen on this M422A1 owned by Ralph Doubek of Wild Rose, Wisconsin.

The Spartan instrument panel of the Mighty-Mite featured only a fuel gauge, speedometer, and ammeter. In spite of other weight saving measures, the standard heavy M Series light switch was used on these vehicles. (Photo courtesy of Daryl Bensinger)

HALF-TON TRUCKS

G-505 Dodge VC

The Dodge VC series trucks were the direct ancestors to the 1/2-ton and 3/4-ton WCs and the later M37s. Known to Dodge by the engineering code T202, they were produced during 1940 in six different varieties.

The various models and the production quantities of these six models are listed here. These numbers are from the Dodge master parts book, and are generally considered to be accurate, but there may be some discrepancies due to prototype work:

Model	Engine	Quantity
VC-1	Command Reconnaissance	2,155
VC-2	Radio	34
VC-3	Closed Cab Pickup	816
VC-4	Closed Cab and Chassis	4
VC-5	Open Cab Pickup	1,607
VC-6	Carryall	24

The spare tire of the VC-6 was carried on the passenger's side of the vehicle. This truck is missing its brush guard. This restored example, like all the VC series Dodges shown here, is owned by Chet Krause of Iola, Wisconsin.

The VC-6 Carryall is among the scarcest wheeled U.S. military vehicles. This is the sole known remaining example of the 24 built.

The closed-cab pickup, known as the VC-3, was a handsome vehicle, especially when fitted with the rear canvas.

The Command Reconnaissance version, VC-1, was the most common variant of the VC trucks. This truck is missing its brush guard, but the brush guards were shipped loose from the factory and could have been omitted on trucks dolled up a bit for parade use.

The unusual open cab of the VC-5 is evident here. The driver's compartment has no sides. This VC-5 still has its brush guard installed. The windshield could be folded down.

HALF-TON TRUCKS

All of the VC series vehicles were powered by the Dodge T202 inline six-cylinder engine. A four-speed transmission was provided, and a single-speed transfer case provided selective all-wheel drive. Strangely, the transmission could not be shifted into first or reverse without first engaging the all-wheel drive. The VC series trucks had disc-type wheels and a large brush guard protected the grille and headlights.

The open cab installed on these trucks was not the same as most military open cabs. Rather, it was more of a firewall and cowl with a platform floor with bucket seats behind it.

Like most pre-and early-war trucks, these vehicles are difficult to find today in restorable condition.

GENERAL DATA

MODEL	VC
NET WEIGHT NET	4,275 lbs.
GROSS WEIGHT	5,220 lbs.
LENGTH	188
WIDTH	74
HEIGHT	88
TIRE SIZE	7.50-16
MAX SPEED	54 mph
FUEL CAPY	16 gal
ELECTRICAL	6 pos
TRANSMISSION	
SPEEDS	4
TRANSFER	
SPEEDS	1

Information above is applicable to the VC5.

ENGINE DATA

ENGINE MAKE/MODEL	Dodge T-202
NUMBER OF CYLINDERS	6
CUBIC INCH DISPLACEMENT	201.3
HORSEPOWER	79 @ 3000 rpm

VALUES

	6	5	4	3	2	1
VC-1 Command Recon	1,000	5,000	10,000	20,000	30,000	60,000
VC-2 Radio	no reported sales					
VC-3 Closed Cab P/U	850	4,000	8,000	17,000	25,000	50,000
VC-4 Cab and chassis	no reported sales					
VC-5 Open cab P/U	750	3,500	7,500	16,000	23,500	45,000
VC-6 Carryall	no reported sales					

The rear area of the pickup-bodied trucks was fitted with troop seats. These troop seats crossed the body rather ran longitudinal to it. The canvas protected both troops and cargo from the elements.

G-505 Dodge WC

The G-505 series of 4x4 trucks were built by Dodge, and represented quite an improvement over the previous VC series. Rather than the civilian look of the earlier vehicles, the WCs had a distinctly military appearance with the grille and brush guard integrated into a single unit. This brush guard was rounded in the center, whereas the later 3/4-ton series trucks had a flat brush guard. The hood, which sloped gently downward toward the front of the truck, was hinged in the center and opened from the sides.

Three different six-cylinder Dodge engines were installed in the vehicles of this series: the T207 217-cid/85-hp engine, the T211, also 217 cid, and the T215 230-cid/92-hp engine. Regardless of the engine installed, the transmission was a four-speed unit, while the transfer case was single speed. The half-ton trucks were not equipped with combat wheels.

The model number of each vehicle changed with the power plant installed. Unique vehicle model numbers were assigned to winch-equipped vehicles.

WC-1, WC-5, WC-12, WC-14, WC-40

These series of vehicles were all essentially pickups with closed cabs and express-type bodies.

The various models of closed-cab pickups, their power plants, production quantities, and details are as follows:

Model	Engine	Quantity	Details
WC-1	T207	2573	Express body longitudinal seats
WC-5	T207	60	Express body less seats
WC-12	T211	6046	Pickups and one less bed
WC-1	T211	268	Pickup
WC-40	T215	275	Pickup

The WC-3 and WC-4 vehicles introduced the open cab to the G-505 WC series of vehicles. The WC-4 shown here was equipped with a PTO-driven front winch, which the WC-3 lacked. This vehicle has been equipped with a flexible machine gun mount. This beautifully restored WC-4 is owned by John Bizal, who is shown driving it.

WC-3, WC-5, WC-13, WC-21, WC-22

These were basically the same vehicles as those listed above, but with open cabs. The various models of open-cab pickups, their power plants, production quantities, and details are as follows:

Model	Engine	Quantity	Details
WC-3	T207	7,808	Express body with transverse seats
WC-4	T207	4,628	Express body with transverse seats and winch
WC-13	T211	3,019	Pickup
WC-21	T215	7,400	Pickup
WC-22	T215	1,900	Pickup with winch

The WC-23 used the same body as the previous models, which was built by Budd, but now was powered by the larger T-215 engine. Unlike most military vehicles, the seats of the command cars were covered in leather. The spare tire was located so that it did not interfere with entry or exit from the vehicle. This restored example is owned by Ralph Doubek.

This WC-13 has had its windshield glass removed to protect the driver from glass fragments in the event of damage, as well as to prevent the glare from giving away the vehicle's location. It was photographed during maneuvers at Ft. Benning, Georgia. (National Archives and Records Administration photo)

The first series of Command and Reconnaissance cars to enter production was the WC-6. This vehicle, registration number 206765, was photographed with all canvas in place. (Photo courtesy of the Patton Museum)

HALF-TON TRUCKS

When the winch-equipped open-cab pickup had its engine upgraded it was designated WC-12. Shown on the driver's side are the pioneer tool rack and liquid container carriers. Neither of these were installed at the factory, but rather were refitted Army-wide. This restored example is owned by Ralph Doubek of Wild Rose, Wisconsin.

WC-20 and WC-41 Cab and Chassis

These vehicles were furnished as chassis and closed-cab units without beds. Most of these trucks were equipped with dual rear wheels and had service bodies mounted on them for use as emergency repair trucks. Thirty of the T211-powered WC-20s were built, and 306 of the T215-powered WC-41s were constructed.

WC-10, WC-17 and WC-26 Carryall

These vehicles were known as "carryalls." They have a totally enclosed passenger's compartment with windows in the sides and rear. In addition to the driver and co-driver's seats, there were two bench seats in the rear of the vehicle. At the rear of the truck was a two-piece tailgate, the top half opening upward, the lower half folding down to the horizontal position. A spare tire was carried on the right running board. Due to metal

Shown here with the stowage compartments closed is one of the 370 WC-43s built, all in 1942. The service bed is well sized to the 1/2-ton chassis, making these handsome vehicles. (Photo courtesy of the Patton Museum)

Initially the new series of half-ton trucks was equipped with closed cabs as seen in this example. The variety of engines installed in the half-ton Dodges makes it difficult to establish specific model numbers without consulting the data plate, registration number, or looking under the hood. The registration number of W-26001 identifies this truck as a WC-1. (Photo courtesy of the Patton Museum)

The WC-10, WC-17, and WC-26 Carryall models all look alike, again differing only in engine. The Carryalls provided comfortable, enclosed transportation to personnel in all types of weather. (National Archives and Records Administration photo)

fabricating limitations of the time, the central portion of the roof is canvas-covered wood.

The WC-10, WC-17, and WC-26 were powered by the T207, T211, and T215 engines, respectively. There were 1,643 WC-10s, 274 WC-17s and 2,900 WC-26s built.

WC-11, WC-19, WC-42 Panel Truck

These vehicles look very much like the carryall, but without the windows in the sides of the rear area. However, they were intended to transport cargo or, in the case of the WC42, communications equipment, so they do not have seats in the rear compartment. Instead of the tailgate arrangement used on the carryall, the rear doors of the panel truck open to the left and right. The WC-42 was powered by the T215 engine. There were more carryalls built than panel trucks. Only 642 WC-11, 103 WC-19, and 650 WC-42s built.

This WC-11's registration number is just eleven digits away from that of the truck below. None of the carryalls or panel trucks were equipped with winches. (National Archives and Records Administration photo)

WC-6, WC-7, WC-8, WC-15, WC-16, WC-23, WC-24, WC-25 Command Reconnaissance and Radio Cars

The WC-6, WC-7, WC-15, WC-23 and WC-24 were Command Reconnaissance Cars. The unique body of these vehicles was designed to permit ease of entry and exit by its passengers, who were usually officers. There was a folding table and map holder mounted on the back of the front seat for use by the rear passengers. An easily

The panel trucks, such as this WC-11, were very similar in appearance to the Carryalls, but lacked the side windows in the rear, and the tailgate was completely different as well. The indentation just behind the door is normally covered by the spare tire. (U.S. Army photo)

HALF-TON TRUCKS

This is another WC-9. Notice the spotlight mounted on the cowl near the driver's door. The vent windows are mounted in the doors — a feature unique to ambulances. (Photo courtesy of the Patton Museum)

antenna mounted above it, and radio equipment inside the vehicle. None of the Radio Cars had winches.

The hazard of the special design of the Command and Radio Cars is that they were easily singled out as targets by opposing forces, a factor that eventually contributed to their elimination.

Model	Engine	Quantity
WC-6	T207	9,365
WC-7	T207	1,438
WC-15	T211	3,980
WC-23	T215	2,637
WC-24	T215	1,412

WC-9, WC-18, WC-27 Ambulance

These trucks had the longest wheelbase in the G-505 series, and a different suspension to provide a smoother ride for the injured personnel. The box-like, totally enclosed, all-steel rear body was insulated and heated and the truck could transport four stretcher patients, or six ambulatory ones. A folding step at the rear of the vehicle assisted passengers in getting inside. Unlike most military ambulances, there was no partition separating the driver's compartment from the patient area.

Engines for the WC-9, WC-18, and WC-27 ambulances were the T207, T211, and T215, and the production numbers were 2,288, 1,555, and 2,579, respectively.

removable canvas top and doors were provided for protection from the elements. The spare tire was mounted on the outside of the center of the vehicle on the driver's side. The WC-7 and WC-24 had PTO-driven front mounted winches.

The similar-appearing WC-8, WC-16, and WC-25 were officially designated Radio Cars. These vehicles had a large 12-volt battery box mounted on the right side of the body, which interrupted the running board with an

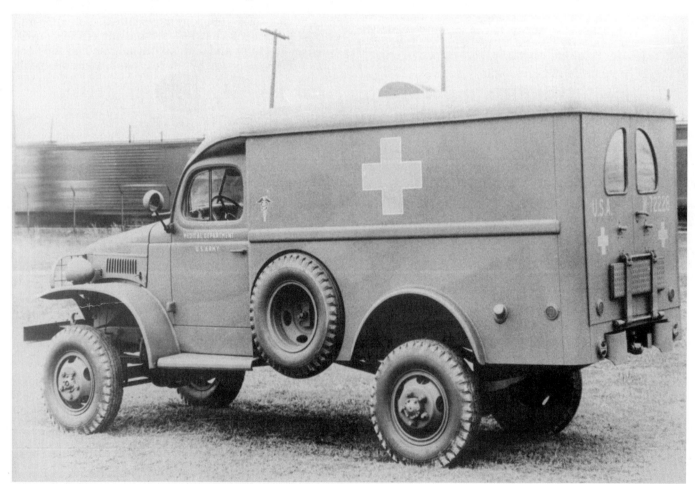

The WC-9 ambulance was built to provide battlefield evacuation of wounded and injured soldiers. Notice the tires do not have the traditional military pattern. The folding rear step is characteristic of military ambulances. (Photo courtesy of Bryce Sunderlin collection)

WC-43 Telephone/Maintenance Truck

These trucks had a utility body that carried a wide variety of telephone linemen's tools for line repair and installation. Army Signal Corps units used these trucks. Only 370 were built, and none had winches.

Among the hardest to find of the half-ton Dodge's are these WC-43 Telephone Maintenance trucks. The cable reel on the roof of the bed is not part of the truck itself, but is part of the equipment used with it. (Photo courtesy of the Patton Museum)

GENERAL DATA

MODEL	WC6/8/15/16/23/25	WC1/5/12/14/20/40/41	WC3/4/13/21/22
NET WEIGHT	4,975 lbs.	4,640 lbs.	4,400 lbs.
GROSS WEIGHT	6,275 lbs.	5,940 lbs.	5,740 lbs.
LENGTH	179	191	191
WIDTH*	75	75	75
HEIGHT	83	83	83
TRACK	59.375	59.375	59.375
TIRE SIZE	7.50-16	7.50-16	7.50-16
MAX SPEED	54 mph	54 mph	54 mph
FUEL CAPY	25 gal	30 gal	30 gal
RANGE	300 mi	240 mi	240 mi
ELECTRICAL	6 or 12 neg	6 neg	6 neg
TRANSMISSION			
SPEEDS	4	4	4
TRANSFER			
SPEEDS	1	1	1

Overall dimensions listed in inches.

MODEL	WC10/17/26	WC11/19/42
NET WEIGHT	4,850 lbs.	4,470 lbs.
GROSS WEIGHT	6,150 lbs.	5,470 lbs.
LENGTH	191 lbs.	191 lbs.
WIDTH*	77	75
HEIGHT	83	83
TRACK	59.375	59.375
TIRE SIZE	7.50 x 16	7.50 x 16
MAX SPEED	54 mph	54
FUEL CAPY	30 gal	30
RANGE**	240	240
ELECTRICAL	6 neg.	12 neg.
TRANSMISSION		
SPEEDS	4	4
TRANSFER		
SPEEDS	1	1

Overall dimensions listed in inches.

ENGINE DATA

ENGINE MAKE/MODEL	Dodge T-215
NUMBER OF CYLINDERS	6
CUBIC-INCH DISPLACEMENT	230.2
HORSEPOWER	92 @3200 rpm
GOVERNED SPEED (rpm)	3200 rpm

VALUES

Values	6	5	4	3	2	1
Open cab pickup	2,750	4,500	7,000	10,000	15,000	18,000
Closed cab pickup	2,750	4,500	7,000	10,000	15,000	18,000
Carryall	2,500	4,500	7,000	12,000	17,000	19,000
Panel	3,000	4,500	8,000	12,000	16,000	18,500
Command	3,750	5,000	8,000	13,000	17,000	20,000
Telephone	no reported sales					
Ambulance	3,000	5,000	9,000	11,000	16,000	19,000
Emergency repair	no reported sales					

SCARCITY

Open cab pickup	2
Closed cab pickup	2
Carryall	3
Panel	4
Command	3
Telephone	5
Ambulance	2
Emergency repair	5

IH M-1-4

When the Marine Corps began shopping for trucks in 1940, they found that most of the "Big 3" automakers' production capacity had already been committed to the U.S. Army. The Army's vehicular requirements were so large that there was little chance of any of the vehicles would be available to the Corps for quite some time.

The Marine Corps turned to International Harvester, the nation's No. 4 truck builder, whose facilities were largely available.

IH designed tactical trucks for the Marines in four weight classes: 1/2 ton, 1 ton, 1 1/2 ton, and 2 1/2 ton. All were 4x4 except for the 2 1/2 ton, which was a 6x6. IH assigned model numbers M-1-4, M-2-4, M-3-4, and M-5-6 to these vehicles.

International assigned the prefix M for military to the model numbers. The first digit is the truck's off-road rating in units of 1,000 lbs., and the last digit is the number of driven wheels.

The M-1-4, discussed here was the 1/2-ton member of the family, and is now quiet hard to find. Production totaled only 1,123 vehicles. All these trucks were of open-cab design, with provision for a canvas top only. There was no provision for sides or doors. International Harvester assigned specific model numbers M-1-4 (214) and (237) to these trucks.

The first order was for 57 plain cargo trucks, four with cargo bodies and radio shielding, and nine ambulances. All of these trucks were built and delivered in 1941.

Subsequent production was of a slightly improved model, designated M-1-4 (237) by IH. These vehicles can be broken down as follows: 97 straight cargo trucks, 78 cargo trucks equipped with radio shielding, 393 ambulances, and 490 ambulances with radio shielding. The U.S. Navy Medical Department used the ambulance models throughout the war, but combat units soon phased out the M-1-4 in favor of the higher-capacity M-2-4.

Even though the Marine Corps initiated production, in August 1942 the U.S. Army Ordnance Department centralized all truck production control, so many of these

While the cargo trucks did not have a long life in forward areas, the abundant ambulance variants did. This truck has a Geneva Cross on the top of its canvas bed cover. (Photo courtesy of the Military History Institute)

Ambulance versions of the M-1-4 had canvas-covered collapsible bodies built by Boyertown. They more closely resembled cargo trucks than they did ambulances. (Photo courtesy of the Military History Institute)

The IH M-1-4 cargo truck normally had an open cab. Ambulance versions were built with bodies by Boyertown, but they more closely resembled cargo trucks than they did ambulances. (Photo courtesy of the Patton Museum).

truck show the Ordnance Department as the procuring agency.

GENERAL DATA

MODEL	M-1-4
NET WEIGHT	4,200 lbs..
LENGTH	190
WIDTH	77
HEIGHT	80
WHEELBASE	113
TIRE SIZE	7.50-16
RANGE	260 mi
ELECTRICAL	6 neg
TRANSMISSION	
SPEEDS	4
TRANSFER	
SPEEDS	2

Overall dimensions listed in inches.

ENGINE DATA

ENGINE MAKE/MODEL	IH GRD-214B	IH GRD-233C
NUMBER OF CYLINDERS	6	6
CUBIC-INCH DISPLACEMENT	214	233
HORSEPOWER	85 @ 3400 rpm	93 @ 3400 rpm

VALUES

	6	5	4	3	2	1
M-1-4	1,700	3,500	5,500	7,000	10,000	14,000

SCARCITY

Scarcity 4+

M274 Mule

The M274 Truck, Platform, Utility, 1/2-Ton is more commonly known as the "Mechanical Mule." Four different companies produced six different varieties of M274 between 1956 and 1970. All M274 vehicles are four-wheel drive and the first five varieties could be driver selected to be regular two-wheel steer or put into a four-wheel steer mode. Despite their small size and odd appearance, the M274 had twice the cargo-hauling ability of a Jeep. However, the top speed of the Mule was only about 15 mph.

Two different versions of air-cooled engines, both rear-mounted, were used over the years to power the

Here a Mule has been wrapped in the cargo canvas of a 2 1/2-ton truck to make an expedient boat for river crossing. (U.S. Army photo)

Mules. The engines were pull started on the first five models with a rope. The first two models (M274 and M274A1) used the Willys A04-53 four-cylinder engine. All subsequent models used the A042 Military Standard engine 2-cylinder engine, which on the final version, the M274A5, was finally equipped with an electric start. The retrofitting of A0-42 engines into earlier M274 and M274A1 vehicles created the M274A3 and the M274A4, respectively.

The Army and Marines used a lot of these in

Many consider the M274A5 the ultimate Mule. This one is mounting a TOW missile launcher. (Photo courtesy of the Patton Museum)

Vietnam. The first five versions were made of magnesium, the last type (M274A5) was made of aluminum. Some of these mules had recoilless rifles mounted on them, and some M274A5s had TOW (Tube launched, Optically tracked, Wire guided) anti-tank missiles mounted on them, but most were used just to haul supplies and soldiers.

An unusual feature was the basket for the driver's feet and the movable steering column. If you had a lot of cargo to haul, the steering column could swing up and the driver then walked behind it and steered while driving in reverse, letting the space where the driver would normally sit be used for cargo. If the driver thought there was a danger of him being seen or shot, the steering column could be swung further down so that the driver could crawl along behind it. The speed and gear controls were located so that the driver could easily reach them regardless of the configuration.

The most unique quality of these vehicles was their ability to be operated normally with a right front tire missing.

Willys began the work on what was to become the Mule during WWII, and was the contractor for the first production models. Later manufacturers included Bowen-McLaughlin-York. Baifield Industries and the defense division (now General Dynamics Armament and Technical Products) of bowling equipment and recreational products giant Brunswick Corp. produced the final two versions.

The height of the steering column in the Mule made it within easy reach of a soldier walking. It could be swung forward and driven in reverse in that manner, allowing the driver's seat to be stowed and cargo placed in its position. (U.S. Army photo)

This is an M274A2 as built by Bowen-McLaughlin-York. (Photo courtesy of the Patton Museum)

This Mule is being used as a platform for the 106mm M40C Recoilless Rifle. (U.S. Army Photo)

A U.S. Army Mule being refueled en route on the road in Vietnam. (U.S. Army photo)

Although they looked small, the M274 family of vehicles had twice the cargo capacity of a Jeep. The M274 and M274A1 were powered by Willys A04-53 four-cylinder engine. (Photo courtesy of the Patton Museum)

GENERAL DATA

MODEL	M274	M274A1	M274A2
NET WEIGHT	795 lbs.	900 lbs.	900 lbs.
GROSS WEIGHT	1970 lbs.	2075 lbs.	2075 lbs.
LENGTH	118.25	119.21	118.25
WHEELBASE	57	57	57
WIDTH	49.75	49.75	49.75
HEIGHT	49.5	49.5	49.5
TRACK*	40.5	40.5	40.5
TIRE SIZE	7.50-10	7.50-10	7.50-10
MAX SPEED	25 mph	25 mph	25 mph
FUEL CAPY	8 gal	8 gal	8 gal
RANGE	107.5	107.5	107.5
TRANSMISSION SPEEDS	3	3	3
TRANSFER SPEEDS	2	2	22
TURNING RADIUS FT	10	10	9-2 R, 9-10 L

MODEL	M274A3	M274A4	M274A5
NET WEIGHT	—	970 lbs.	—
GROSS WEIGHT	—	1970 lbs.	—
LENGTH	118.25	119.21	118.25
WHEELBASE	57	57	57
WIDTH	49.75	49.75	49.75
HEIGHT	49.5	49.5	49.5
WIDTH TRACK*	40.5	40.5	40.5
TIRE SIZE	7.50-10	7.50-10	7.50-10
MAX SPEED	25 mph	25 mph	25 mph
FUEL CAPY	8 gal	8 gal	8 gal
RANGE	107.5	107.5	107.5
TRANSMISSION SPEEDS	3	3	3
TRANSFER SPEEDS	2	2	2
TURNING RADIUS FT	10	10	10

Overall dimensions listed in inches.

ENGINE DATA

ENGINE MAKE/MODEL	Willys AO-4-53	MIL STD AO42
NUMBER OF CYLINDERS	4	2
CUBIC INCH DISPLACEMENT	53.5	42.4
HORSEPOWER	16 @ 3200 rpm	13.5 @ 3000 rpm
TORQUE	30 @ 2100 rpm	26 @ 2300 rpm
GOVERNED SPEED (rpm)	4200	3600

3/4-TON TRUCKS

G-502 Dodge

The 3/4-ton Dodge is probably second only to Jeeps in popularity with collectors of World War II military vehicles. There were a variety of trucks in this series — cargo trucks, ambulances, command cars, even anti-tank weapons.

This series had its roots in the earlier Dodge 1/2-ton G-505 trucks which, while nice, left the military wanting for something more.

The "more" was to be delivered starting in 1942 with these 3/4-ton trucks, which had the Dodge engineering symbol T214. The G-502 series was standardized by OCM item 19107.

In late 1942, the axle differentials were changed from a two-pinion type to a four-pinion type. At about the same time, the radiator and shroud assembly used on the G-507 1 1/2-ton Dodges were adopted for use on these trucks as well, to reduce parts stockage and improve cooling. In March 1943, the ring gear size increased from 8 3/4 in. to 9 5/8 in., and a month later the liquid containers were added.

In mid-1943 the Zenith carburetor was replaced with a Carter. This change occurred between serial numbers 81668308 through 81674100 and again at serial number 81675080. In July 1944, the auxiliary fuel filter in the engine compartment was replaced with a sintered in-tank filter.

WC-51, WC-52 Cargo Truck

These cargo trucks were all built on a 98-in.-wheelbase chassis. The WC-52 vehicles were equipped

The wide stance of these trucks is apparent in this overhead view. The later M-37 series trucks were narrower for greater mobility. Also visible in this photo is the wood plank floor used in both the cargo and carryall versions of the 3/4-ton Dodges. (U. S. Army photo)

This February 1944 photo shows the typical 3/4-ton Dodge WC-51 truck. These vehicles were widely used during and after World War II by the U.S. and other Allied nations. Notice the awkward location of the spare tire. (U.S. Army photo)

with the Braden MU-2 winch. Rather than using frame extensions, as was the case with the postwar M37, the WC series did this by using a longer frame. Thus, the only right way to add a winch to a non-winch vehicle is to replace the entire frame — a job not for the faint of heart.

In May of 1943, a number of minor changes were made, including lower sides for the bucket seats, which made it easier to get in and out of the truck, as well as providing a means of retaining the troop seat backs without the top bows being fitted. At the same time, the front springs were redesigned to reduce breakage, even though only two months earlier an additional leaf had been added to the front springs for the same reason.

This photo was taken at the Studebaker Proving Grounds in January 1944, and shows the typical Dodge WC-52. The Braden PTO-driven winch is visible, as is the large one-piece canvas that covers both the driver's and cargo compartment. (U. S. Army photo)

This profile view illustrates just how difficult it was for the driver to exit on the left side of the vehicle. Also notice that flat grille and almost flat hood characteristic of the 3/4-ton models as compared to the earlier 1/2-ton Dodges. (U. S. Army photo)

The carryall and ambulance trucks had a different hood and cowl than the cargo trucks, which provided a sloping profile. This early WC-53 was photographed in 1942 at the Holabird Quartermaster Motor Base. (National Archives and Records Administration photo)

The WC-53 carryall had a fully enclosed body, although the center of the body roof was canvas-covered masonite, rather than steel. This early carryall, photographed in April 1942, has the small fuel filler characteristic of the early trucks in the G-502 series. These were later replaced by the larger filler, which allowed easier refueling with the 5-gallon fuel cans. The brackets for carrying these cans became a standard feature on these trucks in April 1943. This photo was probably taken in the testing phase. (U. S. Army photo)

3/4-TON TRUCKS

In August of 1943, a more noticeable change was made, when the left front compartment was eliminated, shortening the left side of the bed. This was another effort to make it easier for the driver to get out in spite of the spare tire mounted in the opening. Two months later, the winch wire rope was increased from 3/8 in. to 7/16 in., and a shear-pin change brought the winch capacity up from 5,000 lbs. to 7,500 lbs.

WC-53 Carryall

This truck was intended to provide enclosed transportation to personnel. Although it was totally enclosed, the roof was not solid steel. A large center panel of the roof was made of canvas covered masonite. This was not done to provide a sunroof, but rather due to manufacturing constraints of the time.

Production of these trucks ended in April, 1943, after a total output of 8,400 units. The windows in the doors of these trucks were one piece, as opposed to the two-piece glass used on the WC-54 ambulance.

The WC-53 Special, Field Limousine shown in some books did not actually reach the production stage, with only two prototypes being constructed. Their registration numbers were USA 2092777 and 2092778.

WC-54 Ambulance

This truck more closely resembles its 1/2-ton predecessors than the rest of the series. Production ended in April 1944. Unlike the carryall and radio trucks, the door windows of these trucks have a two-piece arrangement, including the main window and a vent window.

In August 1942, the litter bracket was redesigned to better clear the spare tire housing, which is recessed into the driver's side of the ambulance body. Sometime in mid to late 1943, the fuel filler neck was enlarged to allow fueling from 5-gallon "Jerry" cans, which necessitated slight changes to the left rear part of the body sheet metal.

This interior view of Bruce Gray's restored WC-54 shows the folding seats provided on each wall for ambulatory patients, as well as the upper (hanging) and lower (floor-mounted) litter racks.

The WC-54 was the initial ambulance built on the G-502 chassis, and it became familiar to many wounded GIs. Notice the vent glass in the door, which is not present in the similar door fitted to the carryall. Often the two doors types were interchanged, but the vented window is only truly correct on the ambulance. (U.S. Army photo)

The spare tire of the WC-54 was inset into the driver's side to reduce overall width. The turn signals on this truck were added by the owner, Bruce Gray.

This is a production version of the M6/WC-55. After the M6 was declared obsolete, most of these trucks were converted into WC-52 cargo trucks. When found today this is evidenced by restamped data plates, and often crudely welded-up holes where the various tools, boxes, and racks had been attached. (Photo courtesy of the Patton Museum)

WC-55 Gun Motor Carriage M6

A truly rare vehicle today, the WC-55 trucks when delivered looked very much like a WC-52 with a 37mm M-3A1 field piece stuck in the back, but in fact there were several differences. Among these was its own G-number: G-121. From April 1942 until October 1942, 5,380 of these trucks were built.

These vehicles were intended from the outset to be an intermediate weapon, until better tank destroyers

This May 1942 Aberdeen Proving Ground photo shows a pilot model of the heavily armed WC-55, also known as the M6 antitank gun. Although this truck lacks some of the unique characteristics of the production models of the WC-55, it does show some changes in the basic vehicle. By comparing this vehicle with the WC-51, it is evident how the bed was shortened in August 1943. A storage compartment in the left front of the cargo bed, present on this vehicle, was eliminated, providing more room between the spare and the bed for the driver to exit. Notice how much space there is between the front of the bed and the canvas tie-down hook, compared to the WC-51. Also notice how the shape of the front seats changed as well. This change came in May 1943. (National Archives and Records Administration photo)

could be designed. Once the M8 light armored car was available, the anti-tank guns were removed, and the trucks became cargo trucks. Often times the data plate was even overstamped or replaced with one reading WC-52, and a new registration number was assigned. Usually, the mounting holes for the special gear were welded up during the conversion to the WC-52 type.

WC-56, WC-57 Command and Reconn Cars

The style of these vehicles have made them very sought after by collectors and movie producers. It seems anyone with any importance in a war movie must ride in one of these trucks, probably because the open top allows the star to be seen, and the dual bench seat creates a chauffeur-driven look. The WC-56 did not have a winch, while the WC-57 used the same MU-2 as the WC-52 cargo trucks. Production of these trucks was discontinued in April 1944.

WC-58 Radio Truck

The WC-58 was essentially a WC-56 provided with a full suite of radio equipment in the back seat and a new data plate. Only 2,344 of these were built, making them the scarcest Dodge 3/4-ton command-type vehicles.

WC-59 Telephone Maintenance Truck

Only 607 if these unusual trucks were built, primarily for Signal Corps use. As the name suggests, their job was to help maintain telephone networks. All of these were produced in 1943.

WC-60 Emergency Repair Chassis, M2

The WC-60 chassis was the basis for the M2 Emergency Repair Truck, with the beds being installed by another contractor. These trucks were equivelent to what would later be known as contact maintenance trucks, and wereequipped with an open-topped service-type bed with numerous stowage bins. Its bed resembles, but is not identical to, theWC-61 bed. It is believed that less than 300 of these trucks were built.

WC-61 Light Maintenance Truck

This truck was a revision of the WC-59 maintenance truck body, which now featured a full-width utility body.

The WC-61 was intended to provide Signal Corps crews with a vehicle and equipment for repair of telephone lines. It is among the rarest of the 3/4-ton Dodge vehicles.

When the command car was equipped with a winch, it was known as a WC-57. Unlike later M series vehicles, which had extensions bolted to the frame to mount the winch on, the frames themselves were different on WCs, making it almost impossible for the restorer to add a winch to a vehicle not so equipped from the factory. (National Archives and Records Administration photo)

The WC-64 was developed in part because of the amount of shipping space taken up by the large, box-like body of the WC-54. Known as the "knock-down" ambulance, it was shipped overseas with the patient compartment disassembled. Once assembled, it was not intended to be disassembled again. The comparatively fragile construction of these make them much harder to find today than the WC-54s.

The WC-56 was provided with a convertible top, and could be operated without any top, with just the top in place, or totally enclosed. (National Archives and Records Administration photo)

WC-64 Knock Down Ambulance

These trucks were built from January 1945 until August of the same year, with a production total of 3,500. This design came about as a result of trying to lower the shipping volume of the WC-54 Ambulance. The WC-64 could be shipped "knocked down," or partially disassembled, in considerably less space than the solid-bodied WC-54. Contrary to rumor, these trucks were not meant to be disassembled once they were put together at their destination. These vehicles had a 121-in. wheelbase like the WC-54, but the Knock Down frame was reinforced, probably to compensate for the lack of body strength.

The front end differed from the other trucks of this series by having a different cowl vent, a hot water personnel heater, and a spotlight on the left ahead of the driver's door. The canvas top over the cab was not readily removable. The Knock Downs were supplied with canvas doors with plastic windows, which could be stored in a canvas pocket on the cab top when not in use.

The lower part of the rear body was factory installed on the chassis, while the upper part was shipped boxed for field installation. The lower body had benches over the wheels, which were padded and could be used as seats by ambulatory patients. Alternately, they could serve as litter racks for the more seriously wounded. Under seat storage boxes were provided on both sides fore and aft of the wheel wells. Like the other trucks in this series, the floor of the bed was made of hardwood. The upper, or knock down, portion of the box was steel-sheathed wood construction, the inside surfaces being insulated with cardboard.

There were two hinged litter racks provided in the upper section of the body, which could be sloped to the rear to aid in loading and unloading stretcher patients, or hinged downward to accommodate patients seated on the lower benches.

The rear body had three ventilation blowers, two ceiling lights, a hot-water personnel heater, three rear doors, and a front emergency door. Access was aided with a folding rear-mounted step. There were roll-down windows in the front emergency door, as well as the lockable center rear door.

This May 1942 Holabird Quartermaster Motor Base photo shows what many consider the most desirable of the G-502 series: the command car. With two bench seats, easy entrance and exit (except for the driver), and great visibility, it is ideal for parades. (U.S. Army photo)

GENERAL DATA

MODEL	WC51/52	WC53	WC54
NET WEIGHT	5,645 lbs.	5,750 lbs.	5,920 lbs.
GROSS WEIGHT	7,445 lbs.	7,550	7,720 lbs.
MAX TOWED LOAD	4,000 lbs.	N/A	4,000 lbs.
LENGTH	167	185.75	194.5
WIDTH	82.75	78.75	77.75
HEIGHT	85.5	80 7/32	90.375
WIDTH*	54.125/75.375	54.125/75.375	54.125/75.375
TRACK	64.75	64.75	64.75
TIRE SIZE	9.00-16	9.00-16	9.00-16
MAX SPEED	54 mph	54 mph	54 mph
FUEL CAPY	30 gal	30 gal	30 gal
RANGE	240 mi	240 mi	240 mi
ELECTRICAL	6 or 12 neg.	12 neg.	6 neg
TRANSMISSION			
SPEEDS	4	4	4
TRANSFER			
SPEEDS	1	1	1
TURNING			
RADIUS FT	22	25	26

MODEL	WC64	WC56/57/58
NET WEIGHT	7,000 lbs.	5,375 lbs.
GROSS WEIGHT	8,500 lbs.	7,175 lbs.
MAX TOWED LOAD	4,000 lbs.	4,000 lbs.
LENGTH	192.625	166
WIDTH	84	78.75
HEIGHT	99.375	81.5
WIDTH*	54.125/75.375	54.125/75.375
TRACK	64.75	64.75
TIRE SIZE	9.00-16	9.00-16
MAX SPEED	54 mph	54 mph
FUEL CAPY	30 gal	30 gal
RANGE	240 mi	240 mi
ELECTRICAL	6 neg.	12 neg.
TRANSMISSION		
SPEEDS	4	4
TRANSFER		
SPEEDS	1	1
TURNING		
RADIUS FT	25	22

*Inside/outside width at tires.
Weights and dimensions given are for models without winches. For winch-equipped vehicles, increase weights 295 lbs., and length 9 1/2 in.

ENGINE DATA

ENGINE MAKE/MODEL	Dodge T-214
NUMBER OF CYLINDERS	6
CUBIC INCH DISPLACEMENT	230.2
HORSEPOWER	76 @ 3200 rpm
TORQUE	180 lbs.-ft @ 1200 rpm
GOVERNED SPEED (rpm)	3200

VALUES

	6	5	4	3	2	1
WC-51	1,750	3,250	7,000	10,000	15,000	18,000
WC-52	2,000	3,500	7,500	11,000	16,000	19,000
WC-53	3,000	4,500	8,000	12,000	17,000	19,500
WC-54	3,000	4,500	8,000	12,000	17,000	19,500
WC-55	no reported sales					
WC-56	1,700	3,500	8,000	12,000	17,000	19,500
WC-57	2,000	4,000	9,000	13,000	18,000	20,000
WC-58	3,000	4,500	8,000	12,000	17,000	19,500
WC-59	no reported sales					
WC-60	no reported sales					
WC-61	no reported sales					
WC-64	2,000	4,500	9,000	14,000	19,000	21,500

SCARCITY

WC-51 1
WC-52 1
WC-53 2
WC-54 2
WC-55 no reported sales
WC-56 2
WC-57 2
WC-58 4
WC-59 5
WC-60 5
WC-61 5
WC-64 4

Dodge G-741

With the Dodge G-502 series trucks having been the standard vehicle in that weight class during WWII, it was only natural that the military turned to Dodge once again for a suitable M series replacement. The resultant vehicle was the G-741 series 3/4-ton Dodge, typified by the M37 cargo truck.

Improvements over their WWII-era predecessor included steel doors with roll-up windows, synchronized transmission, and the usual M-series improvements of 24-volt sealed electrical system and fording abilities. They were also slightly narrower and shorter than the earlier trucks.

A Dodge Model T-245 inline six-cylinder 230.2-cid engine provided power for these trucks. The clutch was a Borg and Beck model 11828.

The first production truck was completed in January 1951, and the first series G-741 production ceased in July 1954. These trucks were so popular and successful, however, that the tooling was removed from storage and production of the vehicles, with minor changes, resumed in February 1958 and continued into 1968. None of these trucks were produced in 1955-57. These vehicles were used by the U.S. military through the 1970s.

M37 Cargo Truck

This is one of the most collected postwar military vehicles. The all-steel cargo bed was equipped with troop seats, lazy backs, and top bows to support a canvas cover. The spare tire was carried on the front wall of the bed, and the passenger-side troop seat had a separate

Like most of the tactical vehicles of the 1950s, the M37 could be equipped with a deep-water fording kit. This winch-equipped M37 was photographed at Aberdeen Proving Ground in April 1950 while being tested. It has been fitted with the intake and exhaust extensions that are the core of the deep-water fording kit. (National Archives and Records Administration photo)

The quickest way to spot an M37B1 is the "door-mounted" spare tire, as seen in this May 1961 photograph. The spare actually was mounted on a hinged rack just outside the driver's door. Previous models mounted the spare tire on the inside front wall of the bed. The passenger-side troop seat was notched to clear it. The other changes characteristics to the B1 vehicles require close examination to spot. (National Archives and Records Administration photo)

For extreme cold-weather operation, a fuel-fired heater kit was developed for the M37 as well, as is seen in this December 1952 photograph taken during testing at Fort Churchill, Canada. The insulated blanket on the hood, as well as the winter front over the radiator, were a part of this kit, whose heart was the box mounted on the left front fender. For less frigid areas, a hot water-type heater was developed. Although it was shaped differently and lacked the exhaust pipe of the fuel fired heater, it mounted similarly. (National Archives and Records Administration photo)

3/4-TON TRUCKS

The M42 was the replacement to the WWII-era command cars and carryalls. It was essentially the same truck as an M37, but the canvas over the bed area had flexible plastic windows installed. The bed of the truck was fitted with a step for entry and a map table, among other detail changes. (Photo courtesy of the Patton Museum)

section to accommodate the spare. The truck has a 112-in. wheelbase. A 7,500-lb. capacity Braden LU-4 front-mounted PTO-driven winch was fitted to some of these trucks with bolt-on frame extensions.

M37B1 Cargo Truck

The second series G-741 cargo truck was the M37B1. It is most easily distinguished from the first series by the spare tire outboard of the driver's door. Improvements were also made to the electrical system and transmission. The Braden LU-4 front mounted, PTO-driven winch was fitted to some of these trucks as well.

M42 Command Truck

This truck is very similar to the M37, but the canvas bed covering had side windows, and the bed was equipped with a map table. The rear curtain also had

The M43 hinged upper litter racks have been folded down to act as a backrest for ambulatory patients who could sit on the lower litter racks. The door, which provides passage to the operator's compartment, is also visible. (National Archives and Records Administration photo)

windows and opened in the middle to allow easier entrance and exit. A boarding ladder was also installed to ease access to the bed.

M43 & M43B1 Ambulance

This was the ambulance version of the G-741 series. It was built on a 126-in. wheelbase chassis. Both the M43 and the M43B1 came with the spare mounted adjacent to the driver's door.

V-41 Telephone Maintenance Truck

This truck was built on an M56 chassis, and featured a telephone maintenance and installation body specified by the Armed Services Electro Standards Agency, Fort Monmouth, New Jersey. These trucks are equipped with a 7,500-lb. capacity Braden LU-4 front-mounted, PTO-driven winch. The spare tire is carried internally in the open top bed. The bed has a low tailgate and a center aisle, with four outward-opening storage compartments on either side. There is a ladder rack above the bed and a water cooler mounted on the driver's side. There is a spotlight mounted near the driver's door to assist in night work.

The Federal Stock Number for the V-41/GT is 2320-392-3703. Although the V-41/GT was listed in government manuals as early as February 1952, its specification, MIL-T-10158B, was last updated on June 30, 1957.

M201 & M201B1

The next of this family of vehicles is the M201, FSN 2320-835-8583. It was appearing in manuals by January 1954, and appears to be identical to the V-41/GT.

The M201B1, FSN 2320-630-6801, again essentially is the same vehicle, incorporating all the improvements to the chassis associated with the resumption of G-741 contracts in 1957.

The V-41/GT, M201, and M201B1 all have open-topped beds, which, except for the ladder rack and cooler, are lower than the windshield top of the chassis the beds are installed on.

All three of these vehicles were used to provide telephone system maintenance and cable splicing services. All of these trucks apparently were equipped with winches.

The ambulance version of the G-741 family was the M43. Its body, from the firewall back, was unique, and it was built on the slightly longer M56 chassis. Disregarding completely the lessons of WWII that brought about the WC-64 "knock-down" ambulance, the M43 returned to metal construction. All M43 ambulances have the swing-out spare tire carrier, requiring close examination to differentiate it from the M43B1. (National Archives and Records Administration photo)

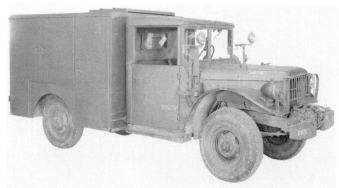

Among the earliest contact maintenance trucks on the G-741 chassis was this CMU-3 fitted with a steel body made by Dunbar-Kapple. Housed between the storage compartments of the enclosed bed was a Hobart PTO-driven welder/generator. (Photo courtesy of Keco Industries)

CMU-3 Contact Maintenance Truck

The first Contact Maintenance member of this family was the CMU-3. Designed for the Corps of Engineers, the CMU-3 design was finalized in December of 1959. Although most documentation shows that these trucks were built on M56C chassis, the data plates indicate that at least some of them are built on the M56B1 chassis. Perhaps data plates reading M56C do not exist. Some of the M56B1 chassis were built in 1958 under contract number 018-15711.

Unlike the 6217 and CMU-6, which have aluminum maintenance beds, the original CMU-3 trucks had an all-steel bed built by the Davey Compressor Company of Kent, Ohio, or by Dunbar-Kapple.

Unlike the open-topped M201, the CMU-3 bed is totally enclosed, and is taller than the truck cab. This bed housed a combination 7.5-kilowatt generator and 200-amp welder built by Hobart, which was driven off the truck driveline by way of a four-belt full-torque PTO. The welder/generator can also be used to slave-start other vehicles.

The list of on vehicle material carried by these trucks was extensive (the overloading is no doubt one of the reasons later trucks had aluminum bodies). In addition to the large welder/generator, there was an electrically powered air compressor, oxygen/acetylene torch set, and a huge variety of mechanic's hand tools carried on board. These trucks were basically used to provide roadside assistance to tactical, engineer, and combat vehicles.

CMU-5 Contact Maintenance Truck

This was an updated version of the CMU-3, and is very similar to the earlier model. The new truck featured an aluminum service bed, rather than the steel bed used earlier. It also had doors that enclosed the rear, instead of the canvas curtain previously used. There were civilian-type taillights recessed into the rear of the bed in addition to the standard military taillights, which were attached to the frame. These trucks have the swing-out spare tire carrier mounted at the driver's door. These contact maintenance beds were supplied by Davey Air Compressor Company.

XM708 3/4-Ton Dump Truck

Another scarce G-741 variant is the XM708 (or E1) dump truck. Like the XM711 wrecker, the XM708 dump

The later CMU-5 featured an aluminum body, as well as the door-type spare tire carrier characteristic of the B1 series vehicles. As can be seen in this photo, contact maintenance trucks carried an extensive, and heavy, array of tools. Notice the CMU-5 lacks the spotlights of the CMU-3. (Photo courtesy of Keco Industries)

In this driver's-side view of the CMU-3, the control panel of the welder is visible. We can also see that the spare tire is not mounted at the driver's door, unlike the CMU-5. (Photo courtesy Patton Museum)

trucks were built on the M53B1 chassis. There were three varieties of these built, according to the SC-2300-IL, July 1969. These were as follows:

— XM708 Dump Truck with Gar Wood GA 2 dump body, FSN 2320-911-507, acquisition cost $6,202.

— XM708E1 Dump Truck with Hardeman dump body FSN 2320-911-5078, acquisition cost of $6,202.

— The final version is the XM708 with winch. Apparently none of the Hardeman-bodied trucks were winch-equipped, as the Federal Stock Number for these units, 2320-926-7154, specifies a Gar Wood body. Despite the addition of a winch, the unit cost was a surprisingly low $6,150.00.

I suspect, but do not know, that the cost figures above do not include the M53B1 chassis. Rather, I suspect that the chassis were government supplied, and the above costs are just for the dump conversion. This would explain the lower cost for the winch-equipped trucks, as they are already equipped with a PTO, which would have had to be added to the others. Ambrose-West, Inc., did these conversions to dump trucks, under contract DAAE07 C-1914.

The XM711 wreckers were built on a special M53B1

The distinctive bodywork of the R-2 is clearly shown here. Never a common vehicle to begin with, the scrap value of the Oneida-built aluminum body led their numbers to be further reduced. The distinctive sloping roof houses a ladder. While the R-2 used the same Braden LU-4 winch as the other winch-equipped trucks in this series, the end of its cable was fitted with a grapnel, rather than a normal recovery hook. (Photo courtesy of Richard Adelman collection)

The XM708 and XM708E1 Dump Trucks were produced in limited numbers and deployed to Vietnam, which is where this photo was taken. The chassis for the XM708 was the 3/4-ton M53B1 chassis, which differed from the normal chassis by being equipped with overload, or helper, springs. The trucks were also the only vehicles in this series to be equipped with power brakes. (Photo courtesy of the Patton Museum)

XM711 Wrecker

Probably the scarcest G-741 variant was the XM711 Wrecker. The PTO on these trucks drove not only the front mounted winch, but also the recovery equipment in the bed. Like the XM708 dump trucks, the XM711s were built on the M53B1 chassis, but lacked the power brake system. This vehicle is on display at the First Cavalry Division Museum at Fort Hood, Texas.

Like the M43 ambulance, the R-2 was built on the long-wheelbase M56 chassis. Here, both types of non-combatants are shown in the service of the Ohio Air National Guard, poised for action near the flight line. (Photo courtesy of Richard Adelman collection)

chassis (also used by the XM708 series dump trucks). These chassis shared the 112-in. wheelbase and driveline with the M37, but had heavier springs and "overload," or helper, springs that came into play when the trucks were heavily loaded.

While the chassis specifications MS51390A is dated June 9, 1967, the final update of the XM711 specification, Military Specification MIL-T-62115, is dated May 13, 1969.

According to Supply Catalog 2300-IL, July 1969, all of the XM-711 wreckers were equipped with the Braden LU-4 front winch. The Federal Supply Number for the truck was 2320-911-5068. The M-53B1 chassis FSN was 2320-440-8674. The government cost of these was $6,165.

Unlike the earlier XM142 Bomb Service Truck, which had an Austin-Western bed with hydraulic crane, the XM-711s were equipped with beds made by the Ashton Power Wrecker Equipment Company. The controls were mounted at the rear of the bed and control the wrecker operation through a series of linkages, just as Ashton's commercial units did.

A unique feature of the XM711, compared to the rest of the G-741 series trucks, is a Hydro-Vac for power brakes. It is mounted on the frame near the driver's side running board. Vacuum for the power assist is taken off of the forward part of the intake manifold, at a port intended for a primer nozzle. The 198 or so of these trucks built each have a payload rating of 3,500 lbs., according the XM-711 data plate. This no doubt required better braking than the standard M37 brake system provided.

R-2 Crash Truck

This diminutive fire truck packs a punch as big as its official title: Truck, Fire, Airplane, Forcible Entry, Type R-2. With the production total of a mere 308 units, the R-2 was never the most common of the G-741 vehicles. Unlike its more common G-741 brother, the M37, the R-2's specialized body was not very versatile. Because the

bodies are made of aluminum, the numbers were to be further reduced by scrapping, until only a handful of intact examples are now known to exist. The scarcity, as well as nobility of purpose, of these vehicles certainly makes them worthy of preservation and restoration. The few that remain are sought after not only by military vehicle collectors, but also by collectors of fire apparatus. The bright red color, reflective markings, and unusual shape makes the R-2 stand out from the ordinary MV.

The R-2s were built by ACF-Brill under contract 22397 on Dodge-built, government-supplied chassis. ACF is American Car and Foundry (builder of tanks, ammunition, etc., in addition to ACF's main business of manufacturing railroad cars) and its Brill subsidiary's main businesses were trolley and bus manufacturing. Oneida Products (the silversmiths) Canastota Division built the aluminum bodies of these trucks.

These trucks were designed to be used in conjunction with Type 0-10 or 0-11 Foam Trucks. The Foam Trucks were to provide a path to the aircraft fuselage through the flames, and the R-2 would supply the tools and equipment to access the aircraft interior and rescue personnel. The meager 20 gallons of bromochloromethane extinguishing agent (discharged not by pumping, but with nitrogen pressurization) would

The quick-opening compartments on either side of the R-2 housed an extensive array of rescue tools. Although equipped with 20 gallons of extinguishing agent, the R-2 was not a fire truck, but a rescue truck intended to extract aircrews from downed aircraft. (Photo courtesy of Richard Adelman collection)

hardly fight a full-fledged aircraft fire. Rather, it was intended to merely get the rescuers the last few feet to the victims.

The R-2 was built on the M56 chassis, which has a 126-in. wheelbase (vs. the 112-in. wheelbase of the M37). These frames had fish belly reinforcements and were equipped with heavier springs than the cargo truck. The chassis for these trucks were produced by Dodge in 1953, under contract number 11939. The government then provided the chassis (and two batteries each) to Brill for conversion into the R-2. These conversions were completed in 1956. Heating, defrosting and other winterization kits could be field installed if needed. The data plate for these controls, as well as the warning light switches, were fitted to all trucks, whether the heater was installed or not.

At the front of the truck was the standard 7,500-lb.-capacity Braden LU-4 PTO-driven winch used on some M37s, but with a grapnel in place of the standard hook. The winch is driven via a double-ended PTO on the truck transmission, the other end of which powers the 230-volt, 180-cycle, three-phase Homelite chain-driven generator mounted in the bottom of the rescue bed. This powered the Mall circular saw, as well as the floodlights used for rescue operations.

Aside from the sea-foam green paint, the interior of the cab area differs from the usual M37s in the following ways:
— The cab doors had a special double-pane insulating glass.
— The arms that hold the windshield open were different than those on any other M-series vehicle.
— There were additional instruments mounted on the cab rear wall to monitor operation of the auxiliary generator.

The unusual sloping roof contained a model ID-1 11- to 20-foot foot extension A-frame ladder made by the Aluminum Ladder Company. The ladder was accessible by opening the rear doors.

Swinging the rear doors open also exposed axes, pry bars, and a variety of other "forcible entry" tools stored on interior surfaces. The open doors also provided access to two fire extinguishers, a Blackhawk model SB-52 porta-power, floodlight, nitrogen cylinder, and the Mall circular rescue saw.

A ladder to access the truck roof was mounted externally on the truck rear, as were both the standard ordnance-type slave receptacle and Air Force-type slave receptacle.

The standard Dodge T-245 230.2-cid six-cylinder engine was equipped with a Pierce Governor Company GC-3939 governor to aid in generator operation. This governor was not the same one that is used in the other G-741 variants, such as the CMU-3 Contact Maintenance truck.

On each side of the bed were two spring-loaded doors — one that swung up, the other down. On the driver's side, the upper compartment contained the communication system, CB extinguishing system, and tool cabinet loaded with rescue and entry tools. The passenger's side compartment opened to reveal even more tools, including bolt cutters, tin snips, a hose reel,

The Navy also had a G-741-based emergency vehicle, the MB-2 Crash Truck. Based on the M56 chassis, the MB-2 had coachwork built by Fred S. Gichner Iron Works of Washington, D.C. Of the reported 200 built, it is not known if any survive intact. This example was photographed in post-Navy service with the West Chicago Fire Protection District. (Photo courtesy of Richard Adelman collection)

and an electrical cable reel.

A Federal Enterprises model 17 24-volt rotating beacon was mounted on the roof of the truck, and the driver's side fender held a Federal model XG siren. These trucks also sported a spotlight on each side of the cab roof.

The empty weight was 4,600 lbs., while the ready-to-work weight was a whopping 7,690 lbs. They were 206 1/4 in. long and 104 13/16 in. tall. These vehicles were in service with the U.S. Air Force and the Navy by 1956.

M506 Hydrogen Peroxide Servicer

This very unusual G-741 variant consisted of an M37

Although the M506 resembles a WWII era bomb truck, in fact it was a hydrogen peroxide servicer for the Redstone missile system.

cargo truck modified by the installation of a monorail supported by an A-frame, a chainfall supported by the monorail, a gasoline-fired heating system, and a liquid nitrogen cooling system. Also mounted were an electric motor and pump assembly, an outflow tank, and a 50-power cable. All of this equipment made the Dodge resemble a WWII-era bomb service truck, although it was designed to support the modern-for-the-time Redstone missile system.

MB2 Crash Truck

These were undoubtedly the least handsome trucks of the G-741 family. Built for the Navy in 1955 by the Fred S. Gichner Iron Works of Washington, D.C., the Dodge M56 cab and chassis the MB2s were based on were barely recognizable. A reported 200 were built, and it is not known if any still exist.

GENERAL DATA

MODEL	M37	M42	M43
NET WEIGHT	5,687 lbs.	6,050 lbs.	7,150 lbs.
GROSS WEIGHT	7,687 lbs.	7,550 lbs.	8,550 lbs.
MAX TOWED LOAD	4,000 lbs.	4,000 lbs.	N/A
LENGTH	184.75	184.75	195.625
WHEELBASE	112	112	126
WIDTH	73.5	73.5	73.5
HEIGHT	89.5	89.75	91.875
WIDTH*	51.25/72.75	51.25/72.75	51.25/72.75
TRACK	62	62	62
TIRE SIZE	9.00-16	9.00-16	9.00-16
MAX SPEED	55 mph	55 mph	55 mph
FUEL CAPY	24 gal	24 gal	24 gal
RANGE	215 mi	215 mi	215 mi
ELECTRICAL	24 neg	24 neg	24 neg
TRANSMISSION SPEEDS	4	4	4
TRANSFER SPEEDS	2	2	2
TURNING RADIUS FT.	25	25	27

MODEL	V41/GT-M201	CMU-3
NET WEIGHT	7,150 lbs.	—
GROSS WEIGHT	9,300 lbs.	—
MAX TOWED LOAD	6,000 lbs.	
LENGTH	203.75	
WHEELBASE	126	126
WIDTH	73.5	73.5
HEIGHT	92.75	89.5
WIDTH*	51.25/72.75	51.25/72.75
TRACK	62	62
TIRE SIZE	9.00-16	9.00-16
MAX SPEED	55 mph	55 mph
FUEL CAPY	24 gal	24 gal
RANGE	215 mi	215 mi
ELECTRICAL	24 neg	24 neg
TRANSMISSION SPEEDS	4	4
TRANSFER SPEEDS	2	2
TURNING RADIUS FT.	5	25

Overall dimensions listed in inches.

Inside/outside width at tires.

All information above is for vehicle without winch (where applicable). For winch-equipped vehicles add 230 lbs. to weights listed, and increase length 4 5/8 in.

ENGINE DATA

ENGINE MAKE/MODEL	Dodge T245
NUMBER OF CYLINDERS	6
CUBIC-INCH DISPLACEMENT	230.2
HORSEPOWER	78 @ 3200 rpm
TORQUE	177 lbs.-ft. @ 1200 rpm
GOVERNED SPEED (rpm)	3200

VALUES

Model	6	5	4	3	2	1
M37	500	1,500	3,000	4,500	7,000	9,000
M42	600	1,600	3,500	5,500	8,000	10,000
M43	700	1,700	3,500	5,500	8,000	10,000
V41/GT or M201	700	1,700	3,500	6,000	8,500	12,000
CMU-3	1,000	1,900	3,500	6,000	8,500	12,000
R-2	1,000	2,000	4,000	6,750	9,500	16,000
MB-2	no known sales					

Note: Winches add $500 to $1,000 to the M37 prices above. All R-2 and CMU trucks have winches, no M43 trucks have winches.

SCARCITY

M37	1
M42	3
M43	2
V41/GT or M201	4
CMU-3 or -5	3
R-2	4

Five XM152 panel trucks were built in 1952, one of which is shown here. Although the trucks were not procured in series by the U.S. military, the Canadian military purchased several of the M152CDN, which differed in details. (Photo courtesy of the Patton Museum)

1-TON TRUCKS

IH Model M-2-4

The International Harvester M-2-4 truck was a 1-ton four-wheel-drive WWII vehicle. These vehicles were supplied to the Navy and Marine Corps. Production of the 1-ton M-2-4 began in 1941 with an order for 584 cargo trucks. The vast majority of these were open-cab cargo trucks, but a few were built with closed civilian "K" cabs with military fenders and hoods. Winches were furnished on 70 of the 584 trucks. The balance of the 10,450 vehicles were open-cab cargo trucks.

The open-cab M-2-4 trucks had very plain open cabs similar to those used on Dodge VC series 1/2-ton trucks, with two bucket seats and no provision for a top or doors. The majority of the trucks were cargo trucks with a narrow cargo box that further made them resemble the WWII Dodge 1/2-ton models. However the rear body was longer than the Dodge and the truck's simple fenders were mounted outside of the bed. The M-2-4 trucks were supplied with top bows, tarpaulins, and troop seats. The

spare tire was mounted on outer right hand side of the cargo bed. The fuel tank was under the seats, a toolbox on the left running board, and a one-piece folding

The rugged, simple construction of the Internationals made them popular with the Marine Corps. This example, owned and restored by Joe and Cheryl Capozzi, is equipped as it would have been when in service. (Photo courtesy of John Adams-Graf)

This photo of the prototype M-2-4 undergoing tests shows the general layout of these vehicles. Production units varied in details. (Photo courtesy of the Patton Museum)

windshield protected the crew. Separate brush guard protected the actual grille and lights during off-road operation. The radiator cap protruded through a hole in the right front of the side-opening hood. Power take-off driven winches were mounted at the front of some vehicles, and the frames of those trucks were longer than the none-winch trucks, rather than having extensions riveted on the ends. The earliest production trucks used civilian instruments, but those were supplanted in later production by the standard round military gauges.

GENERAL DATA

MODEL	M-2-4
NET WEIGHT	5,820 lbs.
GROSS	8,020 lbs.
LENGTH	197
WIDTH	84.5
HEIGHT	89
TRACK	63.5
TIRE SIZE	9.00 x 16
MAX SPEED	45 mph
FUEL CAPY	35 gal
RANGE	260 mi
ELECTRICAL	6
TRANSMISSION	
SPEEDS	4
TRANSFER	
SPEEDS	2

Overall dimensions listed in inches.

ENGINE DATA

ENGINE MAKE/MODEL	International GRD-233C
NUMBER OF CYLINDERS	6
CUBIC-INCH DISPLACEMENT	233
HORSEPOWER	93 @ 3400 rpm

VALUES

	6	5	4	3	2	1
M-2-4	1,700	3,500	5,500	7,000	10,000	14,000

SCARCITY

Scarcity 3+

The protruding, offset radiator cap of the M-2-4 is visible in this photo, as are the lifting rings and tow hooks. (Photo courtesy of John Adams-Graf)

1 1/4-TON TRUCKS

M715 Family

In 1965 the military wanted more all-wheel-drive medium trucks, but the Dodge G-741s then in use were getting expensive. The Army hoped to save money by buying a truck that was closer to being a standard civilian truck in mass production The result was the G-890 series of 1 1/4-ton trucks, which included the M715 — an adaptation of the Kaiser-Jeep "Gladiator" pick-up. The M715 was the first M series tactical vehicle to use primarily civilian commercial components.

In March of 1966, a contract was awarded to Kaiser for 20,680 trucks. This contract included M715 cargo trucks and M725 ambulances. The first trucks rolled of the assembly line in Toledo during January 1967. Additional contracts brought the production total to more than 30,500 M715 series trucks by the time production ceased in 1969.

The Gladiator tooling was used to create the grille, fenders, hood, doors, and cab of the M715 family. Changes to the sheet metal stampings included opening up the upper part of the cab and doors to accommodate the military canvas cab top. Also, the front fenders were cut out to clear the military 9.00-16 tires. The new fold-down windshield resembled the one used on the M38A1.

The cargo bed was an all-new design, unlike that of any other vehicle, military or civilian.

It appears that the M726 is the scarcest production version of these vehicles, followed by the M724, M725, and the common M715. It is unclear if any vehicles were produced with data plates that read M142 instead of M715.

All M715 series trucks were built on the same frame and wheelbase, regardless of body or winch. The

This M715 in the motor pool for maintenance shows the troop seat arrangement and unique cargo bed. Also visible is the padlocked under-bed tool compartment. (U.S. Army photo)

This is an XM715 with winch shown on trial by the Armor and Engineer Board at Fort Knox in October 1966. Although mounted differently, this is the same type 7,500-lb.-capacity Braden LU-4 PTO-driven winch that was used on the G-741 series trucks, such as the M37. (Photo courtesy the Patton Museum)

variations of this series are as follows:

M715

Standard 1 1/4-ton cargo truck, both with and without winch.

M724

Cab & chassis, often equipped with an aluminum contact maintenance body housing, and a combination welder/generator. This body, made by Stewart Avionics, was very similar to the Davey beds used on the Dodge-based CMU-5. All of these trucks were equipped with a winch.

M725

The ambulance variant of the family. The front sheet metal looked like a normal M715, but on the rear was an ambulance body. The body was different from the firewall rear. There was a sliding doorway between the driver's compartment and the rear patient compartment, which was equipped with four stretcher racks. Also provided on the ambulance body was: a surgical light, air ventilators, double rear doors, and a gas heater.

M726

Telephone maintenance truck, built on the same chassis as the M724. On its rear was a utility box body. However, this body differed significantly from the M724. Rather than being enclosed and mounting a generator/welder, it had an open cargo area in the back with outward-facing storage compartments. This bed was much lower than the M724 contact maintenance

This is truly an M724 — simply a cab and chassis. The contact maintenance truck and the M726 were built on this chassis. (U.S. Army photo)

The XM715 is shown with all the canvas removed and the windshield folded down. The unusually shaped box between the seats is the truck's battery box. The fuel filler and spare fuel can be seen in the lower part of the photograph. (Photo courtesy the Patton Museum)

The M725 was the ambulance variant of the G-890 series. The body from the firewall back was unique to this truck. The battery compartment, located between the front seats on the rest of the series, was relocated to beneath lower litter rack on the passenger's side of these trucks. The floodlight mounted on the roof was standard equipment on ambulances. (U.S. Army photo).

When set up to transport, the S-250 shelter was known as the M142. This truck may well have been the pilot model of the M142. (U.S. Army photo)

body. Some of the M726s were equipped with the 8,000-lb. PTO winch and a spotlight mounted on the left corner of the cowling.

GENERAL DATA

MODEL	M715	M724	M725	M726
NET WEIGHT	8,400 lbs.	8,500 lbs.	8,800 lbs.	8,900 lbs.
GROSS WEIGHT	5,500 lbs.	4,800 lbs.	6,000 lbs.	6,500 lbs.
MAX TOWED LOAD	3,590 lbs.	3,590 lbs.	N/A	3,590 lbs.
LENGTH	209.7	209.75	209.75	220.75
WHEELBASE	126	126	126	126
WIDTH	85	85	85	85
HEIGHT	95	80	95	80
TRACK	67	67	67	67
TIRE SIZE	9.00-16	9.00-16	9.00-16	9.00-16
MAX SPEED	60 mph	60 mph	60 mph	60 mph
FUEL CAPY	28 gal	28 gal	28 gal	28 gal
RANGE	225 mi	225 mi	225 mi	225 mi
ELECTRICAL	24 neg	24 neg	24 neg	24 neg
TRANSMISSION SPEEDS	4	4	4	4
TRANSFER SPEEDS	2	2	2	2
TURNING RADIUS FT.	27.5	27.5	27.5	27.5

For winch-equipped vehicles, increase the weight by 500 lbs., and the length by 11 in.

GENERAL DATA

ENGINE MAKE/MODEL	Jeep Tornado
NUMBER OF CYLINDERS	6
CUBIC-INCH DISPLACEMENT	230
HORSEPOWER	132 @ 4000 rpm
TORQUE	198 lbs.-ft. @ 2000 rpm
GOVERNED SPEED (rpm)	4000

VALUES

	6	5	4	3	2	1
M715	500	1,500	3,000	4,500	7,500	9,750
M724	500	1,250	2,000	3,000	5,000	6,000
M725	500	1,500	3,000	4,500	8,000	10,000
M726	500	1,500	3,000	4,500	8,000	10,000
6217	700	1,750	3,000	4,500	7,500	9,750

SCARCITY

M715	1
M724	4
M725	2
M726	4
6217	4

The 6217 contact maintenance truck (above) is often erroneously referred to as an M724. A host of tools and equipment were carried in the compartments, while a large PTO-driven combination welder/generator was mounted inside the bed. (Photo courtesy the Patton Museum)

This is the XM726 1 1/4-ton telephone maintenance truck. Its bed is much different than the 6217 bed, but very similar to the bed of the G-741-based V-41/GT. (U.S. Army photo)

Dodge M880

The M880 series of vehicles were intended to provide the military with a low-cost vehicle to replace the G-741 and G-890 series vehicles in non-tactical duty. The trucks were built by Dodge in 1976 and 1977 and, except for the ambulance, were essentially the contemporary Dodge commercial trucks with a few military modifications.

M880

The base vehicle of the series was the M880 pickup, which was based on the Dodge 3/4-ton W200 pickup. A folding set of steel bows was available to support a cargo cover over the standard civilian bed. A form of the standard military folding troop seat was provided that would fit into the bed's stake pockets.

The trucks were powered by the standard civilian Chrysler 318 V-8, which drove the truck through an automatic transmission. The trucks also had power

This M880 was built after August 19, 1976, as evidenced by the parking lights inboard of the headlights. (Photo courtesy of Memphis Equipment Company)

steering and a civilian-type step bumper on the rear provided the mounting point for the pintle hook. A kit was available to add a 24-volt power system to the trucks. Most of the vehicles did not have military-type lighting systems.

M881

This was an M880 equipped with a 24-volt, 60-amp generating system in addition to the standard 12-volt electrical system of the vehicle.

M882

This was an M881 with the addition of a communications kit.

M883

The M883 was an M881 with an S250 shelter kit. The shelter was mounted inside the trucks standard cargo bed and secured with tie-downs.

M884

A truck with the S250 shelter, 24-volt, 100-amp electrical system and communications kit was known as the M884.

The base vehicle for this series was the M880 pickup. The position of the parking lights under the headlights identifies this as being built prior to August 15, 1976. After that date the parking lights moved inboard of the headlights. (U.S. Army photo)

The M880 series trucks, while achieving the military's goal of providing economical transportation in non-combat areas, lack the appeal of the purely tactical designs that preceded them. (U.S. Army photo)

M885

When an S250 shelter was installed in the base M880, the vehicle was known as the M885.

M886

While the ambulance model used the same sheet metal from the cab forward, the rear bed was especially made for this truck. A sliding door in the rear of the cab allowed the attendant access to the heated rear patient compartment. A pair of double doors in the rear of the body could be opened for patient loading. Five litter patients could be carried.

M887

This was a cab and chassis vehicle, and was commonly used on contact maintenance trucks.

M888

The M888 was a telephone maintenance truck. This truck used the same chassis as the M880, but had a utility bed.

M890

This is essentially the same truck as the M880, but without the all-wheel-drive components. These vehicles were intended strictly for on-road use.

M891

The M891 was a two-wheel-drive version of the M881.

M892

The two-wheel-drive version of the M882 was known as the M892.

M893

There was also a two-wheel drive version of the ambulance built, which was known as the M893. The ambulance body used on the M893 was identical to the ambulance body used on the M886.

From the standpoint of the collector, the civilian lineage of these trucks has advantages and disadvantages. The trucks themselves are economically

Some of the vehicles were supplied as cab and chassis and were then fitted with a contact maintenance body, like this example owned by Sam Werner.

The M886 ambulance had an unmistakable profile. Some of these were adapted for use as communication vehicles. A spotlight was mounted on the front of the ambulance body. For any use other than ambulance, the red crosses would have been removed. (U.S. Army photo)

priced, and parts are readily available through normal civilian channels. However, they lack the mystique of purely tactical vehicles.

GENERAL DATA

MODEL	M880
NET WEIGHT	4,648 lbs.
GROSS WEIGHT	7,748 lbs.
LENGTH	218.7 lbs.
WHEEBASE	131
WIDTH	79.5
HEIGHT	73.9
TRACK	65.2
TIRE SIZE	9.50-16.5
MAX SPEED	70 mph
FUEL CAPY	20 gal
RANGE	225 mi
ELECTRICAL	12 neg
TRANSMISSION	
SPEEDS	3 automatic
TRANSFER	
SPEEDS	2

Overall dimensions listed in inches.

ENGINE DATA

ENGINE MAKE/MODEL	Chrysler
NUMBER OF CYLINDERS	V-8
CUBIC-INCH DISPLACEMENT	318.3
HORSEPOWER	150 @ 4000 rpm
TORQUE	230 lbs.-ft. @ 2400 rpm

VALUES

	6	5	4	3	2	1
M880	500	1,000	1,600	2,200	3,500	4,750
M886	500	1,000	1,800	2,600	4,000	5,000
M888	700	1,200	2,000	2,400	3,800	4,500
M890	300	800	1,200	1,600	2,100	3,000
M893	500	1,000	1,600	2,000	2,500	3,500

SCARCITY

M880 1
M886 2
M888 3
M890 1
M893 3

CUCV Series

The Chevrolet Commercial Utility Cargo Vehicle series replaced the Dodge M880 series. Like their predecessors, the CUCVs were militarized versions of off-the-shelf civilian four-wheel-drive vehicles, although in

The base vehicle of this series is the M1008. Shown here in its cleanest form, it can hardly be differentiated from its civilian counterpart. (Photo courtesy of Tacticaltruck.com)

With the canvas cargo cover in place, and wearing the three-color NATO camo scheme, the M1008 looks more like what it is, a military vehicle. (Photo courtesy of Tacticaltruck.com)

this case the militarization was a little more extensive than it had been with the earlier Dodges.

Production of this series began in 1984. The front axle had lockout hubs. Additional modifications included the addition of a brush guard and towing shackles on the front bumper and a dual 12-and 28-volt 100-amp charging system. The engine was GM's 6.2-liter diesel coupled to a Turbo-Hydramatic transmission. Most models used the New Process NP208 two-speed chain-driven transfer case. All models had non-slip rear differentials.

M1008

The M1008 was the base vehicle of the series, and was essentially a diesel-powered version of the Chevrolet K2500, but with a K3500 front axle. At the rear of the truck was a step bumper with a pintle hook. The cargo bed itself was essentially the civilian model, but with a folding cargo cover and removable troop seats added.

M1008A1

The M1008A1 is the same basic vehicle as the M1008, but it has radio racks installed in the bed, and antenna mounts. As with the M1008, the base civilian 12-volt system was retained for instruments.

M1028

The M1028 was a shelter carrier based on the M1008, with a communications kit and an S-250 shelter kit installed.

The M1009 was based on the civilian Chevrolet Blazer. Although it used the same 6.2-liter diesel engine and automatic transmission as the rest of the series, its axles, tires, and wheels were not as robust as those used in the rest of the series. (Photo courtesy of Tacticaltruck.com)

Unlike the rest of this series, the M1010 did not have a civilian equivalent. The additional electrical load imposed by the air conditioning and lighting systems of the patient compartment required these vehicles be equipped with a 200-amp charging system. (U.S. Army photo)

The pintle hook of the M1008 was mounted on a standard civilian step bumper. The front and rear shackles are attached to the frame. (U.S. Army photo)

M1028A1

This was the same truck as the base M1028, except for its two-speed New Process 205 gear-driven transfer case, which had provisions for a power take-off unit.

M1028A2

This is an M1028A1 with the New Process 205 transfer case and dual rear wheels.

M1028A3

The M1028A3 is an M1028A2, but with a New Process 208 transfer case.

M1031

The M1031 was a cab and chassis only — essentially an M1008 without the bed.

M1009

The M1009 was based on the Chevrolet Blazer and used the standard 1/2-ton chassis components, rather than the heavy-duty suspension components of the rest of this series. The interior of the truck was essentially the same as its civilian counterpart.

The ambulance version of the CUCV series was the

The M1028 shelter carrier was equipped with the S-250 shelter. A variety of communication equipment could be installed within the shelter. (U.S. Army photo)

This front view of the M1008 with canvas erected shows the blackout driving light, NATO slave receptacle, and bridge weight classification plate. (U.S. Army photo)

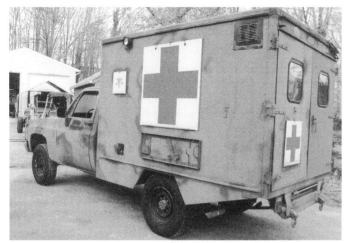

M1010 Ambulance

only member of the series with factory air-conditioning. The custom-built patient compartment was not only heated and air conditioned, but also was equipped with an elaborate air filtration system. A sliding door separated the driver's compartment from the rear patient area. A spotlight was mounted on the cab roof, and the patient compartment had an elaborate lighting system. The various lights, air conditioning, and filtration required a lot of electricity, which was supplied by a 200-amp, 28-volt charging system.

The Red Cross emblems on these ambulances were mounted on removable panels, which are often missing today. Unlike previous similar ambulances, the rear step of the M1010 doesn't fold against the rear doors, but rather slides into the rear bumper. (Photo courtesy of Tacticaltruck.com)

In this M1010, the right-hand side has been set up to transport two litter patients, and the left-hand side is configured to transport four ambulatory patients. (U.S. Army photo)

The boarding ladder is shown here in its deployed position. The shackles are missing from their brackets on this example. (U.S. Army photo)

GENERAL DATA

MODEL	M1008	M1009	M1028	M1010
WEIGHT NET	5,900 lbs.	5,275 lbs.	5,688 lbs.	7,475 lbs.
GROSS	8,800 lbs.	6,475 lbs.	9,288 lbs.	9,555 lbs.
LENGTH	216.5	185.625	216.5	222 13/16
WHEEBASE	131.5	106.5	131.5	131.5
TRACK FRT/REAR	68/65	68/65	68/65	68/65
WIDTH	79.625	79.625	79.625	79.625
HEIGHT	76	75 13/32	76	101
TIRE SIZE	235/85R16	235/85R16	235/85R16	235/85R16
MAX SPEED	65 mph	65 mph	65 mph	65 mph
RANGE	270 mi	250 mi	270 mi	270 mi
ELECTRICAL	12/24 neg	12/24 neg	12/24 neg	12/24 neg
TRANSMISSION				
SPEEDS	3 auto	3 auto	3 auto	3 auto
TRANSFER				
SPEEDS	2	2	2	2

Overall dimensions listed in inches.

ENGINE DATA

ENGINE MAKE/MODEL	Chevrolet
NUMBER OF CYLINDERS	V-8
CUBIC-INCH DISPLACEMENT	379
HORSEPOWER	135 @ 3600 rpm
TORQUE	240 lbs.-ft. @ 2000 rpm

VALUES

	6	5	4	3	2	1
M1008	1,200	2,800	4,000	7,000	8,500	10,000
M1009	1,500	3,000	4,400	7,500	9,000	11,000
M1028	1,000	2,800	4,000	7,000	8,500	10,000
M1010	2,000	3,200	4,800	8,000	10,000	12,000

SCARCITY

M1008 1
M1009 1
M1028 2
M1010 2

HMMWV

After extensive competition, AM General was awarded the contract to build the High-Mobility Multipurpose Wheeled Vehicle in March of 1983. It was intended to replace tactical vehicles in the 1/4- to 1 1/4-ton range, and as the name states, perform a variety of functions.

The initial series was powered by the General Motors 6.2-liter diesel engines, while the latest versions have a GM 6.5-liter engine. The hoods are fiberglass, and the bodies are made of aluminum. The truck has four-wheel independent suspension.

There are a variety of models of these vehicles, in part due to the Army's assigning a different M-numbers to winch-equipped and non-winch-equipped vehicles. This practice was discontinued with the introduction of the A2 series.

The basic vehicle is the M998. This vehicle could be configured as either two or four door using removable panels, and was supplied with a vinyl top and doors. The same truck, when supplied with a front winch, was known as the M1038.

Some of the other vehicles in this series are:

M1037 shelter carrier. This vehicle has heavy-duty suspension components, and special brackets for tying down a shelter in the cargo area. These shelters could be

This M998 has been fitted with an M998A2-type hood. It is configured as a four-man personnel carrier. It has a brush guard installed, and a cover over the rear cargo area. (Photo courtesy of Tacticaltruck.com)

Evacuation of injured personnel is a high priority for the military, and there are three different HMMWV-based ambulance models. Shown here is the M996 two-litter hard top ambulance rigged for airdrop. It is capable of transporting two litter patients, or six ambulatory patients, in air-conditioned comfort. (Photo courtesy of John Adams-Graf)

The M998 could also be configured as two-seat pickup truck. This truck lacks the optional brush guard. (Photo courtesy of AM General Corp.)

The M998 is the base vehicle of the HMMWV series. This one is configured as a four-man troop carrier with a soft-top enclosure. (Photo courtesy of AM General Corp.)

The M1035 is a soft-top ambulance in the style of the M151-based M718 field ambulance that it replaced. This is a U.S. Navy vehicle. (Photo courtesy of AM General Corp.)

The M1037 shelter carrier was designed to transport the S250 communications shelter. These shelters can be used for communications, electronics, or command purposes and are secured firmly to the vehicle. (Photo courtesy of AM General Corp.)

used for communications, electronics, or command purposes.

The M1042 is the same vehicle as the M1037, but is equipped with a winch.

The M1025 is an armament carrier without a winch. The same vehicle with the winch installed is known as the M1026. This mount allows the HMMWV to be armed with a variety of weapons, including the M60, 7.62mm machine gun; M2 .50 caliber machine gun; or the MK 19 Grenade Launcher. The ring mount allows weapons traversal of a full 360 degrees.

When armed with a TOW missile launcher, the winch-equipped vehicle is an M1036; sans winch it is the M966. These vehicles closely resemble the M1025 and M1026, but have a different interior layout, and there is a small blast shield mounted on the TOW carrier.

All the armament carriers have four doors, and a metal slope-backed roof. The doors of all armament carriers are made of composite-reinforced fiberglass.

The two-litter hard-bodied ambulance was tabbed the M996, while the M997 is the hard-bodied four-litter ambulance. The M1035 is a soft-top two-litter ambulance. The M996 and M1035 are air-droppable.

The lack of the distinctive X embossed in the door and the winch on the front gives away the fact that this is an armored M1043A2 or M1045A2. (Photo courtesy of AM General Corp.)

Even more heavily armored, and armed, than the M1025 series is this M1114 up-armored variant. (Photo courtesy of AM General Corp.)

The M997 ambulance is slightly larger than the M996, and has a higher profile. The increased area is visible above the cab of the truck. This added height allows it to accommodate four-litter patients or eight ambulatory patients, again in an air-conditioned and heated compartment. (Photo courtesy of AM General Corp.)

The slant-back M1025 armament carrier is one of the most distinctive members of the HMMWV family. It is protected against splinters, but not opposing direct fire. This vehicle is armed with an MK 19 grenade launcher. (Photo courtesy of AM General Corp.)

1 1/4-TON TRUCKS

The Marine Corps wanted vehicles with additional armor protection, as well as permanently installed deep water fording pipes. The additional armor on the doors of these vehicles made the outer surfaces of the doors flat, rather than showing the X-shaped embossments of the normal trucks. The Marine Corps version of the armament carrier with winch is known as the M1044; without winch it is the M1043. The TOW missile carriers with and without winch are M1046 and M1045, respectively.

The M1097 was developed to fill the need for a vehicle with higher payload and towed load ratings than the M1037 provided. This Heavy Humvee has a reinforced frame, heavier springs, tires and rims and other improvements. Because of the success of the improvements in the M1097, they were incorporated in the M998A1 series.

The M1109 is an armored version of the HMMWV, with the armor provided by O'Gara-Hess & Eisenhardt.

The M998A2 series, introduced in 1984, had numerous improvements in the power train. The engine was the 6.5-liter (400 cubic-inch) diesel, and the automatic transmission was a four-speed unit rather than the three-speed previously used.

Special Operations units are outfitted with these heavily modified HMMWVs. Among the modifications was considerably increased protection for the engine compartment. Also, these are unique among U.S. HMMWVs in that they carry spare tires. Any other vehicles with spares are foreign sales units. (Photo courtesy of AM General Corp.)

The M1097A2 is the base vehicle of this series (despite the name, there is no M998A2 vehicle). It serves as the shelter carrier, prime mover, cargo carrier, and personnel carrier member of the family.

The M1025A2 is the armament-TOW missile carrier in the new series, while the Marine's M1043 and M1045 were carried over into the new series as the M1043A2 and M1045A2.

The soft-top ambulance continued to be produced as the M1035A2 and the four-litter hard-bodied ambulance became the M997A2. The two-litter ambulance was discontinued.

Once again there grew a need for a higher-capacity vehicle, which was answered by the development of the M1113 expanded-capacity truck. The engine was upgraded to a turbosupercharged version of the 6.5-liter, and the gear ratios were changed.

O'Gara-Hess & Eisenhardt used this as the basis for the M1114 armored HMMWV. The M1114's roof mounted ring mount could be used for the venerable M2HB Browning machine gun or more modern weapons such as the 7.62mm M60 or 40mm Mark 19 grenade launcher. Armor provided the crew with protection from 7.62 ammo at ranges over 100 meters, and 4-lb. mines.

The U.S. Air Force purchased similar vehicles, known as the M1116, for use as base security vehicles.

GENERAL DATA

MODEL	M997A2	M1025A2	M1035A2
NET WEIGHT NET	7,770 lbs.	6,780 lbs.	6,100 lbs.
GROSS WEIGHT	10,300 lbs.	10,300 lbs.	10,300 lbs.
LENGTH	204.5	190.5	182.5
WHEELBASE	130	130	130
WIDTH	86	86	86
HEIGHT	102	76	72
TRACK	71.6	71.6	71.6
TIRE SIZE	37 x1 2.5R16.5	37 x 12.5R16.5	37 x 12.5R16.5
MAX SPEED	70	70	70

GENERAL DATA, continued

FUEL CAPY	25	25	25
ELECTRICAL	24 neg	24 neg	24 neg
TRANSMISSION			
SPEEDS	4	4	4
TRANSFER			
SPEEDS	2	2	2
TURNING			
RADIUS FT	25	25	25

MODEL	M1043A2	M1097A2
NET WEIGHT NET	7,264	5,900
GROSS WEIGHT	10,300	10,300
LENGTH	190.5	190.5
WHEELBASE	130	130
WIDTH	86	86
HEIGHT	76	74
TRACK	71.6	71.6
TIRE SIZE	37 x 12.5R16.5	37 x 12.5R16.5
MAX SPEED	70	70
FUEL CAPY	25	25
ELECTRICAL	24 neg	24 neg
TRANSMISSION		
SPEEDS	4	4
TRANSFER		
SPEEDS	2	2
TURNING		
RADIUS FT	25	25

Overall dimensions listed in inches.

Note: Winch-equipped models have payloads reduced by 127 lbs.

ENGINE DATA

ENGINE MAKE/MODEL	GM 6.5
NUMBER OF CYLINDERS	V8
CUBIC-INCH DISPLACEMENT	400
HORSEPOWER	160 @ 3400 RPM
TORQUE	290 lbs.-ft. @ 1700 RPM

VALUES

	6	5	4	3	2	1
Cargo models	4,000	8,000	18,000	30,000	38,000	45,000

SCARCITY

Scarcity 2

The Air Force liked the basic idea of the M1114, but wanted a few changes. The resultant vehicle was this M1116. (Photo courtesy of AM General Corp.)

1 1/2-TON TRUCKS

G-622 Ford

The G-622 Ford trucks, commonly referred to as Burma Jeeps, grew out of the Army's prewar low-silhouette truck program. Although these trucks have a very distinctive appearance, mechanically they are very standard vehicles, and many off-the-shelf parts.

The driver sat alongside the engine, which was offset to the right. The passenger sat to the right of the engine, but unconventionally, the passenger faced the driver.

Production of these trucks began in mid-June 1942. Most of the components were fabricated by Ford's River Rouge plant, but were shipped to the Ford Edgewater, New Jersey, plant for assembly. That changed in January-February 1944 when production was shifted to the Ford Louisville plant so the Edgewater plant could be solely devoted to packaging Ford products for overseas shipment.

Originally intended as foreign aid, but refused by the Russian government, the first 6,001 vehicles were accepted by the Army. One thousand of these trucks were equipped with front-mounted PTO-driven Gar Wood winch.

Although the Ford design was not well received by the Army, the Navy saw this truck as a way around the supply stranglehold the Army had on the G-506 Chevrolet of the same weight class, and began negotiating with Ford in September 1942.

In December 1942, the Navy ordered 1,500 of the model GTBS bomb service trucks. An additional 800

This is the very first Ford GTB. It differs from the production model in that it lacks a blackout-driving lamp, and it has no windshield wiper motors. These trucks' ancestry in the low-silhouette program is apparent in this view. The passenger's seat back has been folded over. (Photo courtesy of the Bryce Sunderlin collection)

were ordered shortly after the first order was delivered in March 1943.

Although the beds of these trucks look very much like the bed of the Chevrolet M-6 bomb service trucks, they differ both mechanically and aesthetically. The GTBS lacks the outward-facing rear seats of the Chevrolet. The hoists were built by Weaver Hoist Manufacturing. Unlike other vehicles in the GTB family, the GTBS had single rear wheels. The GTBS also lacked a front winch.

The Navy also ordered its own version of the GTB cargo truck, the GTBA. These trucks were essentially identical to the Army's GTB trucks, but were generally painted Non-Specular Ocean Gray O-5. These trucks were all equipped with one of two kinds of winches. Some used the same Gar Wood unit as was installed on the GTB, but demand for that winch for use on the CCKW and 1.5-ton Chevrolet forced the substitution of a

The GTBS was the first variant used by the Navy for a bomb service truck. In this photo the single rear tires characteristic of the GTBS are visible. This truck lacks a front winch. (Photo courtesy of the Bryce Sunderlin collection)

Shown here is the prototype for the winch-equipped vehicles. The Gar Wood winch shown here is the same unit that was used on the GMC CCKW and the 1 1/2-ton Chevrolet trucks. With the canvas assembled, the vehicle's normally low profile was increased substantially. (Photo courtesy of the Bryce Sunderlin collection)

Braden winch on some of the trucks. The frames were manufactured to accept either winch.

With only 50 units built, the GTBB Wrecker-Service truck is the rarest of the series. The wrecker body was Marquette model 141 and featured a PTO-driven hoist. Strangely, these trucks lacked a front winch.

The final production variant of this series was the GTBC Improved Bomb Service Truck, Mk II, Model 2. While the hoist mechanism was essentially the same as that used on the GTBS, the chassis had a front winch and dual rear wheels. Production of the GTBC began in September 1943.

Total production for the G-622 family of vehicles was 15,274. This can be broken down as follows:

GTB prototype	3
GTB wo/winch	5,007
GTB w/winch	994
GTBS Bomb Service	2,301
GTBA Cargo	2,218
GTBB Wrecker	50
GTBC Bomb Service	4,701

GENERAL DATA

MODEL	115-in. wb cargo
WEIGHT NET	6,900 lbs.
LENGTH	180.67
WIDTH	86
HEIGHT	100.3
TRACK	68
TIRE SIZE	7.50-20
MAX SPEED	45 mph
FUEL CAPY*	40 gal
ELECTRICAL	6 neg
TRANSMISSION	
SPEEDS	4
TRANSFER	
SPEEDS	2

Overall dimensions listed in inches.

*40-gallon fuel tank fitted to cargo trucks, bomb trucks use a 26-gallon tank.

This is the interior of a GTBC. The cab layout of all the vehicles in the GTB-family was very similar. Notice the sideways-facing passenger's seat. The GTBC was equipped with an electric brake controller, which can be seen mounted on the steering column, just above the instrument panel. (Photo courtesy of the Bryce Sunderlin collection)

The improved Bomb Service Truck, the GTBC, reverted to the dual rear wheels used by the rest of the series, and included a front winch. This winch was the Braden MU-5A model, but the Gar Wood unit was also fitted, and was preferred. This model accounted for about 50 percent of the Navy's GTB series purchases. (Photo courtesy of the Bryce Sunderlin collection)

ENGINE DATA

ENGINE MAKE/MODEL	Ford Military GTB modified 1GA
NUMBER OF CYLINDERS	6
CUBIC-INCH DISPLACEMENT	226
HORSEPOWER	90 @ 3000 rpm
TORQUE	180 lbs.-ft. @ 1200 rpm
GOVERNED SPEED (rpm)	2,870

VALUES

	6	5	4	3	2	1
Cargo truck	1,000	2,000	4,000	8,000	12,000	15,000
Bomb truck	1,000	2,000	4,000	8,000	12,000	15,000

SCARCITY

Cargo truck 4
Bomb truck 4

G-506 Chevrolet

The ton-and-a-half Chevrolet looks very much like a CCKW shorn of its rear axle, but is quiet a different vehicle. Chevy produced about 160,000 of these all-wheel-drive trucks during WWII, far exceeding International and Dodge, who also produced trucks in this size range. More than half of the Chevys were provided to foreign countries. These trucks came with and without winches, and were fitted with a variety of beds for specialized uses. In addition to cargo trucks, Chevrolet built telephone pole auger, bomb handling, crash rescue, and airfield lighting trucks.

All of these trucks used the banjo-style axles, and were powered by the Chevy 235-cid inline six-cylinder engine that would run on gasoline as low as 70-octane. Typical of WWII era vehicles, the four-speed transmission was not synchronized, requiring each shift to be double-clutched. The two-speed transfer case (high and low range), which includes a provision to disengage the front wheel drive, completes the gear train. The data plates were mounted on the map compartment door on 1940 and 1941 models. They moved to the headliner for the rest of the run.

The standard open military cab was never fitted to the Chevy, and all but the bomb service trucks were built with closed cab. There was no provision for the installation of a machine gun ring mount.

The 1942-and-up Chevrolet model numbers, such as G7107, are often used when referring to these trucks. However, the original model numbers were different than in subsequent years. The first contract model numbers are listed below in parenthesis beside the more commonly known 1942-and-up model numbers. The interim model numbers used in late 1941 are in brackets.

G7107 (G4112) [G4174] Cargo

The G7107 was the basic cargo truck with 9-ft. cargo bed. Depending upon date of production, the bed was either steel or wood. Early models used civilian-type instruments, later ones used standard military-type components. These trucks were built on 145-in.-wheelbase chassis.

This photograph was taken outside the Army Engineering Standards Vehicle Laboratory in July 1944. It shows a Chevrolet G7107 equipped with a steel cargo bed. The 1 1/2-ton Chevrolet was unusual because it was only built with closed cabs.(U.S. Army photo)

This November 1944 photo taken at the Studebaker Proving Ground shows the typical 1 1/2-ton Chevy G7107. This particular truck has a steel bed. The liquid container bracket can be seen beneath the fuel filler. (U.S. Army photo)

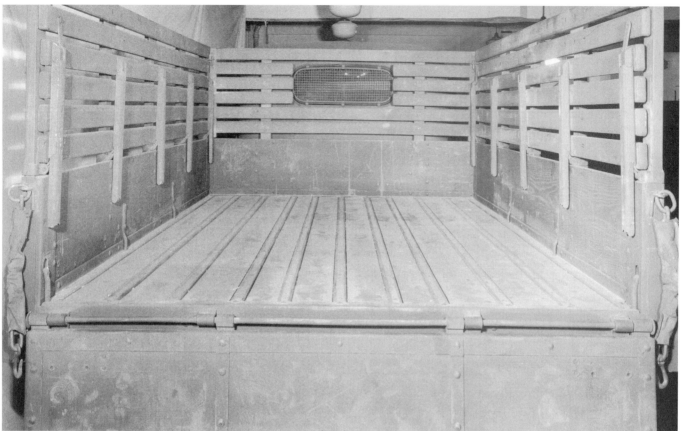

The interior of the wooden cargo bed is shown here. With the troop seats in the stowed position, the truck is ready to receive cargo. (U.S. Army photo)

This Army Engineering Standards Vehicle Laboratory photo taken in January 1944 shows a G7107 with the canvas bed cover. The cargo bed on this truck is made of wood. The stenciling on the side of the canvas indicates it was made for the U.S. Q. M. C. (U.S. Quarter Master Corps), although the maker's name is not legible. (U.S. Army photo)

This totally enclosed truck was known by Chevrolet as the model G7105. The Army used these to transport radios and other sensitive equipment. The dual rear wheels quickly distinguish it from the similar-looking Dodge Carryall trucks. (National Archives and Records Administration photo)

G7117 (G4112) [G4163] Cargo

This was the same truck as the G7107, only equipped with a front-mounted PTO-driven winch. These trucks were built on 145-in.-wheelbase chassis.

G7106 (G4112) [G4152] Dump

The dump truck version of the G-506 was equipped with a single-cylinder hydraulic hoist and sub frame. The bed itself was essentially the same as the cargo bed, but with a dual-action tailgate that could be raised or lowered. These trucks were built on 145-in.-wheelbase chassis.

G7116 (G4112) [G4162] Dump

This is the same truck as the G7106, only it is equipped with the front winch. These trucks were built on 145-in.-wheelbase chassis.

The G7106 dump truck was hard to distinguish from the standard cargo truck, until the bed was elevated as in this October 1941 Holabird Quartermaster Depot photo. (National Archives and Records Administration photo)

This restored G7117 differed from the G7107 only by the addition of a front PTO-driven winch. This truck has had larger 9.00-20 tires installed on it by its owner, Dave Falk, in place of the original 7.50-20 tires.

Coupled here to a 6-ton trailer, the G7113 Chevrolet was used as light general-purpose truck tractor, a role many of them served in on the surplus market as well. (National Archives and Records Administration photo)

The G7173, also known by the Signal Corps nomenclature K43, was often used as a companion to the G7163. It was a telephone line maintenance truck. Several compartments were provided for tool and supply stowage, and the rear winch was also provided with extension shafts to drive an external cable reel. The shaft can be seen extending through the door of the first tool compartment behind the passenger. (U.S. Army photo)

This left rear view of the K44 (G7163) pole setter shows the auger, in the lowered transport position, and its two long operating levers. Also visible are the two stabilizer jacks, in their raised transport position. Near the spare tire is the drinking water cask found on Signal Corps vehicles. (U.S. Army photo)

This overhead view of the K44 shows the equipment stowage. Four auger bits are supplied — the two largest on the driver's side rear, the two smaller on the passenger side front of the bed. Just forward of the two largest augers is the collapsible cable reel, while just inboard of the spare tire is the mounting bracket for a large pole jack (not present), used to extract telephone poles. The large box across the front of the bed houses the rear winch. (U.S. Army photo)

G7113 (G4112) [G4165] Tractor

This vehicle was the truck tractor member of the family. It had a stationary fifth wheel and electric brake controls and was built on 145-in.-wheelbase chassis.

G7105 (G4112) [G4105] Panel

The G7105 was a panel truck, built much like a carryall, with the body continuous from the cab to the rear. There were no side windows, but each of the twin side-opening rear doors was provided with a window.

G7163 (G4112) Pole Setter

The G7163 was used primarily by the Signal Corps. The Signal Corps referred to this truck as a K44. The large transfer case-driven auger could quickly dig a hole the correct size and depth to set power or telephone poles. The winch mounted in the front of the bed was used in conjunction with the auger mast to erect the poles once the holes were dug.

G7173 (G4112) K43

The driver of the fully equipped K43 had to exit out the passenger's side of the vehicle because the long gin poles extended so far forward that they blocked the door. (National Archives and Records Administration photo)

This often served as a companion vehicle for the G7163. Designed for telephone line maintenance, it did not have the auger of the G7163, although it did have the rear winch. Long gin poles were carried, and when stowed in their racks on the left side of the bed they protruded so far forward they prevented the driver from opening his door.

G7123 (G4103) Cab Over

The G7123 was the cab-over-engine model of the 1 1/2-ton Chevy family. Although the sheet metal was different, they were identical mechanically to the conventional trucks. (Photo from the Fran Blake collection)

This truck looks much different from the rest of the family due to its cab-over-engine design, but the power train was the same. The bed was 16 ft. long and equipped with side racks. This truck had a 175-in. wheelbase. The Signal Corps referred to this vehicle as a K-33.

G7127 (G4112) [G4174] Long Wheelbase Truck

This truck is very much like the G7107, but built on a 175-in. wheelbase with a correspondingly longer bed.

G7128 (G4112) M6 Bomb Servicer

These trucks were used in conjunction with M5 Bomb Trailers on airfields to handle bombs. The trailers could be loaded using the hoist and monorail mounted on the rear. The Bomb Trailers, up to five at a time, were towed out to the aircraft together.

This is the only truck in this series with an open cab without doors or solid roof. The M6 was normally equipped with a small canvas roof covering the driver's compartment. In warmer areas the canvas could be removed and the windshield folded down for ventilation. Prior to mid-1943 these trucks were not provided with a spare tire. The earliest trucks were equipped with Beebe chain hoists, while later trucks sometimes used a Holan hoist built by American Coach and Body Co. Braden winches were used briefly, but were found to be inadequate and a modification work order issued to replace them. These trucks were built on 125-in. wheelbase chassis.

Production of the M6 was suspended by the end of September 1944. Its duties were then fulfilled by the CCKW-based M27.

G7103 (G4113) Cab and Chassis

These trucks were supplied as a cab and chassis. Later, various specialized beds could be mounted on them, even though their final use may have been unknown at time of construction. These vehicles had a 145-in.-wheelbase chassis.

G7133 (G4112) Class 135 Crash Trucks

These trucks were built to dispense high-pressure fog and foam to fight aircraft fires. They are very different

This is one of many types of fire trucks built on the G-506 chassis. The nameplate on the side of the hood says Model 110-QMC. This truck was designed to discharge foam, and the hose reel was mounted at the rear behind the large foam tank that constitutes the bulk of the bed. Even though the truck itself is marked as a 110 in this period photo, this very same truck, U.S.A. registration number W-50702, is shown in the April 1949 ORD 3 SNL G-1 supply catalog, and is identified in that publication as a Class 135. (Photo from the Richard Adelmann Collection)

This factory-fresh Bomb Service truck was photographed at the Studebaker Proving Ground in January of 1944. While most of the trucks in the G-506 series were built on 145-in.-wheelbase chassis, these trucks were built on a 125-in. wheelbase, presumably for greater maneuverability in ammo dumps. (U.S. Army photo)

from the Class 325 and 525 pumpers. Because they were not as versatile as a traditional pumper, not many of these have survived today. These trucks were built with a 145-in. wheelbase.

G7133 (G4112) Class 525 Fire Trucks

This was a standard brush and structure firefighting truck built on the same type chassis as the Class 135. However, these trucks had a front-mounted 500-gallons-per-minute fire pump and a traditional fire truck-type bed. Although many of these trucks were cannibalized during the war, hundreds of surplus trucks were provided to communities across the U.S. after the war.

G7143 Field Lighting Truck

There were three types of airfield lighting equipment installed on these chassis: the almost identical J3 and J4 light sets, and the J5. The J3 and J4 had two towers of rectangular lights at the rear of the truck, just behind the transversely mounted generator. The J5 also had two towers, but each had only two lights on it, which were round, and the truck lacked the low apron of the earlier models. These trucks were built on 145-in.-wheelbase chassis.

GENERAL DATA

MODEL	145-in wb cargo	175-in wb cargo	175-in wb COE	125-in wb M6
WEIGHT NET	7,545 lbs.	8,150 lbs.	8,570 lbs.	6,325 lbs.
MAX TOWED LOAD	8,000 lbs.	8,000 lbs.	8,000 lbs.	8,000 lbs.
LENGTH	224	296	286	221
WIDTH	86	86	96	75.75
HEIGHT	106	106	99	91.5
WIDTH	49.25/85.75	49.25/85.75	49.25/85.75	49.25/85.75
TRACK	67.5	67.5	67.5	67.5
TIRE SIZE	7.50-20	7.50-20	7.50-20	7.50-20

MAX SPEED	48 mph	48 mph	43 mph	50 mph
FUEL CAPY	30 gal	30 gal	30 gal	30 gal
RANGE	270 mi	270 mi	240 mi	240 mi
ELECTRICAL	6 neg	6 neg	6 neg	6 neg
TRANSMISSION SPEEDS	4	4	4	4
TRANSFER SPEEDS	2	2	2	2
TURNING RADIUS FT	31	36.5	36.5	27.5

Overall dimensions listed in inches.
*Inside/outside width at tires.

ENGINE DATA

ENGINE MAKE/MODEL	Chevy BV-1001 up
NUMBER OF CYLINDERS	6
CUBIC-INCH DISPLACEMENT	235.5
HORSEPOWER	83 @ 3100 rpm
TORQUE	184 lbs.-ft.@ 1000 rpm
GOVERNED SPEED (rpm)	3100

The basic 145-in.-wheelbase cab and chassis was this G7103. With so many of the Chevys going to foreign nations, many different beds could be found installed on these trucks. (National Archives and Records Administration photo)

Shown here is a Class 525 fire truck, which was built on the Chevrolet Chassis. This particular truck was photographed after it had been transferred to the U.S. Department of Interior, but appears to be unchanged from its military days. The large fire pump mounted behind the front bumper was not required by the foam truck. (Photo from the Richard Adelmann Collection)

VALUES

	6	5	4	3	2	1
Cargo w/steel bed	500	2,000	4,000	6,000	7,000	8,000
Cargo w/wood bed	500	3,000	5,000	7,000	8,000	9,000
Dump	1,000	5,000	7,000	8,000	9,000	10,000
Panel	750	5,000	7,500	8,750	10,500	12,000
M6 Bomb	500	4,500	5,500	7,000	8,000	8,500
Tractor	500	4,000	5,500	6,500	7,500	8,500
Pole setter	2,000	7,000	8,000	9,000	10,000	11,000
Field lighting	1,000	6,500	7,500	8,500	10,000	11,000
LWB cargo	500	3,500	4,500	5,500	6,500	8,000
COE cargo	750	4,000	5,000	6,000	7,000	8,500

For winch-equipped trucks add $250 to $500 to the values shown above.

SCARCITY

Cargo w/steel bed	2
Cargo w/wood bed	2
Dump	3
Panel	3
M6 Bomb	3
Tractor	4
Pole setter	4
Field lighting	5
LWB cargo	4
COE cargo	4

This photo, taken from a technical manual, shows the general layout of the G7143-based J3 and J4 Field Lighting Trucks. Notice the low-hanging rear step, sure to inhibit cross-country operations.

The long-wheelbase version of the Chevy was this G7127, which featured a 15-ft. cargo bed instead of the normal 9-ft. body. (National Archives and Records Administration photo)

The later J5 Field Lighting Trucks differed considerably from their predecessors. Gone is the low-hanging rear step. The bed is accessed from the cab-side running boards.

Many of these Class 525 fire trucks were dismantled during WWII as the Army issued a kit to construct a class 530 fire truck on a CCKW chassis by reusing the pump and valving from a 525. However, if found today, these trucks are usually in good shape, as the fire departments that received them post-WWII typically stored them indoors. (Photo from the Richard Adelmann Collection)

G-507 Dodge 6x6

When the Army increased the size of its rifle squad from eight men to 12 men, a squad could no longer be carried in the 3/4-ton trucks. At the direction of Maj. Gen. Courtney Hodges, Chief of Infantry, the design of the G-502 series trucks was modified to create a 48-in.-longer 6x6 vehicle. Most of the mechanical and some of the sheet metal parts were the same as those used in the 3/4-ton series. However, the transfer was a dual ratio in the 1 1/2-ton version, while a single-speed unit was used on the 3/4-ton trucks.

Although Chrysler's Fargo Division handled government contracts, the trucks were all built at Dodge's Mound Road truck plant in Detroit.

Certain components were strengthened in the design, and many of these changes were incorporated into subsequent 3/4-ton production as well.

Two models — the WC62 and WC63 — of the G-507

were mass-produced. The only difference was that the WC63 was equipped with a Braden MU2 winch. Early models had a Zenith 29-BW-12R carburetor, while later trucks used the Carter ETW-1 carburetor.

About 43,000 of these trucks were produced.

This G-502 is a beautifully restored WC-62 owned by Bruce Gray. The turn signal under the front fender and the license plate holder are not original.

Like its 3/4-ton siblings, the big Dodge's spare tire blocked the driver's entrance.

The long wheelbase of these trucks affords today's collector a much smoother ride than you might expect. They were intended to transport a rifle squad in the canvas-enclosed rear area of the truck.

The WC-63 was essentially the same truck as the WC-62, differing only in its PTO-driven Braden MU-2 winch. Initially, the winch capacity was rated at 5,000-lbs., but an increase in wire rope size from 3/8 to 7/16 in. allowed the rating to be raised to 7,500 lbs. (U.S. Army photo)

International M-3-6

MODEL	WC62	WC63
NET WEIGHT	12,450 lbs.	12,450 lbs.
GROSS WEIGHT	7,250 lbs.	7,250 lbs.
MAX TOWED LOAD	8,000 lbs.	8,000 lbs.
LENGTH	215	224.75
WIDTH	82.75	82.75
HEIGHT	87	87
WIDTH*	54.125/75.375	54.125/75.375
TRACK	64.75	64.75
TIRE SIZE	9.00 x 16	9.00 x 16
MAX SPEED	50 mph	50 mph
FUEL CAPY	30 gal	30 gal
RANGE	240 mi	240 mi
ELECTRICAL	6 neg	6 neg
TRANSMISSION		
SPEEDS	4	3
TRANSFER		
SPEEDS	2	2
TURNING		
RADIUS FT	27	27

Overall dimensions listed in inches.

*Inside/outside width at tires.

ENGINE DATA

ENGINE MAKE/MODEL	Dodge T-223
NUMBER OF CYLINDERS	4
CUBIC INCH DISPLACEMENT	230.2
HORSEPOWER	76 @3200
TORQUE	180 lbs.-ft. @ 1200
GOVERNED SPEED (rpm)	3200

Less well known than the G-507 family of Dodge-built 1.5-ton 6x6 trucks is the International Harvester M-3-6. This very rare truck was produced in extremely limited quantities for the U.S. Marine Corps.

Just as Dodge had stretched its 3/4-ton 4x4 WC-51 design to produce the WC-62/WC-63, International stretched its 1-ton M-2-4 to produce the M-3-6.

The M-3-6 used a Hendrickson rear suspension and Thornton locking rear differentials. Powered by the International 233-cid six-cylinder engine through a four-speed transmission and two-speed transfer case, the truck had impressive off-road capabilities.

Collectors often refer to "open-cab" trucks, and the term certainly applies to the International Harvester designs built for the Marine Corps. (Photo courtesy of the Patton Museum)

This M-3-6 was photographed during testing without its bed. The rugged business-like appearance is typical of International military trucks. (Photo courtesy of the Patton Museum)

G-874 Gama Goat

Throughout the 1950s and 1960s, the Army had ongoing programs to improve its mobility. The Gama Goat grew out of such a program.

The XM561 was built by the Chance-Vought Aircraft Company. It used an articulated coupling between the front and rear sections that allowed body roll, pitch, and turn, while still transmitting power the rear axle. This articulation was designed by Roger L. Gamaunt, whom the vehcle was named after.

The earliest prototypes used an air-cooled Chevrolet gasoline engine, but by the time designed had advanced to the pre-production prototype stage, that power plant had been replaced with a Detroit Diesel 3-53 engine.

After development by Ling-Temco-Vought, the vehicle was classified standard in June of 1966 and bids were solicited for production. Kaiser Jeep and Consolidated Diesel Electric Company joined Ling-Temco-Vought in the bidding. CONDEC was awarded a contract for 14,000 trucks at $14,825 each.

The Gama Goat, though supposedly amphibious, was only marginally successful in the water. The mid-engine machinery layout placed the engine in the operator's compartment, at shoulder level for the driver and co-driver. The resulting noise level of 95 decibels required operators to wear hearing protection.

The vehicles were propelled in the water by their wheels, and both units had bilge pumps installed. Swimming these vehicles can be dangerous, and requires a very slow (2 mph) entry into the water from a

This vehicle is a pre-production prototype, rather than a standard M561. As the M561 neared the end of its service life, the Army issued more restrictions on swimming. Some were deemed not capable of swimming operations. (Photo courtesy of the Patton Museum)

The Gama Goat has outstanding rolling flexibility. The early-type engine housing cover has an angular look. (U.S. Army photo)

The M561 could be operated with no canvas at all. This vehicle has also had it windshield stowed, allowing the lowest possible profile. What appears to be hubcaps on Gama Goats are actually the outboard-mounted brake drums. (U.S. Army photo)

The sloping rear fenders and sloping engine compartment provided extreme flexibility, and kept the Gama Goat's tires in contact with the ground. (U.S. Army photo)

gently sloping firm embankment. Amphibious operations should not be attempted in currents exceeding 4 mph. The aluminum body was foam-filled for additional buoyancy.

The truck had independent coil suspension on the front and rear axles, and transverse leaf on the center axle. Limited-slip differentials were installed in all axles. An unusual feature of these trucks is that they did not carry spare tires. In the event of a flat, one of the center wheels was to be used as a spare and a truss and brace fitted to support the center of the vehicle.

Early vehicles had a cover for their engines made of aluminum sheet with square corners. On later vehicles the engine compartment cover was made of steel, and had rounded corners. The windshield did not fold down as it did on most tactical vehicles, but it was removable. Normally the vehicles are equipped with a vinyl top, but a hard arctic top kit was available. Noise levels in the cab are even higher when it is installed.

An 8,000-lb.-capacity front-mounted winch was available for these vehicles.

Delivery of the Goat began in the early 1970s, and almost immediately the vehicles were subjected to a $5.6-million improvement program to correct problems in the steering and driveline.

Although some M561s were employed in Vietnam, the trucks never really filled their roll as a go-anywhere carrier which, coupled with their reputation for unreliability, lead to their replacement with the HMMWV in the late 1980s and early 1990s.

GENERAL DATA

MODEL	M561	M792
NET WEIGHT	10,200 lbs.	10,200 lbs.
GROSS WEIGHT	7,300 lbs.	7,300 lbs.
LENGTH	226.6	226.6
AXLE SPACING	80.7	80.7
WIDTH	84	84
HEIGHT	90.8	90.8
WIDTH	83	83
TRACK	72	72
TIRE SIZE	11.00-18	11.00-18
MAX SPEED	55 mph	55 mph
FUEL CAPY	28 gal	28 gal
RANGE	420 mi	420 mi
ELECTRICAL	24 neg	24 neg
TRANSMISSION SPEEDS	4	4
TRANSFER SPEEDS	2	2
TURNING RADIUS FT	29	29

Overall dimensions listed in inches.

ENGINE DATA

ENGINE MAKE/MODEL	Detroit Diesel 3-53
NUMBER OF CYLINDERS	3
CUBIC-INCH DISPLACEMENT	159.3
HORSEPOWER	103 @ 2800 rpm
TORQUE	217 lbs.-ft. @ 1500 rpm

VALUES

	6	5	4	3	2	1
All models	2,000	3,000	6,000	8,000	10,000	12,000

SCARCITY

Scarcity 3

Many of the Gama Goats received the four-color MERDC paint scheme. This truck has a soft top, but all the top panels are installed, totally enclosing the cab. (U.S. Army photo)

2 1/2-TON TRUCKS

G-508 AFKWX-353

Some of the more unusual "deuce and a halfs" used by the U.S. military during WWII were the G-508 series AFKWX-353 trucks. They are also one of the harder vehicles to collect, with only 7,235 produced.

Production of these trucks began in 1942, and the truck shared many mechanical components with its contemporary, the CCKW-353. The engine (except for intake and exhaust), transmission, transfer case, axles, and cross-members were all CCKW components. Even the canvas cab cover on the later open-cab models was a CCKW part.

The big advantage these trucks had, in the eye of the Transportation Corps, was that even though the external dimensions were basically the same as the CCKW-353, the trucks had a larger cargo bed. The first 250 trucks had a 15-ft. steel cargo bed. Later production trucks had a wooden cargo bed. Beginning in 1944, the chassis was lengthened by 2 ft. with a corresponding change to the cargo bed. The military-style cargo bed was replaced with

From the rear, the AFKWX-353 resembled a closed-cab CCKW, complete with the toolbox located in the rear bed sill. (Photo from Bryce Sunderlin collection)

This is the AFKWX-353 in its earliest form, with a closed cab and 15-ft. steel cargo bed. (Photo from Bryce Sunderlin collection)

This photo was taken in May of 1942. Although not shown in these photos, a canvas bed cover could be fitted to protect the AFKWX-353 cargo. The cab did not tilt. Engine maintenance was quiet laborious, requiring the removal of much sheet metal. (Photo from Bryce Sunderlin collection)

This is the AFKWX-353 in its final form. The 15-ft. all-steel military style bed has been replaced with a 17-ft. wood cargo bed that looks more like a civilian commercial bed than a military bed. The closed cab has given way to the open-topped, canvas-covered style as well. (U.S. Army photo).

a more commercial bed, and the truck was designated M427. The first 671 trucks had a closed cab (model 1615), the later trucks used a military-style open cab (model 1620). The cargo beds are unique to these trucks, and almost impossible to find.

The first 60 of these trucks, with closed cabs and 15-ft. steel cargo beds, bore registration numbers USA 492732 through 492791. The next 250, also with closed cabs and steel cargo beds, were assigned USA 4209047 through 4209297. The trucks with closed cabs and wooden 15-ft. cargo beds were assigned 4209298 through 4209658, omitting number 4209558.

The open-cabbed trucks with 15-ft. wooden cargo beds were given USA 4209558, USA 4300109 to 4300458, USA 4484334 to 4484952, and USA 4549571 to 4550161. The first 4,000 of the M427 type with the open cab and 17-ft. cargo body were assigned 4738470 to 4742469. The registration numbers of the final 1,000 trucks built, chassis AFKWX-9248 to AFKWX-10247, are unknown.

None of these vehicles were equipped with winches. The U.S, military ceased using these during the 1950s, although they remained in foreign service, including with the French Army, until much later.

GENERAL DATA

MODEL	AFKWX-353	M427
NET WEIGHT	10,800 lbs.	11,950 lbs.
LENGTH	266 1/2	289 1/2
WIDTH	86 1/4	86 1/4
HEIGHT	106	106
TRACK INSIDE	49 1/4	49 1/4
TRACK OUTSIDE	86 1/4	86 1/4
TIRE SIZES	7.50- 20	7.50-20
MAX SPEED	45 mph	45 mph
FUEL CAPY	40 gal	40 gal
RANGE	300 mi	300 mi
ELECTRICAL	6 volt	6 volt
TRANSMISSION		
SPEEDS	5 F, 1 R	5 F, 1 R
TRANSFER SPEEDS	2	2
TURNING		
RADIUS FT	35 R, 34 L	35

Overall dimensions listed in inches.

ENGINE DATA

ENGINE MAKE/MODEL	GMC 270
NUMBER OF CYLINDERS	6
CUBIC-INCH DISPLACEMENT	269.5
HORSEPOWER	91.5 @ 2750 RPM
TORQUE	216 lbs.-ft. @ 1400 RPM
GOVERNED SPEED (rpm)	2750

VALUES

	6	5	4	3	2	1
All models	700	1,500	5,000	10,000	12,000	15,000

SCARCITY

Scarcity 4

Although missing its rear fender, this late AFKWX-353 does have its spare tire and all the cab canvas in place. The sides of this style bed are completely removable, allowing easy side loading with forklifts. (Photo from Bryce Sunderlin collection)

G-508 CCKW

The GMC CCKW is generally considered to be the truck that won WWII. It was a medium-duty all-wheel-drive 2 1/2-ton truck. The CCW was an almost identical truck, but lacked the front-wheel drive.

The trucks were built in both long (164-in.) and short (145-in.) wheelbase versions. The short-wheelbase version was the GMC model CCKW-352, and the long-wheelbase truck was known as the CCKW-353. The CCKW-353 was intended as a general-purpose cargo truck and personnel transport, while the CCKW-352 was built as a prime mover for the Field Artillery, towing 75mm and 105mm weapons. Production was begun initially at the Yellow Truck and Coach plant in Pontiac, Michigan, but in September 1942 another production line was set up in the St. Louis Chevrolet Assembly Plant. In mid-1943, a corporate restructuring caused

Some of the short-wheelbase CCKWs were built with winches, and some had M32 ring mounts installed on them. This truck is one of a fairly small percentage that were equipped with both. (National Archives and Records Administration photo collection)

The CCKW-353 was intended to be a general-purpose transport vehicle. Like the CCKW-352, it was originally equipped with a closed cab. This particular truck is equipped with a PTO-driven self-recovery winch. (Photo courtesy of Bryce Sunderlin collection)

As the war continued, the closed cab of the CCKW-352 gave way to the open cab, and the steel cargo bed was replaced with one of wooden construction, as seen here. (Photo courtesy of Bryce Sunderlin collection)

A driver's-side view of the open-cab CCKW-352. The liquid container bracket on the driver's side running board was also a late-war addition to the production line. (Photo courtesy of Bryce Sunderlin collection)

2 1/2-TON TRUCKS

Yellow Truck and Coach to become General Motors Truck and Coach Division, with an associated change in the data plates.

Some of the trucks were built with winches. The cargo beds were initially steel, but in August/September 1942 the trucks began using wooden beds, and finally in January 1944 a body of composite steel and wood construction began to be used.

The earliest models had fully enclosed cabs, but these were replaced in production during 1942 with the military standard open cab.

The earliest trucks all used axles built by Timken, which had a split differential design. As production levels increased, Timken was not able to supply enough axles, and GMC was authorized to begin using axles of its own design in addition to the Timken units. Trucks built with the Timken axles have serial numbers ending in –1, while those with the GM axles have serial numbers

The fuel tanks on the long-wheelbase CCKW-353 trucks were mounted beneath the bed on the passenger's side. This closed-cab truck sports an M32 ring mount and M2HB .50-caliber machine gun. (National Archives and Records Administration photo)

The military class 335 and 530 fire trucks were conversions done by the military on CCKW chassis. The conversion involved both the mounting of a conversion kit and the cannibalization of a class 325 4x2 fire truck. (Photo courtesy of United States Army Engineer School History Office).

trucks were often grossly overloaded, as the bed was the same size as the cargo bed, but the loads were often much denser. A moveable partition was provided in the dump body that was to be raised when used as a dump truck. This was to contain the load in the rear of the bed to prevent the truck from tipping over when the bed was raised loaded.

— CCKW Water tanker: The CCKW water tanker was intended to transport potable water. The provision was made for heating the tank with exhaust gases to prevent freezing.

— CCKW Fuel tanker: The CCKW fuel tanker had twin 350 fuel tanks mounted on the back. The tanks were emptied by gravity.

This is the only known short-wheelbase dump truck, built on a CCKWX chassis in 1941. (National Archives and Records Administration photo)

ending in –2.

The earliest production trucks were equipped with a 25-amp, 6-volt, positive ground electrical system. In mid-1942 the trucks began to be produced with a 40-amp, negative ground system that was still 6-volts. All these vehicles were equipped with vacuum-assisted power brakes, although two different styles of Bendix Hydro-Vac systems were used.

The CCKW was fitted with a greater array of body types than any other WWII-era vehicles.

In addition to cargo trucks, the following body types were among those installed (this is not a complete list):

— CCKW Dump truck: These trucks look very much like the CCKW cargo trucks, but they were equipped with dumping beds made by either Gar Wood or Heil. These

Extensive testing showed that larger single tires provided better performance off road than did the dual wheels more commonly used. A kit was made available to fit DUKW wheels and tires to CCKWs when extensive off-road use was anticipated. (Photo courtesy of the Patton Museum)

Like the short-wheelbase trucks, the long trucks also evolved into open-cabbed trucks with wooden cargo beds. (Photo courtesy of Bryce Sunderlin collection).

This 1942 photo of a closed-cabbed fuel tanker truck was taken at Holabird, Maryland. The bed actually houses two separate fuel tanks. The racks alongside the tanks were used to store auxiliary fuel cans. (National Archives and Records Administration photo)

This typical CCKW tipper was photographed in 1944 in South Bend, Indiana. Notice the damage to the lower front corner of the bed of this otherwise factory-fresh truck. (U.S. Army photo)

By 1944, GMC was still building fuel tankers, but there had been subtle detail changes, including fitting an open cab. (U.S. Army photo)

Frames were different for trucks that were winch not equipped, and so was the size of the front bumper. (U.S. Army photo)

Certain Army Engineer units were provided with Le Roi air compressors mounted on CCKW chassis. Both open- and closed-cab chassis were used. (Photo courtesy of U.S. Army Engineer School History Office)

The airfield service truck is often confused with the CCKW fuel tanker, but they were two very different trucks. This sleek airfield service truck is owned by Chet Krause.

— CCKW Fuel Service: These trucks were equipped with beds built by Heil. They had a 750-gallon fuel tank, and pumping equipment to fuel and lube aircraft.

— CCKW Air Compressor: Designed for Corps of Engineers use, these trucks were equipped with a Le Roi model 105G compressor driven by a Le Roi model D318 gasoline engine. A clutch connected the engine to the compressor. Tool cabinets surrounded the compressor/engine assembly, forming a walkway. These cabinets held a wide variety of tools, including paving breakers, clay diggers, a chain saw, wood-boring machine, and rock drill, all pneumatically operated. Contrary to other references, the Le Roi

manual lists the capacity of this compressor at 105 cubic feet per minute.

— M27/M27B1 Bomb Service truck: The M27 Bomb Service truck was equipped with a wooden body on which the Earnest Holmes company had installed a frame work and trolley-mounted chain hoist. These trucks were factory-equipped with electric trailer

This truck is easily confused with the M27 family of bomb service trucks. It is a standard CCKW that has been fitted with a wrecker set number 7. The bracing is different, the hoist much heavier, and the monorail much shorter than those on the Bomb Service trucks. (National Archives and Records Administration photo)

The M27B1 as shown here was essentially the same truck as the M27, only in this case the cargo bed was of composite wood and steel construction. Mounted on the sideboards of the bed is sectional railroad-type track (the curved section is visible attached to the inner side of the bed). These tracks were used with a dolly to position the bombs properly under aircraft. (U.S. Army photo)

The tool compartments alongside the Le Roi 105G compressor held a variety of pneumatic construction tools. The compressor had a capacity of 105 cu. ft. per minute, and was powered by its own four-cylinder engine. (Photo courtesy of U. S. Army Engineer School History Office)

brake controls. The M27B1 was the same truck, only with a composite construction bed.

— CCKW Stock Rack: The cavalry still used horses in the early part of WWII, and the Army ordered these trucks to transport them and other livestock.

— Class 530 Fire Truck: The vehicles came from the installation of a conversion kit on a CCKW chassis. The conversion kit was developed to combine a CCKW and a 325 pumper to yield a pumper on a tactical chassis. In September 1944, the designation of this conversion equipment was changed from Class 535 to Class 335. With its front-mounted pump it could discharge up to 500 gpm and up to 250 psi water pressure. Coupled to the all-wheel drive chassis, it was a formidable piece of firefighting apparatus. On December 6, 1945, the Class 530 truck was reclassified as Fire-Fighting Equipment Set Number 18. Some of these conversions were also converted to single rear wheels by installation of DUKW wheels and spacers.

— CCKW Ponton Bolster: The trucks, with bodies made by the Canastota Division of Oneida (who would later build the bodies of the R2 crash trucks), were created to tow slip pole bolster trailers hauling the M4 floating bridge. The trucks had a vacuum-actuated slackless pintle hook, and all had the front winch. Many of

The M27 Bomb Service truck featured this large trolley and hoist mechanism which was used to lift bombs in and out of the body. Notice the spotlight mounted on the front hoist support. The cargo body of the M27 was built of wood. (U.S. Army photo)

Early in the war, a limited number of CCKWs were produced with livestock racks. The vehicle shown here is one of a handful of CCKWX trucks built with stock racks, but the CCKW version was identical externally, except for the rear view mirror mounting. (National Archives and Records Administration photo)

Many of the bomb-handling trucks had the bomb hoist apparatus installed by Chattanooga's Earnest Holmes Company. The trucks shown in the far left of this photograph have had the hoists installed, while the trucks in the foreground await installation of the bomb handling gear. (Photo courtesy of International Towing and Recovery Museum)

these trucks had single DUKW wheels all around, rather than the standard dual rear wheels and smaller tires.

Some trucks were outfitted as mobile kitchens, others had earth-boring equipment installed. Decontamination apparatus was mounted on others, while some were used by medical units as operating rooms, laboratories, or dental units.

Some CCKW trucks were intended to be transported by aircraft, and had their frames split just behind the cab to allow the truck to fit inside contemporary cargo aircraft. Large flanges were bolted together to rejoin the halves.

GENERAL DATA

MODEL	CCKW-352	CCKW-353
NET WEIGHT	10,350 lbs.	11,250 lbs.
LENGTH	244 7/8	256 1/4
WIDTH	86 1/4	86 1/4
HEIGHT	93	93
TRACK INSIDE	49 1/4	49 1/4
TRACK OUTSIDE	86 1/4	86 1/4
TIRE SIZES	7.50-20	7.50-20
MAX SPEED	45 mph	45 mph
FUEL CAPY	40 gal	40 gal
RANGE	300 mi	300 mi
ELECTRICAL	6 volt	6 volt
TRANSMISSION SPEEDS	5 F, 1 R	5 F, 1 R
TRANSFER SPEEDS	2	2
TURNING RADIUS FT	34 R, 34 L	35

Overall dimensions listed in inches.

ENGINE DATA

ENGINE MAKE/MODEL	GMC 270
NUMBER OF CYLINDERS	6
CUBIC INCH DISPLACEMENT	269.5
HORSEPOWER	91.5 @ 2750 rpm
TORQUE	216 lbs.-ft. @ 1400 rpm
GOVERNED SPEED (rpm)	2750

VALUES

	6	5	4	3	2	1
CCKW-352 closed	200	1,200	5,000	8,000	10,000	15,000
CCKW-352 open	200	1,200	5,000	8000	10,000	15,000
CCKW-353 closed	200	1,000	4,000	7,000	9,000	12,000
CCKW-353 open	200	900	3,500	6,000	9,000	12,000
CCKW dump	500	1,500	6,000	9,000	12,000	16,000
CCKW water tank	500	1,000	3,500	7,500	9,500	14,000
CCKW fuel tank	500	1,000	3,500	7,500	9,500	14,000
CCKW airfield svc	500	1,000	3,500	7,500	9,500	14,000
CCKW compressor	800	1,500	6,000	9,000	11,000	16,000
M27/M27B1 bomb	1,000	3,000	9,000	12,000	18,000	20,000
Engineer shop	1,000	3,000	9,000	12,000	18,000	20,000
Ordnance Shop	500	1,000	3,500	7,500	9,500	14,000

SCARCITY

CCKW-352 closed	3
CCKW-352 open	3
CCKW-353 closed	2
CCKW-353 open	2
CCKW dump	3
CCKW water tank	4
CCKW fuel tank	4
CCKW airfield svc	5
CCKW compressor	4
M27/M27B1 bomb	5
Engineer shop	5
Ordnance Shop	4

Note: *Other variants are too rarely sold to establish values.*

The mobile shop shown here is housed in a model ST-5 bed. This is an early shop truck as evidenced by its closed-cab chassis, chevron pattern tires, and use of the ST-5 bed. Seventeen different types of mobile repair shops were mounted in these type trucks. The ST-5 body was superceded by the ST-6 body. (Photo courtesy of United States Army Engineer School History Office).

The engineer-type bodies had sides that opened up, with the lower portion hanging down to form walkways, and the upper portion hinging to form awnings. (Photo courtesy of United States Army Engineer School History Office)

The GMC plant produced only one of these Signal Corps K-53 vans, although others may have been created using cab and chassis. (U.S. Army photo).

G-501 DUKW353

The DUKW was developed by GMC to provide the Army with a means to transport equipment and men from ship all the way to the beach, and some distance beyond, without the need to transfer the cargo. It is a fully amphibious 2 1/2-ton 6x6 truck.

The super-secret Office of Scientific Research and Development received a letter from MG Jacob Devers on March 20, 1942. The project was assigned to Palmer Cosslett Putnam, which contracted on April 21 with the Yellow Truck and Coach Division of General Motors to design build and test the new vehicle. A wooden mockup was completed on April 27, and testing of the pilot model began of June 2, 1942.

The automotive components of the DUKW were based on the G-508 series GMC trucks, but it is less widely known that the hull was designed by 1937 America's Cup winner Roderick Stephens.

The DUKW was standardized in October 1942, and production began immediately at the Yellow Coach plant in Pontiac, Michigan, which was also home to CCKW production. Initially, the truck received only a lukewarm reception from the Army, but a twist of fate was to raise the DUKW's profile within the military.

The DUKW was to be demonstrated to a group of military officers near Provincetown, Massachusettes, in December 1942. Coincidentally, on the night of December 1, a storm of near-hurricane force struck that area. The Coast Guard yawl "Rose," on anti-submarine patrol, began to break up in the storm. A Coast Guardsman aware of the impending DUKW demonstration, contacted Stephens, who took a team of photographers with him in a DUKW and proceeded to sea in the face of the storm and rescued the Rose's crew.

Nevertheless, the DUKW was not fully appreciated by many in the military until after its successful use during the invasion of Sicily. After that, the DUKW's place in history was sealed.

Demand for the DUKW became so great that a second production facility had to be added — this one at the Chevrolet plant in St. Louis. Production totaled 21,147 vehicles by the time production ceased at war's end. Because of its unique abilities, the DUKW was not fazed out of service by the U.S. military until the 1950s.

Because the DUKW was rushed into production,

The DUKW was designed from the outset to mount the M36 ring mount. It is shown here with the M2 HB .50-caliber machine gun mounted. (U.S. Army photo)

Shown here is one of the earlier DUKWs. Notice that the windshield is mounted vertically. In June 1943 the design was changed to have a sloping windshield. The rearmost reflector was moved in February 1943 to prevent it from being obscured by rope fenders. (U.S. Army photo)

Since this is an early DUKW, the spare tire is mounted on the driver's side. In May 1943, the spare tire was relocated to a similar position on the passenger's side. The DUKW used single 11:00-18 tires on combat wheels in all positions. (U.S. Army photo)

This is a later-production vehicle, as can be seen by the sloping windshield and relocated spare tire. However, this truck was built prior to September 1943, when a central tire inflation system was added. In November 1943, when the passenger's side rear view mirror was eliminated. The wheels wells have been fitted with skirts. (U.S. Army photo)

there were many running changes made during the production run. A serious restorer would need to do careful research on their individual vehicle, rather than restoring a vehicle based on the photographs shown here.

GENERAL DATA

MODEL	DUKW353
WEIGHT NET	14,880 lbs.
GROSS	20,055 lbs.
MAX TOWED LOAD	7,500 lbs.
LENGTH	372
WIDTH	98.875
HEIGHT	106
WIDTH*	51.5/75 1/16
TRACK	63.875
TIRE SIZE	11.00-18
MAX SPEED	
LAND	50 mph
WATER	6 mph
FUEL CAPY	40 gal
RANGE	
LAND	240 mi
WATER	50 mi
ELECTRICAL	6 neg
TRANSMISSION	
SPEEDS	5
TRANSFER	
SPEEDS	2
TURNING	
RADIUS FT	35 R, 36 L

Overall dimensions listed in inches.

* *Inside/outside width at tires.*

ENGINE DATA

ENGINE MAKE/MODEL	GMC 270
NUMBER OF CYLINDERS	6
CUBIC-INCH DISPLACEMENT	269.5
HORSEPOWER	91 @ 2750 rpm
TORQUE	216 lbs.-ft. @ 1400 rpm
GOVERNED SPEED (rpm)	2750

VALUES

	6	5	4	3	2	1
All models	3,000	5,000	10,000	14,000	18,000	20,000

The driver's compartment of the DUKW was considerably more complicated than that of the normal land-based cargo truck. The lever on the instrument panel, just to the right of the steering column, controls the central tire inflation system. (U.S. Army photo)

Illustrated here are the major mechanical components of the DUKW. At the far left is the pintle hook, with the winch just above it. The prop and the rudder are visible, and the hydrovac can be seen just forward of the rear axles. (U.S. Army photo)

G-630 Studebaker & Reo US6 Trucks

The US6 trucks were designed by Studebaker Corp, of South Bend, Indiana, to be competitive with the GMC CCKW or the IHC M5-H6 6x6 trucks. Production began in South Bend in June of 1941 and continued through August of 1945, totaling 197,678 vehicles.

These trucks, like the White M3A1 Scout Car and the Ford M8 and M20 armored cars, were powered by the 320-cid Hercules JXD six-cylinder engine. The proper engine for the US6 has the Studebaker spoked logo cast into the manifold. The US6 used the same transmission and transfer case as the GMC CCKW, and even the Timken axles were the same as those used on many of the GMCs.

Most of these trucks have a hardtop cab based on the civilian Studebaker M-series cab. This was not the same as the later M-series military cab. Rather, Studebaker used letters to denote its various truck models, J, K, M, etc. The civilian cab was modified by the addition of a swing-out windshield with top-mounted vacuum wipers, metal interior panels, and military instruments.

Another source of confusion regarding designations for these trucks comes from Studebaker's number system. The U.S. model was built with a number of body codes. These codes were U1 through U13. The brake system employed by Studebaker was not the Hydrovac system that GMC used, but instead was a vacuum-boosted system.

These trucks were produced in short (148-in.) and long (162-in.) wheelbases, and in 6x6 and 6x4 form. Since the 6x4 version was intended for on road use only, its weight classification was 5-ton, whereas the 6x6 version was rated using the traditional off-road system of 2 1/2 tons. During December of 1942, production of the US6 with an open cab was begun. However, this was not to the liking of the major user of the US6 — the Soviet Army — and production reverted to the closed cab in March of 1943, with only about 10,000 of the open-cabbed trucks having been completed.

Reo Motors of Lansing, Michigan, was contracted to build copies of this truck in addition to the output of Studebaker. The 22,204 trucks that Reo built were indistinguishable from the Studebakers, except for the data plates.

All the G-630 series trucks were not six-wheel drive, as can be seen in this view of a Studebaker model US6 6x4 short-wheelbase tractor. Cargo trucks were also built with non-powered front axles. (U.S. Army photo)

While Studebaker developed what was to become the military standard open cab, only a few of the US6s were built with the open cab. The biggest user of the US6, Russia, preferred the closed cab. Open-cabbed US6s are very rare today in the U.S. (National Archives photo)

The vast majority of the US6 models were all-wheel-drive cargo trucks like this one. This vehicle is having its bed mounted in Studebaker's downtown South Bend, Indiana, plant. This is an early production truck, as is evidenced by the Studebaker nameplate on the grille. (Photo courtesy of Bryce Sunderlin collection)

2 1/2-TON TRUCKS

US6   Models
US6   U1 SWB cargo without winch
US6   U2 SWB cargo with winch
US6   U3 LWB cargo without winch
US6   U4 LWB cargo with winch
US6   U5 LWB 750 gallon tanker
US6x4 U6 SWB Semi-tractor
US6x4 U7 LWB cargo without winch
US6x4 U8 LWB cargo with winch
US6   U9 LWB cab and chassis without winch
US6   U10 SWB Rear Dump without winch
US6   U11SWB Rear Dump with winch
US6   U12SWB Side Dump without winch
US6   U13 SWB Side Dump with winch

Note: US6x4 production stopped in July 1945, with the last all-wheel-drive version being built the following month.

GENERAL DATA

MODEL	US6 Cargo	US6 Dump
NET WEIGHT	10,485 lbs.	10,760 lbs.
GROSS WEIGHT	16,095 lbs.	20,760 lbs.
LENGTH	265 1/4	238 5/8
WIDTH	88	88
HEIGHT	88	88
WHEELBASE	157	148
TREAD	62.25	62.25
TIRE SIZE	7.50-20	7.50-20
MAX SPEED	45 mph	45 mph
FUEL CAPY	40 gal	40 gal
RANGE LAND	240 mi	240 mi
ELECTRICAL	6	6
TRANSMISSION SPEEDS	5	5
TRANSFER SPEEDS	2	2

Overall dimensions listed in inches.
Note: Specifications above are for trucks with winch, without winch reduce weight 610 lbs. and length 14 3/4 in.

ENGINE DATA

ENGINE MAKE/MODEL	Hercules JXD
NUMBER OF CYLINDERS	6
CUBIC-INCH DISPLACEMENT	320
HORSEPOWER	86 @ 2800
TORQUE	200 lbs.-ft. @ 1150
GOVERNED SPEED (rpm)	2800

VALUES

	6	5	4	3	2	1
All models	1,500	2,500	6,000	10,000	14,000	18,000

In addition to cargo trucks and tractors, the US6 design could also be equipped as dump trucks or tanker trucks. (National Archives and Records Administration photo)

The US6 was also adapted for use as a fire truck, as shown in this builder's photograph taken by Seagrave Fire Apparatus. (Photo courtesy of Richard Adelman collection)

While the final US6 trucks had metal-enclosed cabs, the beds were made of wood. (U.S. Army photo).

The US6 trucks were built by Reo and Studebaker. This Reo example, ironically, was photographed in December 1944 at the Studebaker Proving Ground. Trucks from the two makers were indistinguishable from each other. (U.S. Army photo).

G-651 International

With the build up of U.S. armed forces prior to the beginning of WWII, purchases of 6x6 trucks from International Harvester began in 1941 with the M-5-6 (M-military, 5,000-lb. capacity, six-wheel drive). Five hundred of these trucks were purchased: 425 SWB without winch, 25 SWB with winch, 25 LWB without winch, and 25 LWB with winch. Production of these vehicles was completed in 1942.

Essentially, all these vehicles were shipped to the Soviet Union, as were some 3,000 LWB cargo trucks lacking the front axle drive (model M-5-6x4). All of these trucks were closed-cabbed vehicles, with the cabs being derived from International's K model civilian trucks. These trucks were powered by the International FBC-318B 318.4-cid straight six-cylinder engine with a five-speed Fuller transmission and an International two-speed, four-shaft transfer case. Hendrickson walking beam suspension was used on all production models.

Once it was decided that the International would be the standard Navy and Marine Corps 6x6, some changes were made and the model became the M-5H-6. The engine was upgraded to the 360.8-cid FBC-361B, the rear axles were equipped with Thornton self-locking differentials, and the tire size increased from 7.50-20 to 8.25 x 20. The locking differentials provided the Internationals with off-road performance superior to that of the CCKW or US6. Most of the USMC vehicles were equipped with a 10,000-lb.-capacity PTO-driven front winch and an open cab.

After 2,782 of these trucks were produced, the engine was again upgraded, this time to the RED-361B — the smallest of the Red Diamond engines produced by International. The front-end sheet metal of the IH was unlike that of the GMC and Studebaker 6x6s, and the hoods of the IH opened from the side in the butterfly-style similar to that of the Dodge G-502 series.

Most of the M-5-6 trucks were equipped with steel military cargo bodies similar to the steel beds used on the CCKW, but the later M-5H-6 trucks used a different cargo bed with a steel floor and either wooden or steel sides. On the long-wheelbase cargo trucks the spare tire was stowed in a recess on the outside of the cargo bed between the cab and the tandems.

The Internationals were fitted with a variety of beds in addition to the cargo beds, including dump, pipeline, tanker, telephone, and fire trucks. More than 30,000 of these trucks were built.

GENERAL DATA

MODEL	M-5H-6 cargo
NET WEIGHT	13,400 lbs.
GROSS WEIGHT	23,400 lbs.
LENGTH	270
WIDTH	88
HEIGHT	98
WHEELBASE	169
TREAD	64.5
TIRE SIZE	8.25-20
MAX SPEED	46 mph
FUEL CAPY	61 gal
RANGE LAND	350 mi
ELECTRICAL	6
TRANSMISSION SPEEDS	5
TRANSFER SPEEDS	2

Overall dimensions listed in inches.
Note: *Specifications here are for trucks with winch, without winch reduce weight 610 lbs. and length 14 3/4 in.*

The Marines used the International 6x6s for many purposes, including adaptation to fire trucks. (Photo courtesy of Richard Adelman collection)

Like their GMC and Studebaker counterparts, the IH 2 1/2-ton trucks also came in a short-wheelbase version for use as an artillery prome mover. (Photo courtesy of the Military History Institute)

Tractor versions of the International, like all the IH short-wheelbase trucks, had their fuel tanks mounted transversely behind the cab. (Photo courtesy of the Military History Institute)

ENGINE DATA

ENGINE MAKE/MODEL	International RED-361-B
NUMBER OF CYLINDERS	6
CUBIC-INCH DISPLACEMENT	360.8 rpm
HORSEPOWER	111 @ 2650 rpm

VALUES

	6	5	4	3	2	1
All models	1,500	2,500	6,000	10,000	14,000	18,000

This International 2 1/2-ton truck is marked for the biggest US user of the IH 6x6s — the U.S. Marine Corps. Once the locking differentials were installed on late rmodels, the M-5H-6 became the most highly mobile conventionally laid-out U.S. 6x6 ever produced. (Photo by James Petralba, courtesy of Fran Blake collection)

G-742

When most people think of post-WWII U.S. 6x6 trucks, the image that comes to mind is that of the G-

The M34 was the base vehicle for the G-742 series. This example was photographed shortly after the trucks were ordered in 1949. (Photo courtesy of the Patton Museum)

742. Developed originally by Reo Motors, and dubbed the Eager Beaver, this truck was also built by a number of other firms.

The U.S. military learned many automotive lessons during WWII, and even before hostilities ceased, it set out to apply these lessons to new vehicles. This process culminated with the Conference on Qualitative Requirements for the Tactical Type Ordnance Transport Vehicles in May of 1949. This conference established, among other things, a need for a new family of 2 1/2-ton 6x6 cargo trucks. Three types were outlined: a 12-ft. body with single tires, 12-ft. body with dual tires, and a 17-ft. body with dual tires. The need for various other vehicles sharing this common chassis was also defined. The specifications of these vehicles had been previously drawn up as Joint Army Navy specification T-712, in December 1948.

Reo completed preliminary work on this series truck by April 1949, and the requirements were finalized in

The M35 introduced the dual rear wheels and bed without wheel wells to the series. In this basic form the series would serve the U.S. Military for more than 30 years. (U.S. Army photo)

2 1/2-TON TRUCKS

May of the same year. Pre-production pilot models were quickly tested, and by 1950 production of these vehicles was in full swing. By the time production ceased in the mid-1980s, the Reo design had been produced by no less than 10 companies, including Reo Motors, Studebaker, Studebaker-Packard, Curtiss-Wright, Kaiser-Jeep, and AM General. The truck's style has become very familiar. Ranging from the M35 cargo truck to variants as exotic as nuclear missile launchers, this chassis mounted dozens of different bodies for specialist use.

The Reo-designed OA-331 inline six-cylinder 331-cid gasoline engine originally powered these vehicles. Later the same power plant was license built by Continental as its model COA-331.

In the late 1950s, the military was keenly interested in developing engines that could run on more than one type of fuel. Aware of this, Continental licensed M-A-N's "whisper engine" design, which utilized a combustion process that Continental dubbed Hyper-Cycle combustion. After extensive tests, this engine was adopted and installed in the G-742 series trucks. This engine was an inline six model LDS-427-2 Multifuel engine, with 427-cid displacement. These engines were able to burn diesel, jet fuel, kerosene, or gasoline, or any combination of these, without adjustment or modification. The cargo truck version of the G-742 series powered by this engine was the M35A1. Initially, trucks with high front axle loadings continued to use the gas engine, due to concern about the considerably higher weight of the Multifuel engine.

The LDS-427-2 was replaced with the LD-465 series of multi-fuel engines in the M35A2 series, which are slightly larger (478 cid) and more reliable. These engines were naturally aspirated, with the exhaust exiting above the righ-side tandems as they had on previous trucks. Later production vehicles used a vertical exhaust, with the muffler beneath the passenger's side of the cab.

Because of the huge amounts of smoke that were characteristic of the LD-powered truck, the LDT-465 series, which is turbosupercharged, was developed. The turbosuper charger on these engines was not intended for power enhancement, but rather to clean up the exhaust. The exhaust stack was vertically oriented and slightly larger than the previous model. No muffler was used. All the Multifuel engines have compression ignition.

A modernization program implemented in the 90's will insure that these trucks will serve well into the new century, now being powered with Caterpillar diesel engines.

All of these trucks can run through water 30 inches deep without modification, and a quickly installed accessory kit will allow the truck to run completely submerged.

A Multifuel engine also powered the M35A2 and M35A2C (drop side, shown here), this time an LDT-465 version. Various exhaust systems were used: horizontal muffled, vertical muffled, and vertical non-muffled. The non-muffled exhaust was used with the turbosupercharged engine. (U.S. Army photo)

The M35A1, although resembling the M35, was greatly improved with the introduction of the LDS-427-2 Multifuel engine and overdrive transmission. This photo of an M35A1 on a test course shows the rear suspension travel. (U.S. Army photo)

Due to its length of service, and popular size, there are more variants of this series than any other vehicle ever in the US Arsenal.

Listed below are some of the more popular versions of these trucks, but this is by no means a complete listing.

CARGO TRUCKS

154-in.-Wheelbase Cargo Trucks

These are what the military refers to as long-wheelbases truck.

The initially cargo truck built was the M34. This truck featured a 12-ft. cargo box with wheel wells to accommodate the 11.00-20 single tires. The superior off-road performance offered by single tires was cause for the military's preference for them at the time.

The M35 was the same vehicle, with dual 9.00 x 20 rear wheels and a cargo bed without wheel wells. It was intended for use primarily on roads hauling cargo, although, like the M34, its bed had fold-down troop seats.

The M35A1 was the first of the Multifuel-powered cargo trucks. The engine was an LDS-427-2, and the transmission was now an overdrive-equipped unit to compensate for the slower-turning compression ignition engine. Like its predecessors, a foot switch engaged the starter.

The M35A2 was the next development, and it was initially powered by the LD-465 478-cid naturally aspirated engine. The LDT-465 turbosuper charged engine, known as the "clean burn engine," superceded this. The starters on these engines have a solenoid mounted on them, which is controlled by a push-button switch on the dashboard.

190-in.-Wheelbase Cargo Trucks

The M36 was the first of the vehicles in this extra-long wheelbase series. Like the M35, it was powered by the OA-331 gasoline engine, and had dual 9:00 x 20 rear wheels. None of the 190-in.-wheelbase cargo trucks have troop seats in the rear, although the sideboards on the bed resemble troop seats. The right side of the bed swings down (drop side) to allow forklift loading of cargo. The M36C was essentially the same truck as the M36, but in its cargo bed there were special appliances for transporting missiles.

The M36A1 was a Multifuel long-wheelbase cargo truck. It was powered by the LDS-427-2 and overdrive transmission.

When the 465 engine series engines were installed in the M36 and M36C-type trucks, they became the M36A2 and M36A2C. All the cargo trucks, regardless of wheelbase, were available with and without PTO-driven front winches.

Like most G-742 series trucks, this M36A2 has a soft-top cab closure. The fuel racks on the front fender of the truck shown are non-standard.

This 1968 Kaiser M36A2 is representative of the longest cargo version of the G-742. The truck shown here, owned by Cecil Jones, is equipped with a hardtop cab enclosure. The passenger's side of the bed of the M36A2 hinged down in two sections to facilitate side loading. (Photo courtesy of Cecil Jones)

142-in.-Wheelbase Trucks

The 142-in.-wheelbase vehicles are referred to as the short wheelbase trucks. These were not built in cargo truck form, but other models discussed later used this wheelbase.

Tractor Trucks

The G-742 series tractors came in two sizes: the M48, which was built on the standard 154 –in.-wheelbase chassis; and the M275, M275A1 and M275A2, which were 142-in.-wheelbase trucks.

The tractor trucks, regardless of wheelbase, were equipped with a fifth-wheel assembly, mounted at the

The fuel tank of the M275 series was a special long unit located on the driver's side in the space normally occupied by a M35's toolbox and spare tire. (Photo courtesy of John Winslow and Bruce Kubu)

The M275 was a shorter-wheelbase tractor, which resulted in a rear arrangement of fuel and air tanks, as well as toolboxes. The version shown here is the later M275A2 model. (Photo courtesy of TacticalTruck.com)

Frame extensions and ramps were mounted at the rear of the M275 chassis to ease coupling with improperly placed trailers. (Photo courtesy of the Patton Museum)

The M48 was the 154-in.-wheelbase tractor version of the G-742. A spare tire was carried behind the cab, and the trucks used the standard fuel tanks and toolboxes. (Photo courtesy of the Patton Museum)

rear of the chassis, which was used to couple to the towed of the semi-trailer. Air hose and electrical cable connections for semi-trailer service were stowed on the airbrake hose support, that was mounted behind the cab. A deck made of nonskid plates bridged the frame between the hose support and the fifth wheel, so the operator could safely connect the inter-vehicular cables. Pioneer tools were stowed on a rack forward of the fifth wheel. Air and electrical connections were also provided on the chassis rear cross-member, near the rear pintle, to allow towing of a standard trailer. The airbrake hand-control valve, used for semi-trailer airbrake control, was mounted on the steering wheel column. The M275 and M275A1 were not equipped with spare tire assemblies or toolboxes. The tools for these trucks were stored in the cab. Gasoline engines powered the M48 and M275, the

This M47 was photographed in almost-new condition. The M47 was a short-wheelbase dump truck using single 11.00 x 20 tires. (Photo courtesy of the Patton Museum)

2 1/2-TON TRUCKS

M275A1 used the LDS-427 engine, and the M275A2 used the various models of -465 Multifuel engines discussed above.

Tractor trucks were available both with and without winches.

Dump Trucks

There were several varieties of dump trucks built in this series. In establishing requirements for these new vehicles, both a single-tired and a dual-tired version of the new 2 1/2-ton truck with a 9-ft. dump body were planned.

By April-May 1953, these two different versions were adopted to replace the World War II the 2 1/2-ton dump trucks.

The new items were as follows:

The M47 was equipped with a 2 1/2-cubic-yard metal dump body secured on a subframe to which the hydraulic cylinder was attached. The hydraulic hoist pump was driven from a transmission power takeoff similar to the unit used to drive the winch. However, the dump truck PTO was equipped with an accessory drive, which provided a rearward-facing output shaft. The hydraulic hoist driver's control lever for dump body operation was located in the cab to the left side and behind the driver's seat. The spare wheel and toolbox were mounted behind the cab. These trucks used a 142-in.-wheelbase chassis and were equipped with 11.00-20 single tires.

The dump truck M59 was similar to the M47, except for the tire size and body width. The M59 was equipped with 9.00-20 dual tires and was about 12 in. wider

Although the M59 looked like a dual-wheeled M47, the bed of the M59 was wider. Note the position of the air reservoirs, common to the M47, M59, and M275. (Photo courtesy of the Patton Museum)

The XM342 was developed to correct problems with the earlier trucks, including the issue regarding bed/wheel positioning. Although the truck used the standard 154-in.-wheelbase chassis, it had repositioned air tanks. (Photo courtesy of the Patton Museum)

Like the M275, the M47 used the long fuel tank on the driver's side in place of the standard passenger's side tank. (Photo courtesy of the Patton Museum)

The M342 helped solve the short-wheelbase dump trucks' inability to transport a squad of men and their gear. (Photo courtesy of the Patton Museum)

The cab protectors of the M47 and M59 were removable to reduce shipping height. The close positioning of the rear of the bed and the rear wheels caused some problems in the eyes of some of the test personnel. (Photo courtesy of the Patton Museum)

Although it is generally believed that machine gun mounts could not be added to dump trucks, this photo shows that, at least in the case of the M342, it was possible. (Photo courtesy of the Patton Museum)

across the body.

After early models of the XM47 2 1/2-ton dump truck had been procured and issued to the field, but before their adoption as the M47, a number of complaints about its operation and the size of its body were received from the field. The body was 3 ft. shorter than that of the WWII 2 1/2-ton dump truck in an effort to prevent the overloading that was common with the earlier CCKW-based trucks.

In April 1953, AFF Board No. 2 tests showed that the M47 and M59 were not only too small to accommodate a squad of combat engineers with full equipment, but also that they were too difficult to load, and discharged their loads too close to the rear axle. Because it was impossible to correct this without a redesign, in February 1954 the Ordnance Corps began a sub-project for the development of a new dump truck with an 11-ft. body, to be designated the XM342.

Like the predecessors, the M342 body was secured on a subframe to which the hydraulic hoist cylinders were attached. Unlike the M47 and M59, which had one lift cylinder each, the M342 was equipped with two hydraulic hoist cylinders. The hydraulic oil reservoir was located in the forward cross-member of the subframe. The hydraulic hoist pump is driven from the transmission power in the same manner as the other models, and the controls are placed and function in the same manner. The M342 used a 154-in.-wheelbase chassis and were equipped with 9.00 x 20 dual tires.

Only the M342 versions were further developed to include Multifuel engines. The dump trucks were available with and without PTO-driven front winches.

Fuel Tank Trucks

Various Fuel Servicing Tank Trucks were built as part of this family: the M49, M49C, M49A1C and M49A2C. The 1200-gallon fuel tank body was divided into 200-, 400-, and 600-gallon compartments. Access to each compartment was through a manhole, equipped with a manhole and filler cover assembly. Side skirts and running boards on each side of the tank body had sockets for mounting top bows and top tarpaulin with end covers to camouflage the fuel tanker as a cargo truck. The tank body sections could be filled or emptied by use of the delivery pump, which was mounted in the rear compartment. The pump was driven from a power

The fuel dispensing and metering equipment was housed behind these doors on the rear of the M49A2C tankers. (Photo courtesy of Memphis Equipment Company)

Fuel supplies are a constant issue on the battlefield, and the M49 series tankers were built to provide fuel transportation and distribution abilities to troops in the field. This is an M49A2C, the final development of the fuel tanker series. (Photo courtesy of Memphis Equipment Company)

take-off mounted on the transfer case. The delivery line gate valve assemblies and two fuel dispensers with nozzle assemblies were provided to control the discharge of fuel. The tank body shell is extended beyond the rear tank bulkhead to form a pump compartment at the rear of the body. The M49 did not have provisions for towing a trailer, but subsequent models did. Tanker trucks M49C, M49A1C, and M49A2C were equipped with an aviation gasoline segregator kit. Tank trucks M49A1C and M49A2C were equipped with LDS-427 and LDS-465 Multifuel engines, respectively.

The M49A2C did not have wheel wells made into the bed. All these trucks used a 154-in.-wheelbase chassis and were equipped with 9.00-20 dual rear tires.

The fuel tankers were available with and without PTO-driven front winches.

Water Tank Trucks

Water tank trucks were included in this series of trucks as models M50, M50A1, and M50A2. The 1,000-gallon water tank body was divided into 400- and 600-gallon compartments. Access to each compartment was through a manhole like that of the fuel tanker, but equipped with inner and outer manhole covers. Each compartment was filled through a filler cover and strainer. Delivery pump and valve controls were mounted in a rear compartment. Tank sections could be filled or emptied by use of the delivery pump that was driven by the transfer case power takeoff. Two delivery line gate valves, two water nozzles, and three discharge hoses were provided to control the discharge of water. An insulated heating chamber below the tank protected the

This March 1952 photo of the top of an M50 shows the placement of the manholes and hatches used to fill the tank. (National Archives and Records Administration photo)

Although the M50 had dual 9.00 x 20 tires, it had wheel wells in the bed. (National Archives and Records Administration photo)

The M50 was built to carry water supplies. (National Archives and Records Administration photo)

Like the M49, the M50 trucks had the pump assembly in the rear compartment. (National Archives and Records Administration photo)

tank or pipes against freezing during severe weather. Like the fuel tanker, the running board and side skirts on each side of the tank had sockets for installation of the top bows and tarpaulin with end curtains for camouflage. On the M50 gasoline engine driven tank truck, proper engine speed was maintained by the engine auxiliary governor during delivery pump operation.

On the M50A1 and M50A2 427 and 465 Multifuel engine tank trucks, proper engine speed during delivery pump operation of 1000 to 1100 rpm was to be observed on the tachometer. This was to be controlled by the operator using the hand throttle. All these trucks used a 154-in. wheelbase chassis and were equipped with 9.00-20 dual rear wheels.

The water tankers were available with and without PTO-driven front winches.

Wrecker Trucks

Two different wrecker-type trucks were built as part of this series: the Light Wrecker Truck M60 and the Crane Truck M108. The M108 was intended for material handling, and the M60 for recovery work. However, it was found that the M60 was too light for many recovery operations, and ultimately both these trucks were replaced in service with 5-ton medium wreckers.

Both trucks had a body platform with an Austin-Western revolving hydraulic crane with an 8,000-lb. lift capacity. The platform was a steel frame surfaced with welded and bolted safety-tread plate. The crane was mounted in an opening in the center of the platform and secured to both platform and chassis frames. Again, sockets were provided along the sides of the platform for

The operator's station of the XM108 was mounted on the side of the boom shipper. It housed controls to maneuver the boom, shipper, and hoist. (Photo courtesy of the Patton Museum)

The XM108 was intended to provide using units with a light, mobile crane for material handling. It lacked the extensive recovery equipment and rear winch of a wrecker. (Photo courtesy of the Patton Museum)

The XM60 bed had sideboards to retain the recovery equipment it carried, and a large winch was mounted in the rear of the bed. (Photo courtesy of the Patton Museum)

installation of top bows and tarpaulin with end curtains for camouflage purposes. Four outriggers were attached to the platform frame, two on each side, to remove the load weight from truck springs and wheels and to stabilize the vehicle during lifting of heavy loads. The operator's compartment was attached to the crane shipper support. The compartment, containing controls for operating the crane, revolved with the crane. The hardtop, windshield and wipers, and cab heater for the operator's compartment could be installed for inclement weather. An engine auxiliary governor was used to hold engine speed at 1700 rpm during crane operation. A hydraulic pump driven from the transfer power takeoff supplied hydraulic pressure for the crane.

Three floodlights were mounted on the wrecker bed for night operation. An electric brake lock was provided to lock the service brake for additional wheel braking action during crane operation.

Lockout bars were installed on the rear springs to relieve springs of extreme weight during lifting and towing operations. Some wrecker crane trucks were equipped with a front winch.

The M60 light wrecker trucks were equipped with a power divider and a 15,000-lb.-capacity rear winch. All these trucks used a 154-in. wheelbase, were gasoline powered, and were equipped with 9.00-20 dual rear tires.

12-ft. Van Trucks

The M109, M109A1, M109A2, M109C, M109A3, M185, M185A1, M185A2, and M185A3 were all van trucks.

The M109A2, M109A3, M185A1, M185A2, and M185A3 were equipped with the multi-fuel engine. All the trucks had 12-ft. van bodies, which were mounted on subsills to raise the body and eliminate the need for

wheel housings. Two side-hinged doors were mounted in the rear of the body. The right door was equipped with a latch that could be padlocked. The left door could be opened only from the inside of the body. Ladders were provided for access to the inside of the van; and access to the roof of the van. The body had side windows with screens and blackout curtains, and a front communication door. The bodies were wired for truck-supplied 24-volt DC or outside supplied 115-volt AC power for lighting, accessories and tools. Heating and ventilating accessories were available to provide satisfactory working conditions in temperatures from 125°F. to -25°F. The body was waterproofed for fording to a depth of 8 ft.

All van trucks were initially equipped with the hardtops. These trucks used a 154-in. wheelbase,

The M109 family went through the various engine upgrades. This example is powered by the LDT-465. Notice the three-window van body. (Photo courtesy of TacticalTruck.com)

The earliest M109 trucks had five windows per side. In later models, this was reduced to three per side. (National Archives and Records Administration photo)

The M109 trucks also had provision for mounting bows, allowing canvas to be fitted to disguise the vehicle as a cargo truck. (National Archives and Records Administration photo)

The M109 canvas could be used as an awning, reducing the temperatures inside the van. (National Archives and Records Administration photo)

gasoline-powered chassis, and were equipped with 9.00 -20 dual tires.

The vans were available with and without PTO-driven front winches.

17-ft. Van Trucks

These van trucks were equipped with the M4 expansible van body. The expansible van body had two rear access doors, and single access doors on either side of the body. Two ladders were provided for access purposes.

The side access doors could be used only when the van body was in the expanded position. The expansible van body was designed to expand to about twice the volume it enclosed when in the retracted or traveling position. This was achieved by expanding side panels, actuated by expanding and retracting mechanisms, and counterbalanced hinged roof and floor sections. All systems, including lighting, heating, air conditioning, and blackout protection were operable in both the expanded and retracted positions.

Four windows, equipped with brush guards, insect screens, and sliding blackout panels, were located in each side panel. Two stationary windows were located in the rear doors. An opening designed to accommodate intercom facilities, normally covered by a removable plate, was located on the left rear panel toward the top.

The telephone entrance jack and the auxiliary power cable entrance power were located on the left rear panel near the bottom. The pioneer tool bracket and power cable entrance receptacle were located on the right rear panel. A bonnet, extending from the front panel of the van, housed the two heating units and the air-conditioning unit. The electrical system included a 24-volt DC circuit for vehicular light operation, and 110-volt and 208-volt circuits for auxiliary equipment operation.

This M292A2 has had its heaters removed, but the final form of the M4 body, with four windows per side, is visible. This truck is powered by an LDT-465 engine.

When fully expanded, the volume of the XM292 bed was almost doubled. The exhaust stacks above the cab were for the heaters. (Photo courtesy of the Patton Museum)

This photo, taken during the XM292 expansion process, shows the sides partially cranked out, and the roof and floor sections swinging into place. (National Archives and Records Administration photo)

A van was needed that was bigger than the M109, so an expansible van was developed. This is a late prototype of the M292, which differed from production units only in detail, including the number of windows. (Photo courtesy of the Patton Museum)

The high voltage was supplied by a M200 trailer-mounted generator towed by the van truck.

The M292 was powered by the gasoline engine, the M292A1 was powered by the LDS-427 engine, and the M292A2 used the LDS-465 Multifuel engine. All these trucks used a 190-in.-wheelbase chassis and were equipped with 9.00-20 dual rear tires.

The expansible vans were available with and without PTO-driven front winches.

Telephone Construction & Maintenance Truck

The V-17A/MTQ body was designed for Signal Corps use during telephone construction and maintenance work and had seven compartments built into the side panels of the body for storage of tools and equipment. The compartments were accessible through hinged doors on the outside of the panels.

Other openings in the side panels provided access to the drum shaft and auxiliary shaft of the rear winch assembly. A collapsible cable reel was installed on this shaft during wire handling operations. A manually rotated revolving platform assembly was mounted on top of the body.

The non-elevating platform was supported by a brake ring frame secured to the front end of the body. A guardrail assembly was welded to the platform as a safety measure. A pole derrick assembly was provided for use when moving, erecting, and pulling poles. This

Although the bed of the V-17A/MTQ looks odd for a military truck, it was based on contemporary civilian designs. Extensive stowage compartments were provided both inside and outside the bed. (Photo courtesy of John Adams-Graf)

RA PD 204514

The companion vehicle for the V-17A/MTQ was the V-18A/MTQ pole setter and earth-boring machine. It was equipped with a large auger to dig holes for telephone poles. (U.S. Army photo)

The V-17A/MTQ was used by the Signal Corps for line work. The rotating platform mounted on the top front of the bed provided access to overhead structures. This truck is missing its brush guard. (Photo courtesy of John Adams-Graf)

V-17A/MTQ was also equipped with two-wheel chock with chain assemblies, two support legs, and a collapsible cable reel.

These trucks used a 154-in.-wheelbase, gasoline-powered chassis and were equipped with 11.00-20 single tires and front winches.

Earth-Boring Machine & Pole Setter Trucks

These trucks were for use by Signal Corps units when building communications lines.

The earlier truck, the V-18A/MTQ, was based on a wheel-well-equipped M34 body modified to mount a rear winch assembly and an earth-boring machine. The rear winch assembly was mounted on the body behind the cab. The earth-boring machine was mounted on the rear end of the body platform. The boring machine received its power from the power divider. A control lever assembly, mounted on the boring machine, controlled the operation of the earth-boring machine. The power divider was operated from the cab through control lever linkage similar to the one used in the V-17A/MTQ. The V-18A/MTQ was also equipped with two support legs and two wheel chocks with chain assemblies. Entry was gained via access steps and grab rings mounted at the rear of the body. These trucks used a 154-in.-wheelbase, gasoline-powered chassis and were equipped with 11.00-20 single tires.

The M764 earth-boring machine and pole setter truck was the Multifuel version of the V-18A/MTQ truck, with additional modifications. The body and auxiliary equipment for this truck were mounted on a modified M45A2 multi-fuel chassis with dual 9.00-20 rear wheels. The rear of the frame of this truck has additional

derrick had three legs, with the center leg consisting of three sections. The top section of the center leg mounted a derrick sheave for use with a winch line from the rear winch assembly.

When the derrick was in the travel position, it was secured in a compartment of the vehicle by two derrick leg hold-down clamp assemblies. With the derrick stowed properly, the driver could not open his door. The rear winch was mounted under a cover in the front end of the body. Power for the rear winch was provided from a transfer case power takeoff. The winch was controlled through a control lever linkage from the truck cab. The

The M764 was the improved model pole setter/earth borer. In addition to a multi-fuel-powered dual wheel chassis, it had a more modern boring machine and hydraulic outriggers. (U.S. Army photo)

reinforcement.

The M764 truck utilized a modified M35A2 cargo body with a clearance opening incorporated in the body floor for the winch mounting frame and boring machine mounting base. Detachable holders were provided on the body for stowage of five earth augers, a collapsible cable reel, pole-pulling jack, and pike poles.

The M764 body utilized the same bows, staves, and body tarpaulin as the M35A2 cargo body. Stave pockets were incorporated between the body side panels and staves. A cutout was provided in the front end curtain to fit over the derrick tube. No rear end curtain was utilized because of the boring machine.

Differences Between the
V-18A/MTQ & M764 Model Trucks

Stowage facilities for the equipment accessories were re-arranged due to the addition of 30-in. earth auger. Additional brackets were added to inside body for stowage of pike poles.

An outrigger hydraulic system was added to operate the outrigger legs mounted at rear of M764 truck. The outrigger legs were used in lieu of the support legs mounted on the V-18A/MTQ truck.

The M764 truck utilized the model HDB2L boring machine. This model machine was an improved version of the HD machine mounted on V-18A/MTQ truck. Major improvements were incorporated in the clutch case assembly, control lever operating handle assembly and linkage, and power leveling drive components. The HDB2L machine was equipped with two-way power leveling and a 16-ft. rack bar.

The M764 and V-18A/MTQ rear winches were similar in construction, with the major differences being in the drum, drive chain idler pulley assembly, mounting frame, and worm drive sprocket configuration. The cable level winder assembly and cable tensioner assembly were added to the basic winch. The winch cable was increased from 7/16 to 1/2-in. diameter. The rear winch cover was not utilized on the M764 truck.

The M764 and V-18/MTQ power-dividers were basically the same, with the differences being in the shifting arrangement of each unit. The re-design and re-location of the forward and reverse speed gears on front output shaft, enabled the M764 power-divider to be shifted directly from the NEUTRAL position to either REAR WINCH or EARTH AUGER positions. The linkage between shifting lever in cab and power-divider was re-designed because of modifications made to the chassis frame crossmembers.

A two-section cab protector, attached to the M764 rear winch mounting frame, was added to the M764 truck. The upper section of cab protector could be removed to reduce the overall height of truck for shipping purposes. Stowage facilities for the body bows and staves, and wheel chocks were incorporated on each side of cab protector. The upper section of protector also served as a support for the boring machine derrick tube, when derrick was in traveling position.

The 30-in. auger was added to the group of 9-, 12-, 16-, and 20-in. earth augers carried by the V-18A/MTQ. The 12-, 16-, 20-, and 30-in. augers were similar in construction with the major differences reflected in the number of blades and thrust plates bolted to the auger frames.

All the M764 and the V-18A/MTQ pole setter trucks were equipped with front winches.

Pipeline Construction Truck

In the early 1950s, a pipeline construction body conversion kit was developed by the Engineer Research and Development Laboratory to convert an M35 cargo truck into a pipeline construction truck.

In 1969, the M756A2 Pipeline Construction Truck

This truck has a pipeline construction conversion kit installed. It is unloading a pumping unit here. (Photo courtesy of United States Army Engineer School History Office)

All the M756A2 trucks had front winches, although this one is missing its cable. Clearance lights were mounted on the cab protectors of these trucks. (Photo courtesy of TacticalTruck.com)

The M756A2 was a purpose-built pipeline truck similar to the earlier conversion kits. (Photo courtesy of TacticalTruck.com)

was tested at the Aberdeen Proving Ground. This truck was factory built, rather than being a field-installed conversion kit, and was based on the Multifuel chassis. Beyond that it was essentially the same as the conversion kit developed many years earlier. The M756A2 pipeline construction body and auxiliary equipment were mounted on a modified M45A2, 2 1/2-ton, 6x6, Multifuel engine-equipped vehicle chassis with dual 9.00 x 20 rear wheels.

The body was an open-top metal body with a wood-metal reinforced wooden flat-bed. This truck body was equipped with a winch and cab protector, rear-mounted winch, two gin poles for constructing an A-frame, two 24-volt flood lights, tailboard roller, custom made tool box, and stiff leg jacks for providing additional vehicle support. Weather protection for personnel and equipment was provided by a cargo body tarpaulin with end curtains supported by top bows. Front and side cargo body panels with racks supported the top bows. These panels and racks were removable for side loading. The side cargo racks had built-in troop seats that allowed the truck to double as a personnel carrier. The body floor was equipped with provisions for mounting two sheaves — one located at the rear, and the other

toward the front of the body floor slightly off-center. Gin pole brackets were provided on each side of the body side frames for securing and carrying the gin poles that made up the A-frame assembly. Tailboard brackets were welded at each rear corner of the body-side frames to accommodate the tailboard roller and allow for rear mounting and stowage of the gin poles.

A winch and cab protector was located between the cab and the pipeline construction body that housed the rear winch and protected the cab. The top portion of the winch and cab protector served as a platform to protect the cab area, and to hold the gin poles during the raising and lowering of the A-frame.

The rear winch provided for the M756A2 pipeline construction truck was a modification of the winch that was used on the front of G-744 series trucks. It was chain driven directly from the transfer power take-off sprocket. A drum sliding clutch was utilized to engage and disengage the winch drum with drum shaft. A shoe-type drag brake worked on the side of the drum to prevent drum spin when free spooling the winch cable. A drum lock poppet was provided to lock the drum when the winch was not operating. This winch had 300 ft. of 1/2-in. cable with a maximum capacity of 20,000 lbs. on the first layer of cable.

To provide illumination for night winch operations, two adjustable 24-volt floodlights were provided — one mounted on each side of the winch and cab protector. A separate switch located on the rear side of each light housing operated each light.

When heavy loads were being lifted with the A-frame mounted over the rear end of the body, telescoping stiff leg jacks were positioned on the ground to support the vehicle. When not being used, these leg jacks were stored and locked in place within their own compartment, located underneath the rear end of the body sub-frame. For rear loading and unloading of skid-mounted equipment and other heavy gear, a built-in roller with auxiliary roller brackets was provided. This unit was mounted across the rear end of the truck body flatbed. Two gin poles were provided for making up the A-frame assembly. The pipeline construction body was designed so that the A-frame could be mounted on the rear or side of the body flatbed. The A-frame could then be power raised and lowered using the rear winch. When not in use, the gin poles for the A-frame were stowed on each side of the body. They were attached to the tailboard brackets by links and secured on each body side by clamps and wing nuts.

All the pipeline construction trucks were equipped with front winches.

Class 530A Fire Trucks

In 1952, Howe Fire Apparatus Company converted an M44 truck chassis into a pumper at the direction of the Detroit Ordnance District. Dakota Fire Apparatus also worked on developing a new tactical pumper. The result of these tests was a new tactical fire truck designated the Class 530A.

The 530A used a front-mounted pump as had its WWII-era, CCKW-based predecessor, and still stowed much of its fire fighting equipment externally.

2 1/2-TON TRUCKS

Class 530B Fire Trucks

No less than four chassis types were used to produce the 530B series fire trucks. The first Class 530B, developed in the late 1950s, continued to use a Reo-type M44 chassis and gas engine similar to that used by the 530A. The difference was that the pump was relocated mid-ships (driven by a transfer case PTO), and the apparatus bed had compartments in which to stow the gear. Initially, the Hesse Carriage Company produced these beds, but in following years similar ones were also produced by a number of makers. Some of these trucks had the pump control panel enclosed, while most of them did not. One theory is that enclosed panel was part of a winterization kit. Regardless, trucks with the enclosed panel are extremely rare.

By late 1964, the 530B fire trucks were being built on a chassis with single 11:00-20 tires and the Multifuel fire trucks engine. These fire trucks seem to be the only application of a Multifuel engine on a single-tire chassis. The first multi-fuel trucks were built on the M44A1 chassis, and the apparatus bed builder, Ward LaFrance, assigned the complete rig the manufacturer's model designation "M44A1WLF."

When the chassis was changed to the M44A2 chassis, the trucks, then built by Fire Trucks Inc., carried the manufacturers model designation "530 BAM." The winterized versions were known as "530

The 530A trucks were the first series of fire trucks built on the G-742 chassis. This Howe builder's photo shows the front-mounted pump and exposed equipment stowage characteristic of this series. (Photo courtesy of Richard Adelman collection)

The 530B retained the single 11.00-20 tires of the 530A, but featured a new enclosed bed and a midship-mounted pump. (Photo courtesy of Richard Adelman collection)

"BAWM." Ward LaFrance built some of these winterized trucks as well, using its own model number "M44A2WLF-W." It was at about this time that the rear tool compartment below the pintle hook was eliminated. Later production trucks used the dual rear wheel chassis with the multi-fuel engine. Ward LaFrance assigned the manufacturer's model number "M45A2WLF" to the units it built, while American Air Filter used the simpler model number "FT-500."

Class 530C Fire Trucks

With the use of the helicopter becoming widespread in Vietnam, there was a need to add aircraft crash and rescue to the Army firefighters' responsibilities. To aid in this, the truck was again updated, becoming the 530C. Improvements included replacing the 500-gpm Hale pump with a 750-gpm Waterous, adding a pump and roll feature, and the distinctive Feecon combination water and foam deck gun, unique to this model. Like the 530B,

Later 530B trucks used dual 9.00 x 20 tires and multi-fuel engines, as shown in this example. Trucks in rear areas such as this one were initially painted a traditional red. This was later changed to a safety yellow paint scheme. (Photo courtesy of Richard Adelman collection)

Fire trucks assigned to forward areas were painted in the standard tactical truck paint scheme, as shown here. The widespread use of helicopters in Vietnam spawned the last version of the 530 series, the 530C. The large nozzle on the roof, capable of dispensing foam, was the identifying characteristic of 530C trucks. (Photo courtesy of Richard Adelman collection)

The stowage compartments are open in this view, exposing some of the extensive array of equipment carried by the 530 series trucks. The 530C as shown here also had a larger capacity pump than the earlier models. (Photo courtesy of the Patton Museum)

the 530C used four 6TL batteries. On previous models, these were mounted in an enlarged battery box beneath the passenger's door. On the 530C, these were relocated to a special heavily insulated box beneath the pump operator's panel.

Though appearing identical to the 530B, the body also changed slightly, growing a couple of inches taller — just enough, in fact, to make the compartment doors not interchangeable. These trucks were built on chassis made by AM General.

Both American Air Filter and Engineered Devices built these trucks. Engineered Devices referred to their truck as the Model 0814, while tAmerican Air Filter

designated their standard version the FT750 and the winterized version the FT750W. Depending upon the type of use expected as the primary role for a truck, it (like the 530B) was equipped with one of three firefighting equipment sets. As with the 530B, this equipment was largely stowed internally.

None of the Class 530 fire trucks had winches and all used the 154-in.- wheelbase chassis.

Compressor Trucks

Certain G-742 series trucks were built with large air compressors mounted in the space normally occupied by cargo beds. These trucks were used by engineer units for

The M45 chassis was the basis for the engineer's compressor trucks. This truck, restored by Everette Doyle, is equipped with the unique Le Roi 210G1 compressor. (Photo courtesy of D. Moss)

The running boards beside the compressor housing are actually tool compartments, which, along with the crosswise box behind the cab, stored the wide variety of tools carried by these trucks. (Photo courtesy of D. Moss)

construction work. All were built on winch-equipped 154-in.-wheelbase, gasoline engine-driven chassis. Two variants are known to exist: the Le Roi 210G1 and the Davey 210 WDS.

Le Roi 210G1

The Le Roi-design compressor was built exclusively for the military. The engine/compressor was based on the Le Roi H844 V8 engine block (as used in gas-burning 10-ton trucks). The driver's side cylinder bank is a 210 cubic-feet-per-minute single-stage compressor, while the four cylinders on the passenger's side provided an engine of 499 cu. in. to power to the compressor bank. At the time they were built, the Le Roi Model 210 compressors were unparalleled in weight and displacement, and they had twice the capacity of the WWII-era units they replaced. By building the engine and compressor as one unit, the space and maintenance needs of a clutch unit were eliminated.

According to Le Roi records, between June 2, 1952, and November 25, 1953, 523 of these units were built for the Army, along with 77 variants for mounting on GMC truck chassis, and 687 similar units for the U.S. Air Force. In addition, during the developmental stage 10 experimental units were built but never shipped. There was no civilian equivalent made.

With its factory-original 15-in. unmuffled exhaust pipe, it produced a unique (and loud) noise that would undoubtedly disqualify it for clandestine operations!

When new, the compressor was delivered with a number of pneumatic tools, including: an air-powered circular saw, air-powered chainsaw, two paving breakers, a sheeting driver, two clay diggers, a pneumatic reversible wood drill, two rock drills, a nail driver and rivet buster, a grease gun set, an air line oilers gun, tire inflating equipment, and dozens of accessories for these tools.

Davey 210 WDS

In the late 1950s, the Davey Compressor Company of Kent, Ohio, built a number of its 210 WDS compressors for the military. These compressors could be mounted on either the M45 chassis, or the WWII era CCKW chassis. Although the tools and performance of the 210 WDS was similar to that of the Le Roi, it used a separate engine and compressor components.

This is the compressor bank of the V-8 that formed the 210G1. (Photo courtesy of D. Moss)

This Davey 210 WDS has been equipped with an Arctic winterization kit. The hose reels have been totally enclosed to prevent moisture from freezing inside, and the insulation blanket is visible on the roof. (Photo courtesy of United States Army Engineering School History Office, Ft. Leonard Wood, Missouri)

Here is the Davey 210 WDS. Like the Le Roi, its capacity was 210 cu. ft. of compressed air per minute. (Photo courtesy of the Patton Museum)

The 210 WDS, like the 210G1, carried an extensive assortment of tools, but these units could also be used to supply air to other equipment. (Photo courtesy of United States Army Engineer School History Office)

Water Purification Trucks

Two different water purification sets have been mounted on G-742-series chassis. The 1,500-gallon-per-hour unit was mounted on the 154-in. chassis, and the 3,000-gallon-per-hour unit was mounted on the 190-in.-wheelbase chassis. All the water purification trucks were equipped with front-mounted, PTO-driven winches. These units were designed to purify local water supplies and yield drinking water.

1,500-gph Unit

The Water Purification Equipment Set, Diatomite Mobile 1500-gph consisted of a water purification unit mounted on a standard. M45 2 1/2-ton truck chassis, a 10-kw engine generator mounted on a standard 1 1/2-ton trailer, two 1,500-gallon collapsible fabric water storage tanks, a 30-day supply of chemicals, three portable centrifugal pumps, and all accessories necessary for continuous operation. The equipment for the water purification unit was assembled in an insulated and heated van body that was mounted on a standard M45 2 1/2-ton truck chassis.

The water purification unit included: a continuous-flow Erdlator-type solid contact clarifier, three chemical feeders for the application of ferric chloride, pulverized limestone, and calcium hypochlorite to the raw water, one constant-rate variable pressure-type diatomite filter with an electrically driven centrifugal pump, a constant rate diatomite slurry feeder, and a panel board for operating control of all the electrically powered

The large driver's side doors opened to form a work platform on these trucks. This truck is being cleaned following a training exercise in Germany. (Photo courtesy of the Patton Museum)

This ERDLator, so named because it was developed by the Engineering Research and Development Laboratory, is a 1,500-gallon-per-hour unit mounted on a M45A1 chassis. These units were used to purify water. (Photo courtesy of Memphis Equipment Company)

components. The 10-kw engine generator that supplied electric power for all the electrically driven equipment was operated and transported on the 1 1/2-ton trailer, and fabric tanks were erected adjacent to the truck-mounted unit, providing a total storage capacity for 3,000 gallons of drinking water.

The complete set was transported in the truck-mounted van body and in the 1 1/2-ton trailer towed behind the truck, with the exception of the chemical supplies. In field operations, storage space for the chemicals was available for only 60 hours of operation.

3,000-gph Unit

The 3,000-gph Water Purification Set was essentially an enlarged version of the 1500-gph unit. It was mounted on a M46 2 1/2-ton truck chassis, with a 10-kw engine generator mounted on a standard 1 1/2-ton trailer. Two 3,000-gallon collapsible fabric water storage tanks, a 30-day supply of chemicals, and three portable centrifugal pumps were also provided.

The equipment for the water purification unit was assembled in an insulated and heated van body that was mounted on an M46-type truck chassis.

The water purification unit included: a continuous-flow ERDLator-type solid-contact clarifier, chemical feeder for adding ferric chloride, pulverized limestone, and calcium hypochlorite to the raw water, two constant-rate variable pressure-type diatomite filters with electrically driven centrifugal pumps, a constant-rate diatomite slurry feeder, and a panel board for operating control of all of the electrically powered components.

Water purification trucks were built on both gasoline and Multifuel-engined trucks.

The 3,000-gallon-per-hour purification units were mounted on M46-type chassis. Shown here is one such unit mounted on an M46A2C chassis. (Photo courtesy of TacticalTruck.com)

Mobile Shop Trucks

The Couse Model MEDL was a general-purpose repair shop mounted on a 190-in.-wheelbase 2 1/2-ton, 6x6 truck chassis. The heated weather-proofed shop enclosed machine shop equipment, a dynamotor-welder driven by the truck's engine, an electrical control cubicle, a motor-driven air compressor, and had storage compartments that contain complete tool kits and accessories that were used in the repair and overhaul of electrical and mechanical military equipment in the field.

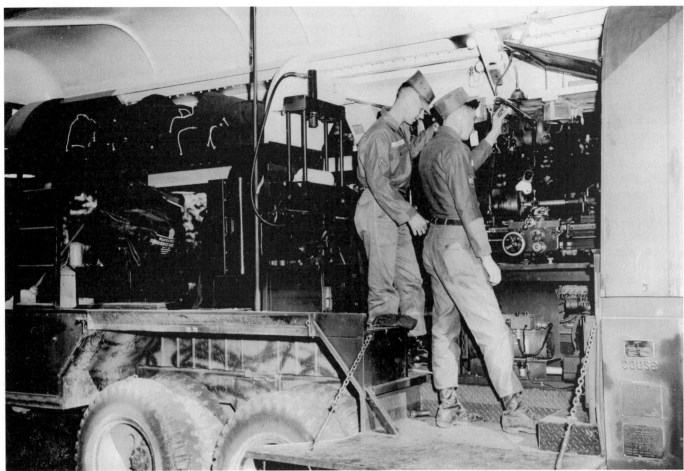

The shop truck van body was fully illuminated for night work, and there was a combination welder and generator powered by the truck engine mounted inside. (Photo courtesy of United States Army Engineer School History Office)

FB 9125-1-1

Initially, the large mobile shop sets were mounted on M46 chassis, like this Shop Set Number 2. However, the great weight of the equipment proved to be too much for the 2 1/2-ton chassis, and later shop sets were built on 5-ton trucks. (U.S. Army photo)

The M46 Shop Truck's unusual shop body opened up, forming a shaded work area and allowing access to the truck's lathe, grinder, drill press, etc. (U.S. Army photo)

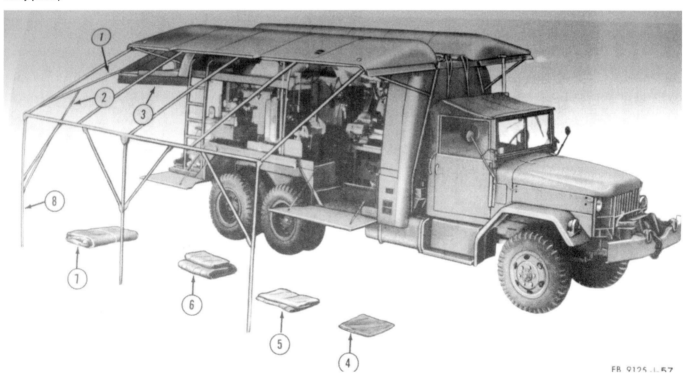

These trucks were supplied with a large canvas tent and framework, which could be attached to the truck to form a large sheltered area during bad weather. (U.S. Army photo)

The dynamotor-welder could also be driven by an external electrical source of power or could be used as an auxiliary power plant.

The sides of the truck were elevated by hydraulic cylinders to provide a shade over the open workshop area.

The extensive array of tools overloaded the 2 1/2-ton chassis, and further developments of this shop set were based on the 5-ton truck chassis

LaCrosse Launcher

The heaviest-armed deuces were the LaCrosse missile launchers.

The LaCrosse missile, built by Martin Marietta, weighed just over 1 ton and was 19 ft. long. It had a range of 11 miles, and flew at a speed of Mach .8. The missile had a wingspan 9 ft. wide across its fins and the fuselage was 20 in. in diameter. The guided missile normally carried a single, 540-lb. shaped-charged warhead, although it could carry high-explosive conventional, chemical and atomic warheads instead.

The operational version of the LaCrosse launcher was the M398. It mounted a more sophisticated helical-railed launcher on the dual-wheel M45 chassis. (U.S. Army photo)

The M387 was the first of the G-742-based rocket launchers. These trucks were built on the single rear-wheeled M44 154-in.-wheelbase chassis, and were used to transport and launch LaCrosse missiles. (Photo courtesy of the Patton Museum)

The M387 missile was lowered to this position during transport. The square launch rail was used for test purposes only. (Photo courtesy of the Patton Museum)

The W40 atomic warhead gave LaCrosse a variable explosive yield in the low kiloton range.

The first G-742-based launcher, the M387 was built on the M44 154-in.-wheelbase, gasoline-powered chassis and was equipped with 11.00-20 single tires. From 1953 through 1957, the LaCrosse was tested using the M387. However, the M387 would not be introduced into service as an operational mount. It was felt that its simple square-section launch rail would not be accurate enough. The M387 was equipped with a PTO-driven front winch.

The operational vehicle issued was the M398 Guided Missile Launcher Truck, Helical Railed. The truck was based on the M45 154-in.-wheelbase, gasoline-powered chassis with dual 9.00-20 rear wheels. The M398 vehicle became the operational mount for the LaCrosse Type I Guided Missile in 1958. With the launcher in the transport position, the M398 was 21 ft.11 in. long overall, 7-ft. 10 in. wide, and 9 ft. 8 in. tall. The helical rail of the M398 launcher gave a 500-degree per second roll to the missile, which improved accuracy compared to the M387-launched missile. The M398 did not have a front winch.

G-742 Accessory Kits

A Gar Wood 10,000 lb.-capacity PTO-driven winch was installed on some of these trucks as mentioned above. In addition to the winch, a variety of kits, including hard tops, hot water and fuel burning personnel heaters, and deep-water fording were produced for these vehicles.

GENERAL DATA

MODEL	154-wb cargo trucks	190-wb cargo trucks
NET WEIGHT *	12,465 lbs.	13,500 lbs.
GROSS WEIGHT *	23,230 lbs.	23,500 lbs.
MAX TOWED LOAD	10,000 lbs.	10,000 lbs.
LENGTH	262	324
WIDTH	96	96
HEIGHT	112	124.5
WHEELBASE	154	190
TIRE SIZE	9.00-20 or 11.00-20	9.00-20
MAX SPEED	58 mph	58 mph
FUEL CAPY	50 gal	50 gal
RANGE LOADED	300 mi	300 mi
ELECTRICAL	24 neg	24 neg
TRANSFER SPEEDS	2	2
TRANSMISSION SPEEDS	5 F	5 F
TURNING RADIUS FT	35.5	45

MODEL	142-wb dump	154-wb dump	142-wb tractor
NET WEIGHT *	14,050 lbs.	15,170 lbs.	11,179 lbs.
GROSS WEIGHT *	24,810 lbs.	26,170 lbs.	23,939 lbs.
MAX TOWED LOAD	10,000 lbs.	10,000 lbs.	36,000 lbs.
LENGTH	235	260.5	228
WIDTH	96	96	94
HEIGHT	101	104.5	99
WHEELBASE	142	154	142
TIRE SIZE	9.00-20 or 11.00-20	9.00-20	9.00-20
MAX SPEED	58 mph	58 mph	58 mph
FUEL CAPY	50 gal	50 gal	50 gal
RANGE LOADED	300 mi	300 mi	300 mi
ELECTRICAL	24 neg	24 neg	24 neg
TRANSFER SPEEDS	2	2	2
TRANSMISSION SPEEDS	5 F	5 F	5 F
TURNING RADIUS FT	35.5	35.5	35.5

GENERAL DATA, continued

MODEL	154-wb van trucks	190-wb van trucks
WEIGHT NET*	15,231 lbs.	20,609 lbs.
WEIGHT GROSS*	20,581 lbs.	25,959 lbs.
MAX TOWED LOAD	10,000 lbs.	10,000 lbs.
LENGTH	263	324
WIDTH	969	96
HEIGHT	130	132
WHEELBASE	154	190
TIRE SIZE	9.00-20	9.00-20
MAX SPEED	58 mph	58 mph
FUEL CAPY	50 gal	50 gal
RANGE LOADED	300 mi	300 mi
ELECTRICAL	24 neg	24 neg
TRANSFER SPEEDS	2	2
TRANSMISSION SPEEDS	5 F	5 F
TURNING RADIUS FT	35.5	35.5

MODEL	154-wb tanker trucks	M108-wb crane trucks
WEIGHT NET*	13,490 lbs.	15,646 lbs.
WEIGHT GROSS*	23,688 lbs.	23,635 lbs.
MAX TOWED LOAD	10,000 lbs.	10,000 lbs.
LENGTH	263	303
WIDTH	96	96
HEIGHT	97	99
WHEELBASE	154	154
TIRE SIZE	9.00-20	9.00-20
MAX SPEED	58 mph	58 mph
FUEL CAPY	50 gal	50 gal
RANGE LOADED	300 mi	300 mi
ELECTRICAL	24 neg	24 neg
TRANSFER SPEEDS	2	2
TRANSMISSION SPEEDS	5 F	5 F
TURNING RADIUS FT	35.5	35.5

Note: All data given above is for gas-powered, dual-wheel trucks. For other engines, adjust as shown below. Data given for trucks without winch, except wreckers, which all had front winches.

Overall dimensions listed in inches.

*Add 650 lbs. to weight on vehicles powered by the Multifuel engine. Add approximately 500 lbs. to weight and 14 in. to length for front winch.

ENGINE DATA

ENGINE MAKE/MODEL	Reo OA-331	LDT-465-1C
NUMBER OF CYLINDERS	6	6
CUBIC-INCH DISPLACEMENT	331	478
HORSEPOWER	146 @ 3400	130
TORQUE	330 lbs.-ft.	305 lbs.-ft.

VALUES

	6	5	4	3	2	1
154-wb Cargo Trucks	800	2,500	4,500	9,000	18,000	25,000
190-wb Cargo Trucks	1,200	3,000	5,000	10,000	19,000	27,000
Dump Trucks	2,000	3,500	5,500	10,500	19,500	27,000
Tractor Trucks	800	2,500	4,500	9,000	18,000	25,000
Wrecker Trucks	2,000	3,500	5,500	10,500	19,500	27,000
154-WB Van	1,200	2,800	5,000	9,500	18,500	26,000
190-WB Van	2,000	3,500	5,500	10,500	19,500	27,000
Tanker Trucks	2,000	3,500	5,500	10,500	19,500	27,000

SCARCITY

154-wb Cargo Trucks	2
190-wb Cargo Trucks	3
Dump Trucks	3
Tractor Trucks	2
Wrecker Trucks	4
154-WB Van	2
190-WB Van	3
Tanker Trucks	3

Notes:

— Values shown for LDT Multifuel engine trucks where applicable.

— Decrease values 30 percent for gas-powered trucks, although scarcity increases.

— Decrease values 30 percent for LDS-427- powered trucks, although extremely scarce.

— Decrease values 10 percent for LD-465 powered trucks, although scarcity increases.

— Values increase 500-1,000 for winch trucks, and a similar amount for hard top cabs.

G-749 GMC

Following World War II, GMC hoped to retain the tactical truck market it had established with its CCKW. When the Reo Motors G-742 became the primary tactical cargo truck, GMC responded by building its own truck and offering it to the government as an alternative. This was the revolutionary M135 (G-749) series of trucks.

These trucks, developed in 1951, featured air-assisted power brakes, automatic transmissions, and oversize single tires. Although this truck was not destined to become the postwar standard bearer for U.S. forces that GMC hoped, it was to be the standard of Canadian Forces for years, as well as the U.S. secondary truck. By the 1980s, as these trucks were becoming the popular "deuce" with collectors, the U.S. military would rediscover the innovations of automatic transmissions and oversize single tires in a new generation of tactical vehicles.

Like all of the M series vehicles designed during this time, these trucks featured a sealed waterproof ignition system, a 24-volt electrical system, and were equipped to ford 30-in. streams. Accessory heater, radio, deep-water fording, hard-top, and gun-mount kits could be installed.

All trucks in this series were powered by GMC's own 302-cid straight six-cylinder gasoline engine. The transmission initially was the GMC 302M Hydro-Matic, but early on it was replaced with the improved 303M.

This M135 cargo truck was photographed just after final inspection at the GMC Yellow Truck and Coach plant. The characteristic holed front bumper is visible, as is the vertical exhaust stack. (GMC Truck and Coach photo)

Both of these units provide four forward and a single reverse speed in either of two ranges. Unlike many automatic transmissions, these units had a rear pump that allowed the truck to be push-started if need be.

Because the transmission had two ranges, the transfer case was a single-speed unit. The axles were also a GM design. Front axle engagement was accomplished by a dog-type clutch that engaged when the rear wheels slipped. There was no provision for manual selection of all-wheel drive. The service brake system was an air-over-hydraulic power-assisted type. In addition to the normal drum-type parking brakes, all production vehicles in this series had an electric parking brake built into the service brake system. Early models had telescoping hidden hood supports. Beginning at serial numbers M211-31388 and M215-4679 a nose-mounted solid hood prop was used. None of these trucks had power steering.

Winch-equipped trucks used the same Gar Wood model CA514 10,000-lb. winch as the G-742 series, although the mounting brackets and winch driveline were different. The front bumper, with its six distinctive lightening holes, was inverted for cable clearance on these trucks. Unlike many military vehicles, the overall length was the same whether it was winch-equipped or not. All trucks in this series, except M135s serial number 10699 and below, had three-piece sheet metal splash guards between the frame and body, the center section of which was omitted on winch-equipped trucks.

The pioneer tools were mounted inside the cab, and an auxiliary fuel container (Jerry can) was mounted on the driver's side step.

M135 Cargo Truck

This was the first vehicle in this series, with production beginning in September 1951. These trucks were equipped with six 11:00-20 tires, and the cargo bed had wheel wells allowing it to be mounted lower to aid in troop entrance and egress. The tailgate had a foldout step to make this even easier. This bed is slightly narrower than was the bed used on dual wheel trucks, so the bows, supports, and canvas were not interchangeable.

This XM135 received some modifications during testing at Aberdeen Proving Ground. Although the truck's sealed windshield didn't see production, the simple hinged hood prop seen here hanging in the center of the brush guard was adopted. (Photo courtesy of the Patton Museum)

The dual-wheel equipped XM211 cargo truck was also demonstrated to the Army Field Forces Board Number Two. Two different-size fuel tanks, differing in length and depth, were used on the G-749 series trucks. The tank shown here is the typical one. Mass production of the dual-wheel version of this truck began before it was officially standardized, resulting in an abundance of XM211 trucks being built. (Photo courtesy of the Patton Museum)

M211 & XM211 Cargo Truck

This was the second vehicle in this series. The 156-in. wheelbase was the same as the M135, but it was equipped with ten 9:00-20 tires. These trucks were intended to be primarily for on-road cargo carrying, as opposed to the more general-purpose M135. As such, the bed had a flat floor (no wheel wells) and was mounted higher than the M135 bed. Also, the tailgate on these models lacked the drop-down step feature, having instead only the simple hoop steps found on most 6x6s.

In addition to the cargo truck versions, the G-749 series included a variety of other styles. This 1956 photo shows an M215 dump truck supplying asphalt to a road-building operation. A single hydraulic cylinder was used to lift the dump bed on these trucks. (Photo courtesy of United States Army Engineer School History Office)

M215 Dump Truck

This truck, built on the dual-wheel equipped M207 chassis, had a shorter 144-in. wheelbase. A single hydraulic cylinder lifted the 2 1/2-cubic yard dump body built either by Gar Wood or by Perfection. Dump controls were located in the cab. The transfer case-mounted PTO was a Chelsea 87C1 model.

M216 Dump Truck

Although this dump truck, built on the M133 chassis, was not used by the U.S. military, it was widely used by Canadian forces and is included here for reference. Unlike the M215, which had 10 9:00-20 tires, the M216 had six 11:00-20 tires.

M217 Gasoline Tanker

The M217 gasoline tanker was equipped with a three-compartment tank body built by the Butler Manufacturing Company. A Blackmer 60 GPM PTO-

The fuel tanker variant of the G-749 was the M217, the prototype of which is shown in this July 1952 view taken at Aberdeen Proving Ground. The tank had three liquid compartments, and the pumping gear was located in a compartment at the rear of the bed. The rotating, folding spare carrier used on the G-749 series, except for the tractors, can also be seen here. (National Archives and Records Administration photo)

This M220 shop van was photographed at Aberdeen Proving Ground in January 1953. Supplied as an empty box, these could be fitted with a variety of repair-shop equipment loads, or with communications equipment. Access to the bed was through two unequal-sized doors on the rear of the body. (National Archives and Records Administration photo)

driven pump was plumbed to empty or fill either the front 200-gallon, center 400-gallon, or rear 600-gallon compartments. The body was equipped with bow sockets to allow bows and canvas to be installed to camouflage the truck as a cargo truck.

M220 Van

The shop van version of the G-749 used a 12-ft. steel-sheathed, wood-lined body built by Superior Coach Company. The body was equipped with three opening windows on each side, and two rear entry doors. The boarding ladder was stored externally on the rear of the truck. The van body had both 24-volt and 110-volt lighting systems.

M221 Tractor

GMC's tractor was equipped with a fifth-wheel coupling made by Drayton Steel Foundry, in addition to

the standard Holland Hitch-built pintle hook used by all trucks in this series. Additional included a trailer brake hand control valve mounted on the steering column, and the "pogo stick" and trailer air connections mounted just behind the cab.

M222 Water Tanker

The M222 water tanker was equipped with a two-compartment tank body built by The Heil Company. A Blackmer 60-gpm PTO-driven pump was plumbed to empty or fill either the front 400-gallon or rear 600-gallon compartments. As with the fuel tanker, the water-tank body was equipped with bow sockets to allow bows and canvas to be installed to camouflage the truck as a cargo truck. An exhaust diverter system was used to route engine exhaust to a heat exchanger in the tank body to prevent the cargo water from freezing.

2 1/2-TON TRUCKS

GENERAL DATA

MODEL	M135	M211	M215	M-17	M220	M221	M222
WEIGHT**	12,330 lbs.	13,170	14,460	14,100 lbs.	—	—	—
LENGTH	269	269	240	266.5	268.75	232.625	266.5
WIDTH	88	96	96	96	96	96	96
HEIGHT	105	112	108	102.25	130.25	102.25	102.25
TRACK WIDTH*	59.5/82.5	58.5/79.5	58.5/79.5	58.5/79.5	58.5/79.5	58.5/79.5	58.5/79.5
TIRE SIZES	11.00-20	9.00-20	9.00-20	9.00-20	9.00-20	9.00-20	9.00-20
MAX SPEED	58 mph	55 mph	55 mph	55 mph	55 mph	55 mph	55 mph
FUEL CAPY	56 gal	56 gal	56 gal	56 gal	56 gal	56 gal	56 gal
RANGE	300 mi	300 mi	300 mi	300 mi	300 mi	300 mi	300 mi

**Without winch, winch equipped vehicles are 410 lbs. heavier.*

Tanker and van trucks were never equipped with winches.

* *Inside/outside width at tires.*

Overall dimensions listed in inches.

ENGINE DATA

ENGINE MAKE/MODEL	GMC
NUMBER OF CYLINDERS	6
CUBIC-INCH DISPLACEMENT	302
HORSEPOWER	130 @ 3200 RPM
TORQUE	262 @ 1200 RPM
GOVERNED SPEED (rpm)	3400

SCARCITY

M135	2
M211	3
M215	3
M217	3
M220	3
M221	4
M222	3

VALUES

	6	5	4	3	2	1
M135	300	900	2,000	5,500	7,000	9,000
M211	300	900	2,000	5,500	7,000	9,000
M215	500	1,200	2,500	6,000	8,000	10,000
M217	500	1,100	2,200	5,800	7,500	9,000
M220	300	900	2000	5500	7000	9000
M221	300	900	2000	5500	7000	9000
M222	500	1200	2500	5800	7500	9000

Because of the shorter wheelbase (a benefit in tight turns), the M221 was equipped with a shorter, deeper fuel tank than those used on other cargo trucks. The M221 tractor trucks were not provided with spare tires. The M221 tractor shown here is coupled to a trailer equipped with a Thermo-King refrigeration unit. (Photo courtesy of the Patton Museum)

4-TON TRUCKS

G-509 Diamond T

The 4-ton Diamond T trucks were originally developed at the behest of the Quartermaster Corps to serve as a prime mover for the 155mm howitzer. However, due to the success of these trucks, they were soon adapted to other roles as well.

Early models of these trucks were all built in the closed-cab version of the Diamond T chassis. While the hood and fenders were strictly military, the cab itself was based on Diamond T's commercial truck cabs. During June and July of 1943, this was replaced with the military-style open cab, which allowed greater visibility and better air defense.

A Hercules RXC 529-cid inline six-cylinder engine powered most of these trucks. The high-torque engine and low gearing of the five-speed transmission and two-speed transfer case allowed a highway towed load rating of 12 1/2 tons.

967, 968, 968A & 968B Cargo Trucks

These trucks were referred to as short wheelbase trucks and were intended to transport personnel, general

This 968 was photographed at Holabird Quartermaster Depot in 1941. Notice that the headlights have their own individual brush guards. (National Archives and Records Administration photo)

cargo, or to act as a prime mover for 155mm Howitzers. Like almost all the WWII cargo trucks, the beds of these trucks initially were made of steel, but were changed to wood construction early on. The two spare tires were carried across the front of the bed.

The Model 967, produced in early 1941, was first in the Diamond T series and was powered by the Hercules RXB 501-cid inline six-cylinder engine. The 967 is easily

This photo shows the first truck in this series, the 4-ton 6x6 Diamond T Model 967. The identifying feature of this series is the brush guard that protects the radiator and headlights (Photo courtesy of the Patton Museum)

distinguished by its one-piece brush guard, which extends to protect the headlamp. Later models have a narrower brush guard, with separate guards for the headlights.

The Model 968, introduced later in 1941, was upgraded to the larger, more powerful Hercules RXC engine.

The Model 968A, which began production in November 1941, featured the military-type instruments instead of the civilian style used previously.

The Model 968B was the final version of the short wheelbase 4-ton Diamond T.

969, 969A, & 969B Wreckers

While 21 wreckers were built on the 967 chassis in 1941, the most well-known Diamond T wrecker was a variant of model 969. The designation was changed to 969A when the instruments and filters were changed to the Military Standard type. The 969B was built for foreign aid requirements, and is most easily spotted by its single headlight and single taillight, along with different paint.

All model 969 trucks were built with closed cabs, while the 969A and 969B were built in both open-and

This 1942 Holabird photo shows the driver's side of the model 968. Notice that the cargo bed on this, as well as the two previous trucks, is made of steel. (U.S. Army photo)

Seen in this view of the same truck are the other spare wheel, the liquid container and its rack, and cargo canvas. The lead chain for the front winch can be seen wrapped around the bumper. Notice that the bed is wooden, but has the King Bee reflectors. (U.S. Army photo)

An early closed-cab truck has the steps mounted on the rear mud guards and the tailgate, which is often missing on these trucks today. Notice the chevron tread design of the tires, characteristic of many early war vehicles. (Photo courtesy of International Towing and Recovery Museum)

This photograph, taken three days after the attack on Pearl Harbor, illustrates the classic lines of the early Diamond T 969 series wreckers. (Signal Corps photograph from the collection of Bryce Sunderlin)

The last wreckers delivered had open cabs. The open-cab design was not adopted to save metal. It actually requires as much or more material as a closed cab. The chief benefit was better visibility of enemy aircraft for the crew. The tire tread is the more common non-directional type. The tires, regardless of tread design, were 9.00-20, 10-ply. (U.S. Army photo)

This truck was fitted with the M36 ring mount and M2HB antiaircraft machine gun. (U.S. Army photo)

closed-cab forms. These trucks were built with a Bendix-Westinghouse air brake system, and a dual 6- and 12-volt electrical system.

The Diamond T wreckers were equipped with the Holmes W-45 H.D. military wrecker bed. This bed was an adaptation of the standard Holmes W-45 twin-boom civilian wrecker. The first of the 6,420 G-509 wreckers to arrive was the model 969 was built in February of 1941. The first unit carried serial number AB1-101. The "A" in the first position of the serial number identifies the bed as a military W45 H.D. model.

The Holmes W-45 wrecker is a twin-boom design with two 5-ton winches mounted behind the cab. Each winch is equipped with 200 ft. of wire rope. The twin-boom design allows side recoveries to be made by swinging one boom to that side, and swinging and tying off the other boom to the opposite side to stabilize the wrecker. There are also stabilizer legs mounted on each

side of the bed, just behind the cab. Typical of U.S. military wreckers, these trucks carried a lengthy list of recovery equipment, including chains, ropes, snatch blocks, cutting torches, and tools.

Unlike the later M series wreckers, which used the truck air brake system as an air source for tire inflation etc, the W-45 left the factory with a self-contained air compressor mounted between the booms. However, the compressor is often missing, even in many wartime photos of these trucks.

In addition to the winches on the Holmes bed, the trucks were also equipped with a 15,000-lb.-capacity Gar Wood winch mounted behind the front bumper.

970 & 970A Trucks

While these trucks look very much like the 967 and 968 series trucks, they are slightly longer. The bed is 16

This October 1943 photo of a short wheelbase Diamond T illustrates how an antiaircraft machine gun mount could be fitted on these trucks. By this time the truck bed was made of wood. (National Archives and Records Administration photo)

The final development of the 968 series trucks is shown in this May 1944 photograph. This truck features a wood body, open cab, and optional anti-aircraft machine gun ring. A pioneer tool rack is mounted beneath the driver's position. (U.S. Army photo)

in. longer, and the wheelbase is 21 in. longer. These trucks were designed to transport pontoons for temporary bridging. The spare tires were carried between the back of the cab and the bed.

972 Dump Truck

The Diamond T chassis was also used as a basis for a dump truck known as the model 972, in addition to its other uses. The spare tires were mounted between the cab and bed. The tailgate could be opened at the top for dumping, or at the bottom for spreading. When the open cab was standardized for the Diamond T, it wasn't initially fitted to the dump. Instead, the trucks were built with the closed cab in order to exhaust the supply of pre-built cabs Diamond T had assembled. When that stockpile was exhausted in September 1943, the dump

This Model 972 dump truck was built sometime between September 1943 and June 1944, as evidenced by its rare combination of open cab and no winch. All the Diamond Ts, except the earliest dump trucks, were built with winches. (U.S. Army photo)

trucks began receiving open cabs. In order to reduce front axle loading, the earliest dump trucks did not have winches. However, at the request of the Corps of Engineers, beginning in June 1944, the dump trucks were also fitted with the front winch.

vans. The trucks were equipped with air brakes and trailer brake controls. The initial production vehicles had very tall closed cabs, but by 1942 production had switched to the military-style open cab.

GENERAL DATA

MODEL	WRECKER	CARGO	DUMP	PONTON
NET WEIGHT	21,350 lbs.	18,450 lbs.	18,050 lbs.	18,450 lbs.
GROSS WEIGHT	—	34,500 lbs.	34,500 lbs.	34,500 lbs.
MAX TOWED LOAD	25,000 lbs.	25,000 lbs.	25,000 lbs.	25,000 lbs.
LENGTH	291.625	297	264.625	297
WIDTH	99.5	95.25	94	96
HEIGHT	116	119	106	119
WIDTH*	50/94	50/94	50/94	50/94
TRACK	72	72	72	72
TIRE SIZE	9.00-20	9.00-20	9.00-20	9.00-20
MAX SPEED	40 mph	40 mph	40 mph	40 mph
FUEL CAPY	60 gal	60 gal	60 gal	60 gal
RANGE	180 mi	180 mi	180 mi	180 mi
ELECTRICAL	6/12 pos	6/12 pos	6/12 pos	6/12 pos
TRANSMISSION SPEEDS	5	5	5	5
TRANSFER SPEEDS	2	2	2	2
TURNING RADIUS FEET	32.5 R, 34 L	37.5 R, 39 L	32.5 R, 34 L	37.5 R, 39 L

Overall dimensions listed in inches.

* Inside/outside width at tires.

For vehicles without winch, reduce weight by 850 lbs.

ENGINE DATA

ENGINE MAKE/MODEL	Hercules RXC
NUMBER OF CYLINDERS	6
CUBIC-INCH DISPLACEMENT	529
HORSEPOWER	106 @ 2300 rpm
TORQUE	342 lbs.-ft. @ 900 rpm
GOVERNED SPEED (rpm)	2300

G-510 Autocar U7144T
G-691 White 444T

These trucks had a cab-over engine design and were all-wheel-drive truck tractors intended to provide rear area transportation services. They were used to tow a variety of semi-trailers, from flatbed to communications

The 109-in. height of these trucks is apparent in this view of a White 444T. The marker lights are visible on the outer corners of the front fenders, and the blackout driving light was mounted just above the driver's side headlight. (U.S. Army photo)

The early closed cab soon gave way to the open cab on the 444T. In addition to opening the top of the cab, the front-end sheet metal was redesigned so the brush guard also acted as the grill. (U.S. Army photo)

A canvas tarpaulin was provided to protect the crew during bad weather. One has been installed for this June 1945 photo. The brake chambers associated with an air-brake system are visible near the rear axle. (U.S. Army photo)

Like many of the tactical vehicles fielded initially by the U.S. military during WWII, the 4-5-ton tractors had an enclosed steel cab based upon their civilian counterpart. The Autocar U7144T is shown here pulling a 2,000-gallon tanker trailer. (National Archives and Records Administration photo)

A bird's-eye view of an open-cabbed Autocar U7144T. The pioneer tools are clearly seen, as are liquid containers added during the production run of the trucks. The spare wheel is in place but, due to rubber shortages, the spare tire is not. (U.S. Army photo)

GENERAL DATA

MODEL	U7144T
NET WEIGHT	12,360
GROSS WEIGHT	21,010 lbs.
MAX TOWED LOAD	20,000 lbs.
LENGTH	203.5 lbs.
WIDTH	95
HEIGHT	112.75
WIDTH*	50.125/93.875
TRACK	72
TIRE SIZE	9.00-20
MAX SPEED	41 mph
FUEL CAPY	60 gal
RANGE EMPTY	540 mi
ELECTRICAL	12 pos
TRANSMISSION	
SPEEDS	5
TRANSFER	
SPEEDS	2
TURNING	
RADIUS FT.	30

Overall dimensions listed in inches.

* Inside/outside width at tires.

ENGINE DATA

ENGINE MAKE/MODEL	Hercules RXC
NUMBER OF CYLINDERS	6
CUBIC INCH DISPLACEMENT	529
HORSEPOWER	112 @ 2200 rpm
TORQUE	368 lbs.-ft. @ 1000 rpm
GOVERNED SPEED (rpm)	2300

There were 11,104 Autocar trucks produced. They were designated G-510, but within Autocar they were known as the Model U7144T. White's model number for its vehicle was 444T and the truck was assigned G-691. White's production total was 2,751 vehicles. Mechanically, both the White and the Autocar were very similar to the Federal 94x43.

GENERAL DATA

MODEL	444T
NET WEIGHT	11,660 lbs.
GROSS WEIGHT	21,010 lbs.
MAX TOWED LOAD	30,000 lbs.
LENGTH	203.5
WIDTH	95
HEIGHT	112.75
WIDTH*	50.125/93.875
TRACK	72
TIRE SIZE	9.00-20
MAX SPEED	41 mph
FUEL CAPY	60 gal
RANGE LOADED	198 mi
ELECTRICAL	12 pos
TRANSMISSION	
SPEEDS	5
TRANSFER	
SPEEDS	2
TURNING	
RADIUS FT.	30

Overall dimensions listed in inches.

* Inside/outside width at tires.

ENGINE DATA

ENGINE MAKE/MODEL	Hercules RXC
NUMBER OF CYLINDERS	6
CUBIC INCH DISPLACEMENT	529
HORSEPOWER	112 @ 2200 rpm
TORQUE	368 lbs-ft. @ 1000 rpm
GOVERNED SPEED (rpm)	2300

G-513 Federal

The Federal model 94x43 was operationally equivalent to the Autocar U-7144-T, even using many of the same major chassis components. The coachwork was completely different, though. The first Federal, the 94x43A, was being based on the commercial products of the time and had an enclosed cab. Later models, the 94x43B and C, were redesigned to incorporate an open cab.

When used by the Signal Corps, the 94x43 was referred to as a K-32. In Signal Corps use the Federals pulled van trailers, while the Transportation Corps used them for general freight service. Federal built a total of 8,119 trucks of this type. Late in the war, Kenworth and Marmon-Herrington were established as producers of these trucks as well.

The Federal 94x43A had a completely enclosed metal cab. A single spare tire was carried behind the cab, and tow hooks were mounted on the front bumper. (National Archives photo)

Canvas tarpaulins were provided with the open-cab 94x43B and C Federal trucks for weather protection, and a tool box was mounted on the right frame rail just behind the battery compartment. (U.S. Army photo)

GENERAL DATA

MODEL	94x43
NET WEIGHT	11,950 lbs.
GROSS WEIGHT	20,220 lbs.
MAX TOWED LOAD	30,000 lbs.
LENGTH	203
WIDTH	95.5
HEIGHT	109
WIDTH*	50/94
TRACK	72
TIRE SIZE	9.00 x 20
MAX SPEED	40 mph
FUEL CAPY	62 gal
RANGE LOADED	280 mi
ELECTRICAL	6/12
TRANSMISSION	
SPEEDS	5
TRANSFER	
SPEEDS	2
TURNING	
RADIUS FT.	27

Overall dimensions listed in inches.

* Inside/outside width at tires.

ENGINE DATA

ENGINE MAKE/MODEL	Hercules RXC
NUMBER OF CYLINDERS	6
CUBIC-INCH DISPLACEMENT	529
HORSEPOWER	112 @ 2200 rpm
TORQUE	368 lbs.-ft. @ 1000 rpm
GOVERNED SPEED (rpm)	2300

The threat of enemy air strikes on convoys made it necessary to develop a means of anti-aircraft defense. Many people don't realize that these weapons were not the exclusive purview of the open-cabbed trucks, but were fitted to closed-cabbed vehicles as well. This 94x43A has been fitted with an M60 truck mount, which was designed expressly for the Federal. (National Archives photo)

The open-cab 94x43 trucks saved slightly on trans-oceanic shipping space, as well as providing better visibility. (U.S. Army photo)

The open-cabbed trucks could also be armed. This example has been given an M57 truck mount. Regardless of mount, the weapons were designed to be operated by the assistant driver, and were only marginally effective when the vehicle was moving. (U.S. Army photo)

"Austere" describes the 94x43B, the model number (along with 94x43C) applied to the open-cab Federal tractors. Built for freight hauling, the trucks had a very business-like look about them. A wooden deck spans the frame rails, making a platform for the operator to stand on when connecting the trailer brake lines. (U.S. Army photo)

5-TON TRUCKS

G-511 Tractor

Autocar built 2,711 U-8144-T trucks between 1941 and 1945 for use predominately in transporting bridge pontons. Its styling was much like the 4-5-ton U-7144-T, and it used the same Hercules RXC engine. All of the U-8144-T trucks were provided with a Gar Wood 3165 winch that was mounted behind the front bumper. The large box behind the cab carried bridging equipment and tools. Early models had a hard cab. Later production came with a soft-topped cab.

Autocar built 607 similar chassis, the U-8144, which were not used for truck tractors. Rather, they were equipped with a van body built by York-Hoover. These vans housed radio and radar equipment. Depending on how the vehicles were equipped, the Signal Corps designated them K30, K31, and K62.

The Autocar U-8144-T was an imposing machine, and its big 12-20 tires and massive axles certainly added to this aura. Given the duty of these vehicles to transport bridging materials, the pioneer tools shown stowed here probably got a lot of use. (U.S. Army photo)

The U-8144-T could be fitted with an antiaircraft ring mount. (U.S. Army photo)

This overhead view shows the Gar Wood winch that all U-8144-T trucks were equipped with, as well as the interior arrangements of the cab and toolbox. (U.S. Army photo)

For operation in inclement weather, a canvas tarp could cover the U-8144-T cab. Of course, this interfered with operation of the machine gun mount. Also visible in this view are the spare fuel cans and tire, as well as the trailer air-brake lines. (U.S. Army photo)

The doors on either side of the large toolbox behind the U08144-T cab opened by swinging down. A spotlight was mounted on the rear of the driver's side of the cab to aid in night work. (U.S. Army photo)

GENERAL DATA

MODEL	U8144T
NET WEIGHT	16,660 lbs.
GROSS WEIGHT	27,120 lbs.
MAX TOWED LOAD	30,000 lbs.
LENGTH	246.5
WIDTH	98
HEIGHT	114.75
WIDTH*	47/97.5
TRACK	72.25
TIRE SIZE	12.00-20
MAX SPEED	45 mph
FUEL CAPY	90 gal
RANGE EMPTY	630 mi
ELECTRICAL	12 pos
TRANSMISSION SPEEDS	5
TRANSFER SPEEDS	2
TURNING RADIUS FT	35

Overall dimensions listed in inches.

*Inside/outside width at tires.

ENGINE DATA

ENGINE MAKE/MODEL	Hercules RXC
NUMBER OF CYLINDERS	6
CUBIC INCH DISPLACEMENT	529
HORSEPOWER	112 @ 2200
TORQUE	368 lbs.-ft. @ 1000
GOVERNED SPEED (rpm)	2300

VALUES

	6	5	4	3	2	1
All models	500	2,500	4,000	7,000	10,000	15,000

G-635 Autocar U-5044

Autocar only built 97 of its model U-5044 tractor — two in 1940 and 95 in 1941. These all-wheel-drive trucks closely resembled the earlier Autocar 4144-T, but had twice the load rating. Powered by Autocar's 377-cid engine, these trucks were used primarily to tow fuel servicing trailers.

The U-5044-T was produced in low numbers, making it very difficult to find today. Even though these trucks were four-wheel drive, as evidenced by the front differential housing visible in this photo, their tires had a highway tread pattern. (National Archives and Records Administration photo)

GENERAL DATA

MODEL	U-5044-T
MAX TOWED LOAD	30,000 lbs.
LENGTH	201
WIDTH	92
HEIGHT	104
TIRE SIZE	9.00-20
TRANSMISSION	
SPEEDS	5
TRANSFER	
SPEEDS	2

Overall dimensions listed in inches.

ENGINE DATA

ENGINE MAKE/MODEL	Autocar
NUMBER OF CYLINDERS	6
CUBIC-INCH DISPLACEMENT	377
HORSEPOWER	100

VALUE: *Only 97 of these trucks were built, and there is no recent record of sales.*

G-639 Mack

The bulk of the 700 G-639 trucks built by Mack were delivered in 1941, although a half dozen were delivered in 1942. While eight were Mack model NJU-2s, intended to tow topographical map unit semi-trailers, the balance of the units were the model NJU-1, intended to tow ponton trailers. However, they were not as widely used as the similar Autocar U-8144T. The eight NJU-2s did not have the large stowage box behind the cab.

The Mack truck and trailer with a ponton load was quite long. The large storage box was accessed by fold-down doors on each side. (National Archives photo)

Although the Mack was not as widely used by U.S. forces as the Autocar ponton tractor, the U.S. did use some. Like the Autocars, the Macks had all-wheel drive to assist in dragging their heavy loads to crossing points. (National Archives photo)

The Mack NJU-1 5-6-ton tractor was intended to haul bridging equipment. (National Archives photo)

GENERAL DATA

MODEL	NJU-1
NET WEIGHT	16,580 lbs.
MAX TOWED LOAD	30,000 lbs.
LENGTH	237
WIDTH	96
HEIGHT	114
WHEELBASE	148
TIRE SIZE	12.00-20
TRANSMISSION	
SPEEDS	5
TRANSFER	
SPEEDS	2

Overall dimensions listed in inches.

ENGINE DATA

ENGINE MAKE/MODEL	Mack EN532
NUMBER OF CYLINDERS	6
CUBIC-INCH DISPLACEMENT	532
HORSEPOWER	136 @ 2400 rpm

VALUES

	6	5	4	3	2	1
All models	500	2,500	5,000	8,000	10,000	15,000

G-671 M426/M426

The M425 was designed by International Harvester, who gave it the model number H-542-9. International built 4,640 of these tractors during 1944 and 1945, 1,200 of which were later remanufactured as M426 tractors. The 117-in.-wheelbase, open-cabbed trucks were powered by International's own Red Diamond 450D gasoline engine.

The interior of the M426 cab was spartan and the instrument panel was located on the center of the dashboard. The truck's twin fuel tanks can be seen here, as can the pintle hook used for towing lunette-equipped trailers. (U.S. Army photo)

The third company involved in the production of the M426 was Kenworth, which produced the example shown here. Despite having a non-driven front axle, this truck had non-directional tread pattern tires mounted all around. (U. S. Army photo)

The M426 trailer air and electrical connections were mounted behind the cab, which was typical of tractor-trucks. Also visible is the vertically mounted pioneer tool rack, as well as liquid container racks and wheel chocks. (U. S. Army photo)

Beefier springs and larger tires distinguished the M426 from its predecessor, the M425. This example, photographed at the Studebaker Proving Ground, was built by the design's originator, International Harvester. The data plates or registration numbers are often the only way to tell the builder. (U.S. Army photo)

The long supply lines involved in the liberation of occupied Europe required vast numbers of trucks to operate. Because of this, Marmon-Herrington was also contracted to build M426 trucks, including the one shown above. In 1945, Marmon-Herrington was also contracted to rebuild 1,200 M425 trucks into the M426 configuration. (U.S. Army photo)

The M426 was an improved version of the M425, which used 11.00-20 tires instead of the M425's 9.00-20 tires. The springs were also heavier on the M426, and there were other detail changes as well. The engine and drive train were the same as those used in the M425. International's model number for the M426 was H-542-11. International built 6,678 of these trucks, while Marmon-Herrington built 3,200 copies and Kenworth 1,100.

The M426, like the M425, was used for general freight hauling.

GENERAL DATA

MODEL	M425	M426
NET WEIGHT	11,400 lbs.	12,100 lbs.
GROSS WEIGHT	24,400 lbs.	25,100 lbs.
MAX TOWED LOAD	30,000 lbs.	30,000 lbs.
LENGTH	199.875	199.875
WIDTH	94.625	97.5
HEIGHT	105	106.75
WIDTH*	49.875/94.625	47/97.5
TRACK	72.25	72.25
TIRE SIZE	9.00-20	11.00-20
MAX SPEED	35 mph	38 mph
FUEL CAPY	80 gal	80 gal
RANGE LOADED	280 mi	240 mi
ELECTRICAL	6 neg	6 neg

This photo, taken in June 1944, shows an International Harvester M425 doing what it was built for — towing a 25-ft., 10-ton semi-trailer. Hundreds of similar combinations were used by the famed Red Ball Express. (U.S. Army photo)

The M425 was designed from the outset as a military vehicle and always had the open-style cab. Notice the spotlight mounted near the driver's door. (U.S. Army photo)

5-TON TRUCKS

TRANSMISSION		
SPEEDS	5	5
TRANSFER		
SPEEDS	2	2
TURNING		
RADIUS FT.	23.5	25.5 R, 25.25 L

Overall dimensions listed in inches.

* Inside/outside width at tires.

GENERAL DATA

ENGINE MAKE/MODEL	IHC RED 450-D
NUMBER OF CYLINDERS	6
CUBIC-INCH DISPLACEMENT	451
HORSEPOWER	124.5 @ 2600 rpm
TORQUE	348 lbs.-ft. @ 800 rpm
GOVERNED SPEED (rpm)	2600

VALUES

	6	5	4	3	2	1
All models	500	1,500	2,500	4,500	8,5000	11,000

This M54A1C had a drop-side cargo bed, which greatly eased loading. The Mack-powered A1 trucks are externally indistinguishable from the Multi-fuel-powered A2s. (Photo courtesy of the Patton Museum)

In its June 20, 1945 report, the Army Ground Forces Equipment Review Board, popularly known as the Cook Board, recommended that the 4-ton and 6-ton classes of 6x6 vehicles then in service be replaced by a standardized 5-ton 6x6. In May 1949 this recommendation was made policy by the Conference on Qualitative Requirements for Tactical Type Ordnance Transport Vehicles.

The Reo-designed G-742 cab was selected for the new vehicles. Due to the the outbreak of war in Korea, production began on these trucks even before pilot models had been submitted for testing. International was awarded the contract and production began at its Ft. Wayne works in January 1951, but it was March 1953 before these vehicles were classified Standard A. Additional vehicles were built by Diamond T through a cooperative agreement with International.

Extensive rear-wheel travel allowed the XM41 to traverse rugged terrain if needed. The single-rear-wheel trucks were preferred for off-road use, while the dual-wheel trucks were intended for primarily on-road use. (Photo courtesy of the Patton Museum)

The XM41 was photographed for the Army Field Forces Board 2 prior to testing. The large 14.00-20 single tires all around and wheel well-type bed make these trucks stand out. (Photo courtesy of the Patton Museum)

In 1952, Mack Trucks also began producing a few of selected models of this series as follows:
— M51 built from 1952 to 1954. Total production: 4,310 units.
— M52 built from 1952 to 1956. Total production: 1,443 units.
— M54 built from 1954 to 1956. Total production: 1,126 units.
— M55 built in 1956. Total production: 85 units.
— M61 built in 1953. Total production: 107 units.

International Harvester and Kaiser-Jeep (later) built the bulk of these vehicles, with Diamond T and Mack production being relatively small.

These vehicles were designed for use over all types of roads, highways, and cross-country terrain, and in all types of weather. The all-steel cab with steel doors was a marked improvement over most WWII-era trucks. They were capable of fording hard-bottom water crossings to a depth of 30 in. without preparation.

A Continental R6602 602-cid gasoline engine powered all these trucks and was connected to a Spicer 6352 five-speed synchromesh transmission with a two-speed transfer case. The transmission speed ranges were selected manually through a shift lever in the driver's

The center portion of the sideboards of the M54A1, like the M54 and M41, folded down to form troop seats. (Photo courtesy of the Patton Museum)

When standardized, the M54E3 became the M54A1. (Photo courtesy of the Patton Museum)

The M55 was the extra-long-wheelbase version of the G-744 series. It had a 20-ft. bed, but unlike the extra-long-wheelbase G-742 trucks, the sides of the M55 bed were not hinged. (Photo courtesy of the Patton Museum)

This is a Multifuel-powered M55A2 restored by Cecil Jones. The truck was built as an M55, but was later re-powered by the military — a common occurrence. The sideboards of the extra-long-wheelbase trucks did not form troop seats. (Photo courtesy of Cecil Jones)

While the shared-cab design of the G-742 and G-744 meant the 5-tons resembled the 2 1/2-ton trucks, the fuel tanks were on opposite sides, aiding identification. (Photo courtesy of the Patton Museum)

The XM54, like the XM41, was tested by Army Field Forces Board 2 at Fort Knox. It is pictured here without the cargo area canvas installed. (Photo courtesy of the Patton Museum)

compartment. Another shift lever in the cab controlled the transfer case. Power was delivered to all wheels by a sprag unit that automatically engaged the front wheels if the rear wheels slipped. Service brakes were air-actuated hydraulic. The cab was enclosed with removable canvas tarpaulins, and the cargo truck bodies were provided with both removable tarpaulins and end curtains. All vehicles are equipped with a spare wheel and tire, and a pintle hook at the rear permits towing of a trailer.

In 1960, Diamond T moved its production to the Lansing plant. Both Diamond T and Reo at that time were subsidiaries of White, and consolidating production facilities was done to save money.

In the late 1950s, the Army had purchased a commercial vehicle powered by a Mack ENDT-673 engine. Tests demonstrated there was considerable potential for a diesel-powered tactical truck. In early 1959, OTAC (Ordnance Tank Automotive Command) recommended that a number of the Mack ENDT-673 engines be procured for evaluation in the M54 truck.

In February 1960, seven M54 cargo trucks were converted to diesel power using the Mack ENDT-673 engine. The ENDT-673 was a basically commercial engine of 211 gross hp at 2,100 rpm. It is a turbosupercharged six-cylinder, valve-in-head, water-cooled, compression-ignition diesel engine. The M54 truck equipped with this engine was known as the M54E3. A Spicer 6453 five-speed synchromesh

The M54E3 was the test bed for installing the Mack ENDT-673 engine in the 5-ton cargo truck. (Photo courtesy of the Patton Museum).

The M52 truck tractor, like the M51 dump truck, was built on the 167-in.-wheelbase chassis. (Photo courtesy of Mack Trucks Historical Museum)

This M52A1 with winch is a Diamond T product. It is one of a group of trucks that were re-powered with the Mack ENDT-673 engine in the early 1960s. (Photo courtesy of TacticalTruck.com)

At the rear of the large all-steel bed on the M328 was a roller to assist with the unloading of the cargo in the absence of a crane. (Photo courtesy of United States Army Engineer School History Office)

transmission was used, which was similar to the 6352, but with different gear ratios befitting the difference in engine speeds.

Seven trucks were also converted to diesel power using the Cummins Model C200-A turbosupercharged compression-ignition engine, which developed 200 hp at 2800 revolutions per minute. The M54 truck equipped with this engine was known as the M54E4.

By January 1962, all the engineering required for installation of both ENDT-673 and C200-A engines in the 5-ton cargo truck had been completed. The modified vehicles were tested at APG for engineering and durability and at Yuma Test Station, Arizona, and Fort Greely, Alaska, for operation in climatic extremes. The U.S. Army Armor Board conducted service tests as well. Although both the M54E3 and the M54E4 met all the standard 5-ton truck performance specifications, it was felt the M54E3 was the slightly superior vehicle, and in June 1962 it was classified Standard A as the M54A1.

From that time through 1963, the M52 and M54 were converted to the Mack ENDT-673 diesel engine. This was a joint project between Mack Trucks and the Diamond T Motor Truck Company. The vehicle model identifications for these units were M52A1 and M54A1, respectively.

The installation of the ENDT-673 was short-lived. After only a year it was decided to use Multifuel engines wherever possible in the tactical vehicle fleet. For the 5-ton, the engine chosen was the LDS-465-1A. With the Multifuel engines installed, the model suffixes changed to A2.

In 1963, Studebaker was awarded a contract to build the G-744 5 ton vehicles. Initially the contract was for 4,159 units with contract extensions bringing the total to 8,493 vehicles. However, before production of the trucks could begin, in February 1964, Kaiser-Jeep bought Studebaker's Chippewa Avenue truck plant, and the G-744 contract. The Army approved the contract transfer

the following month.

The G-744 chassis was the basis for a variety of different trucks. A brief description of some of the different uses follows:

Cargo Trucks

The 5-ton 6x6 cargo truck M41 had a 179-in. wheelbase and used 14:00-20 tires, single rear wheels, and a 14-ft. cargo body mounted on the rear. The cargo body was equipped with troop seats, which made it suitable for transporting troops or cargo. The large tires of the M41 necessitated that wheel wells protrude into the cargo bed.

The 5-ton, 6x6, cargo truck M54 had a 179-in. wheelbase with 11:00-20 tires and dual rear wheels. A 14-ft. flat bed cargo body is mounted on the rear.

The M55 cargo truck had a 7-20-ft. cargo box with fixed sides. The M55 spare wheel carrier was mounted to the truck frame rail between the cab and tandems on the driver's side. All trucks had removable front and side racks, and a hinged tailgate.

Dump Trucks

The 5-ton, 6x6, M51 dump truck was built on a 167-in.-wheelbase chassis with 11:00-20 tires and dual rear wheels. A 5-cubic yard dump body and twin-cylinder

The pilot model of the M51 was built by International Harvester's Fort Wayne, Indiana, works. (Photo courtesy of the Patton Museum)

This is the experimental M51E5, which was used in the power plant tests. The sideboards and troop seats could be mounted in any of the G-744 dump trucks. This allowed these vehicles to double as troop transports for the engineer units. (Photo courtesy of the Patton Museum)

The M51 dump truck was designed to transport 5 cubic yards of material. Two hydraulic cylinders lifted the bed. (Photo courtesy of the Patton Museum)

5-TON TRUCKS

hoist assembly was mounted on the rear of the chassis.

Tractor Trucks

The 5-ton 6x6 tractor truck M52 had a 167-in. wheelbase with 11:00 x 20 tires and dual rear wheels. A fifth wheel assembly, approach plates, and deck plate, suitable for hauling trailers, were mounted on the rear of the chassis. Tractor-to-trailer brake hoses and connections were mounted behind the cab.

Medium Wrecker Trucks

Two different 5-ton, 6x6, medium wrecker trucks were built in this series. Both had a 179-in. wheelbase with 11:00 x 20 tires and dual rear wheels. A hydraulic crane and a winch assembly were mounted on the rear

The M543 was functionally the same as the M62, but its bed was built by Gar Wood. It is easily distinguished by the large hydraulic reservoir in the position that had been occupied by the spare tire on the M62. (Photo courtesy of the Patton Museum)

The M62 used an Austin Western recovery bed, which was selected over five competitors. The new medium recovery vehicle's hydraulically operated boom provided significant labor savings over the WWII-era wreckers. (Photo courtesy of Keco Industries)

The convoy warning lights behind the M62 cab were a common field modification applied to these wreckers late in their service life. Normally, wrecker trucks had an "extra" flashing amber warning light on the left front fender, although it is missing from this example being restored by Joe Shannon. (Photo courtesy of Joe Shannon)

The boom of the M62 was 18 ft. long. For heavy loads with the boom well extended, the boom jacks were put in place as shown here to relieve some of the load on the boom. The maximum lift of the wrecker was 20,000 lbs. (National Archives and Records Administration photo)

The M246 was a tractor wrecker based on the G-744 chassis. Intended primarily for aircraft recovery, its boom would extend up to 26 ft. and, rather than the rear recovery winch, there was a fifth wheel installed to tow low-bed semi-trailers. The M246 was built on a 215-in.-wheelbase chassis. (Photo courtesy of the Patton Museum).

of the chassis. The M62 used an Austin Western crane and the later M543 used a Gar Wood crane. In addition to the 45,000-lb.-capacity rear recovery winch, these trucks had 20,000-lb.-capacity front-mounted self-recovery winches.

In either event, the crane mounted on the medium wreckers was a hydraulically powered unit, with the hydraulic pump being driven via PTO from the truck engine. The front and rear winches were both mechanically driven via PTOs from the truck's driveline. In addition to self-recovery, the front winch could act as an anchor point for rear recovery operations by attaching its line to a fixed object. The rear winch was the heavy-duty recovery apparatus and had a 45,000-lb. pulling capability. Both the front and rear winches were equipped with a level winding devices. The crane, which had a live boom that could be extended hydraulically from 10 to 18 ft., was used for lifting loads up to 20,000 lbs. The rear suspension on the wrecker was different than that of the other G-744 trucks, with a beam above the springs to limit spring deflection.

Tractor Wrecker Trucks

The 5-ton, 6x6 tractor-wrecker truck M246 had a 215-in. wheelbase with 12:00-20 tires and dual rear wheels. A hydraulic crane and a fifth-wheel assembly were mounted on the rear of the chassis. The M246 was based on the M63C chassis and was intended to be used for aircraft recovery operations and towing trailers.

The crane, the boom of which could be extended from 11 1/2 to 26 ft., could lift loads up to 20,000 lbs. One section telescoped hydraulically, but the final section had to be extended manually. The boom was capable of 270-degree rotation and approximately 45-degree elevation.

A fifth wheel, or semi-trailer coupler, was mounted on the rear of M246 tractor wrecker truck in place of the drag winch of the medium wreckers. The base of the fifth wheel pivoted on a walking beam that in turn pivoted on the sub-base. This construction permitted the fifth wheel to move in all planes. The front winch was used to free vehicles if they became mired.

Expansible Van Trucks

The M291 was a 5-ton expansible van truck. The fully enclosed rear van body had sides that could be extended when the vehicle was stationary, almost doubling its volume. Expansible vans transported electronic base stations into the field. In the traveling position, the van truck bodies was 17 ft. long by 8 ft. wide. When in the field, van sides were expanded to almost 14 ft. wide. These trucks were used as communication stations or electronic repair stations, and could be equipped with up to 5,000 lbs. of electronic gear.

Bridge Trucks

The 5-ton, 6x6, M328 bridge truck had a 215-in. wheelbase with 14:00-20 tires and dual rear wheels. The

The M328 was made to transport floating assault bridges. The bulk of the bridge structure was aluminum, and few have been preserved. (Photo courtesy of the Patton Museum)

Machine Shops

Because of its excessive weight, the mounting of the mobile machine shop on a G-742 2 1/2-ton truck chassis was discontinued. Instead, it was mounted on a modified long-wheelbase G-744 chassis. The special contact maintenance body housed a complete repair facility and machine shop. A large generator driven by the truck's engine supplied electricity for the power tools. This generator could also double as a welder. In addition to power tools, these trucks carried many hand tools. Like most Corps of Engineer equipment, it was not assigned an "M-number."

Rocket Launchers

The "Honest John" was a tactical nuclear rocket system developed in the 1950s. The M139 chassis, after extensive modifications, was used as the basis for the launcher. The earliest version of the launcher was the M289. These were built on the M139C and M139D chassis. Modified specifically for transporting the 7.62-mm rocket launcher, they had an axle gear ratio of 10.26:1.00 for increased traction. Front axle loading was of great concern to the designers and, in addition to a reinforced axle housing, these trucks had no front winch.

The M139D had a different rear axle and jack bracket supports, and both the M139C and M139D had modified front cross-members. The M289 launcher had a long launcher rail that extended over the front bumper

bridge transporting truck was equipped with a stake body designed to carry bridge-building materials and equipment such as the M4T6 float bridge or class 60 bridge sections. The truck stake racks could be removed to transport extra wide loads.

The bed of the M328 bridge transporting truck was 20-ft. long and 7-ft. wide. A roller built into the rear edge of the bed was used for loading and unloading bridging equipment. Two hand-operated winches on the left underside of the body and two identical winches under the rear of the body were used to secure the load. The beds for these trucks were built by Hobbs, Perfection, Metro Engineering, and Gresham.

The mobile machine shop, having been deemed too heavy for the G-742 chassis, was mounted on the G-744, which was much better suited for the heavy load. (Photo courtesy of United States Army Engineer School History Office)

The M386 was built on the M139F chassis. Its launch rail was noticeably shorter than that of the M289, and the truck lacked the A-frame brace on the front bumper. (Photo courtesy of Patton Museum)

The M139C chassis, used by the M289, had a reduced normal axle ratio to permit reasonable off-road maneuverability, despite the heavy load. The M289 leaving this landing craft has been prepared for deep-water fording. (Photo courtesy of United States Army Engineer School History Office)

and was supported by an A-type frame at its outer end while traveling.

The later M386 launcher had a short launcher rail and did not require the A-frame support. The M386 was built on the M139F truck chassis with a 6.443:1.00 ratio.

All the Honest John launchers were declared obsolete in 1982.

Note: All data given above are for Multifuel-powered trucks, for other engines please adjust as shown below. Data given for trucks without winch, except wreckers and tractor-wreckers, which all had front winches.

Overall dimensions listed in inches.

*Add 460 lbs. to weight on vehicles powered by the ENDT-673 engine. Subtract 50 lbs. from the gas-powered vehicle weight for Multifuel trucks.

GENERAL DATA

MODEL	179-wb Cargo Truck	215-wb Cargo Truck	Dump Truck
WEIGHT NET*	19,945 lbs.	20,720 lbs.	22,663 lbs.
WEIGHT GROSS*	39,945 lbs.	40,720 lbs.	42,663 lbs.
MAX TOWED LOAD	15,000 lbs.	15,000 lbs.	15,000 lbs.
LENGTH	298.75	386	266.125
WIDTH	97	97.5	97.25
HEIGHT	116	117.5	110 5/8
WHEELBASE	179	215	167
TIRE SIZE	11.00-20	11.00-20	11.00- 20
MAX SPEED	52 mph	52 mph	52 mph
FUEL CAPY	78 gal	78 gal	110 gal
RANGE LOADED	280 mi	280 mi	440 mi
ELECTRICAL	24 neg	24 neg	24 neg
TRANSFER SPEEDS	2	2	2
TRANSMISSION SPEEDS	5 F	5 F	5 F
TURNING RADIUS FEET	20-7	23	19-4 1/2

MODEL	Tractor Truck	Wrecker Truck	Tractor-Wrecker
WEIGHT NET*	18,996 lbs.	33,325 lbs.	32,830 lbs.
WEIGHT GROSS*	43,996 lbs.	45,325 lbs.	48,830 lbs.
MAX TOWED LOAD	30,000 lbs.	20,000 lbs.	20,000 lbs.
LENGTH	257.5	348	352
WIDTH	97	97	97.5
HEIGHT	103.1/8	127 1/8	132
WHEELBASE	167	79	215
TIRE SIZE	11.00- 20	11.00- 20	12.00-20
MAX SPEED	52 mph	52 mph	52 mph
FUEL CAPY	110 gal	78 gal	78 gal
RANGE LOADED	440 mi	200 mi	200 mi
ELECTRICAL	24 neg	24 neg	24 neg
TRANSFER SPEEDS	2	2	2
TRANSMISSION SPEEDS	5F	5 F	5 F
TURNING RADIUS FEET	19-4 1/2	20-9 1/2	23-4

ENGINE DATA

ENGINE	Continental R6602	MACK ENDT-673	LDS-465-1A
CYLINDERS	6	6	6
CID DISPLACEMENT	602	672	478
HORSEPOWER	224	211	175
TORQUE	504 lbs.-ft.	610 lbs.-ft.	425 lbs.-ft.

VALUES

	6	5	4	3	2	1
179-wb Cargo trucks	1,500	4,000	6,500	12,500	20,000	29,000
215-wb Cargo trucks	2,000	4,500	7,000	13,000	21,000	30,000
Dump trucks	2,000	5,000	7,500	13,500	21,500	32,000
Tractor trucks	1,500	4,000	6,500	12,500	20,000	29,000
Wrecker trucks	3,000	6,000	9,000	15,000	25,000	36,000
Tractor-wreckers	3,000	6,000	9,000	15,000	24,000	33,000

Values shown for Multifuel engine trucks.
Increase values by 1,000-2,000 for Mack ENDT-673-powered trucks.
Decrease values 500-1,000 for R6602-powered trucks.
Values increase 500-1,000 for winch trucks and hardtop cabs.

SCARCITY

179-wb Cargo trucks	2
215-wb Cargo trucks	3
Dump trucks	2
Tractor trucks	2
Wrecker trucks	2
Tractor-wreckers	3

The "Honest John" was a tactical nuclear rocket system developed in the 1950s. The earliest version of the launcher was the M289, shown here. (Photo courtesy of the Patton Museum)

G-852 M656 Family

In the early 1960s Ford was awarded a contract to produce a series of 5-ton 8 x 8 vehicles. These vehicles evolved from the XM543E2 program, and the production models were the M656 5-ton 8 x 8 cargo truck, M757 5-ton 8 x 8 tractor, and the M791 5-ton expansible van truck. All of these models were also available with a front mounted self-recovery winch. These trucks were typically used to support the Pershing missile system.

The XM656 had an eight-month testing program, ending in 1964, which involved 40,000 miles of driving.

These trucks were powered by a Continental LDS-465-2 Multifuel engine — the most powerful version of the Multifuel to be placed into production. The engine was coupled to an Allison six-speed automatic transmission. The XM656 differed from production models in details. The lifting shackle brackets were redesigned, and a cup-shaped step was added to the front wheel assembly to make cab access easier.

These trucks had aluminum cabs and bodies, with the cargo body of the M656 having drop sides. Unlike similar-looking civilian trucks, the XM656 had a cab that did not tilt. Engine access was gained by removing a cover in the cab. Power steering was used to move all four front tires, and all eight wheels drove all the time

On the Munson Test Course at Aberdeen Proving Ground, an M656 challenges the vertical wall. The engine of the G-852 family was the LDS-465-2 Multifuel. This engine has the highest horsepower rating of the Multifuel family. It was coupled to a six-speed Allison TX-200-6 automatic transmission. The close proximity of both the exhaust and the engine itself to the driver made it necessary to for crewmen of the G-852 family of vehicles to wear ear protection.

This M656 was equipped with a front winch. (Photo courtesy of the Patton Museum)

This is the M791 expansible van. The frames of these trucks were longer than other G-852s in order to accommodate the standard M4 expansible van body. The box protruding over the cab houses an air conditioner and two heaters. The balance of the bed contained electronic equipment. When in use each side cranked out to almost double the enclosed area of the bed. It was typically used to house launch, control, and communication equipment for the Pershing system.

The M757 tractor is shown here doing what it was built to do — tow the massive M790 Pershing 1a missile erector launcher. This entire family of vehicles was created to support the Pershing missile system, which was eliminated by the Intermediate Range Nuclear Forces (INF) Treaty. This treaty specified that all the launchers and missiles were to be destroyed by May 31, 1991, save for 15 de-milled examples to be displayed in museums. Thus, you are unlikely to locate an M790 trailer for your collection, at least not without triggering an international incident!

through a single-speed transfer case. The trucks had air brakes with outboard drums.

The M757 tractor had dual fuel tanks. The others had only one 80-gallon tank on the driver's side. The frame of the M791 was longer at the rear than that on

Automatic transmissions, first tried in tactical trucks in the GMC G-749 series 2 1/2-ton trucks, offer superior performance in off-road conditions by eliminating the loss of momentum while clutching. This example is a very early truck with the early style lifting shackles and no wheel-mounted front step.

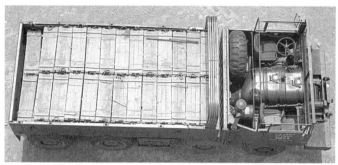

The cab top has been removed from the winch-equipped vehicle in the foreground, revealing how close the cover over the engine was to the driver. The seemingly roomy cab actually houses just the driver, the co-driver, spare tire and the engine. (Photo courtesy of the Patton Museum)

The bed of the M656 was all aluminum, which has caused many to be scrapped for their metal content. This rendering shows how the sides folded down and the bottoms of the troop seats became steps.

the other vehicles, but the wheelbase and spacing were the same on all.

GENERAL DATA

MODEL	M656	M757	M791
NET WEIGHT**	15,330 lbs.	13,500 lbs.	24,500 lbs.
LENGTH	278	278	314
WIDTH*	95.5		98
HEIGHT	116	116	142
TREAD	77.25	77.25	77.25
TIRE SIZES	16.00-20	16.00-20	16.00- 20
MAX SPEED	50 mph	50 mph	50 mph
FUEL CAPY	80 gal	160 gal	80 gal
RANGE	310 mi	620 mi	310 mi
ELECTRICAL	24	24	24
TRANSMISSION SPEEDS	6	6	6
TRANSFER SPEEDS	1	1	1
TURNING RADIUS FT	41.33	41.33	41.33

**Without winch, winch equipped vehicles are 1150 lbs heavier. Overall dimensions listed in inches. Add 21 inches to length for winch equipped trucks.

ENGINE DATA

ENGINE MAKE/MODEL	Continental LDS-465-2
NUMBER OF CYLINDERS	6
CUBIC-INCH DISPLACEMENT	478
HORSEPOWER	195 @ 2800 rpm
TORQUE	425 lbs.-ft @ 2000 rpm
GOVERNED SPEED (rpm)	2,850

VALUES

	6	5	4	3	2	1
M656	1,500	2,500	4,000	6,000	9,000	12,000
M757	1,500	2,500	4,000	6,000	9,000	12,000
M791	1,500	2,500	4,000	6,000	9,500	13,000

G-908 M809

The M809 series of 6x6 5-ton cargo trucks was similar to the earlier G-744 series of 5-ton 6x6 trucks. The principle difference was the Cummins NHC-250 diesel engine. AM General Corp. performed the product engineering development as well as the production of these vehicles. Production of the M809 series began by AM General Corporation in 1970 and continued into the 1980s.

The frame was of conventional construction with two rail-type beams and six reinforced cross-members. All the truck's axles were hypoid single-speed, double-reduction units. The layout of the truck was conventional with the engine at the front, but the hood and engine compartment were longer on these trucks than on the G-744. These trucks used the same standard U.S. military cab that was used on the G-742, G-744, and G-792 series trucks.

There were three different wheelbase chassis used in this series: the long (standard) wheelbase M809 (used for the M813. M813A1, M816 and M815), the short wheelbase M810 (used for the M817 and M818), and the extra-long wheelbase M811/M812 (used for the M814, M819, M820 and M821).

Many accessories for these trucks were available in the form of kits to install the following items: A-frame, hard tops, deep-water fording, winch level wind device, slave receptacle, personnel heater, and a power plant heater. All models except the M820 were available with a PTO-driven 20,000-lb.-capacity winch at the front.

Typical of trucks in this size range, the M813's cargo area could be covered with a tarpaulin. (Photo courtesy of AM General)

The base vehicle of the G-908 series trucks was the M813. (Photo courtesy of AM General)

The M815 bolster truck was one of the more unusual members of the G-908 family. It was used to pull a loaded bolster trailer, or to haul the trailer when unladen. (U.S. Army photo)

The M814 was the extra-long-wheelbase version of the G-908 series. The sides of its bed were fixed, and although the trucks came with sideboards (removed here) they did not have troop seats. (Photo courtesy of Shane G. Deemer, Military Rails Online)

The M813A1 had a drop-side body, as opposed to the fixed-side body of the M813. This allowed easier loading of cargo, such as the fuel cells seen in the rear of the truck. (Photo courtesy of John Adams-Graf)

VARIANTS

M813 Cargo Truck

This was the basic cargo model as described above and could carry 5 tons of cargo across country and 10 tons of cargo on roads. The foldable seats enabled 26 fully equipped troops to be carried.

The M813 truck had a 179-in. wheelbase, 11:00 x 20 tires and a 14 x 7-ft. cargo bed. The M813A1 also had a 179-in. wheelbase, 11:00-20 tires with a 14-foot x 7-foot cargo bed. However, the bed of the M813A1 was of a dropside design with a 147 1/2-in. access opening on each side. These allowed easy loading and unloading using forklifts on the ground. The spare wheel assembly was mounted on the left forward side at rear of cargo box on both M813 and M813A1 cargo trucks. The M814 cargo truck had a 7 x 20-ft. cargo box. The M814 spare wheel carrier was mounted to the truck frame rail between the cab and tandems on the driver's side. All trucks had removable front and side racks, troop seats, and a hinged tailgate.

Bows and tarpaulins could be installed, if required, on each of the three cargo trucks.

The M813, M813A1, and M814 cargo trucks were used to transport equipment, materials, and/or personnel. The M813 and M814 cargo trucks had permanent steel-welded sides. For this reason, they were preferred vehicles for use in transporting bulky payloads that may shift during transit.

The M813 and M813A1 vehicles provided 550 cu. ft. of cargo space, and the M814 vehicle, which is 72 in. longer, provided 744 cu. ft. of cargo space. Some M814 vehicles were equipped with a front winch. This feature

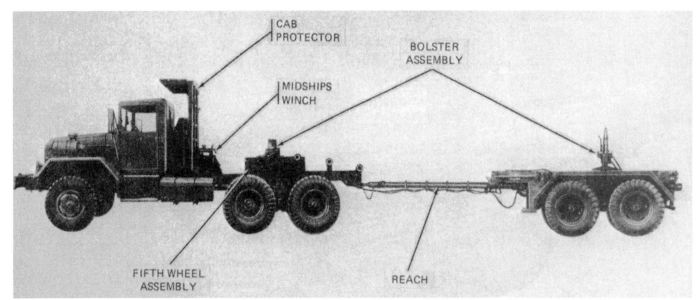

The P-14 bolster trailer was used to haul logs, pipe, poles and other long objects. The M815 truck normally was equipped with a steel hardtop. (U.S. Army photo)

made it more versatile for operations under difficult field conditions.

The M814 cargo truck was not maneuverable in limited spaces

M815 Bolster Truck

The M815 bolster truck and trailer combination was designed to transport utility poles, bridge sections, and logs. The bolster trailer was carried on the rear of the truck when it was not in use.

The M815 bolster truck was equipped with a cab protector, front winch, midships winch, bolster assembly, and bolster trailer carrier. The carrier was connected to the truck frame to support the M796 bolster trailer in the loaded position. Ramps are used for loading and unloading the bolster trailer. Mounting brackets for the ramps were located at the rear section of the trailer carrier.

The bolster trailer M796 (P14) had two bolster assemblies mounted over the midsection of the trailer

The crane operator's station of the M819 could be fully enclosed with a hard top kit. In the absence of the hardtop kit, a canvas tarpaulin and bows were provided for the crane operator. (U.S. Army photo)

frame, an adjustable reach, and a bolster assembly mounted on the reach. The trailer had safety chains, failsafe air-over-hydraulic wheel brakes, separate parking brake for both front wheels, an inter-vehicular electrical cable, two airbrake hoses, and retractable landing gear mounted on its reach.

M816 Medium Wrecker Truck

The medium wrecker M816 was used to return disabled vehicles for repair, and to free mired vehicles. The vehicle crane can be used for lifting operations of up to 20,000 lbs. Common uses for the M816 as a crane included removing and replacing engines, power packs, and gun tubes, and loading and unloading munitions.

The crane mounted on the medium wrecker M816 was hydraulically powered, with the hydraulic pump being driven via PTO from the truck engine. The front and rear winches were both mechanically driven via PTOs from the truck's driveline. The front winch was used primarily for self-recovery if the medium wrecker were to become mired, or for assisting the rear winch by acting as an anchor point. The rear winch was the heavy-duty recovery apparatus and had a 45,000-lb. pulling capability. Both the front and rear winches were equipped with level winding devices.

The crane, which had a live boom that could be extended hydraulically from 10 to 18 ft., was used for lifting loads up to 20,000 lbs. The rear suspension on the wrecker was different than that of the other trucks, having a beam above the springs to limit spring deflection.

The M816 was basically the bed of an M543 wrecker mounted on a new chassis. (Photo courtesy of Shane G. Deemer, Military Rails Online)

The hydraulic reservoir for the 20,000-lb.-capacity hoist is visible in this photo, as is the 45,000-lb.-capacity rear recovery winch with level wind device. (U.S. Army photo)

M817 Dump Truck W/W & WO/W

The M817 dump truck had a steel bed with a 5-cubic-yard dump bed. (Photo courtesy of Memphis Equipment Company)

The M817 dump truck was used to transport materials such as sand, gravel, and stone, or other bulk materials. These vehicles operated on or off the road with load limits up to 10,000 lbs.

Fully loaded, this vehicle could tow trailers with loads up to 15,000 lbs. This vehicle had a welded-steel dump body that was lifted by two hydraulic cylinders. The forward end of the dump body extended up and over the vehicle cab to protect it and the driver from damage during loading. Troop seats were available as well to allow the dump truck to be used for troop transport operations.

The dump bodies on these trucks had a tailgate that could be opened at either the top or bottom, allowing operation as a regular end load-type, rocker- type, or as a spreader-type dump truck.

M818 Tractor, Truck

The M818 tractor truck had a 33-in. standard-sized fifth wheel and was used to haul semi-trailer loads up to 37,500 lbs. maximum. While connected to a semi-trailer, the fifth wheel could pivot up, down, and sideways, to permit operation of the truck and trailer over irregular terrain.

However, the fifth wheel could not pivot more than 21 degrees up, 15 degrees down, or 7 degrees sideways. This meant semi-trailer operations cross-country had their limits.

M819 Tractor Wrecker

The M819 tractor wrecker truck had a hydraulically powered engine-driven crane, a front winch equipped with a level winding device, and a fifth wheel for pulling a trailer. The crane, the boom of which could be extended from 11 1/2 to 26 ft., was used for lifting loads up to 20,000 lbs. One section telescoped hydraulically, the second section did not have power extension. The boom was capable of 270 degrees rotation and approximately 45-degree elevation. The vehicle was used for freeing mired vehicles, lifting materials for loading and unloading operations, and for towing trailers.

The M818 tractor, as well as the dump trucks, used a shorter wheelbase than the cargo trucks. (U.S. Army photo)

This restored M818 tractor, owned by Jim Lurba, has an extension on its fender-mounted air cleaner. (Photo courtesy of John Adams-Graf)

The M819 tractor wrecker was equipped with a longer boom than the M816, and had a rear-mounted fifth wheel instead of a recovery winch. (Photo courtesy of Memphis Equipment Company)

A fifth wheel, or semi-trailer coupler, was mounted on the rear of M819 tractor wrecker truck in place of the drag winch of the M816. The base of the fifth wheel pivoted on a walking beam, which in turn pivoted on the sub-base. This construction permitted the fifth wheel to move in all planes. The front winch was used to free the vehicle if it became mired.

M820 Van Expansible Truck

The M820-type trucks were equipped with a fully enclosed body at the rear that was 8 ft. wide in its normal position.

The M820 expansible van truck had windows, heating and air-conditioning systems, and used outside electric power. The M820A1 expansible van truck lacked windows and air-conditioning but did have a heating system. The M820A2 expansible van truck had windows, hydraulic liftgate, heating, and air-conditioning system.

The M820 and M820A2 expansible vans transported electronic base stations into the field. The M820A1 expansible van could be used for the same things. In the traveling position, the van truck bodies were 17 ft. long by 8 ft. wide. When in the field, van sides were expanded to give a width of nearly 14 ft. They served as communication stations or electronic repair stations. The vans were designed to carry up to 5,000 lbs. of equipment inside. The M820A2 expansible van was equipped with a hydraulic liftgate, which made it the preferred vehicle to use when heavy, delicate electronic equipment had to be moved in or out of the van.

The M811A2 was the chassis that was the basis for

M820, M820A1, and M820A2 Expansible Vans This chassis had a 215-in. wheelbase and used 11:00-20 tires.

M821 Bridge Transport

The M821 was used to carry bridging components and was based on the M812 chassis.

The bridge transporting truck was equipped with a stake body specially designed to carry bridge building materials and equipment such as the M4T6 float bridge or class 60 bridge sections. The truck stake racks could be removed if needed to transport extra-wide loads.

The bed of the M821 bridge transporting truck was 20 ft. long and 7-ft. wide. A roller built into the rear edge of the bed was used to ease loading and unloading of bridging equipment. Two hand-operated winches on the left underside of the body and two identical winches under the rear of the body were used to secure load to the truck.

When the M820 was expanded, the interior volume of the bed almost doubled. The flap in the front has been raised, allowing the air conditioner to draw fresh air. (Photo courtesy of Shane G. Deemer, Military Rails Online)

The M820 expansible van was equipped with a single air conditioner and two diesel-fired heaters in the compartment over the truck cab. (Photo courtesy of Shane G. Deemer, Military Rails Online)

The M821 was the replacement for the G-744 Series M328 bridge truck. It was used to transport the M4T6 float bridge or Class 60 bridge sections. (U.S. Army photo)

The M820A1 lacked the windows and air conditioner of the M820, but was equipped with heaters. (Photo courtesy of AM General)

The power tailgate on the rear of the M820A2 could be powered by PTO, or electrically. This was very handy when moving large pieces of delicate electronic equipment. (U.S. Army photo)

When the ribbon bridge was introduced, special equipment was required to transport the bridge and erection boat. This is an example of one of these transporters. (Photo courtesy of Memphis Equipment Company)

Ribbon Bridge Carrier and Lauching Vehicle

An M809 chassis is also used to carry and launch the Ribbon Bridge system as well as carrying and launching the 27-ft. bridge erection boat.

Shop Equipment, Organizational Repair Truck

A mobile machine shop, often known as the "Batmobile" because of its unusual elevating side doors, which give it the appearance of a bat in flight when opened, was built on a specially modified G-908 chassis. The body housed a very complete repair facility and machine shop. The power tools were powered by a large generator that was driven by the truck's engine. The generator could also double as a welder. In addition to power tools, these trucks carried manyy hand tools. Like most Corps of Engineer equipment, it was not assigned an "M-number," but was known as the SEORLT, or SEARL-118.

GENERAL DATA

MODEL	M813	M813A1	M814	M815
WEIGHT NET**	21,020 lbs.	21,020 lbs.	23,540 lbs.	21,040 lbs.
WEIGHT GROSS**	31,020 lbs.	31,020 lbs.	33,540 lbs.	31,040 lbs.
MAX TOWED LOAD	15,000 lbs.	15,000 lbs.	15,000 lbs.	15,000 lbs.
LENGTH**	319	319	395	317
WIDTH*	97.75	97.75	97.75	97.75
HEIGHT*	117	117	117	118
WHEELBASE	179	179	215	179
TIRE SIZE	11.00-20	11.00-20	11.00-20	11.00-20
MAX SPEED	52 mph	52 mph	52 mph	52 mph
FUEL CAPY	78 gal	78 gal	78 gal	78 gal
RANGE LOADED	350 mi	350 mi	350 mi	350 mi
ELECTRICAL	24 neg	24 neg	24 neg	24 neg
TRANSFER SPEEDS	2	2	2	2
TRANSMISSION SPEEDS	5 F	5 F	5 F	5 F
TURNING RADIUS FT	42-4	42-4	48-7	42-4

MODEL	M816	M817	M818
WEIGHT NET**	35,050 lbs.	23,755 lbs.	20,165 lbs.
WEIGHT GROSS**	42,050 lbs.	337,55 lbs.	35,165 lbs.
MAX TOWED LOAD	20,000 lbs.	15,000 lbs.	37,500 lbs.
LENGTH**	356	289	280
WIDTH*	97.75	97.75	97.75
HEIGHT*	112	112	112
WHEELBASE	179	167	167
TIRE SIZE	11.00-20	11.00-20	11.00-20
MAX SPEED	52 mph	52 mph	52 mph
FUEL CAPY	133 gal	110 gal	110 gal
RANGE LOADED	585 mi	440 mi	440 mi
ELECTRICAL	24 neg	24 neg	24 neg
TRANSFER SPEEDS	2	2	2
TRANSMISSION SPEEDS	5 F	5 F	5 F
TURNING RADIUS FT	42-4	40-7	42-4

MODEL	M819	M820	M820A1
WEIGHT NET**	35,065 lbs.	28,195 lbs.	27,895 lbs.
WEIGHT GROSS**	47,065 lbs.	33,195 lbs.	32,895 lbs.
MAX TOWED LOAD	37,500 lbs.	15,000 lbs.	15,000 lbs.
LENGTH**	359	363	363
WIDTH	97.75	97.75	97.75
HEIGHT	132	138	138
WHEELBASE	215	215	215
TIRE SIZE	12.00 x 20	11.00 x 20	11.00 x 20
MAX SPEED	52 mph	52 mph	52 mph
FUEL CAPY	78 gal	78 gal	78 gal
RANGE LOADED	350 mi	350 mi	350 mi
ELECTRICAL	24 neg	24 neg	24 neg
TRANSFER SPEEDS	2	2	2
TRANSMISSION SPEEDS	5 F	5 F	5 F
TURNING RADIUS FT	48-7	47- 2	47-2

During bridge launch operations, the transporters were backed into the water, and the bridge sections expanded and launched, as seen here. (Photo courtesy of the Patton Museum)

MODEL	M820A2	M821	SEORLT
WEIGHT NET**	30,195 lbs.	28,800 lbs.	32,630 lbs.
WEIGHT GROSS**	32,895 lbs.	35,195 lbs.	38,800 lbs.
MAX TOWED LOAD	15,000 lbs.	15,000 lbs.	15,000 lbs.
LENGTH**	376	382	356
WIDTH	97.75	114	98.5
HEIGHT	138	114	125
WHEELBASE	215	215	215
TIRE SIZE	11.00-20	14.00-20	12.00-20
MAX SPEED	52 mph	52 mph	52 mph
FUEL CAPY	78 gal	78 gal	78 gal
RANGE LOADED	350 mi	350 mi	350 mi
ELECTRICAL	24 neg	24 neg	24 neg
TRANSFER SPEEDS	2	2	2
TRANSMISSION			
SPEEDS	5 F	5 F	5 F
TURNING			
RADIUS FT	47-2	48-7	48-7

Overall dimensions listed in inches.

*** Subtract 665 lbs from weight and 15.5 in. in length for vehicles without winches. Expansible vans do not have winches.*

ENGINE DATA

ENGINE MAKE/MODEL	Cummins NHC250
NUMBER OF CYLINDERS	6
CUBIC INCH DISPLACEMENT	860
HORSEPOWER	240 @ 2100 rpm
TORQUE	685 lbs.-ft. @ 1500 rpm

VALUES

	6	5	4	3	2	1
M813	1,500	3,000	4,000	7,500	13,500	29,000
M813A1	1,500	3,000	5,000	8,500	14,500	30,000
M814	1,800	3,200	5,500	9,500	16,000	32,000
M815	1,800	3,200	5,500	9,500	16,000	32,000
M816	3,500	5,500	9,000	14,000	20,000	36,000
M817	2,000	4,000	6,000	10,000	16,000	31,000
M818	1,500	3,000	4,000	7,500	13,500	29,000
M819	3,500	5,500	9,000	14,000	20,000	36,000
M820	1,800	3,200	5,500	9,200	15,500	31,000
M820A1	1,500	3,200	5,000	9,000	15,000	30,000
M820A2	1,800	3,200	5,500	9,500	16,000	32,000
M821	1500	3,000	4,000	7,500	13,500	29,000
SERL-118	1,500	3,000	5,000	9,500	—	—

SCARCITY

M813	2
M813A1	2
M814	3
M815	4
M816	3
M817	3
M818	2
M819	3
M820	4
M820A1	4
M820A2	4
M821	3
SERL-118	4

M939 Cargo Truck

Development work on military vehicles is never complete. Even as production begins on one vehicle, work goes on to improve it. So it was when the M809 5-ton 6x6 was type classified. Extensive testing of the M809 series in 1970 had shown that product improvements should be carried out in the areas of transmission, transfer case, and brakes.

By the late 1970s half of the Army's 35,000 5-ton 6x6 trucks were at least 10 years old. The replacement for these trucks, officially known as a PIP, for Product Improvement Package, was given the designation

XM939. Two test trucks were built by AM General featuring the Product Improvement Package. After extensive trials of the cargo and semi-trailer tractor prototype vehicles, at last in October 1979 the M939 (6x6) 5-ton cargo truck was type classified. In April 1981, a contract for 11,394 of the new trucks was awarded to

Here is a winch-equipped M925A2 on the left, with the non-winch M923A2 on the right. Notice the additional length between the front bumper and the grill on the truck on the left. The second set of shackles, below the bumpers of both these trucks, are characteristic of the A2 series only.

The A2 vehicles used much larger single radial tires, as did the A1 series, but they also were powered with a different engine than was used in the previous series. This M923A2 was photographed at the MVPA Convention, Fort Lee, Virginia. (Photo courtesy of John Adams-Graf)

Standard-length, winch-equipped trucks with drop-side cargo beds were designated M925. The M925A2 shown here, assigned to the 395th Ordnance Company of Appleton, Wisconsin, has been equipped with a M66 ring mount and a convoy warning light. (Photo courtesy of John Adams-Graf)

This particular M923 has an F36T4-2S shelter in its bed. Visible behind the cab, which has been fitted with the optional hard top, is the spare tire and its handling davit. (Photo courtesy of Keco Industries)

The base vehicle for the Army's new series 5-ton cargo trucks was the M923 cargo truck. The same truck with a fixed-side body was named the M924. (Photo courtesy Keco Industries)

Extra-long-wheelbase vehicles have been developed in every class of 5-ton vehicles since WWII. In the M939 series, the big truck is known as the M927 without a winch, and an M928 when equipped with a winch. Shown here is an M928A1. (Photo courtesy of Bruce Kubu)

Although this truck is does not have its sideboards place, the extra-long-wheelbase truck's sideboards did not have troop seats. These large vehicles were built to haul cargo only. (Photo courtesy of Bruce Kubu)

The dump truck member of this family is the M929, shown here in the A1 version. If this truck was equipped with a front winch, it would be an M930. (Photo courtesy of Bruce Kubu)

AM General Corporation by the U.S. Army Tank Automotive Command.

Production of the new M939 series 5-ton vehicles was begun in 1982 at AM General's plant at South Bend, Indiana.

The dump bed of the M929A1, like that of most military dump trucks, had a cab protector. (Photo courtesy of Bruce Kubu)

Winch-equipped tractors were model M932, while non-winch models were known as M931. The position of the air intake above and behind the cab helped reduce in-cab noise. (Photo courtesy of Bruce Kubu and John Winslow)

Although the initial price tag of the M939 was greater than that of the M809 series, cost (lifecycle) was estimated to be the same as that for M809 vehicles. The two vehicles were produced side by side briefly as the M939 series production began and the M809 production ended.

All the M939 and M939A1 trucks were built by AM General, which had developed the truck. In the mid 1980s the program was up for re-buy as the M939A2, and a team made up largely of former AM General employees put together the successful bid. Immediately after the award, the winners sold the contract to BMY, a division of HARSCO. Bowen-McLaughlin-York (BMY) of York, Pennsylvania, has a long and respectable record of building tracked vehicles dating back to WWII, but had limited experience in wheeled military vehicles. BMY Wheeled Vehicles Division was established in a leased plant in Maryville, Ohio.

The previously used M809's transmission and transfer case had their origins with the gasoline-powered G-744 M39 series trucks. As such they were under capacity and mismatched to the engine/axle ratio of the Cummins-powered M809. This made the engine prone to over-speeding or laboring due to improper gear ratio

Another view of an M932 5-ton truck. (Photo courtesy of Bruce Kubu and John Winslow)

selection. The M939 had an automatic transmission that eliminated these problems — a concept first tried in a U.S. 6x6 with the GMC M135 series of the 1950s. An automatic transmission has been shown to require less driver training, reduce fuel consumption, lessen driver fatigue, and require less maintenance compared to a manual transmission.

The transfer case used by the M939 is pressure lubricated, whereas earlier vehicles relied on splash lubrication. Front axle engagement is controlled by the driver using an air cylinder. Earlier 5-ton 6x6 trucks used an automatic overrunning clutch to engage the front axle. It is not necessary to stop the truck to shift between transfer case ranges.

The M939 uses commercial-type full air brakes, rather than the air-over-hydraulic brakes used on earlier models. The air brakes are self-adjusting and are backed by fail-safe mechanical spring brakes.

Externally, while retaining the conventional layout used by US 6x6s, the truck differs in some obvious ways, especially in the area of the engine hood and the grille. The hood of the M939 is joined to the front fenders and is hinged to tilt forward for easier access to the engine components. Basic maintenance can be carried out from the ground, whereas even opening the hood on the M809 required climbing onto the bumper.

While at a glance the cab itself looks like the standard military one, it however is considerably wider. The M939 is the first tactical truck to meet Surgeon General standards for in-cab noise even with the windows open. Part of the noise reduction was accomplished by relocating the engine air intake and exhaust stack to a position behind the cab from the forward location used on previous models.

The engine used in the M939 and M939A1 was the 855-cid NHC250 Cummins similar to the engine used in M809 series. However, the engine of the M939 was fitted with connectors for engine diagnostic equipment known as ISTE/ICE (Simplified Test Equipment, Internal Combustion Engine). The ease of use of this test equipment, it was hoped, would cut maintenance time and eliminate incorrect replacement of components based on poor diagnosis. The M939 was the first truck built for use with STE/ICE. The M939A2 series vehicles used a smaller turbosupercharged 504.5-cid Cummins 6CTA8.3 diesel engine. Horsepower ratings of the Cummins 6CTA8.3 are equivalent to the NHC-250.

Winch-equipped vehicles use a hydraulically powered winch instead of the mechanical winch driveline used on the older M series vehicles. With hydraulic drive the winch will stop when overloaded and restart when the overload is removed. The older mechanical-winch driveline used on previous vehicles required shear-pin

The exhaust stack used on these M934 expansible van trucks was considerably shorter than that of the rest of the series. This avoided interference with the heater and air-conditioner assembly extending over the cab. (Photo courtesy of the Patton Museum)

replacement when similarly overloaded.

Differences in tires and wheels can help different series of trucks. The initial M939 series used 11.00 x 20 with dual rear wheels. The A1 series vehicles had larger 14.00-20 tubeless tires and single rear wheels.

The A2 series vehicles have single tires, like the A1 series, but the truck has a CTIS Central Tire Inflation System, and steel shields on the wheels to cover the inflation valves.

With their large tires, the A1 and A2 series vehicles earned the nickname Big Foot. A davit behind the cab is used to load and unload the spare tire.

Like most U.S. military trucks, a variety of special-purpose kits were made for the M939 series of trucks. These include: automatic chemical alarm, hot water personnel heater, deep-water fording, bow and tarpaulin cover, electric brake, engine coolant heater, fuel burning heater, hard top closure, and machine gun mount.

VARIANTS

— M923 Cargo Truck, dropside body, standard wheelbase without winch
— M924 Cargo Truck, fixed-side body, standard wheelbase without winch
— M925 Cargo Truck, dropside body, standard wheelbase with winch
— M926 Cargo Truck, fixed-side body, standard wheelbase with winch
— M927 Cargo Truck, fixed-side body, long wheelbase without winch
— M928 Cargo Truck, fixed-side body, long wheelbase with winch
— M929 Dump Truck, short wheelbase, without winch
— M930 Dump Truck, short wheelbase, with winch
— M931 Tractor Truck, short wheelbase, without winch
— M932 Tractor Truck, short wheelbase, with winch
— M934 Expansible Van Truck, long wheelbase, without winch
— M935 Expansible Van Truck, long wheelbase, without winch, with hydraulic lift gate
— M936 Medium Wrecker, standard wheelbase, front and rear winch
— M942 Chassis with cab, for mounting of purpose built bodies, long wheelbase
— M944 Chassis with cab, for mounting of purpose built bodies, standard wheelbase

GENERAL DATA

MODEL	M923	M924	M925	M927
WEIGHT NET	21,470 lbs.	21,470 lbs.	22,750 lbs.	24,300 lbs.
WEIGHT GROSS	31,470 lbs.	31,470 lbs.	32,750 lbs.	34,300 lbs.
MAX TOWED LOAD	15,000 lbs.	15,000 lbs.	15,000 lbs.	15,000 lbs.
LENGTH	307.2	328.7	307.2	383.2
WIDTH	97.5	97.5	97.5	97.5
HEIGHT	115	115	115	115
WHEELBASE	179	179	179	215
TIRE SIZE	11.00-20	11.00-20	11.00-20	11.00- 20
MAX SPEED	63 mph	63 mph	63 mph	63 mph
FUEL CAPY	81 gal	81 gal	81 gal	81 gal
RANGE LOADED	350 mi	350 mi	350 mi	350 mi
ELECTRICAL	24 neg	24 neg	24 neg	24 neg
TRANSFER SPEEDS	2	2	2	2
TRANSMISSION SPEEDS	5 F	5 F	5 F	5 F
TURNING RADIUS FT	38	38	38	46.2

MODEL	M929	M931	M934	M936
WEIGHT NET	23,990 lbs.	20,510 lbs.	28,440 lbs.	37,600 lbs.
WEIGHT GROSS	33,990 lbs.	58,010 lbs.	33,440 lbs.	44,600 lbs.
MAX TOWED LOAD	15,000 lbs.	37,500 lbs.	15,000 lbs.	20,000 lbs.
LENGTH	273	264.5	362.6	362.2
WIDTH	97.5	97.5	97.5	97.5
HEIGHT	111.1	118.6	138	117.6
WHEELBASE	167	179	215	179
TIRE SIZE	11.00-20	11.00-20	11.00-20	11.00- 20
MAX SPEED	63 mph	63 mph	63 mph	55 mph
FUEL CAPY	116 gal	116 gal	81 gal	81 gal
RANGE LOADED	480	460	350	500
ELECTRICAL	24 neg	24 neg	24 neg	24 neg
TRANSFER SPEEDS	2	2	2	2
TRANSMISSION SPEEDS	5 F	5 F	5 F	5 F
TURNING RADIUS FT	39.2	39.2	45.2	39

Overall dimensions listed in inches.

ENGINE DATA

ENGINE MAKE/MODEL	Cummins NHC250	Cummins 6CTA8.3
NUMBER OF CYLINDERS	6	6
CU.-IN. DISPLACEMENT	855	504.5
HORSEPOWER	240 @ 2100 rpm	240 @ 2100 rpm
TORQUE	685 lbs.-ft. @ 1500 rpm	745 lbs.-ft. @ 1500 rpm

VALUES

	6	5	4	3	2	1
M923	3,000	6,000	10,000	18,000	26,000	45,000
M924	3,000	6,000	10,000	18,000	26,000	45,000
M925	3,000	6,500	10,500	18,850	26,850	46,000
M927	3,000	6,500	11,000	19,000	28,000	47,000
M929	3,500	6,500	11,000	19,000	28,000	48,000
M931	2,000	4,000	6,000	10,000	16,000	31,000
M934	2,000	4,000	6,000	10,000	16,000	31,000
M936	4,500	7,000	12,000	21,000	31,000	52,000

SCARCITY

M923	2
M924	2
M925	2
M927	2
M929	3
M931	3
M934	3
M936	3

The wrecker bed of the M936A2 was very similar to that of the M816 and M543, with the hydraulic reservoir mounted on the side of the shipper (photo courtesy of Shane G. Deemer, Military Rails Online)

6-TON TRUCKS

G-535 Mack NM

The series NM was the first military 6x6 built by Mack Trucks Inc. The NM series trucks were 6-ton prime movers intended to tow anti-aircraft artillery and transport the gun crews. The enclosed steel cab of the NM was derived from Mack's civilian model L cab. A midship winch with capstan head was mounted between the cab and the 11-ft. steel cargo bed.

Production of the NM-1 began in 1940 and totaled 87 units. Its successor, the NM-2, was most readily distinguished by its smaller headlights with parking lamps on top. Mack built 107 of the NM-2.

The last of the hard-topped NMs were the 104 NM-3s. As opposed to the straight front bumper of its predecessors, the NM-3's bumper was arched in the center to clear a pintle hook mounted on the front cross member. This was used during artillery emplacement.

Counter to what some references list, beginning with the NM-5 (NM-4 was not a production model), Mack supplied the NMs with an open canvas-topped cab, but the cab did have steel doors. The NM-5 through NM-8

models were equipped with gun carriage brake cylinders. This amounted to an air slave cylinder that would actuate the gun carriage's mechanical brakes. This

The NM series trucks were tall. The hardtop versions stand just over 9 ft. to the top of the cab. The cargo beds of the NM-1 through –3 were steel, and built by Perfection. Beginning with the NM-3, the front bumper, now sans tow hook, was arched to clear a pintle hook mounted on the front cross member. Also, the brush guard of the NM-3 and later trucks was considerably smaller than on the earlier trucks. (Photo courtesy of the Mack Trucks Historical Museum)

The Mack NM-1 (shown here), NM-2, and NM-3 trucks were supplied with Lee tires with highway tread. Initially, the size was 9.75 x 22 in., but soon that was increased to 10-22. The NM-1 and -2 had a flat bumper with tow hooks mounted on the top. (Photo courtesy of the Mack Trucks Historical Museum)

The NM-5 lost its commercially based closed cab in favor of the military-style open cab. Simultaneously, the steel bed was replaced with a wooden bed, still made by Perfection. The midship-mounted winch can clearly be seen in this photo. Notice the tire tread pattern has changed to the military non-directional style. (Photo courtesy of the Mack Trucks Historical Museum)

The front pintle hook can be seen clearly in this photograph, as can be the liquid container racks above the fuel tank. This imposing vehicle is the Mack NM-6. (Photo courtesy of the Mack Trucks Historical Museum)

In July 1944, this NM-7 posed for a portrait at the Studebaker Proving Ground. The capstan head for the midship winch is clearly seen. The spare tires for the NM were carried in the truck bed. (U.S. Army photo)

cylinder was mounted under the right rear frame rail.

By this time (1943), the U.S. military had standardized on the Corbitt-White-Brockway-Ward LaFrance 6-ton 6x6s, so the Macks were supplied as foreign aid. The NM-6 was similar to the NM-5, except for the addition of liquid container racks beside the winch and rifle racks in the cab. Production was 1,060 NM-5 vehicles, 3,240 NM-6s, and 3,888 NM-7s. It is unclear how many NM-8 trucks were built.

GENERAL DATA

MODEL	NM
NET WEIGHT	22,659 lbs.
GROSS WEIGHT	41,959 lbs.
MAX TOWED LOAD	30,000 lbs.
LENGTH	282.375
WIDTH	96
HEIGHT	119
WIDTH*	50.125/94.375
TRACK	74.25
TIRE SIZE	10.00- 22
MAX SPEED	34 mph
FUEL CAPY	80 gal
RANGE LOADED	280 mi
ELECTRICAL	6/12 pos
TRANSMISSION SPEEDS	5
TRANSFER SPEEDS	2
TURNING RADIUS FT	37 R, 35 L

Overall dimensions listed in inches.

* inside/outside width at tires.

ENGINE DATA

ENGINE MAKE/MODEL	Mack EY
NUMBER OF CYLINDERS	6
CUBIC INCH DISPLACEMENT	707
HORSEPOWER	159 @ 2100 rpm
TORQUE	530 lbs.-ft. @ 1000 rpm
GOVERNED SPEED (rpm)	2100

VALUE

	6	5	4	3	2	1
All models	2,500	5,500	9,000	14,000	18,000	25,000

6-Ton 6x6 Trucks

In addition to the Mack NM, the U.S. Army fielded several variations of the 6-ton 6x6 during WWII. The original builder of these trucks was Corbitt, of Henderson, North Carolina. Corbitt began producing its model 50SD6 in 1941, and was soon joined by White, which built identical vehicles with the clever model number of 666 (six tons, six wheels, six-wheel drive). Both the 666 and the 50SD6 were intended to be artillery prime movers. As such, they were equipped with midship winches and pintle hooks on both the front and rear cross members.

In 1942, Brockway joined in the manufacture of 6-ton trucks as well, assigning model number B-666 to its vehicles. While Corbitt's entire production was artillery prime movers, between 1942 and 1944 Brockway built chassis for Quickway Cranes and pontoon and bridge erecting trucks.

Prime mover production at White carried over from 1941 into 1942, at which time they were joined on the assembly line by simple chassis bridge erecting and gasoline tankers, and truck tractors. In 1944, long-wheelbase cargo trucks and chassis for Signal Corps vans were added.

In 1945, FWD Corporation of Clintonville, Wisconsin, was added to the 6-ton truck manufacturing group. FWD completed 168 bridge erecting trucks. Ward LaFrance also built trucks in this series.

To conserve shipping space, the enclosed cab of the early 6-ton models was replaced by the open military-type cab, as seen on this restored example owned by Chet Krause, of Iola, Wisconsin. As with the closed-cab trucks, a machine-gun mount was available for the open-cab models.

These bridge erection trucks were photographed in Japan just prior to their transfer to the Japanese self-defense force. The elaborate hydraulically powered beds on these trucks were built by Heil and given model number M-11. (National Archives and Records Administration photo)

Like Corbitt, White converted to production of open-cabbed trucks, like this bridge truck chassis photographed in April of 1944 at the Studebaker Proving Ground. Like many of the bridge trucks, this truck is equipped with a 25,000-lb.-capacity dual-drum winch. (U.S. Army photo)

This 1945 photograph shows the hoist being used to launch an inflated pontoon during a bridging operation. The bridge trucks had an additional air compressor and air reservoir to inflate these. (Photo courtesy of United States Army Engineer School Office)

The White-built 6-ton trucks were virtually identical to the Corbitt trucks. This White version was photographed in October 1943. (National Archives and Records Administration photo)

In order to conserve steel needed for more critical items during the war, the steel bed of the early trucks was replaced with a wooden bed. Notice the steps on the rear mud flaps, and the spare tires mounted in the bed.

The hoist of this truck is being used to unload panels of a treadway bridge section. The bridge trucks were built on specially reinforced 220-in.-wheelbase chassis. (National Archives and Records Administration photo)

This early Corbitt 6-ton has had an antiaircraft machine-gun mount added above its enclosed cab. This vehicle also has a steel cargo bed — a feature discontinued in 1942. The midship winch is visible between the cab and bed. (National Archives and Records Administration photo)

Only 25 of these huge 2,000-gallon fuel tankers were built by White, making them the scarcest of the 6-ton trucks. They featured self-sealing four-compartment tanks built by Butler. There were provisions to install bows and canvas to camouflage them as cargo trucks. (White Motor Company photo)

Initially, White put its name badge on the grille of its trucks, but this practice was discontinued per government instructions. This early closed-cab prime mover chassis proudly displays its builder's plate. (White Motor Company photo)

The extra-capacity air receivers can be seen in this overhead view, along with the interior arrangement of the cab. This photo was taken by the Engineering Standards Laboratory in February 1944. (U.S. Army photo)

The front-mounted winch came on many of the 6-ton vehicles. The trucks were equipped with a capstan drum on each side of the main winch drum. (White Motor Company photo)

This 6-ton truck has a Quickway 3/8-yard shovel and crane mounted on its 197-in.-wheelbase chassis. The crane mechanism was powered by a separate International U-9 four-cylinder engine. (U.S. Army photo)

After WWII, some of the 6-tons were equipped with stake bodies for bridging equipment similar to the M-series 5-ton trucks. An example of a 6-ton so equipped is shown here. (Photo courtesy of the Patton Museum)

GENERAL DATA

MODEL	C666 CHASSISS	WHITE 666 TANKER	WHITE 666 CARGO	WHITE 666 TRACTOR	CORBITT 50SD6
WEIGHT NET	22,400 lbs.	23,820 lbs.	22,900 lbs.	22,070 lbs.	
GROSS	32,850 lbs.	35,820 lbs.	42,000 lbs.	41,530 lbs.	42,070 lbs.
MAX TOWED LD	—	—	40,000	30,000	40,000
LENGTH	311.625	286	289	278.75	286
WIDTH	114	110.125	96	113.125	97
HEIGHT	134	96	114	113.125	120
WIDTH	48/114	49.125/95.375	50.25/94.25	49.125/113.125	47.5/97
TRACK	81	72.25	72.25	81.125	72.25
TIRE SIZE	14.00-20	10.00- 22	10.00-22	14.00- 20	10.00- 22
MAX SPEED	37 mph	35 mph	35 mph	35 mph	37.5mph
FUEL CAPY	118 gal	80 gal	80 gal	80 gal	80 gal
RANGE LOADED	306 mi	300 mi	300 mi	300 mi	200 mi
ELECTRICAL	6/12 pos	6/12 pos	6/12 pos	6/12 pos	6/12 pos
TRANSMISSION SPEEDS	4	4	4	4	4
TRANSFER SPEEDS	2	2	2	2	2
TURNING RADIUS FEET	44 R, 43L	41	41	41	41R, 42 L

Overall dimensions listed in inches.

ENGINE DATA

ENGINE MAKE/MODEL	HERCULES HXD
NUMBER OF CYLINDERS	6
CUBIC INCH DISPLACEMENT	855
HORSEPOWER	202 @ 2150 rpm
TORQUE	642 @ 900 rpm
GOVERNED SPEED (rpm)	2150

VALUES

	6	5	4	3	2	1
Value, all models	3,000	6,000	10,000	17,000	22,000	30,000

SCARCITY

Scarcity 4

7 1/2-TON TRUCKS

G-532 Mack NO

The NO was a huge vehicle designed to tow 155mm guns and 8-in. howitzers. The NO series was classified as a 7 1/2-ton 6x6, but it shared many components with the postwar G-792 10-ton trucks. The first design, the NO-1, did not go into series production. The NO-2 went into production in 1943 with a total of 403 of the imposing vehicles turned out. These were followed by 97 of the NO-3 model and 1,000 of the NO-6 model. All the NO-3 and NO-6 trucks were supplied to other countries. The final incarnation was the NO-7, 550 of which were supplied to U.S. forces.

All of the production NOs had wooden cargo bodies made by the Schantz Furniture Company. Any found with steel cargo bodies were rebodied during NATO service. Another feature common to all these trucks is the massive Gar Wood 5MB 40,000-lb.-capacity winch. All the NOs were nearly identical.

A hoist was mounted on the rear of the bed, which was used to lift the gun trails of the towed weapon during coupling. The hoist was also used to handle the two huge 12.00-24 in. spares carried in the bed.

GENERAL DATA

MODEL	NO
NET WEIGHT	29,103 lbs.
GROSS WEIGHT	50,000 lbs.
MAX TOWED LOAD	50,000 lbs.
LENGTH	296.75
WIDTH	103
HEIGHT	124.25
WIDTH*	50.75/101.75
TRACK	76.25
TIRE SIZE	12.00- 24
MAX SPEED	32 mph
FUEL CAPY	160 gal
RANGE LOADED	400 mi
ELECTRICAL	6/12 pos
TRANSMISSION SPEEDS	5
TRANSFER SPEEDS	2
TURNING RADIUS FT.	35

Overall dimensions listed in inches.
*Inside/outside width at tires.

ENGINE DATA

ENGINE MAKE/MODEL	Mack EY
NUMBER OF CYLINDERS	6
CUBIC-INCH DISPLACEMENT	707
HORSEPOWER	159 @ 2100 rpm
TORQUE	534 lbs.-ft. @ 800 rpm
GOVERNED SPEED (rpm)	2100

The lone Mack model NO was photographed at Aberdeen Proving Ground in December of 1940. Unlike the production models, the engine side panels of this truck were louvered, and the cab was the traditional Mack C shape. Even with the antique-style cab, the NO was an impressive machine, and the huge winch behind the front bumper did nothing to diminish its brawny look. (National Archives and Records Administration photo)

Although the NO-3s were all supplied for foreign aid, before shipping out this one took part in a War Bonds Drive. Notice the boards protecting the ground from the NO's weight (almost 30,000 lbs.), and the wide five-man cab. (Photo courtesy Mack Trucks Historical Museum)

This NO-2 is an example of the first NO production model. The cab and front-end sheet metal were completely redesigned, the steel cargo body has given way to a wooden bed, and a different model of front winch has been used. (Photo courtesy Mack Trucks Historical Museum)

The NO-6, like the other production NOs, had the traditional military troop seat and side board arrangement. The lower section of the side boards aft of the spares hinged down to provide seating. The rear-mounted derrick is barely visible in this 1944 Studebaker Proving Ground photo. (U.S. Army photo)

Like most of the open-cabbed tactical vehicles of WWII, the NO could be fitted with the M36 antiaircraft machine-gun mount. This filthy example was photographed at the Aberdeen Proving Grounds in February 1943. (National Archives and Records Administration photo)

10-TON TRUCKS

G-116 Wrecker

These robust vehicles have their beginnings in three vehicles built in the late 1930s by the Corbitt Truck Company. In 1940, Ward La France was awarded a production contract, and production began the following year. Later, Kenworth was given a contract to produce a vehicle using identical essential serviceable parts, although the sheet metal on the cab was different. A Continental Model 22R engine powered the trucks by both builders, with the earliest versions having the dual ignition system (two spark plugs per cylinder) characteristic of the fire apparatus that was Ward La France's primary business. Kenworth delivered its first M1 wrecker in mid 1942.

The G-116 series trucks were to be the standard heavy wrecker of the U.S. military throughout World War II and into the 1950s. Regardless of who built the chassis, the recovery equipment was built by Gar Wood Industries, and included a crane with 180 degree traverse. In their final form, the Series 5 Ward La France and model 573 Kenworth parts were completely interchangeable.

The M1 and M1A1, known at various points in their careers as 6-ton or 10-ton wreckers, were the Army's standard wrecker until the 1950s, when the adoption of the M62 caused these to be reclassified as limited standard before they were finally phased out. A limited number of the Ward La France chassis were used as the basis for Class 155 fire and crash truck.

Ward La France Model 1000 Series 1

Starting in 1941, this was the first model to reach mass production. Sixty-nine of these trucks were built under contract W-740-ORD-6294. These trucks, all with the closed cab, had the two 11.25-20 spare tires mounted behind the cab, crosswise on the truck. These were the only trucks of the series to use this size tire. The

This is one of the two test examples of the famed Ward LaFrance M1 wrecker. This photo was taken March 18, 1941. The front-end sheet metal was an adaptation of Ward LaFrance's civilian product. The front winch is hidden between the front bumper and the radiator. One of the spare tires, with directional tread, can be seen behind the cab. (U.S. Army photo)

Series 1 trucks lacked the rear drag winch that was so useful on the later models.

Ward La France Model 1000 Series 2

The Series 2 trucks were fitted with a 47,500-lb.-capacity rear drag winch, a Gar Wood 5M713K, with 350 ft. of rope, in addition to the 20,000-lb.-capacity Gar Wood 3U615 winch mounted behind the front bumper.

The crane was manually operated.

The spare tire mounting was changed. One tire was stored crosswise behind the cab, the other on the passenger's side of the crane base. The first 143 trucks were built in 1941-1942 under contract W-740-ORD-2126. An additional 15 vehicles were later ordered under supplement to the same contract.

The next contracts, also in 1942, were for 61

The Ward LaFrance M1 has a relatively clean, uncluttered look. Notice the siren mounted on the left front fender and the hand wheels for raising, lowering, and rotating the boom mounted on the crane support. (U.S. Army photo)

The boom of the M1 wreckers could be swung to the side for lifting and recovery operations. The wooden sideboards of the bed are visible here, as is the M1's lack of a rear drag winch. The two oxygen bottles and a single acetylene bottle were carried as part of the welding/cutting outfit. The pulley in the socket in the bed rear could be positioned in a variety of ways. (U.S. Army photo)

wreckers, with an order for 300 more right behind it.

The final batch of Series 2 wreckers were built in 1942 under two contracts — one for 150 trucks, and another for 51. Many of these trucks had the unusual chisel-shaped bumper.

Ward La France Model 1000 Series 3

These trucks lacked the front and rear trailer connections found on the earlier models, and the entire run of 365 was supplied to the British as Lend-Lease items.

Ward La France Model 1000 Series 4

The fourth series of the heavy wrecker is readily identifiable by the curved boom of the Gar Wood US5G crane mounted in place of the US5 straight-boomed crane used previously. Although still manually operated, the cranes had a dual-ratio swinger gear for the boom, with the operating wheel moved between shafts on the driver's side of the crane "A" frame to select speed. Inside the cab, the obvious change was the introduction of individual military instruments in place of the civilian type used previously. Four hundred of these vehicles were built. These trucks, built in 1943, also had the

enlarged fuel filler to accommodate field refueling with jerry cans. The front bumper had a chisel-shape design.

Ward La France Model 1000 Series 5

The final Ward La France series was designated Heavy Wrecking Truck M1A1, and delivery began in May 1943. These trucks had a soft-top cab, and the fenders had a flat design. At last the crane, a Gar Wood US6A, was fully power-operated, with the three control levers located beside the "A" frame just behind the driver's door. The crane boom on these trucks reverted to a straight design.

Production began in 1943, and continued throughout the war.

Kenworth Model 570

These vehicles were the Kenworth equivalent to the Ward La France Series 2, with the contract awarded in 1941. The Kenworth design used levers, rods, and bell cranks to actuate the PTO, transfer case, and other components. Ward La France had used cable linkages for these functions. An initial order for 300 units was augmented with an additional 30 purchased under contract W-883-ORD-2582. Early military manuals call

The Series 2 wreckers incorporated a much-needed drag winch on the rear of the truck, as this April 1942 photo shows. In addition to the outriggers on the rear of the chassis to stabilize the truck, these wreckers had boom jacks to support the outer end of the boom during heavy lifting operations. (NARA photo)

these trucks "Heavy Wrecking Truck, M1, Series 2, Kenworth."

and oil filter changes. These 1942-43 production trucks were built under contract W-883-ORD-2716.

Kenworth Model 571

These 100 Model 571 trucks are practically indistinguishable from the model 570. The differences are primarily beneath the hood, in the form of air, fuel,

Kenworth Model 572

This truck retained the closed cab of the 570 and 571, but included the Gar Wood US6A full-power crane. This combination of closed cab and power crane is not

With the second series wreckers, the spare tires were relocated, with one behind the cab and the second on the crane tower. Ward LaFrance would retain this placement for the tires until the introduction of the fifth series wreckers. The long passenger's-side toolbox can also be seen in this February 1942 view. (NARA photo)

The Series 5 Ward LaFrance (and the Model 573 Kenworth) were M1A1 heavy wreckers. In this photo we can see many of the improvements. Most obvious is the military-style open cab. Also visible just behind the cab are the three levers that control the now power-operated crane, and just to the rear of them can be seen the stabilizer legs added to each side and the different tool box and bed arrangement. (U.S. Army photo)

found on any other M1 or M1A1, making these 100 trucks, from the collector/operators standpoint, the most desirable of the entire family of vehicles.

The crane controls were three levers beside the crane A-frame, just behind the driver's door. These were the first Kenworth wreckers with the distinctive chisel-shaped front bumper and the military-style instruments.

Kenworth Model 573

These vehicles were the Kenworth equivalent to the Ward La France Series 5, with the open military cab and flat fenders. The whiffletree and toolboxes are slightly different on these trucks, as well. Production began in 1943, but was stopped due to labor shortages in the Pacific Northwest after only 1,323 trucks were produced. The remaining components were shipped to Ward La France, which may account for the Kenworth-style toolboxes found on some Ward La France wreckers.

GENERAL DATA

MODEL	M1	M1A1
WEIGHT NET	27,330 lbs.	30,000 lbs.
LENGTH	276	348
WIDTH*	99 1/2	99 1/2
HEIGHT	122	117
TRACK INSIDE	50	50
TRACK OUTSIDE	99 1/2	99 1/2
TIRE SIZES	11.00-20	11.00-20

MAX SPEED	45 mph	45 mph
FUEL CAPY	100 gal	100 gal
RANGE	250 mi	250 mi
ELECTRICAL	12 volt	12 volt
TRANSMISSION SPEEDS	5 F, 1 R	5 F, 1 R
TRANSFER SPEEDS	2	2
TURNING RADIUS FT.	44	35

Overall dimensions listed in inches.

ENGINE DATA

ENGINE MAKE/MODEL	Continental 22R
NUMBER OF CYLINDERS	6
CUBIC INCH DISPLACEMENT	501
HORSEPOWER	145 @ 2400 rpm
TORQUE	372 lbs.-ft. @ 1200 rpm
GOVERNED SPEED (rpm)	2400

VALUES

	6	5	4	3	2	1
All models	2,500	3,500	6,500	11,000	14,500	18,000

The Series 5 trucks had a very business-like front end. A whiffletree is affixed to the chisel-shaped front bumper, and the two spares, as well as the torch set, are visible through the windshield. This truck is equipped with a ring mount and .50-caliber machine gun, but this was not always the case. (U.S. Army photo)

This June 1942 Aberdeen Proving Ground photo shows the first Kenworth-produced M1 wrecker. Known by Kenworth as the model 570, it was almost identical to the Ward LaFrance Series 2 trucks, although there were some differences in control linkages. (NARA photo)

This is the Kenworth version of the M1A1. It is almost indistinguishable from a Ward LaFrance M1A1. The whiffletree was slightly different (notice the KW whiffletree lacks the flange across the back present on the Ward LaFrance). The tool lockers varied with manufacturer as well, although a few Ward LaFrances were built with the Kenworth tool lockers to use up excess inventory after Kenworth stopped building the trucks. (U.S. Army photo)

G-642 White 1064

The White 1064 was a 10-ton truck built for on-highway use between 1942 and 1945. The front axle was not powered, and the truck did not have a winch. The cab was the same as that used on the company's model 666 6-ton 6x6. Even though it was capable of hauling a 10-ton load, its top speed was only 35 mph.

Originally developed for use by the British in the Persian Gulf region, the truck was powered by a

Unlike many of its contemporaries, the White 1064 had only single rear wheels. A large truck by the standards of the day, it was intended for on-road use only. A luggage rack was built on the cab roof. Like most vehicles supplied to Britain early in the foreign aid program, this vehicle was painted Coronado tan. (White Motor Company photo)

The wooden construction of the 1064 bed is apparent in this photograph. Steel was deemed a critical material for the war effort, and much effort went into getting the most out of available supplies. (White Motor Company photo)

Cummins HB600 diesel engine. The U.S. Army was supplied some of these vehicles for use on the Alaska Highway. The U.S. vehicles were converted to 12-volt electrical systems.

G-792 10-Ton

When the planners laid out the proposed post-WWII tactical vehicle families, the largest vehicles were the 10-ton vehicles of the G-792 series. Although several types were planned, only the tractor, and to a much lesser extent, the prime mover, entered series production.

Designed and originally produced by Mack, these trucks used many of the chassis components of the WWII-era NO series 7 1/2-ton prime movers. Both the tractor and the cargo truck were initially powered by the massive Le Roi TH-844 V-8 gasoline engine. The vehicles used a non-synchronized combination transmission and transfer case, which, along with the axles, were of Mack design and manufacture.

The M125 was in production for one year only, beginning in 1957 and 1958. It was intended to tow

The early 10-tons had an unusual four-mirror setup. (Photo courtesy of the Patton Museum)

This huge M125 was photographed leaving Mack's Allentown factory via rail. The pioneer rack was mounted on the side of the cargo bed, and the powerful winch is visible behind the front bumper. (Photo courtesy of the Mack Trucks Historical Museum)

This XM125 was photographed in February 1955 at Fort Churchill, Manitoba. The truck has been fitted with an insulated cargo cover, and an insulating blanket on the hood, which are typical components of arctic winterization kits. (National Archives and Records Administration photo)

The M123 had dual rear winches. The two winches were operated in tandem, with their ropes crossed, to guide disabled tanks onto the trailer towed by the tractor. The rear winches were equipped with level-wind devices and cable tensioners. The siren on the left front fender was a popular non-standard item. (Photo courtesy of the Patton Museum, Fort Knox, Kentucky)

This M123 was coupled to a M162 60-ton lowboy for an October 1961 photo. It has had a siren added to it. The relocation of the towing shackles on the front bumper may have been an effort to resolve compatibility issues with the military standard 5-ton wreckers. Ultimately, towing these trucks with the standard wreckers was prohibited. The front wheels on this truck are non-standard. (U.S. Army photo)

This soldier is dwarfed by the M123C being tested at Aberdeen Proving Ground. Later models added a hinged step in the center of the front bumper to provide access to the engine. The M123C had only a single rear winch. (U.S. Army photo)

The dual winch-equipped M123E2 was powered by the V8-300 Cummins diesel engine. In addition to the clearance lamp mounted above the front tire, the M123E2 also had rearward-ffacing turn signal lamps mounted on the rear slope of the front fenders. Finally, the M123E2 was the first vehicle in this series to come equipped with a warning beacon. This amber beacon was mounted on the winch. (U.S. Army photo)

This tractor has a single rear winch and the high-mounted fifth wheel. The trailer these tractors were originally intended to pull, the M15A2, was designed for use with the WWII-era M26 Pacific, which used the same 14-24-in. tires as the M123. While the top frame rails of the M123 are approximately level with the tops of the tires, on the Pacific the frame is taller than the tires. Thus, the M123s fifth wheel was raised to provide a level ride attitude of the trailer. Later M123 models were used with different trailers and the raised fifth wheel was no longer needed. (U.S. Army photo)

A quick distinguishing feature of the diesel-powered trucks is the intake air elbow on the passenger-side engine side panel. Notice the access step folded up neatly in the center of the bumper. (Photo courtesy of the Mack Trucks Historical Museum)

The M123A1C was factory built as a diesel-powered truck. Some diesels, like this vehicle photographed at Aberdeen Proving Ground, had dual horizontal exhausts, as did the gasoline-powered trucks. Others had a single vertical exhaust stack. (U.S. Army photo)

This M123A1C has the vertical exhaust stack, characteristic of a late production vehicle. The slogan on the front bumper is a testament to these trucks' reputation for handling loads well in excess of the designers' intentions.

The spare tire and wheel assembly weighs more than 500 lbs. The davit visible just over the top of the spare on this M123A1C was provided to handle the spare. (U.S. Army photo)

155mm guns and 8-inch howitzers, however it was soon supplanted in that role by high-speed track-laying tractors and self-propelled weapons. Production ceased after only 552 units were built. All the M125s had a huge PTO-driven, front-mounted, 45,000 lb.-capacity winch.

Production of the M123 10-ton tractor had begun earlier, in 1955. All the trucks in this series have fifth wheels made to accept 3.5-in. kingpins, and thus will not couple to conventional semi-trailers. The tractors had either single or dual rear 45,000-lb.-capacity winches, rather than the front-mounted winch of the prime mover. The basic M123 had dual rear winches and a normally mounted fifth wheel. The M123C had a single winch and a low-mounted fifth wheel, and the M123D had the low-mounted fifth wheel and dual winches. Of all gas-powered variations, Mack built a total of 392 trucks when production stopped in 1957.

In June 1965, Consolidated Diesel Electric Company of Old Greenwich, Connecticut, was awarded a contract to produce 1,848 diesel-powered versions of this truck, known as the M123A1C. The same Mack axles and combination transmission and transfer case were used, and the engine was the V8-300 Cummins. CONDEC received a contract for a 1,340 more of these vehicles in June 1967. In June of 1968 Mack re-entered the picture, receiving a contract to build 420 M123A1C trucks. At the same time Mack was also awarded a contract to produce 210 M123E2 vehicles. These were the re-manufacturing of 210 of the gas-engine driven trucks into diesel-powered vehicles with dual rear winches. These conversions were preformed during 1969.

The Cummins engine had a different speed range than did the Le Roi, making downshifting difficult. For this reason, many of these tractors were retrofitted with Williams Exhaust Brakes to aid driveability.

Initially the 10-ton tractors pulled the M15A2 50-ton trailer. Later these trucks also pulled the M172A2, M162, M793, and M747 semi-trailers.

The tractors were phased out of service during the 1990s.

GENERAL DATA

MODEL	M125	M123	M123A1C
WEIGHT NET	31,600 lbs.	32,250 lbs.	29,100 lbs.
LENGTH*	331.5	280	280
WIDTH*	114	114	114
HEIGHT*	111	113	108
TREAD	79	79	79
TIRE SIZES	14.00-24	14.00-24	14.00-24
MAX SPEED	42 mph	42 mph	45 mph
FUEL CAPY	166 gal	166 gal	166 gal
RANGE	300 mi	300 mi	350 mi
ELECTRICAL	24 neg	24 neg	24 neg
TRANSMISSION SPEEDS	5 F, 1 R	5 F, 1 R	5 F, 1 R
TRANSFER SPEEDS	2	2	2

Overall dimensions listed in inches.

ENGINE DATA

ENGINE MAKE/MODEL	Le Roi T-H844	Cummins V9-300
NUMBER OF CYLINDERS	8	8
CUBIC INCH DISPLACEMENT	844	785
HORSEPOWER	297 @ 2600 rpm	300 @ 3000 rpm
TORQUE	725 @ 1700 rpm	580 @ 2100 rpm
GOVERNED SPEED (rpm)	2600	2600

VALUES

	6	5	4	3	2	1
Tractor models	2500	6200	9000	22000	31500	40000
cargo models	2800	8500	11000	25000	34500	45000

SCARCITY

Tractor 3
Cargo 5

12-TON TRUCKS

Diamond T 980 & 981

Production of the Diamond T M20 12-ton 6 x 4 began in 1940. These trucks were originally developed to meet British requirements for a tank transporter. The massive truck was a conventional design, with its Hercules diesel engine housed beneath a hood almost 6 ft. long.

Just to the rear of the cab was a Gar Wood 5M723B 40,000-lb. pull winch. A ballast box was mounted to the rear of the winch and above the tandem axles. Weight was added to this box to increase traction to allow the truck to pull heavy loads.

The earlier Model 980 trucks had 300 ft. of wire rope for the winch, which could be played to the rear to pull disabled tanks onto the trailer. The later Model 981 trucks had 500 ft. of wire rope, and a pulley and fair lead arrangement that allowed the rope to be fed through the front bumper and used for self-recovery.

The powerful diesel engine drove the rear axles through a four-speed Fuller transmission and a three-speed Fuller auxiliary gearbox, which combined to give the truck the ability to tow loads well in excess of its 115,000-lb. rated towing capacity, but its top speed was limited to 23 mph. Air brakes stopped the vehicle.

When combined with the M9 trailer that was designed for it, the vehicle was known as the M19. Although widely used by the British, as well as the Soviets, French and other countries, the vehicle was never classified as Standard by the U.S. military. It was alternately Substitute Standard or Limited Standard, probably because of its non-powered front axle and diesel engine.

Diamond T records indicate 6,554 of these trucks were built. Despite a few reports to the contrary, no records exist that indicate that any engine other than the Hercules diesel was installed in these trucks as part of factory mass production.

GENERAL DATA

MODEL	980/981
NET WEIGHT	26,950 lbs.
GROSS WEIGHT	45,000 lbs.
MAX TOWED LOAD	115,000 lbs.
LENGTH	280
WIDTH	100
HEIGHT	100.5
WIDTH*	48.25/99.75
TRACK	74
TIRE SIZE	12.00-20
MAX SPEED	23 mph
FUEL CAPY	150 gal
RANGE LOADED	300 mi
ELECTRICAL	24 pos
TRANSMISSION SPEEDS	4
AUX TRANS SPEEDS	3
TURNING RADIUS FT.	32.5 R, 36 L

Overall dimensions listed in inches.

* Inside/outside width at tires.

ENGINE DATA

ENGINE MAKE/MODEL	Hercules DXFE
NUMBER OF CYLINDERS	6
CUBIC-INCH DISPLACEMENT	895
HORSEPOWER	185 @ 1600 rpm
TORQUE	665 lbs.-ft. @ 1200 rpm
GOVERNED SPEED (rpm)	1600

VALUES

	6	5	4	3	2	1
All models	1,200	2,500	4,000	8000	12,000	18,000

This brand-new closed-cab Diamond T 981 was photographed at the Studebaker Proving Ground in 1944. The wire rope for the winch has been secured to the front pintle hook. The winch is visible just behind the cab above the fuel tank. (U.S. Army photo)

This restored 981 has the later-style open cab, and its ballast box has been filled with rock to increase traction.

The model 981, with its front fairlead, could also winch from the forward direction, unlike the earlier model 980. In February 1945 this truck was photographed doing just that at the Studebaker Proving Ground. (U.S. Army photo.)

MISCELLANEOUS TRUCKS

G-160 Pacific

The big M-26 tank retriever tractor, popularly known as the Pacific, after its chief builder, Pacific Car and Foundry. However, it was actually developed by the San Francisco-based Knuckey Truck Company in response to a military requirement for a tank recovery vehicle capable of operating in desert. Knuckey was a small firm, whose primary business was building heavy off-road trucks. The 12-ton 6x6 was powered by a huge 1,090-cid displacement Hall-Scott Model 440 engine. This six-cylinder engine's origins go back to a marine engine Hall-Scott had developed in the 1930s.

The Knuckey design was well received by the Army, but in the Army's view, Knuckey lacked the production capacity to fulfill the military's requirements. Pacific Car and Foundry of Renton, Washington, was contracted to refine the design and mass produce it. Pacific assigned the M-26 their model number TR-1. Production lines were set up in Renton plant as Pacific's Sherman tank contract was winding down. This was short-lived, however, as the military decreed that the Renton-Seattle area was a critical labor area due to the shipyards and aircraft industries, and ordered the retriever production moved inland. A location was secured at the Midland Empire Fairgrounds in Billings, Montana, and production of the retrievers was transferred there.

The retriever was originally an armored vehicle intended to operate in combat areas. Later production, designated M26A1, was soft-skinned. After WWII, several vehicles were rebuilt to M26A2 standards, which included a 24-volt electrical system.

This front view is of the prototype M26 built by the Knuckey Truck Company. While the basic design had been worked out, there was some refinement before the vehicles were mass produced. (U.S. Army photo)

GENERAL DATA

MODEL	M26	M26A1	M26A2
NET WEIGHT	48,895 lbs.	27,600 lbs.	27,600 lbs.
MAX TRAIN WEIGHT	108,895 lbs.	108,895 lbs.	108,895 lbs.
LENGTH	306	306	306
WIDTH	130.5	130.5	130.5
HEIGHT	123	123	123
TRACK	98	98	98
TIRE SIZE	14.00 x 24	14.00 x 24	14.00 x 24
MAX SPEED	28 mph	28 mph	28 mph
FUEL CAPY	120 gal	120 gal	120 gal
RANGE LOADED	120 mi	120 mi	120 mi
ELECTRICAL	12 neg	12 neg	24 neg
TRANSMISSION			
SPEEDS	4 F, 1R	4 F, 1R	4 F, 1R
AUX TRANS SPEEDS	3	3	3
TURNING			
RADIUS FT	40	40	40

Overall dimensions listed in inches.

ENGINE DATA

ENGINE MAKE/MODEL	Hall-Scott 440
NUMBER OF CYLINDERS	6
CUBIC-INCH DISPLACEMENT	1,090
HORSEPOWER	240 @ 2000 rpm
TORQUE	810 lbs.-ft. @ 1200 rpm

VALUES

	6	5	4	3	2	1
All models	2,200	4,000	7,000	15,000	19,000	25,000

SCARCITY

Scarcity 4

This is another view of the prototype vehicle. Just visible between the tandems are the chain oilers which lubricated the rear axle drive chains. The vertical exhaust pipe exited just behind the spare tire. (U.S. Army photo)

This view of a Knuckey prototype illustrates just how large the vehicle's cab was. The dual rear retrieval winches behind the cab were used in tandem to pull disabled tanks onto the trailer. (U.S. Army photo)

The soft-skinned M26A1 was introduced later for non-combat use. The M26A1 had glass windshields that folded outward and down, and a canvas cab cover was provided. (Photo courtesy of the Patton Museum)

This September 1944 photo shows a production model M26 vehicle built by Pacific Car and Foundry. Changes from the prototype included: the stowage of the large tow bar on the front, the addition of a large siren and a brush guard, and the addition of a pioneer tool rack on the right front corner. (U.S. Army photo)

A look from behind the prototype M-26 shows the robust construction of the truck. (U.S. Army photo)

Oxygen and acetylene bottles were stowed near the rear of the cab on M26 trucks, with the addition of a large vise near the driver's side step and another pioneer tool rack. Guards have been added to protect the winch controls and around the exhaust stack, which has been slightly relocated. (U.S. Army photo)

The M26 was provided with a large davit and chain hoist for use in repair operations and to handle the heavy spare tire. The A-frame at the rear of the truck could be set up in five different positions for different recovery operations. (U.S. Army photo)

The pintle hook was relocated on the production vehicle, and was a more substantial design. The ring mount for the .50-caliber machine gun is just visible on the roof of the truck. (U.S. Army photo)

Two large spotlights were mounted on the rear of the cab, and the standard military flexible spotlight was mounted above the co-driver's position. (U.S. Army photo)

The shiny M26 shown in this 1949 photograph has had its outer dual wheels removed. Barely visible behind the front bumper is the drum for the 35,000-lb.-capacity front winch. (U.S. Army photo)

The rear forward winch had a shaft extension with a windlass gypsy drum on it. Beside the ring mount was stowed a tripod to allow for ground firing of the .50-caliber machine gun. (U.S. Army photo)

The M26 was well outfitted for handling tanks and other large items. Two large sledgehammers were attached on the driver's side of the cab. The armored hatches could be closed, protecting the cab occupants from splinters and small arms fire. (U.S. Army photo)

Without the cab roof to support it, the front spotlight of the M26A1 was relocated to the center of the windshield. There was an elaborate supporting structure for the machine gun ring and canvas. (U.S. Army photo)

The stowage layout of the M26A1 differed from that of its armored sibling. Gone are the sledgehammers and vise. Barely visible on the back wall of the cab is the folding seat for the machine gun operator. (U.S. Army photo)

The M26A1 was 10 ft., 10 1/2 in. wide. The large roller chains that drove the rear wheels are just inboard of the rear tires. (U.S. Army photo)

In November 1944, this soft-skinned M26A1 was photographed at the Engineering Standards Research Laboratory. Being some 10 tons lighter than its predecessor, the M26A1 had considerably better off-road performance and increased load-carrying capacity. (U.S. Army photo)

Without the cab roof to support it, the front spotlight of the M26A1 was relocated to the center of the windshield. The elaborate supporting structure for the machine gun ring and canvas is also clearly shown here. (U.S. Army photo)

G-268 M249 M250

These trucks were developed specifically to transport the M65 280mm cannon, popularly known as the "Atomic Cannon." Produced during 1952-1953, the first Atomic Cannon went into service in 1952. The last was retired in 1963.

Kenworth Motor Truck Corporation manufactured the T-10 transporter units at its Seattle, Washington plant.

For each M65 carriage there are two T-10 4x4 transporters required. One of these had the cab forward as in normal trucks, and was the lead vehicle, known as the M249. A second truck, with the cab at the rear, supported the rear of the M65. This trailing truck was designated the M250.

Prior to firing, specially engineered hydraulic hoisting equipment on each truck lowered the carriage and mount assembly to the ground. The trucks were then removed. After firing, the same equipment would lift and re-couple to gun carriage to the trucks. The two trucks could transport the weapon at speeds up to 35 mph. The unit as a whole can move forward, backward or sideways since either tractor unit can pull while the other pushes, or they can turn at right angles to the center section and proceed parallel to one another.

The T-10 transporter had a gross vehicle weight rating of was more than 85 tons. Length is 84 ft., 2 in.

The standard military tail lights and liquid container mounted on the rear of the trailing M250 provide another frame of reference to the size of these vehicles. (National Archives and Records Administration photo)

The M65 280mm Atomic Cannon, with its M249 and M250 transporter, was an imposing sight. (National Archives and Records Administration photo)

Not only were the M249 and M250 trucks broad and tall, but when coupled to the M65 mount, yielded a vehicle 84 ft. long. Off-road mobility was limited by not only weight and length, but also the very limited angle of departure. (National Archives and Records Administration photo)

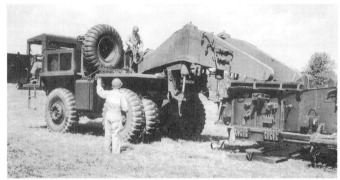

When emplacing the gun, both the tractors were disconnected. Seen here is the leading M249 being re-coupled to the field piece at the conclusion of training exercise. (National Archives and Records Administration photo)

Each tractor unit was powered by an Ordnance-Continental AO-895-4 air-cooled gasoline engine, which developed 375 gross hp.

A forward-facing driver steered each truck, but the front driver controlled the throttle and the brakes of the entire truck-carriage-truck combination.

GENERAL DATA

MODEL	M249	M250
NET WEIGHT	37,293 lbs.	35,341 lbs.
LENGTH	372.5	373.5
WIDTH	123.5	124
HEIGHT	116	103.75
TRACK	85.5	85.5
TIRE SIZE	16.00-25	16.00-25
MAX SPEED	30 mph	30 mph
FUEL CAPY	140 gal	140 gal
RANGE LOADED	150 mi	150 mi
ELECTRICAL	24 neg	24 neg
TRANSMISSION SPEEDS	3	3
AUX TRANS SPEEDS	3	3
TURNING RADIUS FT	40	40

Overall dimensions listed in inches.

GENERAL DATA

ENGINE MAKE/MODEL	Continental AO-895-4
NUMBER OF CYLINDERS	6
CUBIC-INCH DISPLACEMENT	895
HORSEPOWER	375 @ 2800 rpm
TORQUE	775 lbs.-ft. @ 2100 rpm

VALUES

VALUE: *Not enough sales data to report accurate pricing.*

SCARCITY

Scarcity 5

The trailing M250, in the foreground of this photo, was even more bizarre-looking when disconnected than when in train. The forward-facing cab sat at the rear of the vehicle, above the dual rear wheels, while the coupling device was located at the front, over the steering axle. Driving the M250 has been likened to being the tillerman on a big ladder truck. (National Archives and Records Administration photo)

G-861 GOER

During the 1950s, the U.S. Army needed a vehicle that combined increased off-road capability and a high load-carrying capacity. In 1956, the United States Army Armor Board began evaluating large, wheeled, earth moving equipment for potential tactical application. The board felt that these vehicles could be used as a basis for a new series of tactical vehicles.

In 1957, testing began on a number of commercial vehicles, all equipped with articulated steering. As a result of these tests, development contracts were awarded to Clark Equipment Le Tourneau-Westinghouse and Caterpillar for 4x4 all-terrain vehicles of various weight classes.

Clark supplied a prototype in the 5-ton weight class. Le Tourneau-Westinghouse three variants, cargo (XM437), tanker (XM438) and wrecker (XM554). All were in the 15-ton class, but none were placed in series production.

Caterpillar was the winner in this program, and in 1960 was awarded a $5 million contract to design, develop and build eight 8-ton cargo trucks. These were delivered during 1961 and 1962 for testing. In June 1962 two 10-ton wreckers and two 2,500-gallon tankers were added to the contract as well.

In May 1963, another contract was awarded to Caterpillar. The 13 cargo vehicles, eight tankers and two wreckers in this contract were destined to be service test

vehicles. These vehicles were delivered to units in Germany for extensive troop trials during 1964. At the end of the trial period, these were stored until 1966. At that time they were sent to Pleiku, Vietnam, to support the 4th Infantry Division.

In Vietnam the GOER was very successful, establishing a reputation for dependability and operating where no other vehicle could go. In May 1971, Caterpillar Tractor Co. was at last awarded a production contract. This contract was for the purchase 812 M520 cargo vehicles, 117 M553 wreckers, and 371 M559 tankers. Production began immediately, with final deliveries made in June 1976.

Like much of Caterpillar's earthmoving equipment, the GOER consisted of a front and a rear section. An articulated joint that permitted lateral oscillation up to 20 degrees and a steering angle up to 60 degrees connected the units.

The forward section had the cab, with seats for the driver on the left and the vehicle commander to his right, and the engine behind the crew area. The Goer had a moveable windshield and a typical military removable canvas top with separate side curtains.

The vehicle had a six-speed transmission. A short propeller shaft connected the driveline to the front differential and out to the planetary drives in the front hubs. The rear differential was driven through clutch and drive shafts and universals from the front differential. The final drives in the rear wheels are also planetary. The rear-wheels were automatically driven in first and second gears, but were automatically disconnected as the transmission shifted from second to third gear. The operator could manually override this automatic disengagement of the rear wheels if need be. The cargo bed of corrugated construction made up the bulk of the rear section of the cargo GOER. The bed had side and rear doors to allow rapid discharge of cargo. These doors had watertight seals to preserve the GOER's swimming ability. The large cargo area could transport six standard military pallets simultaneously, or one CONEX container and two pallets or 25 55-gallon drums. The standard military-type Gar Wood 10,000-lb.-capacity winch was recessed into the front panel of the cab. Some of the cargo trucks were fitted with a crane for loading and unloading, and were designated M877.

Amazingly, these vehicles were fully amphibious.

This M520 has been fitted with the hard cab typically found in the arctic kit. Its construction equipment lineage is apparent. (Photo courtesy of the Patton Museum)

Shown here is the prototype of the recovery variant, the XM553. The crane operator's station can be seen just behind the driver's station. (Photo courtesy of the Patton Museum)

Water propulsion was via their wheels. Like most U.S. wheeled vehicles, the GOER had special kits to customize it, including: an arctic kit, infra-red driving light kit, wheel chain kit, machine gun kit, and a trailer brake kit.

M553 Wrecker

The general arrangement of the M553 was very similar to that of the M520. However, rather than a cargo box as the second section, the M553 carried a variety of recovery equipment.

Among the recovery gear was a hydraulically operated crane with a maximum lifting capacity of 10,000 to 20,000 lbs., depending on the operating radius. The boom was 6 ft. long, and extendable to 16 ft. A hydraulic pump driven by the engine crankshaft operated the hydraulics. Manually operated outriggers were used to stabilize the truck during recovery operations.

Like the cargo trucks, the M553 also had the standard 10,000-lb. Front-mounted self-recovery winch.

M559 2,500-Gallon Fuel Tanker

The M559 was the tanker variant of the GOER family. It featured a 2,500-gallon stainless-steel tank, pump, military aircraft fuel filler, four pressure discharge outlets, three discharge houses and a large bulk outlet. It can discharge all three hoses simultaneously. The tanker also has a gravity discharge outlet for handling bulk fuel at storage sites.

GENERAL DATA

MODEL	M520	M553	M559
NET WEIGHT	25,430 lbs.	37,870 lbs.	28,100 lbs.
GROSS WEIGHT	41,400 lbs.	45,780 lbs.	46,550 lbs.
MAX TOWED LOAD	20,000 lbs.	20,000 lbs.	20,000 lbs.
LENGTH	380	401.75	375.75
WIDTH	108	108	108
HEIGHT	133.5	139.5	133.5
TRACK	86.5	86.5	86.5
TIRE SIZE	18.00 x 33	18.00 x 33	18.00 x 33
MAX SPEED LAND	30	30	30
MAX SPEED WATER	2.8	2.6	2.6
FUEL CAPY	106	106	106
RANGE	300	300	300
ELECTRICAL	24 neg	24 neg	24 neg
TRANSMISSION			
SPEEDS	6	6	6
TURNING			
RADIUS FT	52.7	52.7	52.7

Overall dimensions listed in inches.

ENGINE DATA

ENGINE MAKE/MODEL	Caterpillar D33T
NUMBER OF CYLINDERS	6
CUBIC-INCH DISPLACEMENT	638
HORSEPOWER	213 @ 2200 rpm
TORQUE	578 lbs.-ft. @ 1550 rpm

VALUES

VALUES: Too few of these vehicles have appeared on the market to establish accurate pricing.

SCARCITY

Scarcity 4

G-903 M746 Transporter

The M746 Heavy Equipment Transporter was a very large 22 1/2 ton 8x8 vehicle that was, along with its M747 trailer, intended to transport heavy tanks. Chrysler did the prototype work for this vehicle, but Ward LaFrance built the production units. Depending upon the source, somewhere between 125 and 200 of these trucks were built between 1973 and 1977. The tandem front axles steer, and are mounted on tapered leaf springs via walking beam bogies, as are the rear axles. High-flotation tires were used all around. The cab top could be removed and the windshield was hinged to fold down to lower shipping height for these vehicles.

This vehicle was replaced in the U.S. military inventory by the M911 C-HET after a relatively brief service life.

GENERAL DATA

MODEL	M746
NET WEIGHT	45,740 lbs.
MAX TRAIN WEIGHT	182,400 lbs.
LENGTH	332
WIDTH	165 reducible to 120
HEIGHT	128 reducible to 120
TRACK	101.625
TIRE SIZE	18 x 22.5, 22 ply
MAX SPEED	38.5 mph
FUEL CAPY	140 gal
RANGE LOADED	320 mi
ELECTRICAL	24 neg
TRANSMISSION	
SPEEDS	5 F
TURNING	
RADIUS FT	45

Overall dimensions listed in inches.

ENGINE DATA

ENGINE MAKE/MODEL	Detroit Deisel 12V71T
NUMBER OF CYLINDERS	12
CUBIC-INCH DISPLACEMENT	852
HORSEPOWER	600 @ 2500 rpm
TORQUE	1,470 lbs.-ft. @ 1600 rpm

VALUES

The M746 is a scarce vehicle that is expensive to operate. Insufficient sales data is available to establish collector's values.

The rounded trailing edge of the XM746 rear fenders was replaced with angular rear fenders on production models. A davit was provided to handle the spare tire. (Photo courtesy of the Patton Museum)

This is a pilot model of the XM746 shown doing what these trucks were intended to do — transport medium tanks over all types of terrain. (Photo courtesy of the Patton Museum)

The M746 was equipped with dual hydraulic winches that could be used to pull disabled tanks onto the deck of the trailer. This M746 is preserved at the Fourth Infantry Division Museum, Fort Hood, Texas.

This overhead view is also of the XM746, but the layout of the equipment remained essentially the same on production models. The absence of a rear view mirror on the passenger's side surely made reversing the behemoth challenging. (Photo courtesy of the Patton Museum)

This XM746 is fitted with a soft top over the crew compartment. Also visible is the amber hazard beacon and the various work floodlights. (Photo courtesy of the Patton Museum)

M911 Heavy Transporter

The M911 Commercial Heavy Equipment Transporter (C-HET) was developed in the mid-1970s as a replacement for the M746 and M123 series vehicles. The military wanted a new truck based on an existing commercial truck. The Oshkosh response was the XM911, which was based on its F2365. In September 1976, a contract for 747 vehicles was awarded to Oshkosh.

The M911 is a very large 8x6 vehicle with an air-suspended helper axle. This axle could be lowered for better weight distribution when the truck was heavily loaded. The trucks were powered by a V8 Detroit Diesel engine with the power being transferred to the axles via a five-speed Allison automatic transmission through a two-speed transfer case.

Behind the two-man steel cab there are two 45,000-lb.-capacity hydraulically driven winches for use when retrieving disabled tanks. The rope on these winches was 1 in. in diameter. Further back was a Holland four-way oscillating fifth wheel that accommodated 3.5-in. kingpins.

This M911 is shown coupled to its usual trailer, an M747. As expensive as this combination is to operate, it's a bargain compared to road marching a tank. Fully operational tanks were often transported by truck. (U.S. Army photo)

The Oshkosh-built M911 provided the Army with what it wanted at the time — a Commercial Heavy Equipment Transporter, C-HET. (U.S. Army photo)

MISCELLANEOUS TRUCKS

GENERAL DATA

MODEL	M911
NET WEIGHT	39,952
MAX TRAIN WEIGHT	191,952
LENGTH	369
WIDTH	98
HEIGHT	140
TRACK	82
TIRE SIZE	14.00-24
MAX SPEED	43.9
FUEL CAPY	150
RANGE LOADED	280
ELECTRICAL	24 neg
TRANSFER SPEEDS	2
TRANSMISSION SPEEDS	5 F
TURNING RADIUS FT	47.1

Overall dimensions listed in inches.

ENGINE DATA

ENGINE MAKE/MODEL	Detroit Deisel 8V92T
NUMBER OF CYLINDERS	8
CUBIC-INCH DISPLACEMENT	736
HORSEPOWER	430 @ 2100 rpm
TORQUE	1,223 @ 1400 rpm

VALUES

	6	5	4	3	2	1
All models	3,000	9,000	18,000	27,000	35,000	65,000

SCARCITY

Scarcity 3

In this view of the XM911, the helper axle has been lowered, as it would be when heavily loaded or in soft soil. The massive tires required the use of an on-board davit to lift the spare tire into position. (U.S. Army photo)

The long nose extending beyond the set-back front axle is evident in this overhead view. By setting back the front axle from the front of the truck, the turning radius was substantially reduced. (Photo courtesy of the Patton Museum)

This XM911 was photographed with its pneumatically controlled helper axle in the raised position, as it would be when unladen or lightly loaded. (Photo courtesy of the Patton Museum)

HEMTT

The M520 GOER series proved the need for a heavy tactical transport vehicle, but it was not suitable for on road use. The HEMTT was developed to provide a vehicle with the Goer's off-road mobility as well as rapid on road transit. After trials, in May 1981, the U.S. Army Tank Automotive Command awarded a $251.13 million five-year contract to the Oshkosh Truck Corporation for production of the 10-ton (U.S.) Heavy Expanded Mobility Tactical Truck (HEMTT). The first prototype was completed in December 1981, with first production vehicles delivered in September 1982.

The HEMTT design incorporated many components of Oshkosh's commercial truck line. These include the Oshkosh truck cab, standard eight-cylinder diesel engine, and a standard four-speed automatic transmission. Some of these components are also found in the similar Marine Corps Dragon Wagon (8x8) vehicles.

The chassis is made of heat-treated carbon manganese steel, which is bolted together with grade eight bolts to increase serviceability. All variations of the HEMTT have heavy-duty front bumper and skid plate, external hydraulic connection, service and emergency air brake connection, slave start connection and trailer electrical connector.

The HEMTT used a two-man two-door forward control cab, giving it an appearance unlike that of most U.S. military vehicles. The cab is of welded-steel construction and includes air-suspension seats for the driver and passenger, seat belts, tinted glass, and a heater and defroster.

Due to its size and weight, a davit is provided to lower the spare wheel from its position at the rear of the cab to the ground. All models of the HEMTT used the Oshkosh 46K front tandem axles, both of which steer. These axles include an inter-axle driver controlled differential, and the driver can disconnect the power to the front axles. These trucks have power-assisted steering.

The angular cab-forward design of the Oshkosh M977 HEMTT makes it look like one of the airport crash trucks built by the same firm than a military vehicle. (U.S. Army photo)

The knuckle-boom crane at the rear of the M977 HEMTT, along with its drop-side cargo body, makes the HEMTT a big improvement over previous military transports. (U.S. Army photo)

The backward rake of the lower portion of the cab gives the HEMTT a 43-degree angle of approach, which is important when operating off-road. (U.S. Army photo)

VARIANTS

M977 Cargo Truck

This is the base vehicle of the HEMTT family. These vehicles include a light-duty hydraulic material handling crane at the rear of the truck. These vehicles were built with and without a 20,000-lb.-capacity midships self-recovery winch that can be used for self-recovery at either the front or rear of the vehicle. The drop side cargo bed is 216 in. long.

M978 Tanker

The HEMTT fuel tanker has 2,500-gallon capacity, and like the cargo version was produced with and without self-recovery winch. It could be used to transport diesel and jet fuel.

M983 Tractor Truck

Known as the Light Equipment Transporter, the HEMTT tractor truck was built either with a self-recovery winch or a material handling crane just ahead of the fifth wheel.

M984 Wrecker

The 984 is similar in layout to the rest of the HEMTT series, but at the rear of the truck is a Grove 14,000-lb.-capacity recovery crane with 9-ft. boom. In addition to the vehicle's self-recovery winch, the M984 also has a 60,000-lb.-capacity drag winch. A small cargo area is provided to transport replacement power packs and other repair supplies.

The M978 tanker has off-road mobility characteristics similar to those of the M977 cargo trucks. (U.S. Army photo)

The M978 tanker truck can transport up to 2,500 gallons of gasoline, diesel, or jet fuel. The truck also has onboard dispensing equipment. (U.S. Army photo)

The M983 tractor has many uses, including towing the Patriot missile system. (U.S. Army photo)

GENERAL DATA

MODEL	M977	M978	M983	M984
WEIGHT*	38,800 lbs.	38,200 lbs.	36,000 lbs.	50,900 lbs.
LENGTH	400.5	400.5	350.5	392
WIDTH	96	96	96	96
HEIGHT	112	112	112	112
TRACK	79	79	79	79
CREW	2	2	2	2
TIRE SIZE	16.00 x R20	16.00 x R20	16.00 x R20	16.00 x R20
MAX SPEED	62 mph	62 mph	62 mph	62 mph
FUEL CAPY	155 gal	155 gal	155 gal	155 gal
RANGE	400 mi	400 mi	400 mi	400 mi
ELECTRICAL	24 neg	24 neg	24 neg	24 neg
TRANSMISSION				
SPEEDS	6F, 1R	6F, 1R	6F, 1R	6F, 1R
TRANSFER				
SPEEDS	2	2	2	2

Weight unladen

Overall dimensions listed in inches.

ENGINE DATA

ENGINE MAKE/MODEL	Detroit Diesel 8V92TA
NUMBER OF CYLINDERS	8
HORSEPOWER	445

VALUES

Current military issue, not commonly available on the collector market.

LARC

The LARC was developed to provide a means to get cargo from supply ships to points inland without benefit of an improved port. LARC stood for "Lighter Amphibious Resupply Cargo." Though many see this as a modern replacement for the World War II era DUKW, it was much larger. LARCs were developed in various sizes, but the LARC-V was the one most commonly seen. Two different firms, Consolidated Diesel Electric and LeTourneau-Westinghouse, built slightly different versions of the LARC-V.

The LARC was powered by a V8-300 Cummins diesel engine very similar to the engine in the M123A1C tractor. The engine was located at the rear of the hull and drove the vehicle through an automatic transmission. The entire body and hull were made of aluminum and more resembled a wheeled barge than a floating truck.

On the upper front of the vehicle was a crew cab that could be enclosed with either a hard or soft top. The steering controls were centered in the cab. The vehicle was quite complex and required extensive training to

Here is a LARC-V operating in the water, again loaded with a CONEX container. The water is calm, and the side curtains are lowered. A rear propeller drove the LARC in the water. (U.S. Army photo)

operate properly. The truck had hydraulic power steering. The engine was mounted in the rear of the vehicle, with the bell housing toward the front of the vehicle. A single-speed transmission was connected to a two-speed transfer case, which drove the four wheels by means of right-angle drives and planetary hubs.

The cargo area was the large flat space on the center deck, and side curtains were installed to protect cargo from the surf if need be. The load capacity of the LARC-V was 5 tons.

GENERAL DATA

MODEL	LARC-V
NET WEIGHT	19,000 lbs.
GROSS WEIGHT	30,000 lbs.
LENGTH	420
WIDTH	120
HEIGHT	122
TREAD	92
TIRE SIZES	18.00 x 25
MAX SPEED	
LAND	30 mph
WATER	9.5 mph
FUEL CAPY	144 gal
RANGE	250 mi
ELECTRICAL	24 neg
TRANSMISSION	
SPEEDS	1
TRANSFER	
SPEEDS	2
TURNING	
RADIUS FT	41.25

Overall dimensions listed in inches.

ENGINE DATA

ENGINE MAKE/MODEL	Cummins V8-300
NUMBER OF CYLINDERS	8
CUBIC-INCH DISPLACEMENT	785
HORSEPOWER	300 @ 3000 rpm

VALUES

Only a few LARCs have appeared on the collector market, making it impossible to determine values.

The LARC-V in the foreground is transporting an M38A1 Jeep, while the one in the background is carrying a Dodge M37. The LARC had no suspension system beyond its oversized tires. (U.S. Army photo)

This is a LeTourneau-Westinghouse LARC-V. It has been loaded with a CONEX container, and its side curtains have been raised in preparation for entering the water. (U.S. Army photo)

WHEELED ARMORED VEHICLES

G-067 M3A1 WHITE SCOUT CAR

The White M3A1 scout car was produced from 1940 until March 1944. Almost 21,000 chassis were built by the White Motor Company in Cleveland, Ohio, then driven to the Diebold Safe and Lock Company, also in Ohio. Diebold fabricated and installed the armor plating, which was 1/4-in. thick and face-hardened. After the armor was installed, the cars were driven back to the White plant for final assembly and inspection. Slightly more than half of these vehicles were supplied to other nations as foreign aid.

Armament was a variety of machine guns mounted by means of trolley and pintle to a skate rail that went completely around the interior of the fighting compartment. Since then, this skate rail has often been removed or the section above the doors cut out. Another frequent civilian modification is cutting a door in the rear armor.

With the canvas removed, the radios and armaments carried by the scout car, as well as the arrangement of the crew seats, are all visible. The right front seat was for the vehicle commander. Although scout cars weren't provided with winches, they all came with unditching rollers mounted on the front bumper. (Photo courtesy of the Patton Museum)

This 1939 Aberdeen Proving Ground photo of the M3A1 pilot model shows the protruding "greenhouse" windshield used on the earliest production vehicles. Also visible are the crossed swords of the cavalry on plaques mounted to the driver's door. Just ahead of the door is the chrome-plated spotlight. Both the latter details are repeated on the passenger's side of the vehicle. (National Archives and Records Adminstration photo)

During the course of production there were various detail changes. The right-hand mounted spotlight was eliminated in favor of a spare fuel can rack, the armored flap over the windshield was modified, and the crossed sword emblems removed from the doors.

The M3A1 was a relatively fast vehicle, but it was lacking in off-road performance when compared to tracked vehicles, and its open top left its crew vulnerable. By 1944, M3A1s were being sold as surplus.

The M3A1 was provided with a canvas covering, shown in this April 1944 Studebaker Proving Ground photo. Gone are the spotlights, externally stored collapsible canvas bucket, crossed sabers, and greenhouse-type windshield of the early models. Instead, there are liquid container carriers and removable windshield glasses. (U.S. Army photo)

White assembled the M3A1 scout car chassis, but the armored body was installed by the Diebold Safe and Lock Co. These chassis, shown at White's Cleveland plant, await transport to Diebold's facility for this work. Notice the large Willard batteries installed, and the unusual tread pattern of the tires. (Photo courtesy of Diebold, Inc.)

GENERAL DATA

MODEL	M3A1
WEIGHT*	9,100
LENGTH	221.5
WIDTH	80
HEIGHT	78.5
TREAD FRONT/REAR	63.25/65.25
CREW	6 TO 8
TIRE SIZES	8.25 x 20
MAX SPEED	50
FUEL CAPY	54
RANGE	250
ELECTRICAL	12 neg
TRANSMISSION SPEEDS	4F 1R
TRANSFER SPEEDS	2
TURNING RADIUS FT.	28
ARMAMENT	1x .50MG
	1x .30MG

Weight unladen

Overall dimensions listed in inches.

ENGINE DATA

ENGINE MAKE/MODEL	Hercules JXD
NUMBER OF CYLINDERS	6
CUBIC-INCH DISPLACEMENT	320
HORSEPOWER	86 @ 2800 rpm
TORQUE	200 lbs.-ft. @ 1150 rpm
GOVERNED SPEED (rpm)	2800

RADIO EQUIPMENT: *Communications was important in the reconnaissance role, and the M3A1 was normally equipped with one of the following sets of radio equipment: SCR-506 or SCR-508 or SCR-510.*

VALUES

	6	5	4	3	2	1
All models	2,500	4,000	8,000	16,000	23,000	28,000

G-136 M8 Greyhound

In June of 1942, design work for a wheeled gun motor carriage, including a rotating turret with a 37mm gun, had been completed, and the resulting 6x6 was designated T22E2. This T22E2 evolved into the M8.

Ford built 8523 the M8 armored cars in St. Paul from March 1943 until May 1945. It was designed to provide high-speed reconnaissance with reasonable protection for the crew. It was later dubbed the Greyhound by the British as a testament to its speed.

The M8 had self-sealing fuel tanks, which frequently deteriorated and have resulted in fuel-system problems for modern-day owners. The Greyhound was armed with a 37mm M6 anti-tank gun mounted in its open topped turret. An M1919A4 .30-caliber machine gun was mounted coaxial with the main gun — a .50-caliber M2 HB machine gun for defense against aircraft or infantry. Initially, the .50 mounted via a trolley and cradle to a M49 ring mount attached to the turret. Later models had a cast-steel socket attached to the rear of the turret, which accepted a pintle.

The racks holding three land mines on either side of the first vehicles were eventually replaced with large enclosed storage boxes. Another change during production was increasing the number of leaves on the front springs from 11 to 13.

The driver's controls had a conventional truck layout. The clutch and accelerator controls were both hydraulic assisted. Nowadays, this hydraulic system

The M8 was armed with a 37mm gun in its turret from the outset, and later models added a .50-caliber machine gun on the turret as well. This is an early vehicle, as evidenced by the mine rack on it side. (U.S. Army photo)

Later M8 models deleted the mine rack in favor of the stowage bin. The example on display at the Patton Museum, Fort Knox, Kentucky, has been restored in the markings of the postwar constabulary, which used these vehicles for patrol purposes. (Photo by D. Moss)

This M8 has the machine gun mount installed on it. A few vehicles were fitted with ring mounts, either at depot or field level, but the mount shown here was designed for this vehicle and was factory installed on much of the production. (Photo courtesy of the Patton Museum)

GENERAL DATA

MODEL	M8
WEIGHT**	14,500 lbs.
LENGTH	197
WIDTH	100
HEIGHT	90
TREAD FRONT/REAR*	67/85
CREW	4
TIRE SIZES	9.00-20
MAX SPEED	56 mph
FUEL CAPY	54 gal
RANGE	250 mi
ELECTRICAL	12 neg
TRANSMISSION SPEEDS	4F, 1R
TRANSFER SPEEDS	2
TURNING RADIUS FT.	28
ARMAMENT MAIN	37mm
SECONDARY	1x .30MG
	1x .50MG

**Weight unladen

*Inside/outside width at tires.

Overall dimensions listed in inches.

often leaks and is the source of frequent maintenance problems for collectors. It is often removed. Those desiring authenticity need to verify its presence when contemplating a purchase.

The hull of the M8 was of welded construction, while the turret was a steel casting.

The crew of four also was armed with 12 hand grenades, six anti-tank mines, 400 rounds of .30-caliber M1 carbine ammo, 1,575 rounds of .30-caliber machine gun ammo, 420 rounds of .50-machine gun ammo, and 50 to 80 rounds (depending upon production date) for the main gun.

The U.S. military used M8s as late as the Korean War, while the French used them in Indochina/Vietnam.

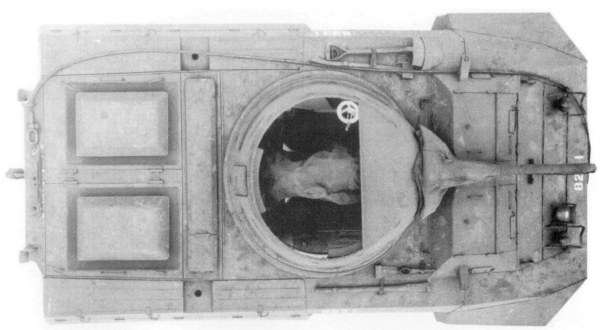

The turret of the M8 was open topped. The breach has been fitted with a canvas cover in this photo, but the dual hatches for the engine compartment are visible. (U.S. Army photo)

When they left the factory, both the M8 and M20 were fitted with hinged fenders on all four wheels. However, these were susceptible to damage and often were removed, either intentionally or accidentally. (U.S. Army photo)

ENGINE DATA

ENGINE MAKE/MODEL	Hercules JXD
NUMBER OF CYLINDERS	6
CUBIC INCH DISPLACEMENT	320
HORSEPOWER	86 @ 2800 rpm
TORQUE	200 lbs.-ft. @ 1,150 rpm
GOVERNED SPEED (rpm)	2800

RADIO EQUIPMENT: *Communications were important in the reconnaissance role, and the M8 was normally equipped with one of the following sets: (SCR-506 or SCR-193T or AN/GRC-9), (SCR-506 or SCR-193T or SCR-608B or RC-99), (SCR-506 or SCR-193T or AN/GRC-9 or SCR-694C and SCR-619 or SCR-610), and (RC-99; or SCR-169 or SCR-610), and (RC-99).*

VALUES

	6	5	4	3	2	1
All models	2,500	4,000	8,000	16,000	23,000	28,000

G-176 M20 Armored Utility Car

Like the M8, the M20 was a six-wheeled armored car built by Ford at its St. Paul plant. The first of the 3,791 of these high-speed personnel carriers was produced in July 1943.

The M20 was also designed to be used as an armored transport for field commanders. Unlike its brother the M8, the M20 had no turret and was an open-topped vehicle. A .50-caliber M2 HB machine gun was used for defense against aircraft or infantry. This gun was mounted via a trolley and cradle to a ring mount attached to the top of the hull. Units built prior to August 1944 were equipped with the ring mount M49, while those built after that date had the improved mount M66. Like the M8, the mine racks of the early M20s were replaced by large storage lockers before production ended in June 1945.

The crew of six also was armed with 12 hand

**1954 M38A1
(RESTORED BY ERIC TEDESCHI)**

**1977 DODGE M886
(OWNED BY LARRY HERMAN)**

**1942 WC58
(RESTORED BY
JOHN BIZAL)**

1944 HALFTRACK M3
(RESTORED BY PAUL BENSON)

**M996 TWO-LITTER
ARMORED
AMBULANCE**

(OWNED BY U.S. ARMY)

1952 M42

**(OWNED BY KEVIN
KRONLUND)**

XM706 ARMORED CAR
(FORT MCCOY, WISCONSIN)

M923A2 5-TON TRUCK
(OWNED BY U.S. ARMY)

1951 WILLYS M38
(RESTORED BY GARY WIRTH)

**1941 WC4
(RESTORED BY JOHN BIZAL)**

**1945 US6
6X4-48**

**(OWNED BY
GUY, CHRIS,
AND LYN
JENSEN)**

**1973 M35A2C AND
1970 S280 SHELTER**

(OWNED BY DAVID BUNDY)

M60A1 ARMORED VEHICLE LAUNCHED BRIDGE (AVLB)

(OWNED BY U.S. ARMY)

M6 HIGH-SPEED TRACTOR

(OWNED BY THE MARSHALL MUSEUM, ZWYNDRECHT, HOLLAND)

1945 AIR-PORTABLE CCKW CARGO DUMP

(OWNED BY KEVIN KRONLUND)

M5A1 HIGH-SPEED TRACTOR, M19 TRUCK TRAILER, AND M20 DIAMOND T

(OWNED BY JOSEPH J. GARBARINO)

1943 GPA

(AL ALLEN)

1945 US6 (LEFT) AND 1945 CCKW 352 SWB

(RESTORED BY KEVIN KRONLUND)

1968 M274

(RESTORED BY JOHN EMERY)

1962 M37

(RESTORED BY HAROLD STANNARD)

1953 R2 CRASH TRUCK

(RESTORED BY MIKE FEATHERS)

grenades, three anti-tank mines, 500 rounds of .30-caliber M1 carbine ammo, and 1,050 rounds .50-caliber machine gun ammo.

Communications was important in the reconnaissance role, and the M20 was normally equipped with one of the following sets: (SCR-506 or SCR-694C or AN/GRC-9) and (SCR-506 or SCR-608 or SCR-510 or SCR-619 or SCR-610), or (AN/VRC-3), or (AN/VRC-3), or (AN/GRC-3,-4,-5,-6,-7, or –8) and (SCR-506).

GENERAL DATA

MODEL	M20
WEIGHT**	12,250 lbs.
LENGTH	197
WIDTH	100
HEIGHT	91
TREAD FRONT/REAR*	67/85
CREW	6
TIRE SIZES	9.00-20
MAX SPEED	56 mph
FUEL CAPY	54 gal
RANGE	250 mi
ELECTRICAL	12 neg
TRANSMISSION SPEEDS	4F, 1R
TRANSFER SPEEDS	2
TURNING RADIUS FT.	28
ARMAMENT MAIN SECONDARY	1x .50MG, 1x .30MG, 1x .50MG

**Weight unladen
*Inside/outside width at tires.
Overall dimensions listed in inches.

ENGINE DATA

ENGINE MAKE/MODEL	Hercules JXD
NUMBER OF CYLINDERS	6
CUBIC INCH DISPLACEMENT	320
HORSEPOWER	86 @ 2800 rpm
TORQUE	200 lbs.-ft.@ 1150 rpm
GOVERNED SPEED (rpm)	2800

VALUES

	6	5	4	3	2	1
All models	5,000	15,000	25,000	35,000	45,000	55,000

An overhead view shows the interior arrangement of the M20 fighting compartment, as well as the temporary windshields, complete with wipers, which could be used by the driver and his assistant. (U.S. Army photo)

Two-piece hatches were provided for the driver and assistant driver on both the M8 and the M20. The tow cable can be seen here. The M20 had its machine gun mounted on a ring mount. (U.S. Army photo)

The M20, like the M8, started out with mine racks like those shown here, but they were eventually converted over to the stowage bins. (Photo courtesy of Patton Museum)

The prototypes of the Commando, and the initial pilot models, had wheel wells cut out in an angular shape as seen here. Later models had rounded wheel wells. The turret of this XM706 was armed with a .30-caliber and a .50-caliber machine gun. Notice the flat-type hatches and protruding periscopes around the hull. (Photo courtesy of the Patton Museum)

G-392 Cadillac Gage Commando

The prototype of the Cadillac Gage V-100 was first tested in June 1962. This armored 4x4 vehicle was powered by a Chrysler 361, similar to the engine fitted to the M113 at that time. The axles are similar to the axles used on M35 cargo trucks, but they have locking differentials. The 14.00-20 tires have a special tread with a run-flat design.

A 10,000-lb.-capacity hydraulically operated winch was mounted internally at the front of the vehicle. The fenders on the pilot models were cut out in an angular manner, while later vehicles had rounded fenders. There was no provision for deepwater fording because the vehicles were completely amphibious without preparation.

Procurement of these vehicles began in 1964, with many of them destined for Vietnam. Their designation was XM706. The first units produced retained the

The XM706E2 lacked the turret of the XM706, instead having an open-top compartment on the roof. The XM706E2 was the version of the V-100 that was most popular with the Air Force. (Photo courtesy of the Patton Museum)

This XM706 is displayed at Fort Leonard Wood, Missouri. The tires were developed specifically for the Commando, and even have "Commando" imprinted in them. The wheel wells are rounded, and the periscopes of the pilot models have given way to vision blocks.

The horn was mounted on the passenger's side of Commando beside the headlight. The firing port is located between the front vision blocks, and the winch is offset rather than centered on the hull. (Photo courtesy of Tacticaltruck.com)

This XM706 is armed with a pair of .30-caliber machine guns in its turret. The Commandos were equipped with self-recovery winches. The rope and guides are visible at the front of the hull.

Although not frequently seen with towed loads, the Commando nevertheless had a pintle hook on the rear of the hull. The rear door is barely visible in this photo on the left rear of the hull. (Photo courtesy of Tacticaltruck.com)

The standardized M706 differed from the XM706 by having one less vision block and firing port on each side, as well as roof hatches for the driver that were raised slightly above the surface of the hull.

The XM706E2, which was popular with the Air Force, is basically an M706 with an armored box in place of the turret, much like the relationship between the earlier M8 and M20 armored cars.

GENERAL DATA

MODEL	XM706	M706	XM706E2
WEIGHT**	13,800 lbs.	13,800 lbs.	13,300 lbs.
LENGTH	224	224	224
WIDTH	89	89	89
HEIGHT	96	96	96
TREAD*	73.5	73.5	73.5
CREW	Up to 11	Up to 11	Up to 11
TIRE SIZES	14.00-20	14.00-20	14.00-20
MAX SPEED	60 mph	60 mph	60 mph
FUEL CAPY	80 gal	80 gal	80 gal
RANGE	400 mi	400 mi	400 mi
ELECTRICAL	24 neg	24 neg	24 neg
TRANSMISSION SPEEDS	5F, 1R	1R, 5F	1R, 5F

The Commando had doors in either side of the hull, as well as in the rear of the vehicle. Notice the unusual brush guards protecting the headlights. (Photo courtesy of Tacticaltruck.com)

angular fender cutouts of the prototypes. These soon gave way on the production line to the rounded fender cutouts. The turret could mount various combinations of machine guns, such as a pair of .30-caliber guns, or one .30-and one .50-caliber, or 7.62mm machine guns instead of the .30s.

TRANSFER SPEEDS	1	1	1
TURNING RADIUS FT.	27	27	27

**Weight unladen
* Width at tires.
Overall dimensions listed in inches.

ENGINE DATA

ENGINE MAKE/MODEL	Chrysler 75M
NUMBER OF CYLINDERS	8
CUBIC INCH DISPLACEMENT	361
HORSEPOWER	191 @ 4000 rpm
TORQUE	325 lbs.-ft. @ 2400 rpm

RADIO EQUIPMENT: *Communications was important in the reconnaissance role, and the Commando was normally equipped with one of the following sets: AN/GRC-8 or AN/VRC-10 or AN/VRC-34.*

VALUES

	6	5	4	3	2	1
All models	5,000	15,000	25,000	35,000	45,000	55,000

SCARCITY

Scarcity 4

LAV

The LAV was built by General Motors of Canada, and is based on a design by Motorwagenfabrik AG (MOWAG) of Switzerland. Completely amphibious, it is powered by the Detroit Diesel 6V53T diesel engine, which gives it a top speed of 60 mph on the road or 6 mph in the water. Although originally intended to by an Army (M1047) item, it has instead become a staple of the Marine Corps armored force, which began purchasing the LAV-25 in 1982. During operation Desert Storm, the Army borrowed 15 LAVs from the Marine Corps. They were deployed as a platoon by the 3/73rd Armor of the 82nd Airborne.

The front four wheels are used to steer. The LAV has selectable eight- or four-wheel drive. In the latter case the rear four are driven. In the water two propellers drive the Piranha. The engine is mounted on the right front, with the driver and winch on the left front.

The basic vehicle, the LAV-25, is armed with the 25mm M242 gun. There is also space on board for 4 to 6 infantrymen.

Other versions have been produced as well. The LAV-C2 is a battalion command and control vehicle. This vehicle does not have a turret, and the rear hull roof has been raised to provide more space inside. Fifty LAV-C2s were produced from January to May 1987. Between September 1985 and December 1986 the Marines purchased 50 LAV-M mortar carriers, which are armed with an 81mm M252 mortar. There is a three-section folding panel in the roof that the mortar fires through.

The TOW missile carrier in this series is the LAV-AT, which has a two-tube missile launcher turret. From January to June of 1987, 96 of these vehicles were manufactured. As with many families of vehicles, there is a recovery version of the LAV — the LAV-R. The LAV-R has a 30,000-lb. drag winch, and a 6,600-lb. capacity hydraulic crane. Only 46 LAV-Rs were produced, all between May 1986 and June 1987. The truck version, known as a logistics vehicle, is known as an LAV-L. It has a raised, opening roof, and a chain hoist for handling cargo. It was in production from November 1985 until August 1986, with a total of 94 vehicles built. Twelve electronic warfare vehicles were built and are known as MEWSS, Mobile Electronic Warfare Support System. The last of these vehicles to be built were the 17 LAV-AD air defense vehicles, which are armed with a 25mm GAU-12 Bushmaster Gatling gun and two quadruple Stinger missile launchers.

GENERAL DATA

MODEL	LAV-25	LAV-C2	LAV-AT
WEIGHT**	24,470 lbs.	23,980 lbs.	24,850 lbs.
LENGTH	252.6	259	251.6
WIDTH	98.4	98.4	98.4
HEIGHT	100.9	110	106
TREAD FRONT/REAR*	85.8/86.8	85.8/86.8	85.8/86.8
CREW	3	7	4
TIRE SIZES	11.00-6	11.00-16	11.00-16
MAX SPEED	62	62	62
FUEL CAPY	71	71	71
RANGE	400	400	400
ELECTRICAL	24 neg	24 neg	24 neg
TRANSMISSION SPEEDS	5F, 1R	5F, 1R	5F, 1R
TRANSFER SPEEDS	1	1	1
TURNING RADIUS FEET	25.5	25.5	25.5
ARMAMENT MAIN	25mm	1x 7.62 MG	2x TOW
SECONDARY			Missile Launchers

MODEL	LAV-M	LAV-R	LAV-L
WEIGHT**	23,520 lbs.	24,980 lbs.	22,760 lbs.
LENGTH	251.6	256	254.6
WIDTH	98.4	98.4	98.4
HEIGHT	84.3	106	109
TREAD FRONT/REAR*	85.8/86.8	85.8/86.8	85.8/86.8
CREW	5	3	3
TIRE SIZES	11.00-16	11.00-16	11.00-16

The base LAV-25 turret houses a 25mm M242 gun. A small group of infantrymen can be carried inside. Notice that the tires on both leading axles steer. (U.S. Army photo)

MAX SPEED	62	62	62
FUEL CAPY	71	71	71
RANGE	400	400	400
ELECTRICAL	24 neg	24 neg	24 neg
TRANSMISSION			
SPEEDS	5F, 1R	5F, 1R	5F, 1R
TRANSFER			
SPEEDS	1	1	
TURNING			
RADIUS FEET	25.5	25.5	25.5
ARMAMENT MAIN			
SECONDARY	1x 81mm mortar	1x 7.62 MG	1x 7.62 MG

**Weight unladen*

Inside/outside width at tires.

Overall dimensions listed in inches.

ENGINE DATA

ENGINE MAKE/MODEL	**Detroit Diesel 6V53T**
NUMBER OF CYLINDERS	6
CUBIC-INCH DISPLACEMENT	318
HORSEPOWER	275 @ 2800 rpm
TORQUE	586 lbs.-ft. @ 2000 rpm

VALUES

Current issue

M93 Fox

The M93 Fox is the U.S. version of the German Fuchs. The Fox is a nuclear, biological and chemical reconnaissance vehicle. A mass spectrometer mounted in the vehicle analyzes samples of air and soil for the presence of these agents. Although they had been contracted for prior to Desert Storm, none of the 48 vehicles had been delivered, so the German government transferred 60 of its vehicles to the U.S. Army.

The M93A1 has improved detection equipment, including the M21 remote sensing chemical agent alarm system. The crew of the M93A1 is three men, one fewer than the M93.

GENERAL DATA

MODEL	M93A1
WEIGHT*	39,200
LENGTH	286.8
WIDTH	117.6
HEIGHT	104.4
CREW	3
MAX SPEED LAND	65
MAX SPEED WATER	6
FUEL CAPACITY	86
RANGE	510
ELECTRICAL	24 neg
TRANSMISSION	
SPEEDS	6

Weight unladen

Overall dimensions listed in inches.

ENGINE DATA

ENGINE MAKE/MODEL	**Daimler-Benz OM 402A**
NUMBER OF CYLINDERS	8
CUBIC-INCH DISPLACEMENT	762
HORSEPOWER	320 @ 2500 RPM

VALUES

Current issue

The M93 Fox is the U.S. version of the German Fuchs NBC vehicle. The base vehicle is the Thyssen Henschel TPz1 armored personnel carrier, which was adapted to a NBC detection role by German forces, then adopted by the U.S. military. (U.S. Army photo)

Section Two:
TRAILERS

1/4-TON TRAILERS

G-529 Trailers

The 1/4-ton trailer is one of the most popular accessories for the Jeep enthusiast, and the most popular versions to couple behind a WWII Jeep are the Willys MB-T and the Bantam T3.

While the Jeep had many impressive characteristics, it was short on cargo capacity. This need was filled by the Quartermaster Corps. which produced 12 pilot models of a 1/4-ton trailer in 1941. After trials, the design was finalized and production contracts awarded to Bantam and Willys. Many people feel that the Bantam award was consolation for it not being made the prime contractor for the Jeep. Willys assigned its model number MB-T (as in MB trailer), while Bantam used the code T3.

Both the Bantam and the Willys used the same type 6.00 x 16 tire and wheel assemblies as were used on the Jeep, with a matching 6-volt electrical system. There were differences between the two brands. The most easily spotted difference was Bantam's use of Gabriel shock absorbers secured with nuts. But on the other hand, Willys used Monroe shocks held on by cotter pins, just as it did on its 1/4-ton trucks. The axle on the Bantam was a solid tube, while the Willys were seamed in the middle.

Late in the war other firms were contracted to build these trailers as well. Among the other builders were Adam Black, Checker, Converto, Crosley, Fruehauf, Gemco, Pacific Fabricating, Springfield Wagon, Strick, Utility, and Transportation Equipment. Production by these firms, plus Bantam and Willys, totaled over 140,000 trailers.

Although often added by civilian owners, and in fact a feature of some of the post-war Bantam production, none of the WWII military trailers were equipped with a tailgate. The WWII trailer is often and easily confused with the post-war M100. However, like the post-war M38 and M38A1, the M100 had 7.00-16 tires and a 24-volt electrical system. Also, the M100 had handles on each of its corners. These trailers are water tight and fully amphibious without preparation.

GENERAL DATA

MODEL	MBT T3
WEIGHT NET	550 lbs.
MAX GROSS	1,550 lbs.
LENGTH	108.5
WIDTH	56
TRACK WIDTH	
INSIDE/OUTSIDE	43/55
TIRES NO. & SIZE	2 6.00-16
BRAKES	parking only
ELECTRICAL	6 or 12 volt

Overall dimensions listed in inches.

VALUES

	6	5	4	3	2	1
G-529 trailer	200	350	550	850	1,200	1,500

SCARCITY

Scarcity 3

This June 1945 Studebaker Proving Ground photo shows a factory-fresh Bantam 1/4-ton trailer. Notice the style of parking brake handle and lack of handgrips on the corners of the bed. These are the characteristics that most readily distinguish the WWII vintage trailer from the postwar M100. (U.S. Army photo)

A tarpaulin was available to protect the contents of the Bantam trailer from the elements. This trailer had its cover fitted when this photograph was taken at Holabird Quartermaster Depot. (National Archives and Records Administration photo)

Willys also produced a 1/4-ton trailer, using bodies supplied by Central Manufacturing. The axle of the Willys trailer differed from that used on the Bantam-built product. (U.S. Army photo)

Willys MB-T trailers had lights and reflectors on the rear, and were fully amphibious, allowing operation behind the GPA as well. (U.S. Army photo)

G-747 M100

When the M-series trucks were introduced, in many cases a new companion trailer was introduced as well. This allowed not only a commonality of 24-volt electrical systems, but in many cases interchangeability of tires, rims, hubs, and brake parts as well. In the case of the new Jeeps, the M38 and M38A1, the new matching trailer was the M100.

The M100 very much resembled the WWII-era MBT,

but was definitely a different unit. One of the most noticeable differences between the M100 and the WWII trailer are the handles on each of the four corners of the M100.

The M100 was a two-wheel general-purpose cargo carrier designed to carry a load of 500 lbs. cross-country on land or water. The body and frame were of one-piece welded construction mounted on a trailer chassis M115. Two drain valves were provided, one in the front, and one in the rear of the floor, to allow water out of the trailer

The early M100 trailers had a box on the front panel, which is often referred to as an intervehicular cable box. However, the manual says the box was designed to stow the tarpaulin. Notice the difference also in the design of the parking brake lever when compared to that of the G-529 series trailers. (U.S. Army photo)

The large interior chests that differentiated the M367 from the M100 can be seen in this view. (U.S. Army photo)

The M100 is quickly distinguished from its WWII counterpart by the handle on each corner of the trailer. (U.S. Army photo)

Later production M100 trailers omitted the stowage box. The landing gear leg was to be swung up and to the rear when the trailer was coupled to its towing vehicle. (U.S. Army photo)

body. These valves had to be closed for fording.

The trailer was equipped with two 24-volt taillights that were operated from the towing vehicle. A cable was provided for connecting the trailer electrical system with the towing vehicle.

The support leg is a movable support that was used to keep the trailer upright when the trailer was not connected to a towing vehicle. A canvas tarpaulin that fastened to hooks welded to the body was provided to cover the trailer top. A metal box was mounted on the left-front body panel of early models. This was used to store the tarpaulin when it was not in use. A hand lever, similar to the one used on M-series 6x6 trucks, was mounted on the right-front body panel and was used to lock the brakes when parking the trailer.

One unusual variation of the G-747 was the Trailer, Maintenance: Telephone Cable Splicer 1/4 ton, Two-wheel M367. These M100s were modified by the installation of two large tool cabinets to carry Signal Corps tools and equipment in the cargo body.

GENERAL DATA

MODEL	M100
WEIGHT NET	565 lbs.
MAX GROSS	1,315 lbs.
LENGTH	108.5
WIDTH	56.25
HEIGHT	42
TRACK WIDTH	
INSIDE/OUTSIDE	42/56
TIRES NO. & SIZE	2 7.00-16
BRAKES	parking only

ELECTRICAL   24 volt
Overall dimensions listed in inches.

VALUES

	6	5	4	3	2	1
M100	200	400	650	900	1,200	1,500

SCARCITY

Scarcity 2

G-857 M416

The M416 was the last of a long line of 1/4-ton trailers, ranging back to the WWII-era G-529. The G-857 series trailers had angular fenders, rather than the rounded fenders used previously. The M416 was a 1/4-ton, two-wheel general-purpose cargo carrier designed to carry a load of 500 lbs. cross-country. The body was of one-piece welded construction, and was bolted to its chassis at 14 lug locations. The M416 chassis was the 1/4-ton two-wheel M569.

The body was watertight and would float the trailer and a 500-lb. load during fording operations. Two drain valves were provided one in the left front, and one in the right rear of the floor, to allow rainwater to escape the trailer. These valves were closed for fording operations. The trailer was equipped with two taillights that were operated by the towing vehicle's electrical system, as are the directional signals. An intervehicular cable was provided for connecting the trailer electrical system with that of the towing vehicle. An "A" frame drawbar was bolted to the frame side members. It served as a mount for the lunette and the support leg. The support leg was a movable support that was used to keep the trailer upright when the trailer was not connected to a towing vehicle. A canvas tarpaulin, which fastened to hooks welded to the body, was provided to cover the trailer cargo. The trailer was designed specifically to be towed by truck, utility: 1/4-ton, 4x4, M151. A two-position bracket for the trailer lunette also makes the trailer

Like all the U.S. military's 1/4-ton trailers, the M416 was fully amphibious, with the hull-like shape of the body performing well in water. (U.S. Army photo)

The M416A1 had an overrunning brake system that the earlier trailers lacked. The system was controlled and distinguished by the large box that attached to the lunette.

One of the scarcest versions of the G-857 family is this M716 cable splicer variant. It differed from the standard M416 by having permanently installed large tool chests in the bed. (U.S. Army photo)

adaptable to being towed by truck, utility: 1/4-ton, 4x4, lightweight, M422.

Anthony, American Air Filter, Stevens, Parkhurst, Johnson Furnace, and Fayette built the M416.

The M416A1 was an improved model that featured an inertia-type overrunning brake. Parkhurst built the M416A1.

Like the M100/M367, there was a Signal Corps version of the M416. It was known as the M716, and was essentially an M416 with tool boxes mounted in the bed.

GENERAL DATA

MODEL	M416
NET WEIGHT	570 lbs.
MAX GROSS	1,320 lbs.
LENGTH	108.5
WIDTH	60.5
HEIGHT	42
TIRES NO. & SIZE	2 7.00 x 16
BRAKES	parking only
ELECTRICAL	24 volt

Overall dimensions listed in inches.

VALUES

	6	5	4	3	2	1
All models	200	350	450	700	850	1,000

SCARCITY

Scarcity 1

The M416 was slightly wider than its predecessor trailers, but the quickest way to distinguish it is the flat-topped angular fenders. This trailer has been modified with a spare tire under the bottom, and a flat steel cover over the cargo area. (Photo courtesy of TacticalTruck.com)

3/4-TON TRAILERS

G-748 M101

The 3/4-ton two-wheel trailer series G-748 was originally developed as a companion for the M37-type trucks. However, this trailer series went on to serve with the M715, the M880, and CUCV series vehicles.

These trailers were built to transport varied types of loads on highway as well as cross-country. At the rear a flat tailgate was hinged to the body. Two handbrake levers at the front of the body could be used to independently lock each of the trailer wheels. A drawbar assembly with lunette was attached to the front of the chassis. A retractable pivoted front support leg was attached to the drawbar bracket, and two taillights were mounted at the rear of the chassis under the body of the trailer.

The M101A1 was almost the same trailer as the M101, but it was slightly different dimensionally, and had an improved electrical system.

The M101A2 used an M116A2 chassis. Like its predecessors, it used a straight axle, but the A2's wheels lug pattern matched that of the M880. It was also equipped with tubeless tires. The M101A2 also introduced the inertia-actuated service brake system to the 3/4-ton trailer series. Many of the M101A2 trailers

also had U-bolt lifting hooks mounted in the trailer sills. The M101A3 had all the features of the M101A2, used an offset axle, and was often towed with a HMMWV.

The G-748 was also the basis for some specialized trailers.

The height of the M101 could be extended with wood-slat sideboards, which were gated at the tailgate. (National Archives and Records Administration photo)

This October 1951 Aberdeen Proving Ground photo of an M101 coupled to an M37 truck shows the trailer with its tarpaulin installed. (National Archives and Records Administration photo)

GENERAL DATA

MODEL	M101
WEIGHT NET	1,340 lbs.
MAX GROSS	3,590 lbs.
LENGTH	147
WIDTH	73.5
TRACK WIDTH	
INSIDE/OUTSIDE	52/72
TIRES NO. & SIZE	2 9.00-16
BRAKES	parking only
ELECTRICAL	24 volt

Overall dimensions listed in inches.

VALUES

	6	5	4	3	2	1
All models	200	400	600	800	1,100	1,500

SCARCITY

Scarcity   2

The ANNMQ1 was a specialized antenna trailer based on the G-748. (Photo courtesy of TacticalTruck.com)

The early G-748 trailers, like this 1967 M101A1, used the same tires and wheels as the Dodge M37 truck. (U.S. Army photo)

1-TON TRAILERS

G-518

The 1-ton cargo trailers were developed initially under the direction of the Quartermaster Corps and the design was standardized in October 1942.

The trailers were intended to be towed by the 1 1/2-ton 4x4 and 2 1/2-ton 6x6 trucks, but in service were towed by vehicles ranging from 3/4-ton trucks on up to track-laying vehicles.

Initially these trailers were of all-steel construction and were built by Nash-Kelvinator, Checker Cab, Gerstenslager, and Ben-Hur.

In June 1942, due to the shortage of steel, the body of the trailer was changed to wooden construction. Simultaneously, the number of builders increased significantly, becoming too extensive to list here. The first wood-bodied trailer was delivered in May 1943, but before the war ended construction reverted to all steel.

GENERAL DATA

MODEL	G-518
WOOD BODY	
WEIGHT NET	1,300 lbs.
MAX GROSS	4,300 lbs.
STEEL BODY	
NET WEIGHT	1,490 lbs.
MAX GROSS	4,300 lbs.
LENGTH OVERALL	145.5
WIDTH	71.125
TRACK WIDTH	
INSIDE/OUTSIDE	51/67
TIRES NO. & SIZE	2 7.50-20
BRAKES	parking only
ELECTRICAL	6 volt

Overall dimensions listed in inches.

VALUES

	6	5	4	3	2	1
G-518 1-ton trailer	300	700	900	1,200	1,500	1800

SCARCITY

Scarcity 2

This trailer built by Hobbs and is representative of the all-steel 1-ton trailers produced toward the end of WWII. (U.S. Army photo)

G-527 Water Trailer

This 1-ton, two wheel, 250-gallon water trailer was developed by the Quartermaster Corps to transport drinking water to troops in the field. It was designed to be towed by vehicles 3/4 ton and up.

Initial production units had baffled steel tanks with a bitumastic interior coating. The tank interior proved to be difficult to clean and the tank material was changed to aluminum in April 1944. The 250-gallon water trailer used the same chassis as the 1-ton cargo trailer, and camouflage kits were available to disguise the tankers as simple cargo trailers.

A hand-operated pump was mounted on the front of the tank for use dispensing the water.

Builders of these trailers included Ben-Hur, Checker Cab, and Springfield Auto Works.

GENERAL DATA

MODEL	KWT
STEEL TANK	
NET WEIGHT	1,500 lbs.
MAX GROSS	3,500 lbs.
ALUM TANK	
NET WEIGHT NET	1,350 lbs.
MAX GROSS	3,350 lbs.
LENGTH	136.5
WIDTH	71.125
TRACK WIDTH	
INSIDE/OUTSIDE	51/67
TIRES NO. & SIZE	2 7.50-20
BRAKES	parking only
ELECTRICAL	6 volt

Overall dimensions listed in inches.

VALUES

	6	5	4	3	2	1
G-527 water trailer	300	600	800	900	1,000	1,500

SCARCITY

Scarcity 3

This Ben-Hur-built water tanker has the supports in place for a tarpaulin, which acts as camouflage to disguise this as a cargo trailer. Any specialized equipment, be it trucks or trailers, seemed to draw an unusual amount of enemy fire, so efforts were made to create a uniform appearance with normal cargo-carrying vehicles. The hand-operated dispensing pump can be seen mounted on the front of the tank. (U.S. Army photo)

1 1/2-TON TRAILERS

G-754 M104

These trailers were part of the postwar Army modernization program, and they replaced the WWII-era 1-ton trailers. These were 1 1/2 ton, two-wheel trailers designed to be towed by a 2 1/2-ton, 6x6 truck equipped with a towing pintle and with a corresponding tire size.

Cargo Trailers M104 and M104A1 and water Tank Trailers M106 and M106A1 have 11:00-20 tires and were towed by M34 and M135 trucks. All other models have 9:00-20 tires and were towed by 2 1/2-ton trucks with the same size tires.

These trailers were designed to be towed over improved roads with a load of 5,500 lbs. at speeds up to 50 mph, and over unimproved roads and average terrain with loads up to 3,000 lbs. and speeds up to 30 mph. They were designed for fording hard-bottom water crossings where the trailer will be completely submerged.

M104

The cargo trailers M104 and M104A1 had seven welded cross-members and a boss welded to two.short cross-members at the front of the frame.

The M104-type trailers were of welded-plate construction. The wheel housing were welded into the body. The body had both a rear and a front tailgate. They were hinged at the floor line and were latched in closed position by hooks of the welded tailgate chains.

Cargo trailer M104 used the 1 1/2-ton, two-wheel, M102 trailer; the M104A1 used chassis M102A1, and the M104A2 used the M102A3 chassis. The M104A1 was the same as the M104, except that the M104A1 did not have a front tailgate, and the body had gusset-type posts in its

The M104 was unusual in that, in addition to the normal tailgate at the rear of the trailer, it also had a front gate. (U.S. Army photo)

sides and a tapered box type at the front and rear.

The front caster could be raised and locked in a mounting bracket, which was welded to the nose of the chassis frame and had a locking handle.

The M105 series lacked a front gate, and also had different reinforcements in the side of the trailer. The trailer shown here is a new M105A2. (U.S. Army photo)

M105

The M105A1 cargo trailer used the M103A1 trailer chassis. The M105A2 cargo trailer used the M103A3 trailer chassis, and the M105A2C cargo trailer used the M103A3C trailer chassis.

All of these trailers were used to transport general cargo on and off highways.

The body was box type with lattice-type side extensions, with tailgate, flat platform, fixed bed, and a straight front. It was equipped with tarp bows and a tarpaulin.

The body construction of the M105A2 was wood and steel rather than the all-steel construction of the other models. The M105A2 was not supplied with support legs or landing gear.

Water Tank Trailers M106, M106A1, & M106A2

The 1 1/2-ton, two-wheel, 400-gallon, M106, M106A1, and M106A2, tanker trailers were used to transport, store, and distribute drinking water.

Each trailer was designed for fording hard-bottom water crossing where the trailer will be completely submerged, and to be towed by single-wheeled 2 1/2-ton, 6x6, M34 or similar vehicle.

Each trailer was equipped with 400-gallon capacity aluminum water tank of elliptical cross section.

Two fenders, one on each side, were provided with extensions in front and rear. The fender and extensions

The M106 was the first of the G-754 tanker trailers. It had 11.00-20 tires, as opposed to the 9.00x20 tires used by the rest of the 1 1/2-ton tanker families. It was equipped with a manually opeated pump, and the hose was carried in a rack on the tongue. (U.S. Army photo)

had non-slip horizontal surfaces.
Differences among models:
— The M106 can be used only with a towing vehicle having an air supply, such as the M34.
— The M106 was equipped with hand water pump and 26-ft. auction hose for filing.
— The M106 had a wood-slat-floored extension at the front of the tank for storing a bell strainer with hose. The extension was flanked on either side by a welded metal faucet box.
— On M106A1, a piping cover plate was located over the piping between the two welded metal faucet boxes at the front of the tank.
— The front caster on the M106 was not interchangeable with the front caster on the M106A1 and M106A2.
— The M106A1 and M106A2 caster was raised and locked in a mounting bracket welded to nose of chassis frame and had a locking handle.

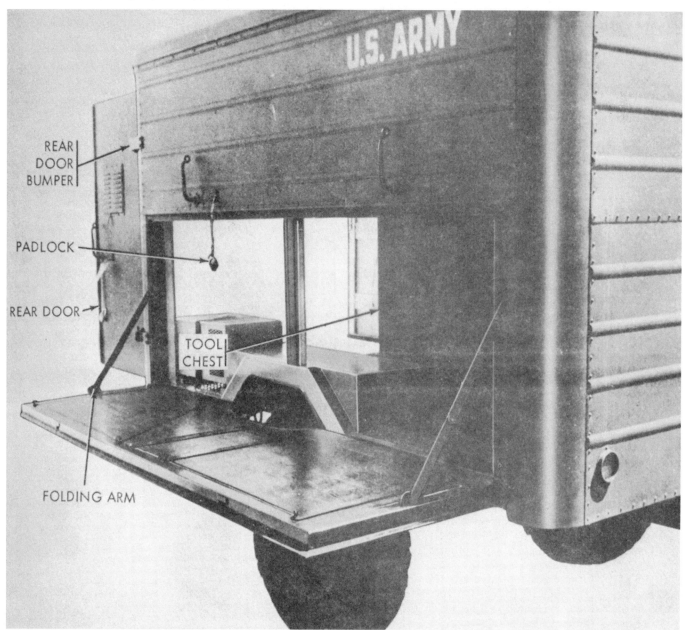

The side openings of the M448 hinged down to provide work platforms, and dual rear doors provided access to the interior. (U.S. Army photo)

— A rear support leg was standard equipment on the M106 only.
— The M106A2 employs two hydraulic wheel cylinders for each wheel service brake.
— The M106 lunette is mounted into the boss welded to the nose of the chassis frame.
— The M106A1 lunette is mounted into a casting welded to the nose of the chassis frame.

Water Trailers M107A1, M107A2 & M017A2C

The M107 series trailers used 9.00-20 tires. The tanker bodies were made of aluminum, and the M107A1, as seen here, lacked the hand pump provision of earlier models. (Photo courtesy of Memphis Equipment Company)

The M107 series trailers had 9.00-20 size tires and were intended to be towed with vehicles with similar size tires. Each trailer was equipped with a 400-gallon aluminum water tank of elliptical cross section.

Like the M106, two fenders, one on each side, were provided with extensions in front and rear. The fenders and extensions have non-slip horizontal surfaces.

The M107 could be used only with a towing vehicle having an air supply, such as 2 1/2-ton cargo trucks. It was equipped with hand water pump and 25-ft. suction hose for filling. The M107 had a wood-slat-floored extension at the front of the tank for storing a bell strainer with hose. The extension was flanked on either side by a welded metal faucet box.

On the M107A1 and M107A2, a piping cover plate was located over the piping between the two welded metal faucet boxes at the front of the tank, and they did not have the hand pump and hose assembly.

The Front caster on M107 is not interchangeable with front caster on M107A1 and M107A2. Caster wheel with bearings was interchangeable.

The caster on the M107A1 and M107A2 was raised and locked in a mounting bracket welded to the nose of chassis frame and had a locking handle.

The support leg was standard equipment on only on the M107.

The M107 lunette was mounted into the boss welded to the nose of the chassis frame. On the M107A1 and M107A2 the lunette was mounted into a casting welded to the nose of the chassis frame.

M107A2 employs two hydraulic wheel cylinders for

each wheel service brake.

The M107A1 water tank trailer used the M103A2 trailer chassis. The M107A2 water tank trailer used the M103A4 trailer chassis, and the M107A2C water tank trailer used the M103A4 trailer chassis.

Each water tank was aluminum and had a 400-gallon capacity. The water tank was mounted on a tank frame that in turn was attached to the chassis frame.

Shop Van Trailer M448

The M448 was designed for use as a mobile paint or battery shop and used a M103A3 trailer chassis.

The van body consisted of framing, folding sides, and rear doors. The van had two leveling jacks that were stowed on the upper rear corner of the left wall. A grounding rod was provided to allow the safe use of electrical equipment. The grounding rod was attached to the trailer chassis. An aluminum ladder, for use to get in and out of the rear door, was mounted on the interior surface of the rear door when not in use.

The body was of riveted aluminum construction and the frame was of welded steel construction. The roof and crown were riveted to the body. The front wall was equipped with an opening to permit mounting of a generating unit when the van was used as a battery shop. A cover assembly covered the opening when it was not needed.

The rear wall of the trailer had double doors for entry of cargo and personnel. The side doors were designed to swing downward to form a working area.

The roof and body were insulated with glass fiber material to provide a comfortable working environment for the crew and protect sensitive equipment installed in the trailer. A cabinet was mounted near the left rear of the van. The drawers of this cabinet were accessible to personnel on the ground with the rear doors open.

When used as a paint shop, the van had a paint storage cabinet mounted inside at the front of the van body.

Two leveling jacks were provided to level the van body and eliminate vibration when stationary. A leveling jack holder was mounted on each rear corner of the van body. The jacks were not intended to lift the van clear of the ground.

GENERAL DATA

MODEL	M104	M104A1	M105A1	M106
WEIGHT NET	2,400 lbs.	2,730 lbs.	2,650 lbs.	2,280 lbs.
MAX GROSS	7,900 lbs.	7,230 lbs.	7,150 lbs.	5,615 lbs.
LENGTH	165.5	165.5	165.5	166.625
WIDTH	83	83	83	93
TIRES NO. & SIZE	2 11.00-20	2 11.00-20	2 9.00-20	2 11.00-20
BRAKES	air/hydraulic	air/hydraulic	air/hydraulic	air/hydraulic
ELECTRICAL	24 volt	24 volt	24 volt	24 volt

Overall dimensions listed in inches.

VALUES

	6	5	4	3	2	1
Cargo models	150	300	500	700	900	1,200
Tanker models	100	300	500	800	1,000	1,400

SCARCITY

Cargo models 2
Tanker models 2

LOW-BED TRAILERS

G-159 M9

The M9 trailer was built specifically to be towed by the Diamond T M20, with the two units combined forming the M19 transporter. This combination was used to recover disabled tanks and other heavy loads. The trailer was fitted with 24 8.25-15 tires. Eight of the tires were on the front axle, which swiveled and joined to an A-frame-type drawbar. The trailer was made of welded steel construction. Hinged loading ramps were located at the rear of the deck, and four steel chocks were also provided. The payload capacity of the M9 was 90,000 lbs. Winter-Weiss was the leading producer of these trailers with a total of 1827. Other builders and their production totals were: Rogers 1,148, Fruehauf 1,632, Checker Cab 344, and Pointer-Williamette 1,192.

This is a true trailer, as opposed to a semi-trailer, which makes it more difficult to back up.

GENERAL DATA

MODEL	M9
NET WEIGHT	20,150 lbs.
MAX GROSS	110,150 lbs.
LENGTH	360
WIDTH	114
TRACK WIDTH INSIDE	
OUTSIDE	6.875
103.125	
TIRES NO. & SIZE	24 8.25-15
BRAKES	air
ELECTRICAL	6

Overall dimensions listed in inches.

GENERAL DATA

	6	5	4	3	2	1
M9 trailer	1,500	2,500	4,000	5,500	6,500	8,500

SCARCITY
Scarcity 3

G-160 M15

The M15 40-ton tank transporter semi-trailer was built by Fruehauf as the companion trailer for the WWII era M26 and M26A1 tractors.

Eight large 14.00-24 tires mounted on combat-style wheels supported the rear of the trailer. The suspension of the M15 consisted of solid walking beams with trunion shafts between the tires. These trailers were provided with full air service brakes, however, there was no parking brake system provided. On the rear of the trailer there were two large hinged ramps that allowed other vehicles to be loaded in the field. These ramps were raised with the tractor's winch, either directly, or by attaching them to the cargo being pulled onto the trailer. The trailer's wheels and tires were retractable to narrow the trailer for shipment.

When uncoupled from the tractor, the front of the trailer was supported by landing gear consisting of two strut and leg supports. On the upper deck at the front of the trailer was a stowage compartment for the block, tackle, and sheaves used in the recovery operations. Cable guides were built into the trailer, and the tractor's winch rope could be threaded through these rollers during recovery operations. Steps were built into the front of the trailer to provide access to the stowage compartment on top of the gooseneck.

The M15A1 had its payload increased from 40 tons to 45 tons, and had hinged covers installed over the rear wheels.

Some of the M15A1 trailers were further modified to the M15A2 standard to cope with the ever-increasing

Here is a factory-fresh M9 45-ton trailer. This particular trailer is a Fruehauf product, although these were produced by a variety of builders. (U.S. Army photo)

The M15A2 was the most heavily reinforced version of the M15 trailers. This trailer's cargo far exceeds the weight of WWII Sherman tanks. (U.S. Army photo)

This new M15 trailer was photographed at the Engineering Standards Vehicle Laboratory in Detroit in September, 1944. (U.S. Army photo)

The removable covers for the rear wheels are stowed on top of the top deck storage compartments of the M15. (U.S. Army photo)

weights of U.S. tanks. Extensive modifications included: heavy reinforcement of the trailer frame, a wider body to accept the larger tracks of the later heavier tanks, installation of track guides, and removal of large stowage compartments on the forward end of the trailer.

These trailers remained in service through the Vietnam war, being towed in later years by the G-792 series tractors.

The new hinged covers covered only the tires, not the entire rear area of the trailer. (U.S. Army photo)

This view of the pilot M15A1 shows the large cable guide rollers at the front of the trailer. (U.S. Army photo)

In this view the M15 wheel covers have been lowered, as have the ramps, into the loading position. (U.S. Army photo)

The M15's two large rear ramps were moveable, and slid on pins. (U.S. Army photo)

The unusual arrangement of the rear wheels of the M15 series trailers is evident in this overhead photo. (U.S. Army photo)

The hinged rear wheel covers of the M15A1 are clearly visible here. This is the pilot model, and ironically still carries the removable covers of the M15, as pointed out by the notation of the wartime editor. (U.S. Army photo)

GENERAL DATA

MODEL	M15	M15A1	M15A2
NET WEIGHT	42,370 lbs.	42,370 lbs.	42,600 lbs.
MAX GROSS	122,370 lbs.	132,370 lbs.	142,600 lbs.
LENGTH OVERALL	461.4375	461.4375	461.4375
WIDTH	150	150	150
TIRES NO. & SIZE	8 14.00-24	8 14.00-24	8 14.00-24
BRAKES	air	air	air
ELECTRICAL	12	12	12

Overall dimensions listed in inches.

VALUES

	6	5	4	3	2	1
M15 trailer	2,000	3,500	5,000	6,500	8,000	9,500

SCARCITY

Scarcity 3

The new rear wheel covers protected the expensive 14.00-24 tires from damage by the tracks of tanks being loaded. (U.S. Army photo)

G-797 M172

The M172 and M172A1, were four-wheel, dual-axle, dual-tired semi-trailers which were used to transport general cargo. The two tubular axles, mounted at the rear, were on walking beam-type suspension.

A fifth-wheel upper plate under the front end of the gooseneck structure housed a reversible kingpin that was accessible through a hinged cover on top of the gooseneck. The double-end kingpin was fitted into the fifth wheel of the towing vehicle to permit the trailer to be towed. When towed by 2 1/2- and 5-ton 6x6 tractors, the normal, commercial-size end of the kingpin was used, but coupling these trailers to the 10-ton tractor required the use of the oversized end.

Two mechanically actuated, retractable, shoe-type

The M172A1 has a deck with only 16 ft. of uninterrupted space, which limits its usefulness. (Photo courtesy of Memphis Equipment Company)

landing gear legs were located on either side near the front. These were used to support the front end of the trailer when it was not coupled to the towing vehicle. The landing gear had a two-speed gearbox with a low and a high gear. A ratchet-type hand crank, located on right side of gooseneck structure, operated the two retractable support legs. The frame structure is the load bed of the semi-trailer. The frame was made of rigidly welded structural steel.

The early type semi-trailer M172 was equipped with commercially designed axles and air brakes. The late type M172A1 was equipped with an Ordnance standard axle, and air-over-hydraulic brakes, with a modified gooseneck kingpin arrangement. Further, the M172 was rated as a 15-ton trailer, while the M172A1 was considered a 25-ton trailer.

GENERAL DATA

MODEL	M172	M172A1
NET WEIGHT	15,500 lbs.	14,860 lbs.
MAX GROSS	45,500 lbs.	64,860 lbs.
LENGTH	406	414
WIDTH	115	115
LOADING HEIGHT	35	39.375
TRACK	82	82
TIRES NO. & SIZE	8 10.00-15	8 11.00-15
BRAKES	air	air
ELECTRICAL	24 volt	24 volt

Overall dimensions listed in inches.

VALUES

	6	5	4	3	2	1
All models	1,000	2,500	4,500	6,500	8,000	9,500

SCARCITY

Scarcity 2

In spite of its short length, the M172A1 can carry heavy loads. This M172A1, coupled to a 10-ton tractor, is transporting an M41 tank. (U.S. Army photo)

G-802 M269/M270

The semi-trailer, low-bed: wrecker, 12-ton, four-wheel M269 and M269A1 were developed in the post-WWII period to be towed by a tractor-wrecker M246 or truck tractor M52, or similar fifth-wheel vehicle.

The trailers were intended primarily for use by the Air Force for transporting new or salvaged aircraft, and for general purpose hauling.

Each semi-trailer had two axles at the rear mounted on a leaf-spring suspension, a fifth wheel upper plate under the front end, and foot-type landing gear that supported the front end when not coupled to a towing vehicle. Two chock blocks were located in brackets welded to the chassis frame beams near the rear end, and a spare tire was carried on a winch-type spare wheel and tire carrier assembly located under the right side of the chassis frame. On the M269 a stowage compartment and toolbox was mounted on top of the gooseneck.

On the M269A1, the gooseneck was modified to include an internal storage compartment. Both the M269 and M269A1 had stake pockets were welded to the inside of the body frame outer rails for hardwood stakes. These trailers had an air-operated brake mechanism controlled from the towing vehicle, and a 24-volt receptacle, 12-volt socket, and 6-volt socket located at the front end.

The M270-series trailers are identical to the M269 series, except they were considerably longer. Like the M269 series, the M270 and M270A1 were designed to be towed by a vehicle equipped with fifth wheel (lower coupler) and to used for transporting new or salvaged aircraft, as well as for general purpose hauling.

Each semi-trailer had two axles at the rear mounted on a leaf-spring suspension. A fifth-wheel upper plate under the front end or nose of the semi-trailer included a kingpin that was fitted into the fifth wheel on a towing vehicle.

A foot-type landing gear supported the front end of the semi-trailer when not coupled to a towing vehicle. The spare tire was carried on a winch-type spare wheel and tire carrier assembly under the right side of the chassis frame. Lights on each semi-trailer were supplied with current by, and operated from, the towing vehicle.

The early-type semi-trailer M270 was equipped with commercially designed axles and air brakes. The later M270A1 was equipped with Ordnance-designed axles, which use air-over-hydraulic brakes.

GENERAL DATA

MODEL	M269	M269A1	M270	M270A1
NET WEIGHT	54,200 lbs.	54,200 lbs.	57,500 lbs.	57,500 lbs.
MAX GROSS	14,200 lbs.	14,200 lbs.	17,500 lbs.	17,500 lbs.
LENGTH	409	409	590.5	596.5
WIDTH	96.75	96.75	96.75	96.75
LOADING HEIGHT	48.75	48.75	49	49
TRACK	72	72	72	72
TIRES NO. & SIZE	8 11.00-20	8 11.00-20	8 11.00-20	8 11.00-20
BRAKES	air	air	air	air/hydraulic
ELECTRICAL	24 volt	24 volt	24 volt	24 volt

Overall dimensions listed in inches.

VALUES

	6	5	4	3	2	1
All models	1,000	2,000	3,000	4,000	5,500	6,500

SCARCITY

Scarcity 2

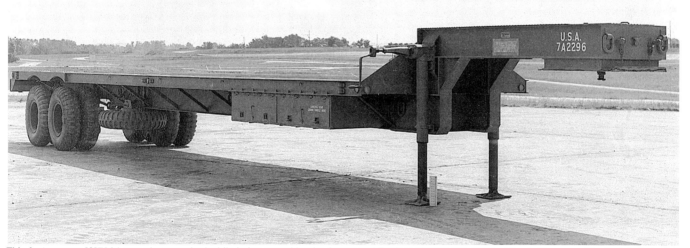

This factory-new M270A1 was photographed while being tested by the Armor and Engineer Board. The M269 series trailers were identical, but shorter. (Photo courtesy of the Patton Museum)

G-904 M747

The M747 was an extremely large low-bed heavy equipment semi-trailer. Originally developed as the companion trailer for the M746 22.5-ton 8x8 tractor, the M747 trailer was considerably more successful than the tractor. In addition to being towed by the M746, the M747 was also frequently coupled to the M123A1C tractor or the M911 C-HET.

Two large aluminum ramps at the rear of the trailer permit loading, and the trailer came with a variety of rigging gear for loading disabled equipment.

The trailer's 24-volt electrical system not only included the normal service and brake lights, but also an amber rotating beacon. The beacon was provided because the trailer is oversize even when unladen.

The oversize kingpin on these trailers prevent them from being towed by conventional civilian tractors.

The spare tire for the M747 trailers is stowed on top of the gooseneck, affording a good view of the wide low-profile tires used on these trailers. (Photo courtesy of Memphis Equipment Company)

GENERAL DATA

MODEL	M747
WEIGHT NET	31,000 lbs.
MAX GROSS	151,000 lbs.
LENGTH OVERALL	513
WIDTH	137
HEIGHT	105
TREAD	102
TIRES NO. & SIZE	16 15-19.5
BRAKES	air
ELECTRICAL	24 volt

Overall dimensions listed in inches.

VALUES

	6	5	4	3	2	1
All models	4,000	6,500	9,000	12,000	15,000	19,500

SCARCITY

Scarcity 3

The XM747 has a stowage location for the recovery and rigging gear provided with these trailers. The ramps were raised with the winches on the tractor. (Photo courtesy of the Patton Museum)

The "shoulders" on the gooseneck actually are guides for wire rope from winches on the tractor. These are used when retrieving disabled equipment. (Photo courtesy of the Patton Museum)

AMMUNITIONS TRAILERS

G-213 M21

The M21 two-wheel, 4-ton ammunition trailer was created after a long period of development as the Ammunition Trailer T33E1 (Modified). It was finally standardized as the Trailer, Ammunition, Two-Wheel, 4-Ton, M21, in November 1943. The design was finalized in January 1944 after additional input from the Field Artillery Board. The initial production order was given to Trailer Company of America, based in Cincinnati. They in turn subcontracted the assembly of the trailer to the Herman Body Co. of St. Louis.

A production pilot model was inspected on March 4, 1944, and after its approval was given for production to begin. This inspection was made on a pilot model that the Trailer Company of America had re-worked to match the latest production drawings. The first production models, however, were not completed by the Herman Body Company until the end of July 1944. An order for the M21 was also given to the Canastota Division of Oneida Ltd., Canastota, New York. Its first production models were completed at the end of September 1944.

These trailers were two-wheeled balanced trailers having specially designed ammunition racks to hold 72 155mm howitzer projectiles, with the powder charges carried above the projectiles.

GENERAL DATA

MODEL	M21
NET WEIGHT	5,300 lbs.
MAX GROSS	13,300 lbs.
LENGTH	144
WIDTH	98
TRACK WIDTH	
INSIDE/OUTSIDE	68/98
TIRES NO. & SIZE	2 14.00-20
BRAKES	air

Overall dimensions listed in inches.

Despite its short, stubby stature and low volume, the M21 carried a heavy load. The box on the front of the body held the fuses for the ammunition. (U.S. Army photo)

The ammo racks were mounted inside the trailer were redesigned late in the war, but were never placed into production.

G-216 M23

The M23 was created for the purpose of carrying a 155mm gun, 8-in. howitzer, or 240mm howitzer ammunition. It was based upon the Ammunition Trailer, T34, built by the Utility Trailer Co., Los Angeles, and the T34E1 built by the Trailer Company of America, Cincinnati. After testing by the Field Artillery Board, it was decided that a modified version of the T34 model would be best suited for the purpose. The modified trailer was designated T34E2.

These trailers had been standardized in March 1944, well before testing was complete, and on May 9, 1944, a production order for these trailers was issued.

The M23 ammunition trailer was a four-wheeled trailer designed to be towed behind the Truck, 7 1/2-Ton, 6x6, Prime Mover, or the Tractor, High Speed, 18-Ton, M4, when used with a Heavy Carriage Limber, M5. Production of the M23 ceased in June 1945.

GENERAL DATA

MODEL	M23
NET WEIGHT	10,000 lbs.
MAX GROSS	26,000 lbs.
LENGTH	224
WIDTH	103.5
TRACK WIDTH	
INSIDE/OUTSIDE	77.5/100
TIRES NO. & SIZE	4 11.00-20
BRAKES	air

Overall dimensions listed in inches.

The M23 trailer was used to transport 155mm gun, 8-in. howitzer, or 240mm howitzer ammunition behind Mack NO trucks or high-speed tractors. (U.S. Army photo)

G-660 M10

The M10 trailers were used for transporting ammunition during WWII. They could be found being towed by vehicles ranging from 2 1/2-ton trucks to tanks.

Essentially a welded-steel, open-topped box mounted solidly on an axle, they were durable trailers, even when carrying heavy loads. A number of footman loops were recessed into the floor for securing the cargo. On the rear of the trailer was a pintle hook to enable multiple trailers to be towed in train. A hole was cut in the tailgate to allow it to clear the rear pintle when it was dropped fully down.

These trailers used six-hole combat rims. On the rear of the trailers were reflectors, blackout and taillights, and a trailer receptacle. A metal box was mounted across the drawbar just forward of the body. This box was used to hold the fuses for the ammunition carried by the trailer.

The small box mounted on the tongue of the trailer was built to store and transport fuses for the ammunition being transported in the main body of the trailer. (U.S. Army photo)

This M10 was built by Youngstown Steel Door Company, a builder of railroad car components during peacetime. The moveable lunette can be seen in this view, as can the front support wheel. The parking brake levers are at each front corner of the cargo box. (U.S. Army photo)

The rear-mounted pintle hook is visible beneath the tailgate, which has a hole cut in it to allow it to be opened fully without interfering with the pintle hook. The bars along the top edge of the trailer sides are intended to support the tarpaulin. (U.S. Army photo)

The cargo box of the M10 was almost perfectly square. Not all M10s had this tread pattern tires. Some of the trailers used the standard military tread. (U.S. Army photo)

AMMUNITIONS TRAILERS

The lunette was mounted on a swivel so that it could be adjusted to different height pintles, and landing gear was provided to support the tongue when the trailer was not coupled to a towing vehicle.

GENERAL DATA

MODEL	M10
NET WEIGHT	2,090 lbs.
MAX GROSS	4,840 lbs.
LENGTH	152.5
WIDTH	85.25
HEIGHT	57.75
TREAD	72
TIRES NO. & SIZE	2 9.00-20
BRAKES	parking only

Overall dimensions listed in inches.

G-660 M332

The M332 replaced the WWII-era M10. Like the M10, it was used for transporting ammunition for field artillery. They could be found being towed by vehicles ranging from 2 1/2-ton trucks to armored personnel carriers.

These trailers have a welded-steel, open-topped box mounted on a framework of rectangular tubular steel. Unlike the M10, the M332 had a spring suspension. A number of footman loops were recessed into the floor for use in securing the cargo. On the rear of the trailer was mounted a pintle hook to enable multiple trailers to towed in train. A hole was cut in the tailgate to allow it to clear the rear pintle when it was dropped fully down. These trailers had all the improvements of the M-series. This includes 24-volt sealed electrical system, standardized components and mounted tires comparable to those used by their towing vehicles.

A metal box was mounted across the drawbar just forward of the body. This box was used to hold the fuses for the ammunition carried by the trailer.

The lunette swiveled so that it could be adjusted to different height pintles, and landing gear was provided to support the tongue when the trailer was not coupled to a towing vehicle.

GENERAL DATA

MODEL	M332
NET WEIGHT	2,750 lbs.
MAX GROSS	5,800 lbs.
LENGTH	148.3
WIDTH	94.825
HEIGHT	63.825
TRACK	80
TIRES NO. & SIZE	2 9.00-20
BRAKES	parking only
ELECTRICAL	24

Overall dimensions listed in inches.

VALUES

	6	5	4	3	2	1
M332 trailer	200	350	550	850	1,200	1,500

SCARCITY

Scarcity 2

TRAILER, AMMO, 1-1/2 TON, 2 WHEEL

MODEL M-332

MFD. BY THE JOHNSON FURNACE CO.

BELLEVUE, OHIO

This photo of a factory-fresh M332 was taken in 1962. Notice the spring suspension and external frame used by the M332. These features clearly distinguished it from the earlier M10. (U.S. Army photo)

MISCELLANEOUS TRAILERS

G-221 2-TON

The M7 trailer was the base unit for the G-221 series. It had a much lower profile and deck height than the other trailers of the era and was originally designed for transporting generators.

These trailers were used almost exclusively by antiaircraft artillery units during WWII. The suspension used a walking beam, with two tires and wheels mounted on either side of the unitized body. No springs were used in the suspension. The tires and wheels were interchangeable with those used by the 2 1/2-ton trucks used as prime movers for this trailer. These trailers had electric service brakes.

A crank on the top of each corner of the body lowered the four leveling jacks, which were employed when the mounted generator was placed in operation. The lunette was adjustable height for use with various towing vehicles.

Clearance lights, reflectors, blackout stoplights, and taillights were mounted on the sides and rear of the trailer. Some trailers were equipped with an adjustable landing wheel under the drawbar. Footman loops and

rope tie downs were riveted around the body for the tarpaulin. The tailgate was heavily constructed for use as a loading ramp.

The M18 was a very similar model that was equipped with a manually operated winch mounted on the trailer's drawbar. It was operated by a large hand wheel on either side of the winch drum. The wire rope from the winch went through the cargo box so generators or other cargo

This image from a technical manual illustrates an M7 doing what it was intended to do — transporting a generator. The leveling jack handles are just visible on the upper corners of the trailers.

The M22 was a totally enclosed director trailer. It had dual rear doors and side window with blackout screen. (U.S. Army photo)

could be pulled up the tailgate and into the trailer. Rather than a tailgate, the M18 had two ramps at the rear. Because it lacked the front leveling screws of the M7, the M18 had a landing leg to support the tongue when disconnected from the prime mover. The M7, M13, and K84 trailers were supplied with bows and tarpaulins to enclose the cargo area.

Hand-operated parking brakes were provided. In addition to generator transport, the M7 was used for antenna mount and radio equipment transport, search light transport, and general cargo transportation.

The M18 trailers had a landing leg under the tongue to support it when disconnected from the prime mover. The winch mounted on top of the tongue was used to pull the cargo into the trailer.

The M13 shown here very much resembled a M7 with bows in place, but it was a different variation for the specific purpose of transporting gun directors.

This M14 trailer built by J. G. Brill provided fully enclosed transportation for gun directors. The front leveling jacks are shown here supporting the tongue of the trailer. (U.S. Army photo)

Model M13, M14, M22

These trailers transported and housed gun directors for antiaircraft artillery and related equipment. These directors were electro-mechanical systems for computing gun-laying data continuously when firing on attacking enemy aircraft. A separate trailer transported the generator necessary to operate the system. The M14 and M22 trailers had metal tops that were insulated and equipped with a gasoline-fired heating unit. A ventilation fan was also provided. The M14 and M22 had two rear doors above the tailgate, and five windows with screens and sliding blackout panels were provided. The M22 had a wooden floor; the others had a steel floor.

Model M17

This model was the same basic trailer as the M7, but was modified for carrying the quad .50-caliber machine gun mount, M45. This was the same type mount as the M16 and M16A1 halftracks carried.

Fruehauf Trailer Company, Kriger, and J.G. Brill Company built this series of trailers during World War II.

GENERAL DATA

MODEL	M13	M14	M22
WEIGHT NET	4,400 lbs.	—	—
MAX GROSS	7,850 lbs.	8,900 lbs.	8,900 lbs.
LENGTH	190	191.875	191.875
WIDTH	96	96	96
HEIGHT	94.5	99.5	99.5
TRACK WIDTH			
INSIDE/OUTSIDE	75.5/92	75.5/92	75.5/92
TIRES NO. & SIZE	4 7.50-20	4 7.50-20	4 7.50-20
BRAKES	electric	electric	electric
ELECTRICAL	6 volt	6 volt	6 volt

MODEL	M7	M18
WEIGHT NET	4,150 lbs.	4,000 lbs.
MAX GROSS	8,448 lbs.	8,194 lbs.
LENGTH	191.875	198.25
WIDTH	96	96
HEIGHT	25.825	63
TRACK WIDTH		
INSIDE/OUTSIDE	75.5/92	75.5/92
TIRES NO. & SIZE	4 7.50-20	4 7.50-20
BRAKES	electric	electric
ELECTRICAL	6 volt	6 volt

Overall dimensions listed in inches.

G-678 M30

These semi-trailers were intended primarily as a bulk hauler for fuel. The Transportation Corps operated these trailers, and each was equipped with a rear pintle hook. These pintle hooks, along with converter dollies, were used to allow operation in trains consisting of a truck-tractor, 4-5 ton, 4x4, one semi-trailer and one full trailer.

Six manufacturers produced these trailers, known as the M30, and the design was based on one developed for an Army Air Force refueler. The makers involved were Davis Welding, Heil, Keystone, Krieger Steel, Independent, and Progress.

The fuel trailers were provided with dispensing equipment consisting of two gravity hose assemblies, and an engine-driven pump and hose assembly. This arrangement allowed the servicing of six vehicles or the

The wide stance of the landing legs provided for the G-678 series is apparent in this photograph taken at the Studebaker Proving Ground in 1944. Notice the fire extinguisher carried on the side of the trailer — crucial on fuel trailers such as this. (U.S. Army photo)

filling of six containers simultaneously. The pump and hose assemblies were constructed so that they could be used for filling the trailer as well.

GENERAL DATA

MODEL	M30
NET WEIGHT	6,750 lbs.
MAX GROSS	18,950 lbs.
LENGTH	240
WIDTH	96
HEIGHT	93
TRACK WIDTH	
INSIDE/OUTSIDE	50.125/93.875
TIRES NO. & SIZE	4 9.00-20
BRAKES	air
ELECTRICAL	6 neg

Overall dimensions listed in inches.

VALUES

No reported sales

G-750 12-TON

The M127 family consists of the 12-ton, four-wheel semi-trailers M127, M127A1, and M127A1C. These vehicles are intended to transport general cargo. Their construction consisted essentially of a body and frame of welded construction mounted on the 12-ton, four-wheel M126 or M126A1.

The body frame was made of pressed-steel side rails, cross members, and short cross members, and was welded together with the chassis frame to form one integral unit.

The semi-trailer chassis M126, M126A1, and M126A1C consisted of two drop-frame I-section longitudinal frame rails and intermediate cross members, along with an upper fifth wheel plate, kingpin, two axles at the rear mounted on a leaf-spring suspension. Taillights, brakes, and foot-type landing gear were provided.

Stake semi-trailers M127 and M127A1 were of similar body frame construction, except that semi-trailer M127A1 was equipped with chains to support the panels and lifting rings for hoisting the semi-trailers. Semi-trailers M127A1 and M127A1C are similar, but the M127A1C is equipped with a voltage control box mounted on the underside of the body. The M127 had commercial-type axles and airbrakes, while the other vehicles in this group had military-type axles and air over hydraulic brakes.

ORD E4072

A tarpaulin was provided to protect the M27 cargo from the weather, or from enemy observation. The tarpaulin has been installed in this photo.

The M127 stake-bodied semi-trailers were among the most abundant of the military's general cargo trailers. Their simple rugged construction has given them a long service life. The sideboards were easily removed to convert the trailer into a flatbed. (Photo courtesy of TacticalTruck.com)

The M128 van-type trailers afforded even better weather protection and cargo security. (U.S. Army photo)

The M128 family consisted of the M128, M128A1, M128A1C, and the M128A2C. These trailers had van-type bodies and were mounted on the same types of chassis described above. The M128A1C had turn signals, mud flaps, and dock bumpers. All of these trailers had a body framework made of square steel tubing, and an interior lining of 1/4-in. plywood. The outside is sheathed in 22-gauge corrosion-resistant steel. The trailers have hardwood floors. A ladder was carried on the rear door to be used entering and exiting the trailer.

All the G-750 series trailers were intended to be pulled by 5-ton tractors.

GENERAL DATA

MODEL	M127	M128
NET WEIGHT	13,840 lbs.	15,220 lbs.
MAX GROSS	37,840 lbs.	39,220 lbs.
LENGTH OVERALL	345.5	348.25
WIDTH	96.75	96.75
HEIGHT	105.5	143.625
TREAD	72	72
TIRES NO. & SIZE	8 11.00-20	8 11.00-20
ELECTRICAL	24 volt	24 volt

Overall dimensions listed in inches.

VALUES

	6	5	4	3	2	1
Flatbed trailer	500	800	1,200	2,000	3,000	4,000
Van trailer	500	800	1,500	2,500	4,000	5,000

SCARCITY

Flatbed trailer	2
Van trailer	2

G-751 Series

The G-751 series trailers were developed in the 1960s to be towed by 2 1/2-ton tractors.

The M118 series trailers were 6-ton stake body trailers built on the M117 series chassis. These were flatbed trailers with removable sideboards made of eight 1-in. oak boards. There was a landing gear at the front of the trailer to support it when uncoupled from the tractor.

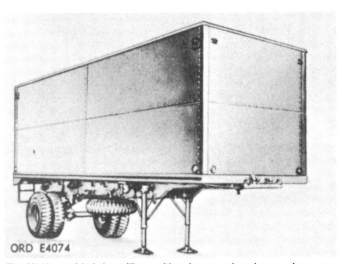

ORD E4074

The M119 provided the military with a large enclosed general-purpose cargo trailer. (U.S. Army photo)

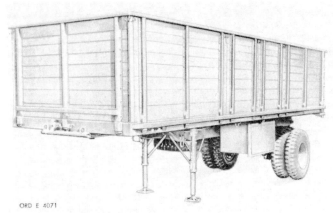

ORD E 4071

The large M118 stowage box for the tarpaulin was mounted underneath the left side of the trailer, with the spare beneath the right side. (U.S. Army photo)

This USMC M118A1 was a 1967 Loadcraft product. The removable hardwood sideboards with steel supports are plainly visible. (U.S. Army photo)

Under the floorboard there is a box to stow the tarpaulin. The M117 chassis was equipped with commercial-type air brakes and the M117A1 had military-style air-over-hydraulic brakes.

The M119 series trailers were 6-ton van body cargo trailers. Like the M118 series, they are constructed on the M117 series chassis. The outer body is constructed of steel sheet, with plywood interior panels. Mechanically it is identical to the M118 series.

GENERAL DATA

MODEL	M118	M119
NET WEIGHT	7,140 lbs.	7,140 lbs.
MAX GROSS	23,340 lbs.	23,340 lbs.
LENGTH OVERALL	275.75	274.625
WIDTH	94.75	92.625
HEIGHT	132.625	103.25
TRACK WIDTH		
INSIDE/OUTSIDE	47.375/92.625	47.375/92.625
TIRES NO. & SIZE	4 9.00-20	4 9.00-20
ELECTRICAL	24 volt	24 volt

Overall dimensions listed in inches.

Note: The M118 has commercial-type air brakes, the M118A1 has air-over-hydraulic brakes.

VALUES

	6	5	4	3	2	1
All models	400	600	800	1,000	1,500	1,800

SCARCITY

Scarcity 2

G-755 M131

Fuel has always been a major concern for the mechanized Army, and the G-755 series tankers were built with that in mind. These trailers, designed to be towed by the M52-type tractors, transport 5,000 gallons of fuel. An engine-driven pump, capable of discharging 225 gallons per minute, was provided for off-loading the fuel.

The M131 had commercial-type air brakes, while the other trailers in this group (M131A1, M131A1C and M131A2) used military-type air-over-hydraulic brakes.

The M131A1 looked very similar to the M131, but had air-over-hydraulic brakes, rather than the straight air brakes of the M131. (U.S. Army photo)

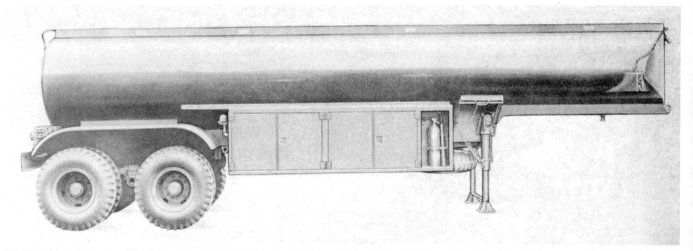

The M131A2 introduced a different appearance to the M131 series. Gone was the rear pump compartment, replaced with an underbelly compartment. (U.S. Army photo)

The M131A5C, like the M131, resembled its contemporary civilian equivalents. (Photo courtesy of TacticalTruck.com)

The M131 resembled the civilian tankers of the era, with a low-hanging rear apron that contained the pumping equipment. (U.S. Army photo)

The M271 had an unusual two-lunette drawbar. The short sideboards on the trailer could be easily removed when hauling its primary cargo, telephone poles. (National Archives and Records Administration photo)

GENERAL DATA

MODEL	M131	M131A1	M131A2	M131A5C
WEIGHT NET	14,850 lbs.	14,280 lbs.	12,400 lbs.	14,250 lbs.
MAX GROSS	45,390 lbs.	44,780 lbs.	42,900 lbs.	43,750 lbs.
LENGTH	352.5	351.5	380	376
WIDTH	96.75	96.75	97.8	95.5
LOADING HEIGHT	109	109	107	106.5
TIRES NO. & SIZE	8 11.00-20	8 11.00-20	8 11.00-20	8 11.00-20
BRAKES	air	air-hydraulic	air-hydraulic	air-hydraulic
ELECTRICAL	24 volt	24 volt	24 volt	24 volt

Overall dimensions listed in inches.

VALUES

	6	5	4	3	2	1
All models	1,000	2,000	2,500	4,000	6,000	8,500

SCARCITY

Scarcity 2

G-782 M271

The M271 was developed for Signal Corps use transporting poles. The Signal Corps knew this trailer as the V-13/GT. While its primary function was to transport poles in support of the V-18A/MTQ polesetter, the trailer did have low removable sideboards that permitted it to transport other gear used by signalmen. The tongue of the trailer was telescopic, reaching from 123 in. to 489 in. To transport the poles, the electrical and air systems

In this view the sideboards have been removed and the telescoping drawbar extended in preparation of transporting poles. The extra long electrical and airlines were stored coiled on racks on the sides of the drawbar when the trailer was operated in the short configuration. (National Archives and Records Administration photo)

had extra-long connections to accommodate the changing length. The G-782 series trailers were equipped with various load restraint devices. These trailers had air-over-hydraulic brake systems and 24-volt tail and stop lights

In this view of the M271 the sideboards have been removed and the telescoping drawbar extended in preparation of transporting poles. The extra-long electrical and air lines were stored coiled on racks on the sides of the drawbar when the trailer was operated in the short configuration. (National Archives and Records Administration photo)

MISCELLANEOUS TRAILERS

GENERAL DATA

MODEL	M271/M271A1
NET WEIGHT	2,430 lbs.
MAX GROSS	9,430 lbs.
LENGTH	
EXTENDED	271
RETRACTED	120
WIDTH	82.5
HEIGHT	62.5
TIRES NO. & SIZE	2 11.00-20
BRAKES	air/hydraulic
ELECTRICAL	24 volt

Overall dimensions listed in inches.

VALUES

	6	5	4	3	2	1
All models	200	500	700	950	1,100	1,250

SCARCITY

Scarcity 2

G-813 M310

The 3 1/2-ton M310 Cable Reel Trailer, known as the K37-B by the Signal Corps, was used by the Signal Corps during construction and maintenance of telephone and telegraph lines. The M310 was the companion trailer for the V17A/MTQ truck. Its unusual shape allows it to transport a reel of cable in the vertical position. The trailer had stub axles, which permitted the reel to extend near the ground. The trailers had an air-over-hydraulic brake system, no electrical system, parking brakes on each wheel, and could be completely submerged.

GENERAL DATA

MODEL	M310 K-37-B
NET WEIGHT	2,520 lbs.
MAX GROSS	9,520 lbs.
LENGTH	149.5
WIDTH	88.75
HEIGHT	71
TRACK	76.25
TIRES NO. & SIZE	2 11.00-20
BRAKES	air/hydraulic
ELECTRICAL	24

Overall dimensions listed in inches.

No rear lights were installed on the M310. The unusually shaped trailer was designed to move reels of wire. (U.S. Army photo)

VALUES

	6	5	4	3	2	1
All models	400	800	1,000	1,200	1,500	1,800

SCARCITY

Scarcity 3

G-816 M345

The M345 was a very large flat-bed trailer frequently used by engineering units, who towed the trailer behind 5-ton trucks. The M345 was built of structural and pressed steel, and had a deck length of 23 ft. Landing gear was provided under both ends of the trailer. These trailers had standard military air-over-hydraulic brake systems, and 24-volt electrical systems. The trailers were supplied with chock blocks in lieu of parking brakes.

GENERAL DATA

MODEL	M345
NET WEIGHT	11,260 lbs.
MAX GROSS	37,260 lbs.
LENGTH	333.5
WIDTH	98
HEIGHT	55.5
TRACK WIDTH	
INSIDE/OUTSIDE	52/96.75
TIRES NO. & SIZE	8 11.00-20
BRAKES	air/hydraulic
ELECTRICAL	24 volt

Overall dimensions listed in inches.

VALUES

	6	5	4	3	2	1
All models	15,000	20,000	25,000	30,000	35,000	45,000

SCARCITY

Scarcity 2

The M345 was surely an impressive trailer, but its 55 1/2-in. deck height made loading it challenging. (U.S. Army photo)

G-819

The M313 was a van-type semi-trailer, in the 6-ton, four-wheel range with an expansible body. It was designed to provide a mobile semi-trailer van shop with expanding sides for the installation of maintenance shop sets to be used by personnel maintaining and repairing military equipment in the field. It consisted of an expansible van body similar to that used on the M291 and M292 trucks mounted on a M295A1 chassis. It was intended to be towed by M52 5-ton 6x6 tractor, or similar vehicle.

The van body was of double-wall construction consisting of an outer aluminum skin and an inner plywood covering. It was insulated between the inner and outer wall members for temperature control. The van body was designed to expand to approximately twice

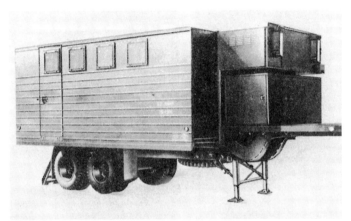

This M313 is shown with the body in its extended position, ready for operation. The upper box on the front of the van body housed two fuel-burning heaters and an air conditioning unit. (U.S. Army photo)

the volume it enclosed when in the retracted or traveling position. This was achieved by using expanding side panels actuated by expanding and retracting mechanisms, and counterbalanced hinged roof and floor sections, which formed extensions of the floor and of the roof when the van body was in the expanded position.

The van body was provided with electrical system lights and service receptacles, two gasoline-burning heaters, stabilizing or leveling jacks, and two aluminum ladders. It had double doors in the rear wall. A blackout relay was actuated by the door-operated switches to provide blackout protection when the doors were opened. There were doors in each side and at the rear of the van, and four windows in each side.

The M447 and M447C expansible vans were similar in design to the M313, but lacked the side doors and had fewer windows. Like the M313, the M447 was designed to provide a mobile semi-trailer van shop with folding sides for the Army, as well as for use as a field spare parts carrier. It was intended for the installation of maintenance shop sets to be used by personnel maintenance and repairing military equipment in the field.

The trailer was suitable for use on highway or cross-country. It was mounted on a M295 or M295A1 semi-trailer with a 6-ton, four-wheel chassis. The M52 5-ton 6x6 tractor, or a similar vehicle, towed it. It was comprised of a van body constructed of electrically welded angle iron.

These trailers had double rear doors, and two full-length side panels that were sectionalized longitudinally so that the lower half hinges downward to form an extension of the floor, and the upper half hinges upward to form a roof extension. Protection from the weather was achieved when canvas side curtains were attached. The van body was provided with an electrical system, including lights and power outlets and two fuel-burning

The M447 had no side doors and a different window arrangement than the M313. (Photo courtesy of the Patton Museum)

MISCELLANEOUS TRAILERS

heaters. The trailers had stabilizing or leveling jacks, guardrails, and ladders, and were fully insulated.

The M447C was the same as the M447, except that the M447C was equipped with an air conditioner.

GENERAL DATA

MODEL	M313	M447
NET WEIGHT	14,700 lbs.	15,500 lbs.
MAX GROSS	28,700 lbs.	23,000 lbs.
LENGTH	324	323
WIDTH RETRACTED	96	94.5
WIDTH EXPANDED	170	175
TRACK BETWEEN DUALS	72	72
TIRES NO. & SIZE	8 9.00-20	8 9.00-20
BRAKES	air/hydraulic	air/hydraulic
ELECTRICAL	24 volt	24 volt

Overall dimensions listed in inches.

VALUES

	6	5	4	3	2	1
All models	400	600	800	1,000	1,500	1,800

SCARCITY

Scarcity 3

G-815 & G-820

The M349 and M349A1 semi-trailers were van-type refrigerated two-wheel trailers in the 7 1/2-ton class. Mechanical differences resulted in the trailers being assigned to two different ordnance groups. The M349 was G-815 and the M349A1 was G-820. The M349 and M349A1 were used to provide refrigerated storage space for perishable items, both fresh and frozen, under all weather conditions. Many were used in Vietnam.

The aluminum body and subframe were mounted on a steel undercarriage supported by semi-elliptic springs that were attached to a single dual wheel standard 14,000-lb.-load-rated Ordnance axle. The semi-trailer had vertical screw-type front landing gear, an interior and exterior lighting system, a braking system, spare wheel, fixed ladders and platform, toolboxes, battery box, and auxiliary equipment. After the introduction of the M349A1, the M349 was reclassified as Limited Standard.

GENERAL DATA

MODEL	M349	M349A1
NET WEIGHT	7,970 lbs.	8,600 lbs.
MAX GROSS	22,790 lbs.	30,600 lbs.
LENGTH	284	277
WIDTH	96.375	96
HEIGHT	129.875	129.875
TREAD	70	70
TIRES NO. & SIZE	4 9.00-20	4 9.00-20
ELECTRICAL	24 volt	24 volt

Overall dimensions listed in inches.

NOTE: *The M349 has commercial-type air brakes, the M349A1 has air-over-hydraulic brakes.*

VALUES

	6	5	4	3	2	1
All models	400	600	800	1,000	1,500	1,800

SCARCITY

Scarcity 3

By modern standards the M349 series trailers were small. This is a 1967 M349A4. (Photo courtesy of TacticalTruck.com)

CONVERTER DOLLIES

G-676 M365

These dollies, built by Springfield Auto Works as well as Production Engineering, were used to convert semi-trailers of up to 10 tons capacity into full trailers. This allowed the trailers to be towed by any adequately sized vehicle with a pintle hook, rather than solely by truck tractors.

GENERAL DATA

MODEL	M365
WEIGHT	3,380 lbs.
LENGTH	114
WIDTH	95.5
HEIGHT	54
WIDTH	
INSIDE/OUTSIDE	45.5/95.5
TRACK	70.5
TIRES NO. & SIZE	4 11.00-20
BRAKES	none
ELECTRICAL	none

Overall dimensions listed in inches.

G-695 K-83

Fruehauf built these dollies for the signal corps. They were used to convert model K78A and K78B Signal Corps semi-trailers into full trailers. This allowed the trailers to be towed by any adequately sized vehicle with a pintle hook, rather than solely by truck tractors. These unusual dollies had their support leg under the rear, rather than the usual position under the drawbar. Also, the drawbar is hinged but lockable so that it can be repositioned for various pintle hook heights.

GENERAL DATA

MODEL	K83 & K83A
WEIGHT	3,000 lbs.
LENGTH	147
WIDTH	94
HEIGHT	53.5
WIDTH	
INSIDE/OUTSIDE	50/94
TIRE NO. & SIZE	4 9.00-20
TRACK	72
BRAKES	none
ELECTRICAL	yes

Overall dimensions listed in inches.

The M365 was the Army's heavy-duty converter dolly during WWII. Notice the overload springs mounted above the normal springs on this example built by Springfield Auto Works. (U.S. Army photo)

CONVERTER DOLLIES

This photo from a technical manual shows the unique rear landing gear used by Signal Corps converter dolly K83. (U.S. Army photo)

G-708 M363

The dollies, built by Fruehauf, and known within the company as a Model DC3, were used to convert semi-trailers of up to 15,000 lbs. gross weight into full trailers. This allowed the trailers to be towed by any adequately sized vehicle with a pintle hook, rather than solely by truck tractors.

GENERAL DATA

MODEL	M363
WEIGHT	1,765 lbs.
LENGTH	112.75
WIDTH	83.625
HEIGHT	46.5
WIDTH	
INSIDE/OUTSIDE	47.625/83.625
TRACK	65.625
TIRES NO. & SIZE	4 7.50-20
BRAKES	none
ELECTRICAL	none

Overall dimensions listed in inches.

VALUES

	6	5	4	3	2	1
All models	200	400	7,000	1,200	1,500	18,000

SCARCITY

Scarcity 3

RA PD 137823

The M363 was among the lightest-duty converter dollies used during WWII. (U.S. Army photo)

G-800 M197

The G-800 6-ton converter dolly was intended to replace the WWII-era M364 unit. Like the WWII unit, it was designed to convert semi-trailers into full trailers. The M197 used commercial-type axles and air brakes, while the M197A1 used an ordnance-type axle and an air-over hydraulic-brake system. These dollies use the standard M-series wheels and tires. They have no electrical system.

GENERAL DATA

MODEL	M197	M197A1
NET WEIGHT	2,970 lbs.	2,880 lbs.
MAX GROSS	14,970 lbs.	14,970 lbs.
LENGTH	112	112
WIDTH	92.625	92.625
HEIGHT	53	53
WIDTH		
INSIDE/OUTSIDE	47.375/92.625	47.375/92.625
TRACK	70	70
TIRES NO. & SIZE	4 9.00-20	4 9.00-20
BRAKES	air	air/hydraulic

Overall dimensions listed in inches.

VALUES

	6	5	4	3	2	1
All models	200	400	700	1,000	1,400	1,800

SCARCITY

Scarcity 2

The M197 was a relatively light-duty dolly, and could be manhandled into position if necessary. It had brakes, but no lights. (Photo courtesy of TacticalTruck.com)

G-800 M198

The M198 series was the big brother to the M197 and was rated at 8 tons. Its purpose was the same as the other converter dollies — to allow semi-trailers to be towed either with pintle hook equipped trucks, or in trains behind a single prime mover — usually a 5-ton class vehicle. The M198 used a commercial axle with air brakes, while the M198A1 used a military-style axle with air-over-hydraulic brakes.

GENERAL DATA

MODEL	M198	M198A1
NET WEIGHT	3,500 lbs.	3,500 lbs.
MAX GROSS	19,500 lbs.	19,500 lbs.
LENGTH	115	115
WIDTH	96.75	96.75
HEIGHT	56	56
WIDTH		
INSIDE/OUTSIDE	47.5 /96.75	47.5/96.75
TRACK	72	72
TIRES NO. & SIZE	4 11.00-20	4 11.00-20
BRAKES	air	air/hydraulic
ELECTRICAL	none	none

Overall dimensions listed in inches.

VALUES

	6	5	4	3	2	1
All models	200	400	700	1,000	1,400	1,800

SCARCITY

Scarcity 2

The M198 8-ton dolly was equipped with a front landing leg, but this example is simply resting on its lunette. (Photo courtesy of Memphis Equipment Company)

G-811 M199

GENERAL DATA

MODEL	M199
NET WEIGHT NET	7,700 lbs.
MAX GROSS	43,700 lbs.
LENGTH	150
WIDTH	114.75
HEIGHT	59
TRACK	82
TIRES NO. & SIZE	8 14.00-20
BRAKES	air
ELECTRICAL	24

Overall dimensions listed in inches.

VALUES

	6	5	4	3	2	1
All models	400	800	1,100	1,600	2,200	2,800

SCARCITY

Scarcity 3

This overhead view shows large size of the M199 and all its components. The M199 was capable of transporting heavy loads both on road and cross-country. (U.S. Army photo)

The M199 series was the largest of the post-WWII converter dollies, and was rated at 18 tons. In addition to dual wheels, it had tandem axles, and used 14.00 x 20 tires. This permitted very large semi-trailers to be converted into full trailers. Due to the weight distribution and tandem axles, the M199 did not require any landing gear, and none was provided. The dolly did have a 24-volt electrical system and full air brakes.

Section Three:
TRACKLAYING VEHICLES

This section of the book is devoted to fully tracked vehicles. In addition to tanks, there are gun motor carriages (self-propelled guns), high-speed tractors, and carriers, which are essentially tracked trucks.

The Ordnance Department's carefully developed "G-number" system does not work as well with tracked vehicles as it does with wheeled vehicles, at least from the collector's standpoint.

Prior to November 9, 1950, the U.S. Army classified tanks on the basis of their weight: light, medium, and heavy. After that date the designation was based on the caliber of the vehicle's main gun.

Tracked vehicles offer special challenges and expenses for the collector. First, there is the problem of transportation. While trucks can be driven or towed, and a wrecker can handle even basket case trucks with relatively little trouble or expense, this is not the case with most tracked vehicles. Even in operating order it is not usually practical to drive the vehicle as a means of transporting it. Steel tracks can eat up pavement, and rubber tracks wear, and are expensive. Many vehicles become oversize loads when hauled, necessitating permits, and their weight in most instances means that something larger than a pickup, often much larger, is needed as the towing vehicle.

Relatively few tracked vehicles are traded in the collector market.

ARMORED PERSONNEL CARRIERS

M75

The M75 was produced by FMC and International Harvester. The production can be separated into two large groups, early vehicles (International serial number 7 through 376 and FMC serial 1007 through 1326, lower numbers were test units) and late vehicles (IHC 377 through 1006 and FMC 1,327 to 1,736).

The engine of the M75 consisted of the 375-hp AO-895-4 Continental engine coupled to a CD-500 cross drive transmission. The taillight mounting, shock absorber arrangement, and fuel tank were among the components that were changed on later models. There were two doors on the rear of the vehicle for troops to use, while the commander had a roof-mounted cupola with an M2 HB machine gun. The driver had a hatch on the upper sloping armor.

The M75 proved itself in combat in Korea in 1953,

The M75 was a large vehicle. The driver and commander both have their hatches open in this photo, and the exhaust pipe running across the front of the vehicle roof can be seen. The hatches at the rear of the roof could be opened to allow troops to fire from the safety of the vehicle. (Photo courtesy of the Patton Museum)

This T18E1 interior was essentially the same as the early M75 interior. The driver's seat is barely visible on the front left. (Photo courtesy of the Patton Museum)

but with a cost of $72,000 each, it was too expensive to be procured in the huge quantities the Army wanted.

GENERAL DATA

MODEL	M75
WEIGHT*	41,500 lbs.
MAX TOWED LOAD	14,000 lbs.
LENGTH	204.5
WIDTH	112
HEIGHT	119.75
TRACK	87
STD TRACK WIDTH	21
MAX SPEED	44.5 mph
FUEL CAPY	150 gal
RANGE LAND	115 mi
ELECTRICAL	24 neg
TRANSMISSION SPEEDS	2
TURNING RADIUS FT.	pivot

Overall dimensions listed in inches.

Fighting weight

ENGINE DATA

ENGINE MAKE/MODEL	AO-895-4
NUMBER OF CYLINDERS	6
CUBIC-INCH DISPLACEMENT	896
HORSEPOWER	295 @ 2660 rpm
TORQUE	672 lbs.-ft. @ 1850 rpm
GOVERNED SPEED (rpm)	2800

VALUES

	6	5	4	3	2	1
All models	2,000	5,000	8,000	12,000	16,000	20,000

SCARCITY

Scarcity 3

M59

The M59 improved on the M75 in several of ways. It was less expensive, amphibious, and had a rear ramp which could be lowered, allowing quick loading and unloading. There was a small personnel door installed in

At the rear of the M59 was a large ramp that swung down to allow the transportation of large cargo, or the quick egress of the troops inside. A traditional hinged personnel door was mounted in the center of the ramp. (Photo courtesy of the Patton Museum)

This soldier is making adjustments to one of the GMC 302 engines that powered the M59. The carburetor of the left engine is visible just above his hands. Also visible is the interior of the ramp-mounted personnel door mentioned earlier. The troop seats, shown here in the lowered position, could be raised and a Jeep driven inside the truck. (Photo courtesy of the Patton Museum)

A late production M59 demonstrates its amphibious capabilities. With only its tracks for propulsion, the M59's maximum speed in calm water was 4.3 mph. (Photo courtesy of the Patton Museum)

Beginning with M59 serial number F2942, the externally mounted .50-caliber was replaced with the M13 cupola. The M13 allowed the commander to sight and fire the machine gun from inside the carrier. Unlike the external mount, which fed the weapon from traditional 150 ammunition boxes, the M13 had an integral 735-round ammunition container. (Photo courtesy of the Patton Museum)

the rear ramp, so it did not have to be lowered for the crew to entire or exit. With the ramp down, a Jeep could be driven inside.

Instead of the single large engine and cross-drive transmission of the M75, the M59 used a pair of GMC 302 straight-six engines and 300MG Hydra-Matic transmissions similar to those used in the G-749 series 6x6 trucks. In emergency situations, the M59 could operate on a single engine, but it was slow going. Even with both engines running the M59 was seriously underpowered.

Though underpowered, the M59 was capable of climbing a 60-percent (30-degree) grade. (Photo courtesy of the Patton Museum)

GENERAL DATA

MODEL	M59	M84
WEIGHT*	42,600 lbs.	47,100 lbs.
MAX TOWED LOAD	14,000 lbs.	14,000 lbs.
LENGTH	221	221
WIDTH	128.5	128.5
HEIGHT	94	94
TRACK	103	103
STD TRACK WIDTH	21	21
TOP SPEED LAND	32 mph	27 mph
TOP SPEED WATER	4.3 mph	6.5 mph
FUEL CAPY	136.5 gal	136.5 gal
RANGE LAND	120 mi	100 mi
ELECTRICAL	24 neg	24 neg
TRANSMISSION		
SPEEDS	2	2
TURNING		
RADIUS FT.	pivot	pivot

Overall dimensions listed in inches.

*Fighting weight

ENGINE DATA

ENGINE MAKE/MODEL	GMC 302
NUMBER OF CYLINDERS	6
CUBIC-INCH DISPLACEMENT	301.6
HORSEPOWER	127 @ 3350 rpm
TORQUE	254 lbs.-ft. @ 1800 rpm
GOVERNED SPEED (rpm)	3400

VALUES

	6	5	4	3	2	1
All models	2,000	5,000	8,000	12,000	16,000	20,000

SCARCITY

Scarcity 3

Shown in this October 1961 photograph is an early production M59 armored personnel carrier. Notice the commander's machine gun is mounted externally to the cupola. The trim vane, necessary for amphibious operations, is shown stowed against the front of the hull. (U.S. Army photo)

M113 Family

M113

The Army standardized the M113 in April 1959, and production began by FMC in 1960. It has been the U.S.'s standard Armored Personnel Carrier since production began, and continues to serve not only the U.S. Armed Forces, but those of many other countries as well.

The hull of the M113 vehicles was made of aluminum armor. There was a hydraulically operated ramp in the rear, which had a personnel door mounted in it. The driver's position was in the left front, and the engine was

The M113 in its original form was amphibious, but barely. As later models gained weight, swimming the vehicles became forbidden except in emergency combat situations. The lifting ring just visible on the forward hull at the waterline is the identifying feature of true M113s. (U.S. Army photo)

When the Army made diesel its fuel of choice, the M113 was readily adapted through the installation of a 6V53 Detroit Diesel engine, becoming the M113A1. (Photo courtesy of the Patton Museum)

The M113A1E1 introduced many features made standard on later models. The M113A1E1 had great improvements in engine cooling and the suspension system. (U.S. Army photo)

Like the M113, the M113A1 was equipped with a pintle-mounted .50-caliber machine gun. (U.S. Army photo)

to the driver's right. The driver was provided with four M17 periscopes, and his hatch had provision for an M19 infrared periscope as well. The commander's station is behind the driver and engine, and he had a cupola equipped with five M17 periscopes and an M2 HB machine gun. There were provisions for 11 passengers to ride in the carrier.

An unusual feature of the M113 was the hydraulically tensioned track. The M113 was amphibious, being propelled in the water by its tracks, but there was only 14 in. of freeboard when the vehicle was in the water.

A Chrysler 75M V-8 engine driving through an ALLISON TX200-2 transmission powered the M113. There were 4,974 M113s built for the U.S Armed Forces, and 9,839 supplied to other countries.

M113A1

The ink was hardly dry on the initial production contracts for the M113 when work began on a diesel-powered version. After trials of various versions, a version powered by the General Motors 6V53 V-6 diesel engine was standardized as M113A1 in May 1963. The V-6 diesel's power was transmitted to the track through an Allison TX-100 automatic transmission and a DS-200 controlled differential.

M113A2

The M113A2 was a result of the quest for even greater improvements in performance. It had an improved suspension system, engine-cooling system, and there was an added provision for external fuel tanks rather than the traditional interior tanks. The new fuel system used identical dual armored tanks mounted on either side of the door, which increased the vehicle length by 17 in. and its weight by 900 lbs.

The power train was upgraded with the addition of a turbo-supercharger to the engine, and the replacement of the TX-100 and DS-200 with an Allison X200-3 cross drive transmission. With the cross drive transmission, the steering levers of previous models were replaced with a steering wheel and brake pedal.

While in this basic form the M113A2 looked much like its predecessor, it had the capability to use rear-mounted external fuel tanks instead of the traditional internal ones. (U.S. Army photo)

The M132A1 self-propelled flame thrower was one of the most fearsome weapons ever mounted on the M113 platform. Not visible is the 7.62 coaxial mounted machine gun. (U.S. Army photo)

The M113A3 was been fitted with the P-900 applique armor kit, resulting in the first truly noticeable change to the vehicle's form since its inception. (U.S. Army photo)

ARMORED PERSONNEL CARRIERS

M113A3

The M113A3 further improved upon the platform. The X200-3 transmission was replaced by the X200-4, and the external fuel tanks, an option on the M113A2, became standard on the M113A3. The M113A3 could be equipped with the P-900 armor kit for greater protection.

M106 107mm Self-Propelled Mortar

The M106 was essentially an M113 with a round roof hatch through which the rear-firing mortar, which was mounted below on a 90-degree traversing mechanism, fired. A base plate for the mortar was stowed on the rear outer left side of the hull, allowing the weapon to be

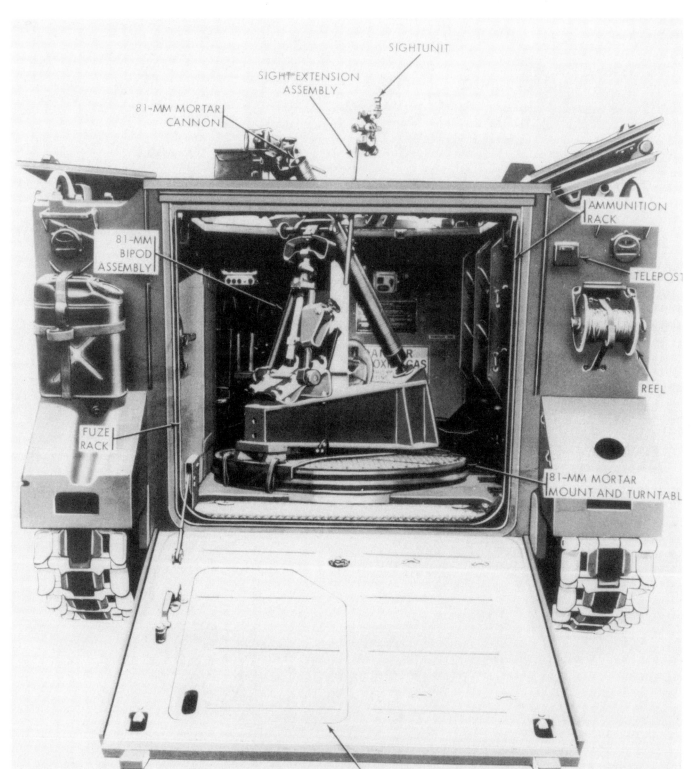

The interior arrangement of the 81mm mortar-armed M125 is shown in this technical manual illustration. The M125 did not carry the mortar base plates externally like the M106. (U.S. Army photo)

removed from the vehicle and fired.

Procurement of the Chrysler gas-powered M106 began even before the type had been standardized. Of the 860 units FMC built, 589 went to U.S. forces. The balance headed overseas.

M106A1 107mm Self-Propelled Mortar

When the base M113 vehicles changed from gasoline-driven units to diesel-powered machines, so did the mortar carrier, becoming the M106A1. The U.S. military received 982 of these, with a further 334 provided for overseas sales.

M106A2 107mm Self-Propelled Mortar

When the M113 was again upgraded, becoming the M113A2, the M106 followed suit, getting the same upgrades and becoming the M106A2.

M125A1 81mm Self-Propelled Mortar

The M125A1 was essentially the same vehicle as the M106A1, but was armed with an 81mm mortar instead of the 107mm mortar. The smaller mortar was able to traverse a full 360 degrees, rather than the 90 degrees of the 107.

M125A2 81mm Self-Propelled Mortar

Like the M106, the M125 was again upgraded along with the M113A2, getting the same upgrades and becoming the M125A2.

M577

The need for a mobile command post was so great that limited production of the M577 was scheduled even before the first prototype had been delivered. From

The 107mm mortar of the M106-series mortar carriers could be dismounted from the vehicle and, using the base plate assembly secured to the side of the hull, be fired from a fixed position. This allowed the vehicle to be used for other purposes. This M106A2 is in firing position with the roof hatches open. Mortar rounds can be seen stowed in the ammunition racks inside the vehicle. (U.S. Army photo)

The additional height of the M577 is evident here. The welded seam indicates where the roof would be on a normal M113. Bows and posts that support the tent are stowed on the back of the command post. (Photo courtesy of the Patton Museum)

The auxiliary generator, which powered the electronic gear of the command post, can be seen on the upper hull of the XM577. (Photo courtesy of the Patton Museum)

The tent added considerable space to the command post of the M577, but that space was not protected by armor. (Photo courtesy of the Patton Museum)

The XM163 Vulcan Air Defense System, with its six-barreled Gatling gun, was capable of delivering tremendous firepower against air or ground targets. (U.S. Army photo)

ARMORED PERSONNEL CARRIERS

December 1962 through May 1963, 270 M577s were produced by FMC. In November 1963, production began on the M577 and continued into 1964, with 674 being delivered.

The M577 was basically an M113 with the personnel compartment roof raised 25 1/4 in. so the average service man was able to stand upright inside. The M577 did not have the commander's seat and cupola in the crew compartment like the M113. Instead, the commander had a simple folding hatch. Two 60-gallon tanks replaced the single 80-gallon tank used on the M113, with one mounted on each side of the interior to support a folding table.

The M577 had a heater for the crew compartment, interior lights, interior blackout lights, and a large tent that could be attached to the rear of the vehicle to provide more floor space. Radios were mounted on the left and front walls of the crew compartment. The M577 carried a dis-mountable 28-volt generator to power all its electrical equipment.

M577A1

Like the rest of the M113 family of vehicles, the M577 was upgraded to diesel power in the early 1960s, becoming the M577A1.

M577A2

When the M113A2 was introduced, the M577A1 followed suit, becoming the M577A2. Not only were new vehicles produced, but when older units were overhauled they were upgraded to the new standard as well.

M577A3

When the RISE power package was created for the M113 family, the M577A2s were upgraded again, becoming M577A3s. In addition to the more powerful engine, the gasoline-driven auxiliary generator of the earlier models was replaced with a slightly larger diesel-powered unit.

The M901 TOW missile launcher was designed to protect armor and mechanized infantry from enemy armor. The launcher held two missiles, with an additional 10 stowed in the hull. (U.S. Army photo)

M1068

The M1068 was a modified version of the M577A2. Known as the Standard Integrated Command Post System, it transported the Army Tactical Command and Control System. A new tent was created for this vehicle, which was illuminated. The auxiliary generator for this unit was a 5-kilowatt diesel-powered unit. M1068A3 was the designation given to the M1068 when modified by the installation of the RISE power pack.

M901 TOW Missile Launcher

The TOW (tube launched, optically tracked, wire guided) missile is one of the most effective anti-tank weapons in the U.S. arsenal, and the M113 family was the basis for a carrier for this weapon system. Emerson Electric Company developed the vehicle that became the M901. Known as the "Hammerhead," it had 10 TOW missiles stored in the hull, and two more transported in the launcher itself.

When upgraded to accommodate the TOW 2 and TOW 2A missiles, the vehicle classification was changed to M901A1. When the RISE power pack was installed, the vehicle became M901A3.

M981 FIST-V

The Fire Support Team Vehicle (FIST-V) is designed to provide artillery support to mechanized infantry and armor units. Based on the M113A2, the FIST-V incorporated many components of the M901. In addition to the Emerson Electric TOW missile launcher, the M981 is armed with a 7.62mm machine gun in the commander's cupola. With the RISE power pack installed, the M981 is known as the M981A2.

M132/M132A1 Flame Thrower

The effectiveness of the flamethrower as a weapon against enemy emplacements is unquestioned. No doubt this was a factor in the desire to mount the E31R1 fuel and pressure unit in the body of an M113 carrier. The E36R1 flame gun dispensed the flame. This combination was standardized as the M10-8 flamethrower, and when mounted in the M113 chassis it became the M132 self-propelled flamethrower. With the standardization of the diesel-powered personnel carrier M113A1, the M132 also became diesel powered, and this version was known as the M132A1.

The M981 FIST-V was a more advanced TOW launcher. Its shape was different from the earlier M901. (U.S. Army photo)

M163 Vulcan Air Defense System

The M163 20mm self-propelled antiaircraft artillery gun resulted from the marriage of the M113A1 personnel carrier and the Air Force Vulcan 20mm Gatling gun. The electrically driven gun can fire up to 3,000 rounds per minute. The M113A1 was modified with the addition with a lock-up suspension to stabilize the vehicle, becoming the M741. The weapon installation consisted of the M168 20mm gun, M157 gun mount, automatic lead computing sight M61, and AN/VPS-2 radar set. Modifications to the gun mount changed its designation to M157A1, and caused the weapon system to be re-designated M163A1. Improvements to the engine cooling changed the base vehicle designation to M741A1.

The M168 is capable of firing 3,000 rounds per minute, and the vehicle only carried 1031 rounds. To conserve ammunition, there was a low firing rate, which could be selected by the operator. At the low rate the weapon fired "only" 1,000 rounds per minute. At the high rate setting ammunition consumption was limited by the weapon system. Bursts could be fired only in groups of 10, 30, 60, or 100 rounds.

XM734

The XM734 was the Army's attempt to create an infantry fighting vehicle out of the M113 family. The XM734 had vision blocks and firing ports installed in the sides and rear of the vehicle. The old fuel tank was removed, and a new 100-gallon tank installed on the vehicle centerline. This fuel tank served as the base for the new seats for 12 troopers. The M113 cupola was removed and replaced it with an M74c cupola equipped with twin .30-caliber machine guns. Very few of these vehicles were built.

This XM734 was photographed in Vietnam. The vision blocks and pistol ports characteristic of this model are plainly visible. (Photo courtesy of the Patton Museum)

GENERAL DATA

MODEL	M113
WEIGHT*	22,615 lbs.
MAX TOWED LOAD	24,000 lbs.
LENGTH	191.5
WIDTH	105.75
HEIGHT	98.25
TRACK	85
STD TRACK WIDTH	15
MAX SPEED	40 mph
FUEL CAPY	80 gal
RANGE LAND	200 mi
ELECTRICAL	24 neg
TRANSMISSION SPEEDS	2
TURNING RADIUS	12 ft. 7 in.

Overall dimensions listed in inches.

*Fighting weight

ENGINE DATA

ENGINE MAKE/MODEL	Chrysler A-710-B
NUMBER OF CYLINDERS	90-degree V-8
CUBIC-INCH DISPLACEMENT	361
HORSEPOWER	215 @ 4000 rpm
TORQUE	332 lbs.-ft.@ 2800 rpm
GOVERNED SPEED (rpm)	3900

VALUES

	6	5	4	3	2	1
All models	3,000	6,000	10,000	14,000	19,000	25,000

SCARCITY

Although abundantly produced, current usage has kept this family out of collectors' hands

M114 Family

The M114 was intended to be a reconnaissance vehicle for armored cavalry units. However, its relatively poor cross-country performance prevented it from being successful in this role. The major shortcoming was that its hull extended forward of the tracks, which caused it to hang up when crossing ditches.

The M114 was lightweight, with its armor being welded 5083 aluminum alloy. It was fully amphibious, and air transportable. Water propulsion was provided by its shrouded tracks. With its low profile, there was only space for four — the driver, commander, observer, and a single passenger.

The M114 series was built by Cadillac, and the power train consisted of a Chevrolet 283 V-8 engine and 305MC Hydra-Matic transmission. The suspension system had torsion bars attached to four road wheels on each side. The band-type tracks were driven by front sprockets, with tension controlled by the rear idler wheels.

On early models the commander had a cupola with an externally mounted .50-caliber machine gun. On later models this was replaced by a turret-type arrangement. The commander's hatch was on the left side of the hull roof. The driver was provided a hatch just forward of the commander's. The observer had a hatch on the right side of the hull, just behind the commander's position. The observer was provided with two pedestal mounts for his .30-caliber machine gun, which was replaced with a 7.62mm M60 machine gun early in the vehicle's production. The rear of the hull had a large circular door.

The first 615 vehicles produced in 1962 were classified as T114. The turret-type machine gun mount was added to the next 600 units and the classification changed to T114E1. In 1963, these were reclassified as M114 and M114A1, respectively, and another 2,495 M114A1s were produced in 1963 and 1964.

The turret of the M114A1 was intended to mount the 20mm gun M139, but that weapon was still under development when the T114A1s and M114A1s were produced, resulting in their mounting the .50-caliber machine gun. When the 20mm weapon became available, some were fitted to M114s and M114A1s. Those vehicles were reclassified as M114E2 and M114A1E1.

An M114A1 equipped with a turret mount for the commander's .50-caliber machine gun allowed him to fire the weapon from inside the vehicle. The original M114 machine gun installation required the commander to expose himself to hostile fire in order to operate the weapon. (U.S. Army photo)

The M114A1E1 packed considerably more firepower than the standard M114-type vehicle. Its M27 cupola was armed with the 20mm gun M139, and it was power operated. (U.S. Army photo)

ARMORED PERSONNEL CARRIERS

GENERAL DATA

MODEL	**M114**
WEIGHT*	14,749 lbs.
LENGTH	175.75
WIDTH	91.75
HEIGHT	91.125
TRACK	72.75
MAX SPEED	40 mph
FUEL CAPY	110 gal
RANGE LAND	300 mi
ELECTRICAL	24 neg
TRANSMISSION	
SPEEDS	3
TURNING	
RADIUS FT.	32

Overall dimensions listed in inches.

*Fighting weight

ENGINE DATA

ENGINE MAKE/MODEL	**Chevrolet**
NUMBER OF CYLINDERS	V-8
CUBIC-INCH DISPLACEMENT	283
HORSEPOWER	160 @ 4600 rpm
TORQUE	210 lbs.-ft. @ 2400 rpm
GOVERNED SPEED (rpm)	4600

VALUES

	6	5	4	3	2	1
All models	6,000	10,000	18,000	24,000	36,000	40,000

While often referred to as an armored personnel carrier, the M114 was properly known as the M114 Armored Command and Reconnaissance Carrier. This November 1962 photo shows the M114 climbing the 60-percent grade on a test course. (U.S. Army photo)

The circular rear hatch, unique to the M114 family, is visible in the rear of a true M114. The commander's .50-caliber machine gun was trained to the front here, while the observer's 7.62mm M60 was turned across the hull. Notice the location of the pioneer tools, and the horizontal position of the spare fuel can. (Photo courtesy of the Patton Museum)

Bradley

The Bradley family of vehicles consists of three primary vehicles: the M2 Infantry Fighting Vehicle, the M3 Cavalry Fighting Vehicle, and the Multiple Launch Rocket System.

The only differences between the early M2 and M3 vehicles visible to the casual observer is the absence of side firing ports on the M3. These ports were for use with the M231 5.56mm Firing Port Weapon, which is a modified version of the M16A1 Assault Rifle. It was planned that six infantrymen plus an operate crew would fight from inside the M2. The M3, being a reconnaissance vehicle, housed fewer men.

M2 Bradley

The M2 Bradley had a two-man turret offset to the right of the centerline. The rear of the vehicle was equipped with a large rear ramp, which was fitted with an emergency door in the left side. The troopers were provided three periscopes positioned between the rear ramp and the rooftop cargo hatch, and two periscopes on each side of the hull above the side firing ports. Inside, there were five stowage racks for TOW missiles.

The Bradley is amphibious after preparation. The vehicle's turret houses a 25mm Bushmaster chain gun with a 7.62mm M240C machine gun mounted coaxially. On the side of the turret was a two-tube TOW missile launcher. The vehicle had to be halted before the TOW missiles could be fired. There were two four-tube smoke grenade launchers mounted on either side of the turret

face. The GE 25mm chain gun (so named because it is chain driven off a 1.5-hp electric motor) could fire single shots, or at rates of 100 or 200 rounds per minute, as selected by the gunner. Its dual feed mechanism allowed the gunner to instantly switch between high-explosive and armor-piercing ammunition.

The vehicle was powered by a Cummins VTA-903 500-hp diesel engine.

M2A1 Bradley

The M2A1 designation was given to vehicles which were upgraded to fire the TOW 2 missiles and included a gas particulate NBC filtration system. The M2A1 also added space for a seventh infantryman just behind the center of the turret.

M2A2 Bradley

The M2A2 was a more heavily armored version of the Bradley. The front-mounted trim vane was replaced with steel applique armor. The vertical hull sides and bottom were also better armored, and there were fittings on this applique armor to allow for the attachment of either passive or explosive reactive armor tiles. When the armor tiles were fitted, the vehicle's weight increased by about 3 tons.

Spaced laminate armor covered the upper run of track and protected the rear of the hull. Unfortunately, the hull side firing ports were covered by this new applique armor. However, the two in the rear ramp were retained. Kevlar liners were added internally to protect men inside from splinters. The number of infantrymen passengers was reduced to six again. The position

The M2 Bradley was well armed with a 25mm Bushmaster chain gun, a 7.62mm coaxial machine gun, and a two-tube TOW missile launcher. There were two four-tube smoke grenade launchers also mounted on either side of the turret face. (U.S. Army photo)

While the M2 Bradley was to be an infantry fighting vehicle, the similar M3 shown here in M3A2 form was to be a cavalry reconnaissance vehicle. (U.S. Army photo)

While the M2 Bradley resembles a late production M113, it is a much larger and heavier vehicle. The trim vane fitted to early model vehicles can be seen here. (U.S. Army photo)

directly behind the driver in previous models was deleted, as was that position's periscope.

The U.S. Army rebuilt many M2s and M2A1s to the M2A2 standard. After additional testing in 1987, the internal arrangement was changed again, and the number of troops carried reverted to seven.

The engine was upgraded to a 600-hp Cummins VTA-903T to handle the additional weight.

M2A2ODS Bradley

The most recent upgrade to the M2A2 family is the M2A2ODS. Improvements included: an eye-safe carbon dioxide laser rangefinder, global positioning system, anti-missile countermeasure device, combat identification system, and thermal viewer for the driver. This program involved 1423 Bradley vehicles.

M2A3 Bradley

The M2A3 is the most electronically sophisticated of the Bradley family. Among its electronic upgrades are the 1553 databus, central processing unit, and information displays for the vehicle commander and squad leader. These improvements made the M2A3 compatible with the intervehicular communication systems used by M1A2 Abrams tank and AH-64D Apache Longbow helicopter.

The commander's station is equipped with an independent thermal viewer, as well as the Improved Bradley Acquisition System (IBAS). The IBAS is a new integrated sight unit that allows automatic gun adjustments, automatic bore sighting, and tracking of dual targets. The CITV and integrated sight are both second-generation FLIR systems. The roof was reinforced

This M3A2 is conducting a firing trial of its most lethal weapon — the TOW missile launcher. (U.S. Army photo)

with titanium armor. These vehicles were manufactured by rebuilding older M2A2 Bradleys.

M3 Bradley

The M3 was basically the same vehicle as the M2, sans firing ports, and with a different interior arrangement. The M3 was built to be a cavalry scout vehicle for M1 Abrams-equipped armored formations. Instead of being filled with armed troops, its passenger compartment was occupied by two observers and a scout motorcycle. The M3 also carries 600 more rounds of ammunition for the Bushmaster and five more TOW missiles than the M2. Without the infantry squad, the firing port weapons, and the firing ports themselves, were not needed and were eliminated.

M3A1 Bradley

The M3 Bradley received the same improvements as the M2 did, and when the M2A1 was fielded, so was the M3A1. The cavalry fighting vehicle included NBC protection for the entire crew. Four periscopes mounted in the cargo hatch proper replaced the three periscopes on the rear deck. The passenger compartment's two right-side periscopes were eliminated.

M3A2 Bradley

Once again, when the IFV was improved, so was the cavalry fighting vehicle. Like the M2A2, the M3A2 had improved armor protection. The observers were repositioned to the left side of the vehicle's passenger compartment, and the missile stowage was relocated.

Like the M2A2, the M3A2 was upgraded after Operation Desert Storm. An eye-safe carbon dioxide laser rangefinder, GPS, combat identification system, missile countermeasure device, and thermal viewer for the driver were added. The vehicles so updated were classified as M3A2ODS.

M3A23 Bradley

Just as it had been earlier, the M3A2 was upgraded alongside the M2A2. Fitted with the same improvements installed on the M2A3, the cavalry vehicle became the M3A3.

M270 MLRS

The chassis of the Bradley was lengthened to form the basis of the Multiple Launch Rocket System. This chassis was known as the M993 Multiple Launch Rocket System carrier. Upon this chassis was mounted the M270 ground vehicle mounted rocket launcher. The launcher housed two rocket pods — each loaded with six 227mm M26 rockets. These rockets could be fired one at a time or in rapid sequence. The M26 rocket has a range of 32 kilometers, and carries 644 M77 submunitions each. A three-man crew consisting of driver, gunner, and section leader served the weapon system.

GENERAL DATA

MODEL	M2A3	M3A3
WEIGHT*	64,000 lbs.	64,000 lbs.
LENGTH	258	258
WIDTH	129	129
HEIGHT	117	117
TRACK	96	96
STD TRACK WIDTH	21	21
MAX SPEED	38 mph	38 mph
FUEL CAPY	175 gal	175 gal
RANGE LAND	250 mi	250 mi
ELECTRICAL	24 neg	24 neg
TURNING		
RADIUS FT	pivot	pivot

Overall dimensions listed in inches.

*Fighting weight without armor tiles (tiles add (8,000 lbs.)

ENGINE DATA

ENGINE MAKE/MODEL	Cummins VTA 903T
NUMBER OF CYLINDERS	V-8
CUBIC-INCH DISPLACEMENT	903
HORSEPOWER	600 @ 2600
TORQUE	1,025 lbs.-ft. @ 2350 rpm

The member of the Bradley that packs the biggest punch is the M270 Multiple Launch Rocket System. It consists of two rocket pods each loaded with six 227mm M26 rockets. The M26 rocket has a range of 32 kilometers, and each carries 644 M77 submunitions. (U.S. Army photo)

AMPHIBIOUS LANDING VEHICLES

G-156 LVT(1)

The unusual nomenclature used on these, as well as similar vehicles, is a result of their procurement under Navy auspices. The first of these tracked landing vehicles, designed by Donald Roebling, was the LVT(1), built by the Food Machinery Corporation (FMC). The total production of this version of the landing vehicle was 1,225 units.

Early LVT(1)s had three widely spaced windows on the cab front, whereas later models had the three windows side by side. A six-cylinder Hercules engine, driving the tracks through a Spicer transmission powered the vehicle. There was no tailgate. Entrance and egress were over the side.

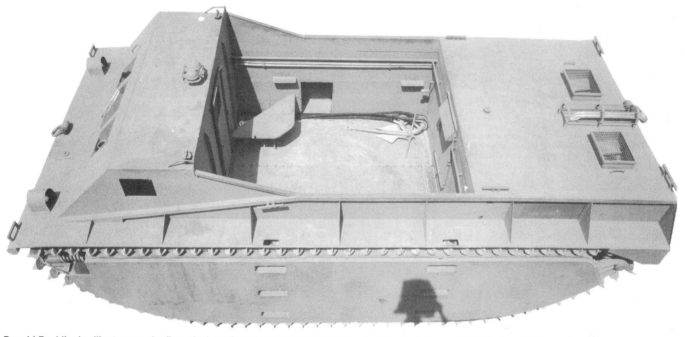

Donald Roebling's alligator was the first of a long line of successful tracklaying landing vehicles used by U.S. Armed Forces. One of its shortcomings, however, was its relatively small cargo carrying space for such a large vehicle. In the floor of this LVT(1) is its anchor. (National Archives and Records Administration photo)

Steps were cut into the sides of the LVT(1) for personnel to use when entering. (National Archives and Records Administration photo)

The major shortcoming of the LVT(1) is shown here. With the engine compartment mounted in the rear, and tracks on the sides, there was no place for a door. Thus, all cargo, whether human or material, had to go over the sides. Cumbersome with freight, it was even worse for personnel during assaults, requiring soldiers to expose themselves to hostile fire to disembark. (National Archives and Records Administration photo)

GENERAL DATA

MODEL	LVT(1)
NET WEIGHT	17,300 lbs.
GROSS WEIGHT	21,800 lbs.
LENGTH	258
WIDTH	118
HEIGHT	97.5
MAX SPEED LAND	12 mph
MAX SPEED WATER	6.1 mph
FUEL CAPY	80 gal
RANGE LAND	150 mi
ELECTRICAL	24 neg
TRANSMISSION	
SPEEDS	3
TRACK WIDTH	10.25

Overall dimensions listed in inches.

ENGINE DATA

ENGINE MAKE/MODEL	Hercules WXLC3
NUMBER OF CYLINDERS	6
CUBIC-INCH DISPLACEMENT	404
HORSEPOWER	146

VALUES

No reported sales

SCARCITY

Scarcity 5

G-167 LVT(2)

The Landing Vehicle, Tracked (2) was an improvement over the earlier series. It was larger, faster, heavier, had greater cargo capacity and an improved suspension. Instead of the Hercules engine of the LVT(1), the LVT(2), like many tracked vehicles of the time, was powered by the Continental W-670 radial. FMC,

Graham-Paige, St. Louis Car Co. and Borg-Warner combined to produce 2963 from 1942 through 1945.

Like the LVT (1), the LVT (2) was unarmored, being built of mild steel. There was, however, a discontinuous Tourelle (skate) ring mounted around the cargo compartment. This allowed the vehicles to be armed with .30- and .50-caliber machine guns for self-defense.

The cargo compartment had a less-than-ideal layout. Since there was no tailgate or ramp, entrance was gained by climbing steps cut into the side of the hull. Cargo had to be lifted over the sides, and the vehicle's heavy driveshaft passed directly through the center of the cargo area.

These vehicles were used by both the Army and the

The short forward skate rail is clearly visible in this photo. The tow cable is shown here stowed on the rear of the hull, but some crews repositioned them along the upper edge of the hull for easier access when at sea. Also, using units tended to obliterate the large star on the side, feeling it acted as an aiming point for opposing forces. (National Archives and Records Administration photo)

Marines, and quite probably were subject to more extensive modifications by their crew than any other vehicle. Virtually no two were alike after having been in the field.

GENERAL DATA

MODEL	LVT2
NET WEIGHT	24,400 lbs.
GROSS	30,250 lbs.
LENGTH	313
WIDTH	130
HEIGHT	98
MAX SPEED LAND	20 mph
MAX SPEED WATER	7.5 mph
RANGE LAND	150 mi
TRANSMISSION	
SPEEDS	5F1R
TRACK WIDTH*	14.25

Overall dimensions listed in inches.

ENGINE DATA

ENGINE MAKE/MODEL	Continental W670-9A
NUMBER OF CYLINDERS	7
CUBIC-INCH DISPLACEMENT	668
HORSEPOWER	250 @ 2400 rpm
TORQUE	584 @ 1800 rpm

VALES

No reported sales

SCARCITY

Scarcity 5

The LVT (2) shown here is an early production model, based on the four step pockets in the side. Later vehicles had only two per side. The uneven height of the machine gun is a result of the discontinuous ring, the short forward section was mounted higher than the side and rear section. (National Archives and Records Administration photo)

G-168 LVT(A)(2)

This was the first of the armored, landing vehicle tracked. Mechanically, the LVT(A)(2) was a LVT(2), but the sheet metal of the cab and hull were replaced by armor. The now armored cab had an escape hatch in the roof, and like the LVT(2), there were two windows in the front of the cab. Because of the added weight of the armor, the cargo capacity was 1000 lbs. less than the LVT(2). Only 450 of the LVT(A)(2) were built.

G-209 LVT(4)

The LVT(4) was a tremendous advancement over the LVT(1) and LVT(2) vehicles. At last the engine was relocated forward, allowing room for a rear cargo drop ramp. The manually raised and lowered ramp provided a means to get troops out of the vehicle without them having to climb over the side, and also allowed easy transportation of smaller vehicles such as Jeeps and anti-tank guns.

The redesigned vehicle also had a substantially larger cargo area. Four different cabs were used on the 8,348 LVT(4) vehicles that were produced: a basic unarmored cab, and three different armored cabs. The windshield of the earliest armored cab resembled that of a half-track in function if not form, with an armored panel that could be raised to allow direct vision. The next version had a .30-caliber ball-mount machine gun for use by the co-driver, while the third version eliminated the moveable armored panel, replacing it with a fixed

The biggest single improvement on the LVT(4) was its folding rear ramp, which allowed protected egress of troops carried ashore, the driving on and off of small vehicles, and the unloading of boxed cargo without lifting it over the sides. (U.S. Army photo)

The engine of the LVT(4) was positioned in the front of the vehicle. Two flexible .50-caliber machine guns are mounted at the front of the cargo bay. On either side of the cargo area are two flexible .30-caliber machine guns. (U.S. Army photo)

panel with vision blocks. The addition of the ball mount brought the total of machine guns fitted to five, with all models having two .50-caliber and two .30-caliber flexible mounts in the cargo area. The last LVT(4)s produced had an escape hatch for the driver in the hull side wall. The LVT(4) was not an armored vehicle, but separate applique armor kits could be installed.

GENERAL DATA

MODEL	LVT(4)
WEIGHT*	36,400 lbs.
LENGTH	314
WIDTH	128
HEIGHT	98.5
TRACK	114
STD TRACK WIDTH	14
MAX SPEED LAND	15 mph
MAX SPEED WATER	7 mph
FUEL CAPY	140 gal
RANGE LAND	150 mi
RANGE WATER	100 mi
ELECTRICAL	12 neg
TURNING RADIUS FT	30

Overall dimensions listed in inches. Measured with main gun facing forward, and antiaircraft machine gun mounted.

Fighting weight.

ENGINE DATA

ENGINE MAKE/MODEL	Continental W670-9A
NUMBER OF CYLINDERS	Radial 7 cylinders
CUBIC-INCH DISPLACEMENT	668
HORSEPOWER	250 @ 2400 rpm
TORQUE	578 lbs.-ft. @ 1600 rpm
GOVERNED SPEED (rpm)	2400

VALUES

No reported sales

G-214 LVT(A)(1)

In order to provide armored support for troops during the initial stages of a landing, it was necessary for the U.S. to develop an amphibious tank. The LVT(A)(1) was the first of these.

It was based on the hull and drive train of the LVT(2), with the addition of a superstructure supporting a turret mounting a 37mm gun and coaxial .30-caliber machine gun. There were also two .30-caliber machine guns in the superstructure roof that were manned through hatches. A total of 509 of these vehicles were built by FMC.

GENERAL DATA

MODEL	LVT(A)(1)
WEIGHT NET	29,050 lbs.
GROSS	30,000 lbs.
LENGTH	313
WIDTH	128
HEIGHT	121
MAX SPEED LAND	25 mph
MAX SPEED WATER	7 mph
RANGE LAND	125 mi
TRANSMISSION SPEEDS	5F, 1R
TRACK WIDTH	14.25

Overall dimensions listed in inches.

ENGINE DATA

ENGINE MAKE/MODEL	Continental W670-9A
NUMBER OF CYLINDERS	7
CUBIC-INCH DISPLACEMENT	668
HORSEPOWER	250 @ 2400 RPM
TORQUE	584 lbs.-ft. @ 1800 RPM

VALUES

No reported sales

SCARCITY

Scarcity 5

Although the turret of the LVT(A)(1) looks very much like the turret of the M3-series Stuart tank, it was not the same. The LVT(A)(1)'s turret lacked a bustle, among other differences.

The LVT(A)(1) provided a much-need amphibious tank for use during Pacific invasions. It was based on the LVT(2), with the addition of a turret. This vehicle is on display at the Patton Museum, Ft. Knox, Kentucky.

LVT(A)(4) & LVT(A)(5)

The LVT(A)(1) was somewhat successful, proving the soundness of the concept of the amphibious tank, but it also showed that the 37mm gun was not up to the task at hand. The LVT(A)(4) addressed this by mounting a new turret with a 75mm howitzer. When first produced in 1944, the turret had a ring mount and a M2 HB machine gun mounted on it. Later, the ring mount and M2 were eliminated, replaced by a .30-caliber gun on each side of the turret.

When power traverse for the turret was added in April 1945, the vehicle was redesignated LVT(A)(5). The new turret was power operated and featured a turret basket.

VALUES

MODEL	LVT(A)(4) & LVT(A)(5)
WEIGHT	40,000 lbs.
LENGTH	314
WIDTH	128
HEIGHT	122.5
TRACK	114
MAX SPEED LAND	15 mph
MAX SPEED WATER	7 mph
FUEL CAPY	140 gal
RANGE	150 mi
ELECTRICAL	12 neg
TRANSMISSION	
SPEEDS	5
TURNING	
RADIUS FT	30

Overall dimensions listed in inches. Measured with main gun facing forward, and antiaircraft machine gun mounted.

VALUES

ENGINE MAKE/MODEL	Continental W670-9A
NUMBER OF CYLINDERS	7 radial
CUBIC-INCH DISPLACEMENT	668
HORSEPOWER	250 @ 2400 rpm
TORQUE	578 lbs.-ft. @ 1600 rpm
GOVERNED SPEED (rpm)	2400

VALUES

No reported sales

SCARCITY

Scarcity 5

The rear of the hull of the LVT(A)(4) was plain, except for the pintle hook and exhaust stacks. (U.S. Army photo)

The 75mm howitzer that armed the LVT(A)(4) seems to be aimed at the cameraman in this photograph. The driver's vision port is open, as are the hatches. (U.S. Army photo)

The LVT(A)(5) provided much-needed mobile fire support during invasions with its howitzer and machine guns able to engage multiple targets simultaneously. (Photo courtesy of the Patton Museum)

Late LVT(A)(4)s and LVT(A)(5)s had dual .30-caliber air-cooled machine guns. These weapons were mounted on either side of the turret. (U.S. Army photo)

When operating in the water, the LVTs did not have a great deal of freeboard. (Photo courtesy of the Patton Museum)

In addition to a turret basket to support the turret crew, another improvement in the LVT(A)(5) was a vision block on the turret rear. (U.S. Army photo)

The LVT(A)(4)'s turret had a small bustle, which is visible here. (U.S. Army photo)

The unusual design of the LVT(A)(4)'s track shoes is visible here, as are the heavy welds joining the armor comprising the hull. (U.S. Army photo)

LVTP5

The LVTP5 was created to replace the WWII-era LVTs. It was developed in 1951 and production began in August 1952 by the Ingersoll Products Division of Borg-Warner.

The LVTP5 was much larger than its predecessors. The front of the hull was of an inverted-V shape that greatly improved in-water performance. Unlike the earlier LVT, the LVTP5 had its tracks mounted low on the hull much like a tank, rather than the all-round track design used previously. The upper return run of track was via an internal return channel. The V-shaped bow could be lowered to form a ramp for loading and unloading cargo and up to 34 infantry troops (25 for water operation). An additional large hatch and two smaller ones over the passenger compartment provided alternate means of loading and unloading.

The crew and passenger compartment was at the front of the vehicle, with the driver's position at the front above the left track channel. On the opposite side was the vehicle commander's station. A machine gun cupola was available and could be installed at the front of the vehicle between the driver's and commander's hatches. The engine was located at the rear of the vehicle and two more small roof hatches provided access to the engine compartment.

The LVTP5 vehicle tracks were made with inverted grousers in order to propel the vehicle while it was in water. These grousers also served as center guide teeth for the track. The road wheels on the LVTP5 were mounted in pairs, with the center guide teeth running between them. This arrangement meant that each LVTP5 used 36 road wheels per track, One wheel of each pair was of conventional design, with a solid rubber tire mounted on a metal wheel. Under normal conditions, the rubber tire bore the weight of the vehicle. The other wheel was steel-rimmed and absorbed shock loads and heavy loads

Improvements were made to the LVTP5's engine air intake and exhaust system, which resulted in the new

This LVTP5 has been equipped with the .30-caliber machine gun turret on the top. Among the improvements of the LVTP5 was its totally enclosed cargo and personnel compartment. (Photo courtesy of the Patton Museum)

AMPHIBIOUS LANDING VEHICLES

classification of LVTP5A1. Externally, the two models can be differentiated by the A1's large housing on the vehicle's rear roof above the engine.

LVTH6

The LVTH6 was the fire support version of the LVTP5 landing vehicle. The hulls of both types of vehicles were identical, but the LVTH6 had a turret armed with a 105mm howitzer. The turret was installed over the cargo compartment in the area where the LVTP5's upper cargo hatches were located. The vehicle commander, gunner, and loader were located in the turret, which was equipped with power traverse and main gun elevation. There were two hatches in the turret — one for the commander and one for the loader.

The LVTH6 provided amphibious troops with needed artillery support. A .30-caliber machine gun was mounted coaxially with the 105mm howitzer in the turret. (Photo courtesy of the Patton Museum)

Although initially developed by Ingersoll, the LVTP5 vehicles were also produced by FMC, Pacific Car and Foundry, Baldwin-Lima-Hamilton, and St. Louis Car Company. Production by all builders totaled 1,123 vehicles. (Photo courtesy of the Patton Museum)

338 STANDARD CATALOG OF U.S. MILITARY VEHICLES

As with the LTP5, the LVTH6s engine air intake and exhaust systems were modified, and the vehicles became LVTH6A1s.

LVTR1

The LVTR1 was developed in 1954 to act as the recovery and maintenance variant of the LVTP5 family. Equipment for this role included a 60,000-lb. drag

This LVTE1 photo helps illustrate the size of this entire family of vehicles. The tractor towing it is an M123-series 10-ton truck — itself a very large machine. (U.S. Army photo)

The LVTH6 was provided with stowage for 151 rounds of 105mm howitzer ammunition. One of the stowage racks is visible in this view of the vehicle front with the ramp down. When the LVTH6 was operating in water, the ammunition carried was reduced to 100 rounds. (Photo courtesy of the Patton Museum)

The distinctive mine plow of the LVTE1 certainly gives the vehicle a menacing look (U.S. Army photo)

winch. A separate hoist winch, a five CFM air compressor, and a General Electric welder were installed in the cargo compartment. The welder could also be used as a battery charger to slave start other vehicles.

The drag winch was powered by a Willys four-cylinder 48-hp MD engine of the type used in the M38A1 quarter-ton Jeep. This engine was also mounted in the cargo compartment. A boom was mounted on the front of the vehicle that could be erected and used for ordnance maintenance and materials handling. The crew chief acted as the crane operator. The boom had a capacity of 8,000 lbs. when used with a single line, or 14,000 lbs. when rigged with a two-part line.

Once again, modifications were made to the engine's

The rear of this entire family of vehicles was rather plain. There was a towing cable stowed on the rear plate, and four taillights mounted high on the vehicle. (Photo courtesy of the Patton Museum)

air intake and exhaust system, making the vehicle the LVTR1A1.

LVTE1

Like many families of tactical vehicles, the LVTP5 family had an engineer version, known as the LVTE1. It was easily distinguished by its large, toothed, V-shaped excavator blade was mounted on the front of the vehicle. This blade could be lowered to the ground and used to clear a 12-ft.-wide path through a minefield. Buoyancy tanks filled with plastic foam were fitted to the rear of the blade. This allowed the LVTE1 to maintain level trim in the water in spite of the large appendage.

Inside the cargo compartment were two pallets that could be hydraulically raised through the overhead hatches. These pallets each carried a rocket-propelled line charge used to clear a path through mine fields. Once fired, the used line charge pallet was ejected over the right side of the hull. Like some of the LVTP5s, the LVTE1 mounted a machine gun cupola between the commander and driver positions.

Late-production LVTE1s were powered by the same Continental AVI-1790-8 12-cylinder, fuel-injected gasoline engines found on the M48A2 tank.

The U.S. Marine Corps was the biggest user of this family of vehicles, although the U.S. Army also had some examples.

GENERAL DATA

MODEL	LVTP5
WEIGHT	87,780 lbs.
LENGTH	356
WIDTH	140.5

HEIGHT	103
TRACK	114
MAX SPEED LAND	30 mph
WATER	6.8 mph
FUEL CAPY	456 gal
RANGE	190 mi

Overall dimensions listed in inches. Measured with main gun facing forward, and antiaircraft machine gun mounted.

ENGINE DATA

ENGINE MAKE/MODEL	Continental LV-1790-1
NUMBER OF CYLINDERS	12 90-degree V
CUBIC-INCH DISPLACEMENT	1,790
HORSEPOWER	704 @ 2800 rpm
TORQUE	1,440 lbs-ft. @ 2000 rpm

VALUES

No reported sales

SCARCITY

Scarcity 5

LVTP7

In the summer of 1967, the first of the prototypes of the LVTP7 was completed by FMC. Like its predecessor the LVTP5, the LVTP7 was a fully enclosed vehicle. However, it was a very different shape and design. The drive sprocket was at the front, and the ramp at the rear. This was the opposite layout of the LVTP5. Rather than using the tracks for propulsion in the water, the LVTP7 used a water jet on either side of the vehicle.

The driver and infantry troop commander were both provided with cupolas on the left side of the hull, while the vehicle commander had his own weapon station on the right side of the hull that was armed with a M139 20mm gun and a coaxial 7.62 machine gun. The assistant driver's position was behind the infantry troop commander. Roof hatches to provide overhead access to the cargo compartment. As a result of a program that not only came in on time, but below the cost estimates, the Marines began issuing the LVTP7 in 1972.

In the early 1980s, a service life extension program (SLEP) was instituted to improve the reliability, communications, and safety of the LVTP7. The GM 8V53T engine, used in the original version, was replaced with the Cummins VT400 diesel engine with an FMC HS-400-3A1 transmission. The hydraulic systems that powered the weapons were replaced by electric motors, which eliminated the danger of hydraulic fluid fires. Improvements were made to the suspension and shock absorbers and the fuel tank improved. A fuel-burning

smoke generator system was added to the vehicles, and eight smoke grenade launchers were mounted around the weapons station. The headlight recesses were round on these vehicles, compared to the square recess used previously. FMC converted 853 of the old vehicles to the new standard in addition to building 333 new ones.

Inside, an improved instrument panel was installed, as was a night vision device and a new ventilation system. Originally designated the LVTP7A1, the vehicle was changed by the Marines in 1984 to the AAVP7A1. About that time the original weapon station was replaced with a new system from Cadillac Gage that was armed with both a .50-caliber machine gun and a 40mm automatic grenade launcher.

GENERAL DATA

MODEL	AAV7A1
WEIGHT	56,552 lbs.
LENGTH	321.3
WIDTH	128.7
HEIGHT	130.5
MAX SPEED LAND	30 mph
MAX SPEED WATER	6 mph
FUEL CAPY	171 gal
RANGE	300 mi

Overall dimensions listed in inches.

ENGINE DATA

ENGINE MAKE/MODEL	Cummins VT400
NUMBER OF CYLINDERS	8 90-degree V
CUBIC-INCH DISPLACEMENT	903

VALUES

Current use

SCARCITY

Current use

Part of the latest upgrades to the LVTP includes a provision for applique armor, as seen in this photo. (Photo courtesy United Defense, LP)

CARRIERS

G-154 M28 Weasel

In May of 1942, the Studebaker Corporation of South Bend, Indiana, was contracted to create a vehicle for use by the proposed Special Service Force. Just two months later, shrouded in great secrecy, the first test of the resulting Studebaker Weasel, in the form of the T-15, was performed on a glacier near Mt. Columbia in British Columbia, Canada.

After trying a variety of tracks, and changes in other details, the T-15 was reclassified as the M28 Weasel. Its engine was modified and borrowed from a Studebaker Champion. To supply power for radio equipment, the vehicle had a 12-volt electrical system. It's three-speed transmission is coupled to a two-speed steering differential.

The rack on the right side of the M28 was for stowing the crew's skis. The soft-top cab enclosure was no doubt welcomed by crews operating the M28 in cold weather. (Photo courtesy of the Patton Museum)

The unusual canted road wheels that were characteristic of the M28 Weasel can be clearly seen on this example, owned and restored by the Military Vehicle Preservation Group of Spooner, Wisconsin.

The Weasel was originally conceived as a snow vehicle, and many were camouflage-painted accordingly. (Photo courtesy of the Patton Museum)

The M28 had two seats with the engine mounted backward in the rear of the vehicle. The drive sprockets and steering differential were mounted at the front of the vehicle. Eight road wheels were mounted on two springs on each side of the vehicle. These road wheels were mounted with a distinct inward cant at the bottom. In 1943 the M28 was dropped in favor of the M29.

GENERAL DATA

MODEL	M28
WEIGHT GROSS	4,600 lbs.
LENGTH	128
WIDTH	60
HEIGHT	67
STD TRACK WIDTH	18
MAX SPEED	30 mph
FUEL CAPY	25 gal
RANGE	155 mi
ELECTRICAL	12 neg
TRANSMISSION	
SPEEDS	3
AXLE/TRANSMISSION	
SPEEDS	2

Overall dimensions listed in inches.

ENGINE DATA

ENGINE MAKE/MODEL	Studebaker Champion
NUMBER OF CYLINDERS	6
CUBIC INCH DISPLACEMENT	169.6
HORSEPOWER	65 @ 3600 rpm
TORQUE	130 lbs.-ft. @ 1800 rpm
GOVERNED SPEED (rpm)	Not governed

VALUES

	6	5	4	3	2	1
M28	1,000	4,000	7,000	9,500	12,000	14,500

SCARCITY

Scarcity 4

G-179 M29 & M29C Weasel

The M29 was a tremendous improvement over its predecessor, the M28. Essentially the same Studebaker Champion engine was used, but with the conventional automotive layout. The engine was mounted in front, with the transmission attached to it. A driveshaft transmitted the power to the rear steering differential.

Seating was increased from two to four, the tracks

had an improved design, and the number of road wheels was doubled. The suspension system was vastly improved as well.

The tracks were further improved in mid-production when their width was increased from 15 to 20 in.

The M29's instrument panel is visible to the right of the driver's seat. Just above the steering lever is the tiller mounted on the dashboard, and at the far right in the open engine compartment is the generator and carburetor mounted on the engine. (U.S. Army photo)

The purpose of the flotation tanks is shown in this photograph of an M29C undergoing testing at the General Motors Proving Ground in September 1944. Extensive testing of the Studebaker-built Weasel was done here, while vehicles of many manufacturers, including GM, were tested at the equally impressive Studebaker Proving Ground. (U.S. Army photo)

The Weasel was designed to traverse snow. Vehicles being shipped to areas with high snowfall amounts were painted in this snow camouflage scheme. Even the canvas cab cover was camouflage. (U.S. Army photo)

The M29's drive sprocket was at the rear of the vehicle, and the engine in front. A spotlight was just forward of the windshield. (U.S. Army photo)

The M29C had flotation tanks added in both front and rear. The front tank was fitted with a surf shield, shown folded backwards into the stowed position in this photograph. This vehicle is missing its track aprons. (Photo courtesy of the Patton Museum)

Studebaker built 4,476 of the M29 before switching production to the M29C.

M29C

Adding another dimension to the Weasel's mobility, the M29C was fully amphibious. Floatation cells were added to both the front and rear of the vehicle, track aprons were installed, and dual rudders were mounted on the rear. The rudders were controlled by a tiller control operated by the driver. The Weasel was propelled in the water by its tracks, which gave it a top speed of 4 mph in calm water. The M29C was the most abundant of the Weasels, with 10,647 produced. Many of these had

their flotation tanks and rudders removed in the field, essentially making them M29s.

The Weasel's unique abilities kept it in the Army inventory until the early 1960s.

GENERAL DATA

MODEL	M29	M29C
WEIGHT	3,725 lbs.	4,778 lbs.
LENGTH	126	192.125
WIDTH	61	67.25
HEIGHT	71	71
TRACK	45	45
STD TRACK WIDTH	15	20
MAX SPEED	36 mph	36 mph
FUEL CAPY	35 gal	35 gal
RANGE	175 mi	175 mi
ELECTRICAL	12 neg	12 neg
TRANSMISSION SPEEDS	3	3
AXLE/TRANSMISSION SPEEDS	2	2
TURNING RADIUS FT.	12	12

Overall dimensions listed in inches.

ENGINE DATA

ENGINE MAKE/MODEL	Studebaker Champion
NUMBER OF CYLINDERS	6
CUBIC-INCH DISPLACEMENT	170
HORSEPOWER	65 @ 3600 rpm
TORQUE	130 lbs.-ft. @ 1800 rpm
GOVERNED SPEED (rpm)	Not governed

VALUES

	6	5	4	3	2	1
M29	1,000	3,000	5,500	7,500	10,000	12,500
M29C	1,000	3,500	6,000	8,000	11,000	13,500

SCARCITY

M29	3
M29C	4

The M29C also had rudders mounted on the rear. In this photograph the rudders have been folded up into a stowed position. The rudders were stowed like this to prevent damage during overland operations. The vehicle's splash shield is down in this photo. (U.S. Army photo)

This group is undoubtedly a Weasel collector's dream. This Signal Corps photo of a group of M29Cs was taken at Manila, the Philippines. Some of them have their surf shields swung up, between the stowed and usable condition, and one has its canvas cab cover fitted. All of them have their pioneer tools in place, and in the foreground we can see the cover next to the driver's seat. Under that cover is the Studebaker Champion engine. (National Archives and Records Administration photo)

G-245 M76 Otter

The M76 Otter was built to provide the military with a lightweight amphibious carrier with a higher load capacity than the Weasel. The Otter had a totally enclosed, insulated aluminum body, and space for eight passengers plus the two-man crew, or a 3,000-lb. cargo. There were hatches in the roof, and a pair of doors on the back for loading and unloading of passenger or cargo. The crew was provided with doors on either side.

The Otter had a propeller mounted below the pintle hook for use in the water, and the fuel tanks were mounted externally. The location of the fuel tanks and external stowage varied during the production run. They were centered on the hull side on early vehicles, and shifted to the rear of the hull sides on late models. All Otters had a 5,000-lb.-capacity winch mounted in the rear compartment under a seat.

The Marines used the Otters in limited quantities in Vietnam.

GENERAL DATA

MODEL	M76
WEIGHT	12,162 lbs.
MAX TOWED LOAD	6,000 lbs.
LENGTH	188
WIDTH	98
HEIGHT	108
TRACK	68
STD TRACK WIDTH	30
MAX SPEED LAND	28 mph
MAX SPEED WATER	4.5 mph
FUEL CAPY	70 gal
RANGE LAND	160 mi
ELECTRICAL	24 neg
TRANSMISSION SPEEDS	2
TURNING RADIUS	pivot

Overall dimensions listed in inches.

*Fighting weight

ENGINE DATA

ENGINE MAKE/MODEL	Continental AOI-268-3A
NUMBER OF CYLINDERS	4 opposed
CUBIC-INCH DISPLACEMENT	269
HORSEPOWER	127 @ 3200 rpm
TORQUE	225 lbs.-ft. @ 2600 rpm
GOVERNED SPEED (rpm)	3200

VALUES

	6	5	4	3	2	1
All models	3,000	5,000	9,500	14,000	16,000	20,000

SCARCITY

Scarcity 3

On the driver's side of the M76 was a second fuel tank, as well as a spare tire. The horn and blackout driving light are just forward of the driver's door. (Photo courtesy of the Patton Museum)

The M76 Otter was not only an unusually shaped vehicle, it had some unusual features as well. The road wheels were fully pneumatic tires, much like those on passenger cars, and the fuel tanks were mounted externally on the sides of the hull. One can be seen here as the bulging protrusion at the rear of the body. Also visible are the axe and mattock pioneer tools. (U.S. Army photo)

G-299 M116 Husky

The Husky was designed by the Pacific Car and Foundry Company as part of a program to replace the Weasel. Pacific went on to build four pilot models, and three pre-production pilots. However, the Blaw-Knox Company got the contract to build the 197 production units. The M116 was rated with a load capacity of 1 1/2 tons and was powered by a Chevrolet V8 driving a Hydra-Matic transmission.

The lightweight welded aluminum hull was topped with a fiberglass cab, which had two hatches in its roof for the driver and co-driver to enter. The engine was positioned behind the driver, with the cooling air coming from a grill in the roof and exhausting through a grill on the right side of the vehicle.

All Huskies had a front-mounted winch and were completely amphibious without preparation. The M116 was propelled through the water by its tracks. A hinged door in the rear of the hull provided entrance and exit to the cargo space. The cargo area floor was moveable and could be raised to provide a flat floor or lowered to provide troop seats. A canvas cargo cover and bows could cover the cargo space, or a hard winter top could be mounted.

XM733

The XM733 was basically an armored version of the M116. It was open topped and could be fitted with a variety of weapons. Pacific Car and Foundry produced 93

The rear door of the hardtop hinged at the top, folding downward to mate with the upward folding tailgate integral with the hull. A pintle hook was provided for towing trailers or sleds. (U.S. Army photo)

The M116 Husky was the answer to the Army's desire for a lightweight amphibious carrier. This vehicle was photographed in the Pacific Car and Foundry Company plant, and such such details as the front-mounted winch found on all Huskies, and the wide track the provided superb flotation in snow, mud and sand.

This view of the M16 Husky shows the pioneer tool stowage and placement of the spare fuel cans, as well as the bottom-hinged rear tailgate.

Though not actually an M116, but an T116E1 pilot vehicle, this vehicle shows how the the optional rear hardtop enclosure was fitted to the vehicle. The hatch in the roof allowed the overhead loading of cargo. (U.S. Army photo)

of these for the Marine Corps to use in Southeast Asia beginning in 1966.

M116A1

Although Pacific Car didn't get to build the M116s for the Army, it did get the contracts to build 111 of the M116A1 for the Navy and Marine Corps.

GENERAL DATA

MODEL	M116
WEIGHT*	10,600 lbs.
LENGTH	188.1
WIDTH	82.1
HEIGHT	79.1
TRACK	58.5
STD TRACK WIDTH	20
MAX SPEED LAND	37 mph
MAX SPEED WATER	4.2 mph
FUEL CAPY	65 gal
RANGE LAND	300 mi
ELECTRICAL	24 neg
TRANSMISSION	
SPEEDS	4F
1R	
TURNING	
RADIUS FT.	8

Overall dimensions listed in inches.

*Fighting weight

ENGINE DATA

ENGINE MAKE/MODEL	Chevrolet
NUMBER OF CYLINDERS	V-8
CUBIC-INCH DISPLACEMENT	283
HORSEPOWER	160 @ 4600 rpm
TORQUE	210 lbs.-ft. @ 2400 rpm
GOVERNED SPEED (rpm)	4600

VALUES

	6	5	4	3	2	1
All models	3,500	8,500	14,000	18,000	22,000	28,000

SCARCITY

Scarcity 4

M548 Carrier Family

M548

The M548 carrier was developed to meet a Signal Corps requirement for a carrier for the AN/MPQ-32 counter-battery radar system. The M548 was built using automotive components of the M113A1 family of vehicles. Although the vehicle was not used for the reason originally conceived, it did fill a variety of rolls. It was used as an ammunition carrier for the M107, M108, M109, and M110 self-propelled artillery pieces, as well as a Lance missile carrier.

M548A1

The improvements made to the M113A1 that resulted in the M113A2 were also applied to the M538, resulting in the M548A1. The M548A1 also had a 1,500-lb.-capacity chain hoist added in the cargo compartment to ease placement of ammunition and cargo.

M548A3

Many of the M548A1s were rebuilt with the 6V53T turbosupercharged engine and Allison X200-4 cross-

The XM474 Pershing missile carrier was the genesis for the entire family of vehicles that became the M548 series. With the excellent road system in Europe, the primary theater of deployment for the Pershing, it was later decided to transport the missile by truck. The G-852 series of 5-ton 8x8 trucks were developed for this purpose. (U.S. Army photo)

As was the case with most soft-topped M-series vehicles, a hardtop was available for the M548 that would totally enclose the cab. This preserved M548, displayed at the Iola Vintage Military Vehicle and Gun show in 2002, is owned by R.A. Schmidt. Some of its cargo bows have been removed.

drive transmission as used in the M113A3. These changes not only made driver training easier, but also made the Carrier's performance equal to that of the Army's frontline fighting equipment.

M667

The M667 was built to be a carrier for the Lance missile system, and was based on the M548 family. Its cab was much narrower than the full-width cab of the M548. The M667 had a counterbalanced loading ramp at the rear, and suspension lockouts to make the vehicle more stable during the loading and unloading of delicate missile components. The M667 was the basic vehicle for the M688 loader/transporter and the M752 launcher.

M688

The M688 was the loader/transporter for the Lance missile. It was based on the M667 and featured a low-profile, narrow cab.

M752

The M752 looked very much like the M688, but was the launcher component of this missile system. The entire Lance system was declared obsolete and disposed of in 1992.

This M667 has been equipped as an M688 loader/transporter for the Lance missile system. It is shown here climbing a vertical wall on a test course in February 1968. The angle shows its load of two Lance missiles in its cargo bay. FMC built 168 of these for U.S. use, and an additional 163 for foreign sales. (U.S. Army photo)

The M548 cargo carrier was fully amphibious, being propelled in water by its skirted tracks. As shown here, it could be fitted with an antiaircraft machine gun on a ring mount over the cab. Vinyl covers were supplied for both the cargo and crew areas, and a 20,000-lb.-capacity self-recovery winch was inset in the front of the hull. (U.S. Army photo)

The M730 Chaparral transported and launched four infrared guided surface-to-air missiles. This one is shown prepared for launch, its cargo bows removed and stowed on the front of the vehicle, and the blast shield deployed over the cab and engine compartment. (U.S. Army photo)

This M667 is set up as an M752 self-propelled Lance missile launcher. During firing operations the cab roof retracted vertically. The Lance missile system was declared obsolete in 1992. (U.S. Army photo)

CARRIERS

M727 Hawk Missile Carrier

The M727 utilized the power train and suspension of the M548 cargo carrier, but it was equipped with the M754 guided missile launcher. It transported and launched three Hawk surface-to-air missiles. The M501 loader/transporter was used to reload the launcher. Blast deflectors were installed to protect the cab and power train of the vehicle from missile exhaust gases during launching. The vehicle's suspension was equipped with a lock system to stabilize it during the loading and launching sequences. These vehicles were not amphibious.

M730 Chaparral SAM System

The M730 consisted of a modified M548, upon which was installed the four-rail M54 launch and control system. The Chaparral missile itself had a range of about 11 miles. It is sighted optically by the gunner, and uses an infrared guidance system to home in on its target. Blast shields are provided for the carrier, which the crew unfolds prior to launching to protect the cab and engine from the missile exhaust.

When the engine cooling system was improved on the M548, it was also improved on the M730, which then became the M730A1. The addition of the RISE power package and NBC protection caused the classification to be changed again, this time to M730A2. The front winch was deleted from the M730A2.

GENERAL DATA

MODEL	M548A1
WEIGHT*	28,300 lbs.
LENGTH	232
WIDTH	105.75
HEIGHT	110.75
TRACK	85
STD TRACK WIDTH	15 mph
MAX SPEED LAND	35 mph
FUEL CAPY	105 gal
RANGE	300 mi
ELECTRICAL	24 neg
TRANSMISSION	
SPEEDS	3F, 1R
TURNING	
RADIUS FT.	14

Overall dimensions listed in inches.

*Fighting weight

ENGINE DATA

ENGINE MAKE/MODEL	GM 6V53
NUMBER OF CYLINDERS	6
CUBIC-INCH DISPLACEMENT	318
HORSEPOWER	212 @ 2800 rpm
TORQUE	492 lbs.-ft. @ 1300 rpm

VALUES

	6	5	4	3	2	1
All models	2,500	6,500	12,000	15,000	20,000	23,000

SCARCITY

Scarcity 3

This photo of the XM727 Hawk missile launcher taken in February 1965 shows the blast shield that protected the cab and engine. (U.S. Army photo)

GUN MOTOR CARRIAGES

M7 Priest

The M7 Priest family of vehicles was designed to provide armored units with highly mobile organic artillery support. Mechanically, the initial vehicles were based on M3 medium tank components, while later production used M4 Sherman components. The name was derived from the pulpit-like appearance of the antiaircraft machine gun ring and mount.

Between April 1942 and August 1943, American Locomotive Company built 2,814 of these self-propelled guns. There were at least three variations in the ammunition stowage of these early vehicles.

Experience in battle showed there was room for improvement, and between March and October of 1944 American Locomotive (ALCO) built 500 more vehicles, and Federal Machine and Welder Company built 176. The most readily visible difference between the early and late models was the addition of fold-down armor along the sides and rear of the fighting compartment.

Simultaneously, Pressed Steel Car Company was building 826 M7B1 self-propelled guns. The M7B1 was very similar to the late M7s, but it was based on M4A3 components. Because of this they were grouped as G-199 vehicles, while the M7 was a G-128 vehicle. Like the late M7, the M7B1's lower hulls were built of mild-steel

The M7B1 used M4A3 automotive components, while the M7s used M4 components. The M37B1 also improved protection for the gun crew by increasing armor height in the from of folding flaps — one of which can be seen here folded down. (Photo courtesy of the Patton Museum)

This late-production M7 was photographed while on training maneuvers. The low side armor is apparent when comparing this photo with those of later models. (Photo courtesy of the Patton Museum)

GUN MOTOR CARRIAGES

plate, not armor.

To increase the elevation of the howitzer for better use in the rugged terrain of Korea during the 1950s, many vehicles were converted to the M7B2 configuration. This was done by raising the gun mount and machine gun ring. All this resulted in a very different frontal appearance.

GENERAL DATA

MODEL	M7	M7B1
WEIGHT	52,000 lbs.	50,000 lbs.
LENGTH	237	247.5
WIDTH	117	113.5
HEIGHT	104	102
TRACK	83	83
STD TRACK WIDTH	16 9/16	16 9/16
CREW	7	7
MAX SPEED	24 mph	26 mph
FUEL CAPY	176 gal	168 gal
RANGE	85 mi	85 mi
ELECTRICAL	24 neg	24 neg
TRANSMISSION		
SPEEDS	5F, 1R	5F, 1R
TURNING		
RADIUS FT.	31	31

ARMAMENT MAIN	105mm	105mm
FLEXIBLE	1x .50	1x .50

Overall dimensions listed in inches. Measured with main gun facing forward, and antiaircraft machine gun mounted.
*Fighting weight.

ENGINE DATA

ENGINE MAKE/MODEL	Continental R975C1
NUMBER OF CYLINDERS	9 radial
CUBIC-INCH DISPLACEMENT	973
HORSEPOWER	350 @ 2400 rpm
TORQUE	840 lbs.-ft. @ 1700 rpm
GOVERNED SPEED (rpm)	2400

COMMUNICATION EQUIPMENT: M238 flag set.

VALUES

	6	5	4	3	2	1
All models	7,000	15,000	18,000	25,000	31,000	37,000

SCARCITY

Scarcity 4

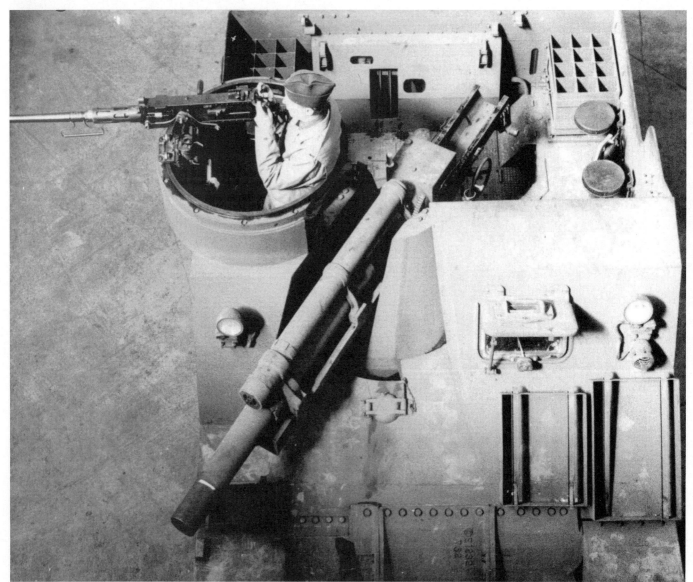

The three-piece differential housing that was characteristic of the earliest production vehicles, as is the pulpit-like antiaircraft machine gun mount that inspired the M7's name, Priest. The main gun has been traversed to its right-most limit in this photograph. (U.S. Army photo)

The cylinders arranged around the perimeter of the open-topped fighting compartment of the M7 contain 105mm ammunition. In this photo the driver's vision hatch is open to provide a clear view as the vehicle prepares to tackle the hill climb test at Aberdeen Proving Ground. This is the first vehicle assembled by American Locomotive Company. (U.S. Army photo)

The final development of the Priest was the modification in the 1950s of some vehicles to the M7B2 standard. (U.S. Army photo)

M10 Tank Destroyer

The M10 Tank Destroyer was based on the automotive components of the diesel-powered M4A2 Sherman tank. Production of the 4,993 Wolverines ran at the Fisher Tank Arsenal from September 1942 through December 1943. The main armament for these vehicles was the 3-in.-gun M7.

Ford Motor Company produced a similar vehicle, known as the M10A1, based on the gasoline-powered M4A3 from October until September 1943. Ford built 1,038 of these. Fisher also built 375 M10A1s and another 300 without turrets, which were later converted to the Gun Motor Carriage M36.

Three different versions of turrets were mounted on the M10 series vehicles. Originally, the turret had no counterweights on the rear but, due to the imbalance caused by the gun, it was difficult to rotate the turret when on a grade. Field units improvised various types of counterweights in an attempt to overcome this deficiency. Eventually, new vehicles were factory equipped with two 1,800-lb. counterweights attached to the turret rear to correct this. Later, the rear of the turret was redesigned and new counterweights were made with a small amount of storage space in them.

Counter to the usual Army policy, the diesel-powered M10s were deployed overseas, while the gas-powered versions were retained in the U.S. for training use.

Later, many of these retained M10s were rebuilt into M36 Gun Motor Carriages. Eventually, some of the M10s were rebuilt with 90mm guns, becoming M36B2 Gun

The M10 was intended to be a fast vehicle designed to knock out enemy tanks, but improved German armor meant that an up-gunned vehicle was required, leading to the M10-based M36. (Photo courtesy of D. Moss)

Two large 1,800-lb. weights were designed to mount on the rear of the turret of the M10 to correct the weight imbalance problem. This vehicle, on display at the Patton Museum, has these weights attached. (Photo courtesy of D. Moss)

The M10, which was long displayed at the Aberdeen Proving Ground's "Mile of Tanks," was shown in transit mode. The "Mile of Tanks" has since been removed and placed in storage. (U.S. Army photo)

The M10 Tank Destroyer was based on the automotive components of the diesel-powered M4A2 Sherman tank, and the lineage is apparent in the suspension. The main armament for these vehicles was the 3-in. gun M7.

M19 Twin 40mm

The M19 was originally designed to provide a highly mobile medium antiaircraft artillery piece. Cadillac began production in April 1945, but by war's end only 300 had been built and production stopped.

The chassis was based on a lengthened M24 light tank chassis with the engine relocated to just behind the driver's compartment. At the rear of the vehicle was a power-operated turret mounting twin Bofors 40mm antiaircraft cannons. Each clip-fed barrel was able to fire 120 rounds per minute. With only 352 rounds carried by the M19 itself, and a possible 320 more in the M28 trailer, accurate sighting was imperative. The addition of a 200-amp auxiliary engine-driven generator and the relocation of the radio equipment to blisters on the turret resulted in the new designation M19A1.

The M19A1 provided antiaircraft defense for the Army into the 1950s.

Motor Carriages. The British rearmed some of their M10s with a 17-pounder Mk V, yielding a very effective tank killer that was dubbed the Achilles IIC. None of the Achilles were used by U.S. forces.

GENERAL DATA

MODEL	M10	M10A1
WEIGHT*	65,200 lbs.	64,000 lbs.
LENGTH	286.3	286.3
WIDTH	120	120
HEIGHT	114	114
TRACK	83	83
CREW	5	5
MAX SPEED	25 mph	26 mph
FUEL CAPY	165 gal	168 gal
RANGE	200 mi	115 mi
ELECTRICAL	24 neg	24 neg
TRANSMISSION		
SPEEDS	5	5
TURNING		
RADIUS FEET	31	31
ARMAMENT MAIN		
FLEXIBLE	3 in.	3 in.
1x .50	1x .50	

Overall dimensions listed in inches. Measure with main gun facing forward, and antiaircraft machine gun mounted.

*Combat weight

ENGINE DATA M10

ENGINE MAKE/MODEL	GMC 6046 or 6046D Diesel
NUMBER OF CYLINDERS	12
CUBIC-INCH DISPLACEMENT	850
HORSEPOWER	375 @ 2100 rpm
TORQUE	855 lbs.-ft. @ 1300 rpm
GOVERNED SPEED (rpm)	2100

ENGINE DATA M10A1

ENGINE MAKE/MODEL	Ford GAA
NUMBER OF CYLINDERS	V-8 60 degree
CUBIC-INCH DISPLACEMENT	1,100
HORSEPOWER	450 @ 2600 rpm
TORQUE	950 lbs.-ft. @ 2100 rpm
GOVERNED SPEED (rpm)	2600

RADIO EQUIPMENT: *The M10 was equipped with SCR 610 radio set, RC99 interphone, and a M238 flag set.*

VALUES

	6	5	4	3	2	1
All models	7,000	15,000	25,000	35,000	45,000	60,000

SCARCITY

Scarcity 4

GENERAL DATA

MODEL	M19	M19A1
WEIGHT	39,000 lbs.	41,165 lbs.
LENGTH	228.8	228.8
WIDTH	115	115
HEIGHT	117	117
WIDTH*	80/1 12	80/1 12
TREAD	96	96
TRACK WIDTH	16	16
CREW	6	6
MAX SPEED	30 mph	30 mph
FUEL CAPY	110 gal	110 gal
RANGE	85 mi	100 mi
ELECTRICAL	24 neg	24 neg
HYDRAMATIC		
TRANSMISSION		
SPEEDS	4	4
TRANSFER		
SPEEDS	2	2
TURNING		
RADIUS FT.	23	pivot

The M19 being has the smooth, rounded shape and turret characteristic of the early vehicles. (Photo courtesy of the Patton Museum)

The blister added to the turret of the M19A1 housed the radio equipment. This equipment was previously located in the hull, but was relocated on the A1 due to the addition of an auxiliary generator. (U. S. Army photo)

The M19 family's twin 40mm Bofors antiaircraft cannons were also used with devastating effect against enemy infantry. The vehicle's automotive lineage to the M24 Chaffee is apparent in this April 1949 view of an M19A1. The five road wheels per side were attached to torsion bars. (U.S. Army photo)

ARMAMENT   2x 40mm   2x 40mm

Overall dimensions listed in inches.

*Inside/outside width at tires.

ENGINE DATA

ENGINE MAKE/MODEL	2 x Cadillac 44T24
NUMBER OF CYLINDERS	V-8 90-degree
CUBIC-INCH DISPLACEMENT	349
HORSEPOWER	110 @ 3400 rpm
TORQUE	240 lbs.-ft. @ 1200 rpm
GOVERNED SPEED (rpm)	Not governed

RADIO EQUIPMENT: *The M19 was equipped with the SCR 510 or AN/VRC-5. The M19A1 was equipped with the AN/VRC-5, as well as either the SCR 593, or AN/GRR-5. Those vehicles equipped with the SCR 510 were fitted with the RC99 interphone set with four stations.*

All vehicles were equipped with the M238 flag set.

VALUES

	6	5	4	3	2	1
All models	5,000	11,000	16,500	27,000	38,000	50,000

SCARCITY

Scarcity 5

M36 Series

The M36 was developed to provide the military with a better-armed tank destroyer to cope with the increasingly heavy German armor.

The 3-in. gun of the M10 was not deemed adequate, so the M36s were equipped with a 90mm originally developed for antiaircraft work. The M36 was basically an M10A1 with a new turret to accommodate the larger weapon.

In November 1943, the Army asked that Fisher convert 500 of the M10A1s then under construction into M36 90mm Gun Motor Carriages. Two hundred of the M1A1s were too far along to convert, but the remaining 300 were converted between April and July of 1944.

Demand for the new M36s was so great that an additional 500 M10A1s were shipped by the Army starting in June 1944 to Massey-Harris and converted to M36 standards using Fisher-built turrets.

The invasion of France proved the superiority of the M36 over the M10A1 and prompted Alco to perform 413 conversions.

Fisher built 187 M36B1 Gun Motor Carriages by placing the M36 turret on the hulls of M4A3 Sherman tanks, with the necessary changes in ammunition storage.

Alco's Canadian subsidiary, Montreal Locomotive

The M36 was basically an upgunned M10 Tank Destroyer. The new gun was a 90mm weapon, and its gun tube seemed disproportionately large for the chassis. (Photo courtesy of the Patton Museum)

The M36, like the M10, had an open-topped turret. To provide protection against grenades and shrapnel, various metal covers, as shown above, were tried. The main gun travel lock, hull stowage, and anti-aircraft weapon mount were all standard. (Photo courtesy of the Patton Museum)

The M36B1 was the result of a joining of the M36 turret with the hull of a M4A3 tank. There were 187 of these hybrid vehicles built. (Photo courtesy of the Patton Museum)

Works, began conversion work on 200 M10A1s in May 1945. With no more M10A1s available for conversion, the M10 chassis began to be used. The resultant M36B2s were converted by both Alco and Montreal, with production totaling 672 and 52, respectively.

GENERAL DATA

MODEL	M36	M36B1	M36B2
WEIGHT	61,000 lbs.	68,000 lbs.	66,000 lbs.
LENGTH	294	294.5	294
WIDTH	120	104.5	120
HEIGHT	125.625	104.5	110
TRACK	83	83	91
CREW	5		
MAX SPEED	26 mph	26 mph	25 mph
FUEL CAPY	192 gal	168 gal	165 gal
RANGE	155 mi	115 mi	115 mi
ELECTRICAL	24 neg	24 neg	24 neg
TRANSMISSION			
SPEEDS	5	5	5
TURNING			
RADIUS FT.	31	31	31
ARMAMENT MAIN			
FLEXIBLE	90mm	90mm	90mm
	1 x .50	1 x .50	1 x .50

Overall dimensions listed in inches. Measured with main gun facing forward, and antiaircraft machine gun mounted.

ENGINE DATA

ENGINE MAKE/MODEL	Ford GAA
NUMBER OF CYLINDERS	V-8 60 degree
CUBIC-INCH DISPLACEMENT	1,100
HORSEPOWER	450 @ 2600 rpm
TORQUE	950 lbs.-ft. @ 2100 rpm
GOVERNED SPEED (rpm)	2600

RADIO EQUIPMENT: *The M36 was equipped with an SCR 610 radio set, RC99 interphone, and M238 flag set.*

VALUES

	6	5	4	3	2	1
All models	7,000	15,000	25,000	35,000	45,000	60,000

SCARCITY

Scarcity 4

G-158 M12

In 1941, development work started on a 155mm self-propelled gun. The vehicle was based on the M3 Medium Tank chassis, with the engine relocated forward to a position just behind the driving compartment. All of the new vehicles had the three-piece differential housing,

At the rear of the M12 was a large hydraulically lowered spade. When in the transport position, as shown here, the spade formed a seat for two crew members. As the M12 was intended to be emplaced well behind the front lines, not much consideration was given to providing armor protection to the crew. (Photo courtesy of the Patton Museum)

but it was tilted slightly forward to align it with the relocated engine. There was a hydraulically operated spade mounted at the rear, which was lowered during firing to anchor the vehicle against the recoil. When retracted into the travelling position it provided a seat for two of the six crewmen.

A pilot vehicle was built by Rock Island Arsenal, and after testing and modification, the M12 was placed into production by the Pressed Steel Car Company. The 100-unit production run came between September 1942 and March 1943. Though a few M12s were used by training units, most were placed in storage until February 1944, when the first of 74 of them were shipped to Baldwin Locomotive Works to be improved based on further tests and usage in training. This work continued until May 1944.

The massive 155mm field piece filled the hull of the M12, allowing only 10 rounds of ammunition to be carried. Each M12 had an M30 ammunition carrier supplied with it to transport additional ammunition. The M30 was essentially a M12 sans main weapon. (Photo courtesy of the Patton Museum)

The M12 was the Army's first successful attempt at a 155mm self-propelled gun. The chassis was based on that of the M3 medium tank, with some modifications. (Photo courtesy of the Patton Museum)

GUN MOTOR CARRIAGES

Three slightly different WWI surplus weapons were mounted, depending upon availability: the M1917, the M1917A1, and the M1918M1. The M1917 was French built, the M1918 was U.S. built, and the M1917A1 had the French gun tube with the U.S. breech.

GENERAL DATA

MODEL	M12
WEIGHT*	59,000 lbs.
LENGTH	266.5
WIDTH	105.3
HEIGHT	113.5
TRACK	83
STD TRACK WIDTH	16 9/16
CREW	6
MAX SPEED	24 mph
FUEL CAPY	200 gal
RANGE	140 mi
ELECTRICAL	24 neg
TRANSMISSION	
SPEEDS	5F, 1R
TURNING	
RADIUS FT.	31
ARMAMENT	155mm

Overall dimensions listed in inches. Measured with main gun facing forward, and antiaircraft machine gun mounted.
*Fighting weight.

ENGINE DATA

ENGINE MAKE/MODEL	Continental R975C1
NUMBER OF CYLINDERS	9 radial
CUBIC-INCH DISPLACEMENT	973
HORSEPOWER	350 @ 2400 rpm
TORQUE	840 lbs.-ft. @ 1700 rpm
GOVERNED SPEED (rpm)	2400

COMMUNICATION EQUIPMENT: The M12 carried an M113 flag set.

VALUES

No reported sales

SCARCITY

Scarcity 5

When the M12 was fired, the spade was lowered into the ground to anchor the vehicle against the 155's tremendous recoil. (Photo courtesy of the Patton Museum)

As the layout of the M12 was not symmetrical, the right side of the fighting compartment was lower than the left. A large travel lock was provided to support the gun tube. (Photo courtesy of the Patton Museum)

G-163 M18 Hellcat 90mm

Production of the M18 Hellcat began in June 1943. At that time the vehicle was known as the T70. It was reclassified as the M18 in March 1944. Production continued until October 1944, by which time 2,507 had been produced by Buick. Units between serial numbers 685 and 1,096 were modified with a different gear ratio. Those with serial numbers were below 685 were to be returned to the factory, where 640 of them were rebuilt

as M39 Armored Utility Vehicles.

The open-topped turret was constructed of welded armor and mounted a 76mm gun. The hull was also made of welded armor, and housed a driver and assistant driver, both of whom had controls with which to drive the vehicle.

The armor of the M18 was very light and could be penetrated by a .30-caliber machine gun at 75 yards. The M18's greatest defense was its speed. With a top speed of 50 mph, the M18 could strike quickly, and hopefully withdraw before the enemy would be able to respond. The torsion-bar suspension of the M18 provided a smooth ride, even at high speeds.

The M18 was a lightweight, high-speed tank destroyer built by Buick. Its torsion-bar suspension set the standard for U.S. tracked vehicle suspensions for years to come. This M18 on display at the Fourth Infantry Division Museum in Fort Hood, Texas, has a muzzle brake. (The barrel without one is on an adjacent vehicle).

Here is another view of the Fourth Infantry's M18 being repainted. Even 60 years after it was built, the M18 Hell Cat has a modern appearance.

GUN MOTOR CARRIAGES

G-232 M40 & M43

The success of the M12 155mm self-propelled gun sparked a desire for more of this type weapon. However, supplies of the WWI surplus rifles were exhausted, and the only available gun type was the 155mm M1. The M1 was more powerful than the M1917 — probably too powerful for the M12 chassis.

A new chassis was designed based on late model Sherman components, including the horizontal volute suspension system. The hull was wider than that used by the tank, so adapters were cast to extend the width of the differential housing.

The vehicle was designated T83 during testing, and production began by Pressed Steel Car Company in February 1945, even before the vehicle had been standardized as 155mm Gun Motor Carriage M40, which occurred in May 1945. Production of the T83/M40 totaled 418 pieces.

The 8-in. howitzer M1 was trial mounted on this

chassis very early in the development, with satisfactory results. These vehicles were referred to as T89 Howitzer Motor Carriages until standardized as M43 in November 1945. The T89 was designed to be readily convertible to a 155mm Gun Motor Carriage, with a reversible travel

The 155mm gun of the M40 fired a 95-lb. shell 25,175 yards. As this M40 on display at the Patton Museum shows, the long tube of the 155 extended well past the end of the vehicle's hull.

The M43 was essentially the same vehicle as the M40, but mounted an 8-in. howitzer. The howitzer fired a 240-lb. projectile, and had a range of 10.5 miles. The barrel of the howitzer was substantially shorter and did not extend beyond the hull.

The M43 on display at the First Calvary Museum, Fort Hood, Texas, shows the G-232 vehicles were equipped with a rear-mounted recoil spade to prevent the carriages from moving when firing.

lock and ammo racks able to handle either shell. Pressed Steel's original order was for 576 pieces, but when the war ended only 24 had been produced, and a further 24 were converted from M40 155mm Gun Motor Carriages. Because they were built so late in WWII, only one of each type actually saw use in combat in that war, although they were to see much more extensive use in later conflicts.

GENERAL DATA

MODEL	M40	M43
WEIGHT	81,000 lbs.	80,000 lbs.
LENGTH	357	289
WIDTH	124	124
HEIGHT	129.75	129.75
TRACK	101	101
STD TRACK WIDTH	23	23
CREW	8	8
MAX SPEED	24 mph	24 mph
FUEL CAPY	215 gal	54 gal
RANGE	107 mi	107 mi
ELECTRICAL	24 neg	24 neg
TRANSMISSION		
SPEEDS	5	5

TURNING		
RADIUS FT.	41.5	41.5
ARMAMENT	155mm	8 in.

Overall dimensions listed in inches.

ENGINE DATA

ENGINE MAKE/MODEL*	Continental R975C4
NUMBER OF CYLINDERS	9 radial
CUBIC-INCH DISPLACEMENT	973
HORSEPOWER	400 @ 2400 rpm
TORQUE	940 lbs.-ft. @ 1700 rpm
GOVERNED SPEED (rpm)	2400

RADIO EQUIPMENT: *There were two possible radio combinations mounted in these vehicles. One was a SCR 610 set with RC99 interphone, the other was the SCR 608B with integral interphone.*

VALUES

No reported sales

SCARCITY

Scarcity 5

The G-232 vehicles were based on components of the late-production M4 tank. They used the R975 engine, and as can be seen here, and the later horizontal volute suspension system. Like its predecessor, the M12, it had an open-topped fighting compartment. (U.S. Army photo).

G-236 M41 Howitzer

Massey Harris produced only 85 of the 155mm Howitzer Motor Carriage M41 before the order was cancelled due to the war ending. The first combat use of the M41 came during the Korean war. The motor carriage was based on the slightly lengthened chassis of the M24 light tank, which utilized the proven twin Cadillac engines. The main gun was the 155 mm howitzer M1, and it was provided with an elevation range of +45 to –5 degrees.

A spade was provided at the rear of the chassis to anchor the howitzer against recoil. Only 95 of these were produced before WWII ended and the order was cancelled. (Photo courtesy of the Patton Museum)

The M41 was based on the components of the M24 light tank. This parentage is apparent in this view showing the suspension and glacis plate. (Photo courtesy of the Patton Museum)

GENERAL DATA

MODEL	M41
WEIGHT	42,500 lbs.
LENGTH	230
WIDTH	112
HEIGHT	96
TRACK	96
TRACK WIDTH	16
CREW	5
MAX SPEED	30 mph
FUEL CAPY	110 gal
RANGE	96 mi
ELECTRICAL	24 neg
HYDRAMATIC	
TRANSMISSION	
SPEEDS	4
TRANSFER	
SPEEDS	2
TURNING	
RADIUS FT.	18
ARMAMENT	155mm

Overall dimensions listed in inches.

ENGINE DATA

ENGINE MAKE/MODEL	2 x Cadillac 44T24
NUMBER OF CYLINDERS	V-8 90-degree
CUBIC-INCH DISPLACEMENT	349
HORSEPOWER	110 @ 3400 rpm
TORQUE	240 lbs.-ft. @ 1200 rpm
GOVERNED SPEED (rpm)	Not governed

RADIO EQUIPMENT: *In addition to the flag set M238, the M41 carried one of the following radio sets: SCR 510, SCR 610, or SCR 619. A three-station RC99 interphone set handled internal communications.*

VALUES

No reported sales

SCARCITY

Scarcity 5

G-238 M37 105mm

The G-238 series was the M37 105mm Howitzer Motor Carriage, which was designed to replace the M7 as a highly mobile self-propelled field piece. It used the modified chassis of the M24 light tank as its foundation. Late in WWII, 150 of these were produced, but none saw combat until the Korean conflict. A .50-caliber M2 HB mounted on a T107 ring was provided for close in and antiaircraft defense.

GENERAL DATA

MODEL	M37
WEIGHT	46,000 lbs.
MAX TOWED LOAD	10,000 lbs.
LENGTH	216
WIDTH	118
HEIGHT	95
TREAD	96

The drive train components of the M37 were adapted from those of the M24 light tank as can be seen in this January 1946 photograph. The top bows are strapped to the hull side, and on the ring mount is the familiar M2 HB machine gun. (U.S. Army photo)

The drive train components of the M37 were adapted from those of the M24 light tank as can be seen in this January 1946 photograph. The top bows are strapped to the hull side, and on the ring mount is the familiar M2 HB machine gun. (U.S. Army photo)

GUN MOTOR CARRIAGES

STD TRACK WIDTH	16
CREW	7
MAX SPEED	30 mph
FUEL CAPY	110 gal
RANGE	100 mi
ELECTRICAL	24 neg
HYDRAMATIC	
TRANSMISSION	
SPEEDS	4
TRANSFER SPEEDS	2
TURNING	
RADIUS FT.	18
ARMAMENT	105 mm
1x .50	

Overall dimensions listed in inches. Measured with main gun facing forward, and antiaircraft machine gun mounted.

ENGINE DATA

ENGINE MAKE/MODEL	2 x Cadillac 44T24
NUMBER OF CYLINDERS	90 degree V-8
CUBIC-INCH DISPLACEMENT	349
HORSEPOWER	110 @ 3400 rpm
TORQUE	240 lbs.-ft. @ 1200 rpm
GOVERNED SPEED (rpm)	Not governed

VALUES

No reported sales

SCARCITY

Scarcity 5

G-253 M42 Duster

Cadillac completed the vehicle that was to be the basis of the M42, the T141, in August 1951. American Car and Foundry (ACF Industries) delivered its rendition of the T141 the following April. Both vehicles were based on the components in the M41 tank program. In October 1953, after an extensive test program, the T141 was standardized as the M42.

The M42 was armed with dual automatic Bofors M2A1 40mm antiaircraft cannons. The cannons were well proven by many services during WWII. The earliest production vehicles had conical-shaped, naval-style flash suppressors on the gun muzzles, but later vehicles used a three-prong type. The earliest production vehicles had doors in the hull between the driver's and commander's hatch. These doors could be opened, along with the hatches, to allow ammunition to be passed from the hull to the turret. These doors were eliminated on later vehicles. A .30-caliber machine gun was pintle mounted on the side of the turret for close in defense.

The Duster was served by a crew of six. The driver

The M42 muzzle covers are in place and the cover is on the .30-caliber machine gun. The stowage location for the liquid container and the gun cleaning rods on the right side of the vehicle. This is a later-production vehicle, judging by the angular shape of the fenders and lack of sand shields. (Photo courtesy of the Patton Museum)

This is an early production Duster. Notice the squared off front fenders and sand shields over the tracks, two features that were discontinued early. The conical flash suppressors were another short-lived feature. The guns are shown at their full 87-degree elevation. (U.S. Army photo)

Even with only half the four-man turret crew in place, the M42 was cramped. A socket for mounting the .30-caliber machine gun is visible on the turret rear, with another on the right side of the turret. The cradle and pintle are shown installed in this position. The vehicle has the later three-pronged flash suppressors. (Photo courtesy of the Patton Museum)

and commander rode in the hull, and a four-man gun crew: two loaders to feed the voracious appetite of the weapon, a sight setter, and a gunner. These crewmen rode in the open-topped turret.

The addition of fuel injection to the AOS-895-5 engine caused the vehicles so equipped to be classified as M42A1.

With the speed of aircraft increasing, the usefulness of the Duster as an anti-aircraft weapon became questionable. However, during the Vietnam conflict, the Duster, with its twin Bofors cannons, was employed very effectively against enemy troop formations. Even in dense jungle, the heavy 40mm shell was devastating.

GENERAL DATA

MODEL	M42	M42A1
WEIGHT*	49,500 lbs.	49,500 lbs.
MAX TOWED LOAD	5,000 lbs.	5,000 lbs.
LENGTH	250.25	250.25
WIDTH	126 15/16	126 15/16
HEIGHT	112.125	112.125
TRACK	102.5	102.5
TRACK WIDTH	21	21
MAX SPEED	45 mph	45 mph
FUEL CAPY	80 gal	80 gal
RANGE	100 mi	100 mi
ELECTRICAL	24 neg	24 neg
TRANSMISSION SPEEDS	2	2
TURNING RADIUS FT.	pivot	pivot

Overall dimensions listed in inches. Guns facing forward.
*Fighting weight.

The Bofors cannons on M42 vehicles had a maximum rate of fire of 120 rounds per barrel per minute. The stowage boxes on top of the fenders provided space for some of this ammunition. (U.S. Army photo)

This October 1961 photo shows the final incarnation of the M42 series — the M42A2. (Photo courtesy of the Patton Museum)

ENGINE DATA

VEHICLE MODEL	M42	M42A1
ENGINE MAKE/MODEL	AOS-895-3	AOSI-895-5
NUMBER OF CYLINDERS	Opposed 6	Opposed 6
CUBIC-INCH DISPLACEMENT	895.9	895.9
HORSEPOWER	500 @ 2800 rpm	500 @ 2800 rpm
TORQUE	955 lbs.-ft. @ 2400 rpm	955 lbs.-ft. @ 2400
GOVERNED SPEED (rpm)	2800	2800

VALUES

	6	5	4	3	2	1
All models	5,000	8,000	11,000	18,000	24,000	32,000

SCARCITY

Scarcity 3

G-258 M52

The M52 project was begun in 1948 as the T98 105mm Howitzer Motor Carriage. By July 1951 the project was known as the T98 105mm Self-Propelled Howitzer. Testing of the pilot vehicles began at Aberdeen Proving Ground in October 1950.

The welded turret of the T98 could be power or manually traversed 60 degrees either side of center, and the T96 howitzer it mounted could move vertically through a range of –10 to +65 degrees. The five-man crew all rode inside the turret, with the driver on the turret's left front. On the right rear corner of the turret was a raised cupola for the vehicle commander or section chief. He was provided with a pintle-mounted .50-caliber machine gun.

105-MM HOWITZER MOTOR CARRIAGE, M52

This view of a factory-fresh M52 shows the driver's cupola and periscopes. Notice the unusually shaped guards protecting the lights, and the shrouds over the mufflers. The driver's door is in the turret side. (Photo courtesy of the Patton Museum)

This M52 has moved into position and is preparing to fire. The rear of the armored turret opened and a deck for the gun crew swung down from the hull. (Photo courtesy of the Patton Museum)

From this angle we can see the redesigned commander's cupola and machine gun mount that was incorporated in the M52. Notice the pioneer tool and equipment stowage on the hull and turret. (Photo courtesy of the Patton Museum)

A Continental AOS-895-3 engine with an Allison CD-500-3 cross-drive transmission powered the vehicle.

The testing of the T98 revealed several flaws, which were later corrected. The biggest changes were the increase in turret ring size from 69 to 73 in., and the redesign of the front hull. The improved vehicle was classified T98E1, and production of 684 vehicles began in January 1951. After further modifications, including the elimination of the power elevation and traverse system, the vehicles were deemed suitable for issue in 1955, and the classification changed to 105mm Self-Propelled Howitzer M52 in November of the same year.

The M52 shared many automotive components with the M41 tank family, and when the tank engines were upgraded to the fuel-injected AOSI-895-5, so were the howitzers, becoming the M52A1.

GENERAL DATA

MODEL	M52	M52A1
WEIGHT*	53,000 lbs.	53,000 lbs.
LENGTH	228.375	228.375
WIDTH	123 15/16	123 15/16
HEIGHT	130 37/64	130 37/64
TRACK	102.5	102.5
STD TRACK WIDTH		
MAX SPEED	35 mph	42 mph
FUEL CAPY	179 gal	179 gal
RANGE	100 mi	100 mi
ELECTRICAL	24 neg	24 neg
TURNING		
RADIUS FT.	pivot	pivot

Overall dimensions listed in inches. Measure with main gun facing forward, and antiaircraft machine gun mounted.

* Fighting weight.

ENGINE DATA

VEHICLE MODEL	M52	M52A1
ENGINE MAKE/MODEL	AOS-895-3	AOS-895-5
NUMBER OF CYLINDERS	Opposed 6	Opposed 6
CUBIC-IN. DISPLACEMENT	895.9	895.9
HORSEPOWER	500 @ 2800 rpm	500 @ 2800 rpm
TORQUE	955 lbs.-ft. @ 2400 rpm	955 lbs.-ft. @ 2400 rpm
GOVERNED SPEED (rpm)	2800	2800

VALUES

No reported sales

SCARCITY

Scarcity 5

G-259 M53 & M55

The G-259 family of vehicles looked like the M52 105mm Self-Propelled Howitzer on steroids. The styling and layout of the vehicles was the same, but while the M52 was based on the automotive components of the M41 tank, the G-259 was based on the automotive components of the M48 tank.

As with its little brother, the M53's engine and transmission were located in the front of the vehicle, while the large turret was at the rear. The AV-1790-7B engine and CD-850-4B transmission powered these vehicles, which were built by Pacific Car and Foundry. The M53 was armed with a 155mm cannon, while the M55 mounted an 8t-in. howitzer. Since they utilized the same chassis, many M53s were converted to M55s during the Vietnam War.

GENERAL DATA

MODEL	M53	M55
WEIGHT*	96,000 lbs.	98,000 lbs.
MAX TOWED LOAD	5,000 lbs.	5,000 lbs.
LENGTH	402	311.375
WIDTH	140	133
HEIGHT	140	136.625
TRACK	110	110
STD TRACK WIDTH	23	23
MAX SPEED	30 mph	30 mph
FUEL CAPY	380 gal	380 gal
RANGE	160 mi	160 mi
ELECTRICAL	24 neg	24 neg
TRANSMISSION		
SPEEDS	2	2
TURNING		
RADIUS	pivot	pivot

The engine and transmission on the G-259 family vehicles were mounted in the front of the vehicle, as is evidenced by the placement of the drive sprocket seen here. At 96,000-plus lbs. each, the G-259s were among the heaviest vehicles fielded by the U.S. military for many years. (Photo courtesy of the Patton Museum)

The M53 can be distinguished from the M55 most readily by the length of the gun tube. The M53's 155mm barrel extends beyond the end of the hull as seen here, where the 8-in. armed M55 does not. (Photo courtesy of the Patton Museum)

Overall dimensions listed in inches. Measure with main gun facing forward, and antiaircraft machine gun mounted.

* Fighting weight.

ENGINE DATA

ENGINE MAKE/MODEL*	Continental AV-1790-5B,5C,5D
NUMBER OF CYLINDERS	90-degree V
CUBIC-INCH DISPLACEMENT	1791.75
HORSEPOWER	704 @ 2800
TORQUE	1440 lbs.-ft. @ 2000
GOVERNED SPEED	2800

VALUES

No reported sales

SCARCITY

Scarcity 5

G-279 M44

The development of the M44 was a troublesome proposition. The vehicle was designed to use as many of the automotive components of the M41 light tank as possible. Initially known as the T99E1, the M44 went into production before testing had been complete. At that time the fighting compartment was enclosed. Fumes during firing were among the major problems, and production was stopped after only 250 units were built.

The vehicle was redesigned and became the T194 Self-Propelled Howitzer. Among the changes were the opening of the top of the fighting compartment and the replacement of the main T97E1 howitzer with the T186E1 howitzer.

New production began on the T194 and the 250

T99E1 vehicles were rebuilt into the T194 configuration as well. The T194 was reclassified as the 155mm Self-Propelled Howitzer M44. When the engine was changed to the fuel-injected AOSI-895-5, the designation changed to M44A1.

GENERAL DATA

MODEL	M44	M44A1
WEIGHT*	62,500 lbs.	64,000 lbs.
LENGTH	242.5	242.5
WIDTH	127.5	127.5
HEIGHT	122.5	122.5
TRACK	102.5	102.5
MAX SPEED	35 mph	35 mph
FUEL CAPY	150 gal	150 gal
RANGE	76 mi	76 mi
ELECTRICAL	24 neg	24 neg
TURNING		
RADIUS FT.	26	26

Overall dimensions listed in inches. Measure with main gun facing forward, and antiaircraft machine gun mounted.

*Fighting weight.

ENGINE DATA

VEHICLE MODEL	M44	M44A1
ENGINE MAKE/MODEL	AOS-895-3	AOS-895-5
NUMBER OF CYLINDERS	Opposed 6	Opposed 6
CUBIC-INCH DISPLACEMENT	895.9	895.9
HORSEPOWER	500 @ 2800 rpm	500 @ 2800 rpm
TORQUE	955 lbs.-ft. @ 2400 rpm	955 lbs.-ft. @ 2400
GOVERNED SPEED (rpm)	2800	2800

VALUES

No reported sales

SCARCITY

Scarcity 5

The M44 had an open-topped fighting compartment. It also had a removable windshield and .50-caliber machine gun. (Photo courtesy of the Patton Museum)

The rear door of the M44 swung down and formed a deck to serve the weapon from, while ammunition racks swung out, freeing up space in the fighting compartment. (U.S. Army photo)

This howitzer has been raised to its full 65-degree limit. The torsion-bar suspension and shock absorbers are clearly visible. (U.S. Army photo)

A canvas cover was provided for the M44 fighting compartment to protect the crew and breach from bad weather. (U.S. Army photo)

G-288 M50 Ontos

Few military vehicles have been as well named as the M50 "Ontos." Ontos is Greek for "thing" and the name fits this vehicles well. It does not look like a tank, and is too small to be an APC. It is just a thing.

With six M40A1C 106mm recoilless rifles on a central turret, it looks more like a sci-fi creation than a combat vehicle. While the firepower of the rifles could be devastating, the shortcoming was that, while the vehicle crew could fire each of the six 106mm weapons once from inside the protective armor, one of the crew had to go outside the vehicle in order to reload. Under enemy fire, or in the event of the feared nuclear attack, this would have been suicidal. In any event, the armor of the M50 was thin, providing little protection beyond small arms and shrapnel. The rifles were mounted high on the vehicle, allowing the crew to use berms and other cover to protect the vehicle while still allowing them to engage the enemy.

The armor on all sides was sloped in an attempt to provide the maximum protection afforded by the plates. The downside was that this made the interior of the Ontos even smaller, crowding the three-man crew. Originally, a six-cylinder inline gasoline GM SL12340 engine was coupled to a XT-90-2 transmission, driving the tracks from front sprockets. This provided a maximum on-road speed of 30 mph, but a driving range of only 150 miles with the 47-gallon internal fuel tank.

The later M50A1 Ontos used a Chrysler HT-361-318 V-8 water-cooled engine. It developed 180 hp at 3,450 rpm and drove the tank through an Allison XT-90-5 transmission. The M50A1s are most easily identified by the addition of air intake louvers in the hull engine, and transmission access doors.

Allis Chalmers produced the first of 297 vehicles in 1955 for the U.S. Marine Corps. Pproduction was completed in November 1957. The Ontos was used in Vietnam, primarily in an anti-personnel role.

GENERAL DATA

MODEL	M50
WEIGHT*	19,050 lbs.
LENGTH	150.75
WIDTH	102.25
HEIGHT	83.875
TRACK	73
STD TRACK WIDTH	20
CREW	3
MAX SPEED	30 mph
FUEL CAPY	47 gal
RANGE	150 mi
ELECTRICAL	24 neg
TRANSMISSION SPEEDS	5
TURNING RADIUS FT.	pivot
ARMAMENT	6 x 106mm

The upper outside 106mm recoilless rifle on each side of the Ontos (rifles 2 and 5) was designed to be quickly dismounted for ground use. These two tubes had M8C .50-caliber spotting rifles mounted on top of them. This type of spotting rifle was also mounted on top of tubes three and four. Barely visible in the center of the Ontos is an M1919A4 .30-caliber machine gun provided for self-defense. (Photo courtesy of the Patton Museum)

While this vehicle looks like an M50 Ontos, it is actually a T165 development model. The suspension and rear doors were different, but the general layout remained the same in the production model. (Photo courtesy of the Patton Museum)

4 x .50-cal spotting

Overall dimensions listed in inches. Measured with main gun facing forward and anti-aircraft machine gun mounted.
*Fighting weight.

ENGINE DATA

ENGINE MAKE/MODEL	GMC 302
NUMBER OF CYLINDERS	6
CUBIC-INCH DISPLACEMENT	301.6
HORSEPOWER	127 @ 3350 rpm
TORQUE	254 lbs.-ft. @ 1800 rpm
GOVERNED SPEED (rpm)	3400

RADIO EQUIPMENT: *The Ontos was equipped with an AN/PRC-10 radio set.*

VALUES

No reported sales

SCARCITY

Scarcity 5

G-289 M56 Scorpion

Production of the 325 M56 Scorpion self-propelled anti-tank gun was begun in 1957 by Cadillac at its Cleveland defense products plant. The Scorpion, with its crew of four, and armed with a 90mm gun, was intended to be an air-mobile anti-tank weapon. Powered by Continental six-cylinder horizontally opposed gasoline

The four-man crew of the Scorpion traveled in the weather, as shown in this November 1966 photograph. The road wheels of the M56 suspension were pneumatic tires, much like on a passenger car. (U.S. Army photo)

The M56 Scorpion driver used a small windshield, complete with wiper, cut into the gun shield. The main gun travel lock is not being employed in this view. (Photo courtesy of the Patton Museum)

engine developing 200 hp, the Scorpion had a top speed of 28 mph, and a range of 140 miles.

The lightweight and basic design of the M56 omitted weather protection for the four-man crew. To the left of the manually elevated and traversed main gun was the driver's station and controls, with a windshield incorporated in the gun splinter shield. To the driver's left was the radio equipment, which formed the base of the commander's seat. The other two crew members rode on the other side of the breech.

The hull was aluminum, with the splinter shield the only real armor on the vehicle.

The main 90mm M54 gun was supplied with 29 rounds of ammunition. The ammunition could be of AP-T, APC-T, HEAT, HEAT-T, HEP-T, WP, TP-T, HVAP-T, or HVTP-T types. When firing, the gun was served by the gunlayer and driver from positions on the vehicle, while the rest of the gun crew was on the ground.

The running gear of the M56 was unusual because it featured pneumatic tires on the four road wheels on each side. In U.S. service, the Scorpion was used by the 82nd and 101st Airborne Divisions only from 1957 until 1970, including service in Vietnam. A few were also supplied to South Korea, Spain, and Morocco as well. Ultimately, the gun was deemed too powerful for the chassis. When the gun was fired, the recoil would lift the front of the vehicle off the ground and the muzzle blast would kick up huge amounts of dust, revealing the vehicle's position.

The M56 ammunition was stowed in a compartment under the breach. The tremendous recoil of the 90mm gun has forced the return idler to the ground while taking all the upward travel out of the front suspension. (Photo courtesy of the Patton Museum)

The M56 exhaust stack was routed out almost directly under the gun shield, and the deck at the rear of the hull served as a platform for the loader. In this view the gun tube is properly secured for travel.

GENERAL DATA

MODEL	M56
WEIGHT*	15,500 lbs.
LENGTH	230
WIDTH	101.5
HEIGHT	81
TRACK	78
STD TRACK WIDTH	20
MAX SPEED	28 mph
FUEL CAPY	55 gal
RANGE	140 mi
ELECTRICAL	24 neg
TRANSMISSION	
SPEEDS	2
TURNING	
RADIUS FT.	9

Overall dimensions listed in inches. Measure with main gun facing forward, and antiaircraft machine gun mounted.

* Fighting weight.

ENGINE DATA

ENGINE MAKE/MODEL	Continental AOI-402-5
NUMBER OF CYLINDERS	6 Opposed
CUBIC-INCH DISPLACEMENT	402
HORSEPOWER	200 @ 3000 rpm
TORQUE	355 lbs.-ft. @ 2750 rpm

VALUES

	6	5	4	3	2	1
All models	3,000	8,000	13,000	20,000	28,000	35,000

SCARCITY

Scarcity 5

G-295 M107 & M110

These two vehicles shared the same chassis and the difference between models was strictly in armament. The vehicles were equipped with torsion-bar suspension and five dual rubber-tired road wheels on each side. The drive sprocket was at the front and the fifth road wheel acted as the idler. The return run of track ran on top of the road wheels. The vehicles were powered by a Detroit Diesel Model 8V-71T diesel engine and an Allison XTG-411-2A cross-drive transmission at the front of the hull.

Deliveries of the M107 175mm self-propelled gun from Pacific Car and Foundry began in 1962. The big gun was mounted on a rotating mount at the rear of the open vehicle. The mount could be rotated 30 degrees either side of center, and the gun elevated to 65 degrees. A crew of 13 men served the weapon. Five men rode on the M107, with the balance riding in the M548 ammo carrier that accompanied it. A spade at the rear of the hull anchored the vehicle during firing.

FMC and Bowen-McLaughlin-York produced the M107 in later years. Regardless of who built them, the M107, with its incredibly long gun tube, was unmistakable. With a range of approximately 20 miles, the M107 was used extensively in Vietnam for long-range bombardment. Its projectile weighed about 175 lbs.

The 8-in. howitzer-armed version, the M110, was produced concurrently with the M107. Like the M107, the M110 was produced by Pacific Car and Foundry, FMC and BMY. The M110 was also used extensively in Vietnam. Though its range was only about half that of the M107, its 200-lb. round had a reputation for greater accuracy and ease of use than the 175mm round.

In 1976, the M110 was supplanted by the M110A1, which had a much longer barrel and increased range. The addition of a muzzle brake allowed an increase of powder charge, which further increased the range. The self-propelled howitzer was known as the M110A2, and all the U.S. Army and Marine Corps M107s were rearmed as such.

GENERAL DATA		
MODEL	M107	M110
WEIGHT*	62,100 lbs.	58,500 lbs.
LENGTH	444.8	294.4
WIDTH	124	124
HEIGHT	136.8	115.6
TRACK	106	106
STD TRACK WIDTH	18	18
CREW	5	5
MAX SPEED	34 mph	34 mph
FUEL CAPY	300 gal	300 gal

The distinctive long gun tube of the M107 is apparent in this view with the gun in firing position. Because of the length of the barrel, the gun was drawn to the rear of its mount when the vehicle was traveling. Even then there was considerable barrel overhang. (U.S. Army photo)

RANGE	450 mi	450 mi
ELECTRICAL	24 neg	24 neg
TRANSMISSION		
SPEEDS	4F, 2R	4F, 2R
TURNING		
RADIUS FT.	pivot	pivot
ARMAMENT MAIN	175mm	8 inch

Overall dimensions listed in inches. Measured with main gun facing forward, and anti-aircraft machine gun mounted.

*Fighting weight.

ENGINE DATA

ENGINE MAKE/MODEL	GM 8V71T
NUMBER OF CYLINDERS	8
CUBIC-INCH DISPLACEMENT	567.4
HORSEPOWER	345 @ 2300 rpm
TORQUE	980 lbs.-ft. @ 1700 rpm

VALUES

No reported sales

SCARCITY

Scarcity 5

The M110A1 featured a longer howitzer than the M110, but still nowhere near the length of the M107's gun. These camouflage painted M110A1s are conducting a firing exercise in this view. (U.S. Army photo)

This M110 is firing on the range at Yuma during tests. The radical difference in barrel length between the original configuration of the M110 and the M107 is readily apparent. (U.S. Army photo)

This new-looking M110 is being loaded onto an M15A2 trailer somewhere in Vietnam. In the background is an M548 cargo carrier, the M110's support vehicle. (U.S. Army photo)

G-296 M108/109

Development of this family of vehicles began in the late 1950s. Early on there was an M108 variant that was armed with a 105mm howitzer, but it was soon discontinued in favor of its companion vehicle, the 155mm howitzer-armed M109. Production of both vehicles began in 1962. Production of the M108 ended in 1963, while production of the M109 continued until 1969. All the M109s were built in the Cleveland tank plant but, depending on the contract and year of manufacture, the builders were Cadillac Motor Car division of General Motors, Chrysler Corporation, and Allison Division of General Motors.

The Army purchased 1,961 M109s and the Marines bought 150 more, all of which were armed with the T255E4 155mm weapon. However, the XM1119 propelling charge used for maximum range was hard on both the vehicle and crew.

The M109A1 corrected this by installing the longer-barreled XM185 weapon. Very little modification to the vehicle was necessary to accomplish this. In 1972, large-scale conversion of the M109 fleet into the M109A1 configuration began, with the resultant vehicles were issued to troops in 1973.

In 1974, new production of the M109A1 began anew, this time by Bowen-McLaughlin-York. The new vehicle was designated M109A1B.

After the vehicles had been used in the field, requests for changes began to flow in, many of which were incorporated in the M109A2. A new gun mount was

installed, the flotation equipment removed, and the turret bustle enlarged for more ammo storage. From 1976 through 1985, 823 of these new vehicles were supplied to the Army. Many of the earlier M109A1 and M109A1B vehicles were also updated to this new standard, and these rebuilt vehicles were classified M109A3.

In the mid-1980s, the M109 family was upgraded to include nuclear, chemical, and biological (NBC) protection for the crew. As the M109A2 and M109A3 vehicles received these upgrades they were reclassified as M109A4.

The most up-to-date version of the M109 is the M109A6 Paladin. First delivered in April 1992, the Paladin had improved armor, armament, increased ammunition stowage, and NBC equipment, including micro-climate cooling for the crewmen. The biggest change was the automatic fire control system, which included automatic gun laying and power-assisted semiautomatic loading. The Paladin can go from road march to pinpoint firing in less than 60 seconds.

The M109A5 was the poor man's M109A6, and was usually supplied to reserve units. The M109A5 was an older vehicle upgraded with the new M284 howitzer in the M182 mount as used on the Paladin. Both the M109A5 and M109A6 weapons have a maximum range of 30 kilometers.

GENERAL DATA

MODEL	M108	M109
WEIGHT*	46,221 lbs.	52,461 lbs.
LENGTH	240.7	260.4
WIDTH	124	124
HEIGHT	129.1	129.1
TRACK	109	109

STD TRACK WIDTH	15	15
CREW	5	6
MAX SPEED	35 mph	35 mph
FUEL CAPY	135 gal	135 gal
RANGE	220 mi	220 mi
ELECTRICAL	24 neg	24 neg
TRANSMISSION		
SPEEDS	4F, 2R	4F, 2R
TURNING		
RADIUS FT.	pivot	pivot
ARMAMENT	105mm	155mm
(FLEXIBLE)	1 x .50	1 x .50

Overall dimensions listed in inches. Measured with main gun facing forward, and antiaircraft machine gun mounted.

*Fighting weight.

ENGINE DATA

ENGINE MAKE/MODEL	GM 8V71T
NUMBER OF CYLINDERS	8
CUBIC-INCH DISPLACEMENT	567.4
HORSEPOWER	345 @ 2300 rpm
TORQUE	980 lbs.-ft. @ 1700 rpm

VALUES

No reported sales

The M109A1 was armed with the XM185 155mm howitzer, which had a noticeably longer gun tube than its predecessor. The vast majority of the M109 fleet was upgraded to the M109A1 configuration in 1972-1973. As seen here, G-296s earlier than the M109A2 were provided with flotation equipment for amphibious operations. (U.S. Army photo)

This is the short-lived 105mm howitzer-armed M108, which was produced for only about a year. (Photo courtesy of the Patton Museum)

The M109 was armed with the larger 155mm howitzer, and variants of it have been produced on and off for 40 years. Notice how much larger the main weapon is on this compared to the M108, yet still the muzzle barely extends beyond the hull. (U.S. Army photo)

The M109A2 shown here lacked the flotation equipment of its predecessors, but featured an improved gun mount and an enlarged turret bustle. (Photo courtesy of United Defense)

The M109A6 Paladin is the latest generation of the M109 family. It has many improvements in weaponry, gun training, and survivability over the earlier models. (Photo courtesy of United Defense)

HALFTRACK VEHICLES

G-102 M2 & M3

Collecting U.S. halftracks can be quite challenging because so many varieties have been built. The halftrack was probably modified into different configurations more than any other vehicle, some even before leaving the factory. Many halftracks were built as one model, only to be converted into another before being shipped to using troops. Then it was often either field or depot rebuilt into

another form. Extensive remanufacturing programs in this country confuse things even more. It is possible for a given vehicle to have had three or more model numbers during its service life.

The M2 halftrack, like the M3 halftrack, has its roots in the T14 halftrack. The White Motor Company of Cleveland built the T14 in early 1940. In September of the same year, the M2 was standardized. Concurrently, the Diamond T Motor Car Co developed a version with the body and frame lengthened 10 in. to the rear, and it became the M3. The M4 was a mortar carrier based on

The early M2 as can be identified by the fender-mounted headlights and lack of mine racks on the side. This particular vehicle is equipped with the Tulsa PTO-driven winch behind the front bumper. It is shown with the canvas in place, which is unusual for halftracks. (Photo courtesy of the Patton Museum)

This M2 is equipped with the side-mounted mine racks required after August 1942. The M2HB machine gun and two water-cooled .30-caliber weapons are visible. A pioneer tool rack has been mounted on the side, and the radio antenna mount is visible in the center of the vehicle. The storage compartment door is open, revealing ammunition boxes stacked inside. This vehicle has an unditching roller on the front bumper. (Photo courtesy of the Patton Museum)

This Autocar-built M3 was photographed prior to testing at the Studebaker Proving Grounds. This vehicle is a later-production vehicle as evidenced by the factory-installed mine racks and the demountable headlights mounted on the radiator armor. (U.S. Army Photo)

The M2A1 introduced the ring mount for the heavy machine gun in the right front corner of the crew compartment. The .30-caliber machine guns were provided with three sockets, allowing mounting on the driver's side center, rear center or, as shown, centered on the right side of the crew compartment. The rear of the crew compartment is forward of the rear of the track, characteristic of the M2 and M2A1. (U.S. Army Photo)

The interior of the M3 was arranged to perform its role as a personnel carrier. Behind the troop seats are twin fuel tanks. (Photo courtesy Patton Museum)

the same chassis. All of these were to be powered by the White 160A engine.

In an unusually cooperative move, representatives from three firms, White, Diamond T and the Autocar Company, as well as the Ordnance Department, formed the Half-track Engineering Committee. Since the demand for halftracks was greater than any one builder could meet, this committee was charged with not only designing halftracks, but also ensuring that all parts except armor plate were interchangeable.

M2

In May 1941 White delivered 62 M2s, the first of 11,415 to be built by White and Autocar. The M2s were armed with an M2 heavy-barrel .50-caliber machine gun, and two water-cooled .30-caliber M1917A1 machine guns. These weapons were mounted via trolleys on a skate rail that surrounded the interior of the vehicle. In later production the pair of water-cooled weapons gave way to a single air-cooled M1919A4 .30-caliber machine gun. Tripods were stored externally on the rear of the vehicle so these weapons could be dismounted and used on the ground.

The M2 had a bottom-hinged door just behind the driver's door, and another one in a similar location on the other side of the vehicle. These doors provided access to large ammunition storage compartments. These compartments were also accessible from inside the halftrack by opening the top of the compartments. These compartments were used in the M2s role as an artillery prime mover. Two 30-gallon fuel tanks were mounted in the rear of the crew compartment, one on either side. Seats in the rear compartment provided seating for eight.

M3

While work on the M2 was going on, Diamond T went about the business of building M3 personnel carriers. The first was delivered in May 1941. White and Autocar joined in later until their combined production reached 12,391 vehicles.

In addition to the lack of the side storage doors of the M2, distinguishing characteristics were a door in the rear armor, and a body that extended beyond the end of the tracks. On the M2, the run of the tracks extended beyond the rear of the body. The twin fuel tanks of the M3 were moved forward into the location occupied by the ammunition compartments on the M2. There was

The pulpit mount is clearly shown in this Engineering Standards Vehicle Laboratory photo of an M3A1. A full compliment of mines is shown in the racks. While this vehicle is equipped with a winch, some came with an unditching roller instead. (U.S. Army photo)

seating for 10 in the rear of the vehicle, plus another seat between the driver and co-driver.

A pedestal-mounted, air-cooled M1919A4 was provided in the crew compartment for defense. M3s, like the M2s, were provided with bows and canvas to protect the crew from the weather, but these were not popular because they hindered the use of the weapons.

The front of the M2s and M3s were fitted with either an unditching roller like that on the M3A1 Scout Car, or a Tulsa Model 18G 10,000-lb. self-recovery winch.

Unlike their German counterparts, American halftracks had their front wheels driven through the vehicles transfer case. The rear of the halftrack was driven by means of a drive sprocket at the front of the suspension. The track itself, developed by Goodrich, was made of rubber molded around steel cables with steel crosspieces with center guides attached. In many of today's remaining vehicles, cracks in the rubber have allowed moisture to reach the steel components, which rust, in turn forcing the rubber away and greatly shortening the life of the track.

In late 1942, it was decided to add mine racks to both sides of the vehicles. Not only were these added to vehicles under production, but instructions were also issued to install these racks on vehicles already fielded. On the M3 they ran the full length of the crew compartment, while on the M2 they extended from the rear of the ammunition compartment doors to the rear of the body.

The use of halftracks as a basis for artillery introduced new problems, including the destruction of the headlights by the muzzle blast. This lead to the replacement of the early fender-mounted headlights with demountable armor-type headlights attached to the side of the radiator armor.

M2A1, M3A1, M5A1

In mid-1942, the Ordnance Committee recommended that the skate rail on the M2 be replaced with a ring mount. The new ring mount, the M49, not only replaced the M2's skate rail, but also the pedestal mount of the M3 and the International Harvester M5.

The new vehicles were classified M2A1, and M3A1, and M5A1. In addition to the ring mount and its M2HB Browning, there was a pintle socket installed on each side and the vehicle rear for installation of the single M1919A4 air-cooled .30-caliber machine gun.

There were fewer A1 vehicles made than their predecessors. Only 1,643 M2A1s were built, along with 2,862 M3A1s. However, the number of M3A1s was bolstered by the conversion of 1,360 75mm Gun Motor Carriage M3s into M3A1 personnel carriers.

M3A2

The M3A2 was supposed to become the standard U.S. halftrack, but only five pilot models, converted from M3A1s, were built.

M4 Mortar Carrier

The mortar-carrier halftrack was the exclusive product of the White Motor Company. From August 1941 until October 1942, 572 of the M4 81mm mortar carriers

Military vehicles in a combat-ready situation are laden with gear, even before their crew begins "personalizing" the equipment. This photo shows the crew of a M3 and the gear that went with the vehicle standing ready for inspection. (Photo courtesy of the Patton Museum)

The downward-folding windshield armor used by the M3 75mm Gun Motor Carriage is evident in this photo, as is the notch in the armor to clear the muzzle. (Photo courtesy ot the Patton Museum)

were built. The M4 was based on the M2 and retained the M2's skate rail and trolley-mounted M2HB machine gun. A door was installed in the rear armor. The mortar was supposed to be removed from the halftrack for firing, except for emergency situations. The side stowage boxes characteristic of the M2 were retained in the M4, configured to stow 28 rounds of 81mm mortar ammunition each. Additional racks in the crew compartment brought the total rounds carried to 96.

M4A1 Mortar Carrier

Once the M4 was in the hands of the troops, it became obvious that the crews were not going to unload the heavy mortar through the small door and under the

skate rail before firing it. Remarkably, the Army relented on this, and redesigned the vehicle to allow a greater range of traverse for the mortar. The new configuration was dubbed the M4A1, and production ran from May 1943 to October the same year, totaling 600 vehicles. Most M4s in the field were upgraded to the M4A1 standard as well.

M21 Mortar Carrier

The mortar in the M4 and M4A1 was mounted so that the tube faced the rear of the vehicle. Once again, this didn't sit well with the using troops, and the 2nd Armored Division relocated the mortars in their vehicles to fire forward. Once again, Ordnance followed suite and a new 81mm mortar carrier, the M21, was created. Rather than being based on the M2 as was the M4, the

This is the halftrack that wasn't — the M3A2. Only pilot models were built. To find one today would be a collector's coup. The device that looks like a ladder mounted on the side served two purposes; it was both a tie-down point for the canvas cover, and a storage bin for other gear. (U.S. Army photo)

This photo shows why so many M4 crews chose not to dismount the 81mm mortar before firing. Notice how the skate rail crosses the rear door opening, making for a very small passage. The M4's lineage to the M2 is evident in this photo. Notice the rear "porch" characteristic of M2-based vehicles. (U.S. Army photo)

This overhead shot of an M4A1 shows the cozy quarters that these crews traveled, worked, and lived in. The mortar, its ammunition, and the halftrack's communication equipment are all clearly shown. Also visible are the full mine racks, and the top bows stored across the rear of the vehicle. (U.S. Army photo)

The M21 mortar carrier is based on the larger M3, and that the mortar has been repositioned to fire forward rather than rearward. There was no skate rail for the .50-caliber machine gun, so it was pedestal mounted in the rear of the vehicle. (U.S. Army photo)

This rear three-quarter view of the M21 shows how the rear storage racks could be utilized and gives a clear view of the machine gun and antenna mounts. (U.S. Army photo)

M21 was based on the M3. White built 110 of these new vehicles between January and March of 1944. The M21's machine gun was pedestal mounted behind the mortar, rather than on a skate rail as in the M4.

M3 75mm Gun Motor Carriage

The T12 was developed by a team lead by Major Robert Icks (whose collection of information on armored fighting vehicles has been invaluable to this and many other researchers). It consisted of an M1897A4 75mm howitzer mounted on an adapted M3 chassis. Eighty-six of these new tank destroyers were built in August and September of 1941 by the Autocar Company.

To create the T12, the M3s glass windshield was removed, and the windshield armor reconfigured to hinge down onto the hood. It was also notched to clear the barrel when the howitzer was in the traveling position.

The fuel tanks were relocated to the rear of the crew compartment and the seats and subfloor of the M3 were replaced with a new subfloor with ammunition stowage for the 75mm weapon.

HALFTRACKS

In October 1941, the T12 was standardized as the 75mm Gun Motor Carriage M3. A change in mount for the howitzer brought about a new classification of M3A1 in July 1942. Production began in February 1942 and continued until April 1943, with 2,116 of the M3 and M3A1 built. However, 1,360 of them were rebuilt into M3A1 personnel carriers before being issued.

Because of the success mating the 75mm howitzer and halftrack chassis, it was decided to try the same tactic with a U.S.-built version of the British 6-pounder. The difference between the U.S. and British versions was in the thickness of the gun tube and the bore length. The

This is one of the 80 T28E1 Multiple Gun Motor Carriages built by Autocar. This one had an open gun mount. (U.S. Army photo)

This view shows the interior arrangement of the T48 57mm Gun Motor Carriage. The large box across the rear was the ammunition ready rack, which held 20 rounds of 57mm ammo. Below it was stowage for another 60 rounds, with a further 20 in a floor compartment. (Photo courtesy of the Patton Museum)

The T19 105mm Gun Motor Carriage poses here for its official portrait. This is an early vehicle as is evidenced by the early style headlights, which were easily damaged by the muzzle blast from the main gun. (Photo courtesy of the Patton Museum)

This snappy trooper is posing next to the T30 75mm Howitzer Motor Carriage. Notice the directional tires on the front bumper. Like all halftracks mounting field pieces, it had a windshield that was hinged at the bottom rather than at the top. (Photo courtesy of the Patton Museum)

The M13 was an effective antiaircraft weapon with its dual M2 HB .50-caliber machine guns mounted on power-operated turrets. There are hinged armor flaps on the rear of the body. (Photo courtesy of the Patton Museum)

windshield was modified, as it had been for the M3 75mm Gun Motor Carriage, to hinge at the bottom. The hood was reinforced to withstand the muzzle blast of the 57mm firing close over it, and seating was provided for a

crew of five men — two in the front, three in the rear. Diamond T built 962 of these vehicles.

Although originally intended for British use, they only got 30 of them. Russia, on the other hand, received 650 of them. The U.S. Army got one. Chester Tank Depot converted the remaining 281 into M3A1 personnel carriers.

T19 105mm Howiter Motor Carriage

Diamond T built 324 of the T19 from January through April 1942. Again, it was based on the M3 halftrack chassis with the reconfigured folding windshield. Some of these vehicles were used in Sicily, North Africa and France, but by July 1945 they had been declared obsolete. Bowen and McLaughlin converted 90 T19s into M3A1 personnel carriers in July of 1945.

T30 75mm Howiter Motor Carriage

White built 500 of these vehicles, armed with the 75mm howitzer M1A1 during 1942. However, even before all of them had been delivered, 108 of them were

This new Autocar M15A1 Multiple Gun Motor Carriage was photographed at the Studebaker Proving Grounds. The demountable headlights and unditching roller are plainly visible, as are the unusual canvases protecting the gun mount and driver's compartment. (U.S. Army photo)

Unlike the T28E1, the sides and front of the gun mount of the M15 Multiple Gun Motor Carriage were protected by armor. In this view we can also see the seats for the gun crew. (U.S. Army photo)

converted into M3 personnel carriers.

M13 Multiple Gun Motor Carriage

With the emergence of the airplane as a dominant force on the battlefield, there came a need to protect troops and equipment from aerial attack. The T1E4 was designed to do just that, and was standardized as the Multiple Gun Motor Carriage M13. An M33 Maxson power-operated turret was installed in the crew area of a halftrack based on the M3 personnel carrier. The upper sections of the side and rear armored halftrack body were hinged to allow the twin .50-caliber M2HB a wider field of fire to engage airborne and ground targets. The Maxson turret was self contained, having batteries and generator.

Although White built 1,103 M13s between January and May 1943, only 139 actually saw service. The balance were converted to Multiple Gun Motor Carriage M16s.

T28E1 Multiple Gun Motor Carriage

This vehicle was conceived as a dual-purpose weapon for use against tanks or aircraft. It was armed with a 37mm M1A2 automatic cannon and two .50-caliber water-cooled machine guns. Autocar built 80 of these halftracks in July and August of 1942. Seventy-eight of them were immediately deployed to North Africa with the 443rd Antiaircraft Artillery, Automatic Weapons Battalion, Self Propelled.

M15 Multiple Gun Motor Carriage

The M15 was similar to the T28E1 and used the

same 37mm M1A2 automatic cannon. The most visible difference was the partial enclosure of the of weapons in armor. The machine guns on the M15 were air-cooled M2HBs, rather than the water-cooled models used on the T28E1. The gun mounts were classified as M42. The M15 was built by Autocar from February to April 1943. There were 500 of these vehicles built, but the type was declared obsolete in August 1945.

M15A1 Multiple Gun Motor Carriage

When the supply of M3E1 carriages that were used in the construction of the M15 was depleted, a new vehicle was developed to use the 37mm M3A1 carriage. The new mount was classified as M54, and the new motor carriage using this mount was classified as M15A1. On the M15 the twin-50s were mounted above the main gun, but they were mounted below it on the M15A1. Autocar built 1,652 of these vehicles between October 1943 and February 1944. By the end of WWII the M15A1's classification had been down graded to Limited Standard, yet the M15A1 soldiered on through the Korean war.

M16 Multiple Gun Motor Carriage

The M13 Multiple Gun Motor Carriage was an effective weapon, but there was a desire to increase its firepower. The Maxson turret was redesigned to support four machine guns rather than two, and the hinged armored sides were notched to clear the ammo cannisters regardless of turret position. The mount was raised 6 in. from the floor so the machine guns could be fired horizontally. White built 2,877 M16s between May

1943 and March 1944. In addition to these, 568 M13s and 109 T10E1 twin 20mm Multiple Gun Motor Carriages were converted to M16 Multiple Gun Motor Carriages.

All early M16 Multiple Gun Motor Carriage were equipped with the front-mounted PTO-driven Tulsa winch.

M34 40mm Gun Motor Carriage

Very similar to the M16 was a group of 321 halftracks modified in England on the orders of Col. John Bruce Medaris, First Army Ordnance Officer. Medaris went on to become a Major General, and was a leader in missile development before retiring to become president of the Lionel Corp.

The first army's shops removed the quad .50 mounts from M51 trailers and placed them in the rear of a variety of halftracks, including both M2 and M3 types.

M16A1 Multiple Gun Motor Carriage

At the outbreak of the Korean War there was a shortage of 37mm ammunition, so 104 M15A1 Multiple Gun Motor Carriages were converted to M34 40mm Gun Motor Carriages at ordnance depots in Japan. The twin .50s and the 37mm M1A2 gun were replaced with a single 40mm Bofors antiaircraft cannon. The resulting vehicle, the M34 Gun Motor Carriage, was classified

The M16A1 vehicles were conversions, usually based on M3 personnel carriers. As such, they had a rear door mounted into the bed, and the rear armor lacked the folding upper sides.

limited standard in September 1951 and was intended to be used more against massed infantry formations than against aircraft.

There were not enough M16 Multiple Gun Motor Carriages in the Army's inventory to meet the

GENERAL DATA

MODEL	M2A1	M15A1*	M16	M3	M3A1	M4	M4A1	M21
WEIGHT*	15,100 lbs.	18,385 lbs.	18,640 lbs.	15,500 lbs.	15,300 lbs.	14,430 lbs.	15,750 lbs.	15, lbs.500
LENGTH	241.625	236.5	256	249.625	249.625	250.75	250.75	244.875
WIDTH	87.5	89	77.875	87.5	87.5	77.5	87.5	87.25
HEIGHT	100	104	88	89106		89.375	89.375	87
WIDTH**	51 13/16	51 13/16	51 13/16	51 13/16	51 13/16	51 13/16	51 13/16	51 13/16
	75 13/16	75 13/16	75 13/16	75 13/16	75 13/16	75 13/16	75 13/16	75 13/16
TIRE SIZES	8.25-20	8.25-20	8.25-20	8.25-20	8.25- 20	8.25-20	8.25-20	8.25-20
MAX SPEED	45 mph	40 mph	45 mph	45 mph	45 mph	45 mph	45 mph	45 mph
FUEL CAPY	60 gal	60 gal	60 gal	60 gal	60 gal	60 gal	60 gal	60 gal
RANGE	210 mi	210 mi	210 mi	210 mi	210 mi	210 mi	210 mi	210 mi
ELECTRICAL	12 neg	12 neg	12 neg	12 neg	12 neg	12 neg	12 neg	12 neg
TRANSMISSION								
SPEEDS	4	4	4	4	4	4	4	4
TRANSFER								
SPEEDS	2	2	2	2	2	2	2	2
TURNING								
RADIUS FEET	29.5	29.5	30	29.5	29.5	30	29.5	29.5

Overall dimensions listed in inches.
** Inside/outside width at tires.
*Dimensions for roller equipped vehicle.
Winch-equipped vehicles are 430 lbs heavier, and 6 1/8 in. longer than roller equipped vehicles. Dimensions shown are for winch-equipped vehicles unless otherwise noted.

ENGINE DATA

ENGINE MAKE/MODEL	White 160 AX
NUMBER OF CYLINDERS	6
CUBIC-INCH DISPLACEMENT	386
HORSEPOWER	127 @ 3000 rpm
TORQUE	325 @ 1200 rpm
GOVERNED SPEED (rpm)	Not governed

VALUES

	6	5	4	3	2	1
M2	1,500	4,000	9,500	15,000	22,000	29,000
M2A1	1,500	4,000	9,500	15,000	22,000	29,000
M3	1,500	4,000	9,500	15,000	22,000	29,000
M3A1	1,500	4,000	9,500	15,000	22,000	29,000
M4	1,500	4,000	9,500	15,000	22,000	29,000
M4A1	1,500	4,000	9,500	15,000	22,000	29,000
M16	2,500	6,000	14,000	20,000	29,000	38,000

SCARCITY

M2	3
M2A1	3
M3	3
M3A1	3
M4	3
M4A1	3
M16	4

requirements for the Korean campaign, so Bowen and McLauglin were contracted to convert 1,662 M3 personnel carriers into M16A1 Multiple Gun Motor Carriages. A new mount, the M45F, was installed. In addition to having folding armor "bat wings" to protect the gun crew, the M45F was also 6 in. taller than the M45D mount used on the M16. This raised the mount enough to allow it to fire over the non-folding sides of the former M3 halftracks. Because they were originally M3 personnel carriers, the M16A1s had a rear door — a feature lacking on actual M16s.

M16A1

The features of the M16A1 proved so successful that they were added to 419 actual M16s. The resulting vehicles became known as M16A2.

G-147 Harvester

While the International Harvester halftracks look similar to the G-102 vehicles built by the original halftrack-manufacturing group (White, Autocar, Diamond T), they are very different vehicles. The International-built units have welded bodies rather than the G-102's bolted construction, and were powered with the 451-cid International RED-450-B engine rather than the White 160AX used by the others. The rear corners of the bed on the International models are rounded, where as the others had square corners.

Very few parts were interchangeable between the G-102 and G-147 series vehicles, and for this reason most of the International production was supplied for lend-

lease purposes, although a few were used by U.S. troops. Many of these vehicles had a 10,000-lb. capacity PTO-driven winch mounted behind the front bumper. Those not so equipped were provided with an unditching roller.

M5 Personnel Carrier

The first three of 4,265 model M5 vehicles (the IH equivalent to the M3) were finished on November 9, 1942, and delivered, along with 37 more, on December 21, 1942. Fifty-seven percent of these vehicles were to be built with a front mounted PTO-driven winch. The balance were to be equipped with unditching rollers.

M5A1 Personnel Carrier

When the ring mount was introduced in lieu of the skate rail on the M5, the model designation was changed to M5A1. The remaining 2,894 vehicles on M5 contracts were built as M5A1s, in addition to 65 vehicles ordered as such. Production of the M5A1 began on August 13, 1943.

M9A1 Car, Half Track

This was the IH version of the M2. Unlike the M2/M3 series, the bodies of the M5 and M9 were the same size. Beginning with a production pilot model built on March 17, 1943, 3,433 M9A1s were built, like all the IH halftracks, at the Fort Wayne Works. Half of the M9A1 vehicles were equipped with winches, with the balance having rollers. No M9 halftracks were built.

M14 Multiple Gun Motor Carriage

The first production M14 Multiple Gun Motor Carriage armed with the Maxson M33 twin .50-caliber machine gun was completed three days after Christmas 1942. A total of 1,605 of these vehicles were built, and all were equipped with the front-mounted winch. Changes

This April 1944 photo shows a fully equipped International M5A1 personnel carrier. It has a comparatively smooth body due to the welded construction. (U.S. Army photo)

made to the bodywork to accommodate the weapons installation included: changing the body sills and floor plates, hinging the top 9 in. of the side and rear armor, and providing for ammunition and equipment stowage.

M17 Multiple Gun Motor Carriage

These were originally ordered as the M14 Multiple Gun Motor Carriages. A total of 1,000 of these vehicles were completed, instead, with the M45 quad .50 mount, and designated the M17 Multiple Gun Motor Carriage. Production of these vehicles began on December 15, 1943.

GENERAL DATA

MODEL	M5A1
WEIGHT*	15,100 lbs.
LENGTH	241.625
WIDTH	87.5
HEIGHT	100
TIRE SIZES	9.00-20
MAX SPEED	42 mph
FUEL CAPY	60 gal
RANGE	125 mi
ELECTRICAL	12 neg
TRANSMISSION	
SPEEDS	4
TRANSFER	
SPEEDS	2
TURNING	
RADIUS FEET	29.5

Overall dimensions listed in inches.
Winch-equipped vehicles are 430 lbs. heavier, and 6 1/8 in. longer than roller-equipped vehicles. Dimensions shown are for winch-equipped vehicles unless otherwise noted.
* Inside/outside width at tires.
** Dimensions for roller-equipped vehicle.

ENGINE DATA

ENGINE MAKE/MODEL	RED 450B
NUMBER OF CYLINDERS	6
CUBIC-INCH DISPLACEMENT	450
HORSEPOWER	130 @ 2600 rpm

VALUES

	6	5	4	3	2	1
M5	1,500	4,000	9,500	15,000	22,000	29,000
M5A1	1,500	4,000	9,500	15,000	22,000	29,000
M9	1,500	4,000	9,500	15,000	22,000	29,000

This overhead view of an M5A1 shows off the rounded rear corners of the hull, as well as the sockets for side or rear mounting the .30-caliber machine gun. The big .50-caliber machine gun is mounted on the M49 ring mount. (U.S. Army photo)

This February 1944 photo of an M9A1 halftrack with winch was taken at the Engineering Standards Research Laboratory. Externally, the M5A1 and M9A1 were very similar, but the interior arrangements were different. (U.S. Army photo)

The folding side armor of the M14 Multiple Gun Motor Carriage is shown in this photo. This was necessary to provide a broad field of fire for the twin .50-caliber machine guns mounted in the M33 turret. (Photo courtesy of the Patton Museum)

The M14 had a large stowage box mounted on the hull rear. This photo also shows the interior layout of the Multiple Gun Motor Carriage. All IH Multiple Gun Motor Carriages were equipped with front winches.

HIGH-SPEED TRACTORS

G-096 M2

One of the earliest high-speed tractors in the Army's inventory was the M2 7-ton high-speed tractor built by the Cleveland Tractor Company (Cletrac). The M2 was very popular with the Army Air Force, and many of the 8,510 built were used at airfields. In addition to being useful as a "tug" around the airfield, it also had a large air compressor mounted on the rear that was very useful for airing up the tires and landing gear of various aircraft. The drawbar was designed to transfer as much weight as possible from the towed object to the tractor to increase the tractive effort available.

GENERAL DATA

MODEL	M2
WEIGHT*	14,700 lbs.
LENGTH	163
WIDTH	69
HEIGHT	64
TRACK	73.5
TRACK WIDTH	14
MAX SPEED	22 mph
FUEL CAPY	33 gal
RANGE	100 mi
ELECTRICAL	12 neg
TRANSMISSION	
SPEEDS	4F, 1R

Overall dimensions listed in inches.

*Loaded weight.

ENGINE DATA

ENGINE MAKE/MODEL	Hercules WXLC3
NUMBER OF CYLINDERS	6
CUBIC-INCH DISPLACEMENT	404
HORSEPOWER	160 @ 3000 rpm
TORQUE	312 lbs.-ft. @ 1200 rpm

VALUES

	6	5	4	3	2	1
All models	1,200	3,000	6,000	8,500	11,000	14,000

SCARCITY

Scarcity 3

The large object on the right front fender is the 1,000-watt, 110-volt DC belt-driven generator that was standard equipment on the M2. On the rear of the tractor is the PTO-driven 1,000-psi air compressor. (U.S. Army photo)

More commonly seen around airfields than on the front line, the Cleveland Tractor M2 was a very useful and versatile piece of equipment. (U.S. Army photo)

The M2 compressor is clearly visible in this unusual view with the cab cover in place. Also visible are the airlines and high-pressure (1500 psi) air cylinder laying on the front fender, and towing pintle on the rear under the compressor. (U.S. Army photo)

This photo, taken by the Engineering Standards Research Laboratory, shows the M2's rear-mounted spotlight, dual rear towing pintles, and second air cylinder. (U.S. Army photo)

There was little wasted space on the M2s, with accessories mounted on almost every inch of the tractor that was reachable from the ground. (U.S. Army photo)

This early model M2 has no brush guard. The belt-drive arrangement for the auxilliary generator is shown, as is the front 7,500-lb. capacity winch and the Cleveland Tractor "Cletrac" logo on the radiator. (U.S. Army photo)

G-150 M4 18-Ton

Allis-Chalmers developed and built the M4 18-ton high-speed tractor to tow artillery and carry the crew as well as ammunition. The M4s were configured to carry either of two load classes. The Class A load was 90mm or 3 inch-ammunition; the Class B load was 155mm, 240mm, or 8-in. ammo. The tractors had a built-in crane and hoist for handling the ammunition. At the rear of the vehicle there was a PTO-driven 30,000-lb. pull winch.

Production began in March 1943 and continued through June 1945, with a total of 5,552 units assembled. It was decided that the tractor needed wider tracks. This was done by adding duck-bill extensions to the ends of the track shoe. This necessitated the moving of the suspension units out from the hull. Only 259 units in this configuration, classified M4A1, were built, all between June and August 1945.

Some of these vehicles were modified to carry more munitions, reducing the crew from eleven to eight. These modified vehicles were identified by adding a C suffix to their model number.

In 1954, Bowen-McLaughlin began a rebuilding program on the M4 tractors. These updated tractors were classified M4A2.

GENERAL DATA

MODEL	M4	M4A1	M4C	M4A1C	M4A2
WEIGHT*	31,400 lbs.	31,400 lbs.	31,400 lbs.	31,400 lbs.	31,400 lbs.
MAX TOWED LOAD	38,700 lbs.	38,700 lbs.	38,700 lbs.	38,700 lbs.	38,700 lbs.
LENGTH	209.75	209.75	209.75	209.75	209.75
WIDTH	97	97	97	97	97
HEIGHT	107.875	107.875	107.875	107.875	107.875
TRACK	80	80	80	80	80
TRACK WIDTH	16 9/16	16 9/16	16 9/16	16 9/16	16 9/16
MAX SPEED	35 mph	35 mph	35 mph	35 mph	35 mph
FUEL CAPY	125 gal	125 gal	125 gal	125 gal	125 gal
RANGE	100 mi	100 mi	100 mi	100 mi	100 mi
ELECTRICAL	12 neg	12 neg	12 neg	12 neg	12 neg
AUOTMATIC TRANSMISSION					
SPEEDS	3	3	3	3	3
TURNING RADIUS FT	18.5	18.5	18.5	18.5	18.5

Overall dimensions listed in inches.
*Fighting weight.

ENGINE DATA

ENGINE MAKE/MODEL	Waukesha 145GZ
NUMBER OF CYLINDERS	6
CUBIC INCH DISPLACEMENT	817
HORSEPOWER	190 @ 2100 rpm
TORQUE	600 lbs.-ft. @ 1200 rpm
GOVERNED SPEED (rpm)	2100

VALUES

	6	5	4	3	2	1
All models	900	2,400	3,000	4,500	8,500	12,000

SCARCITY

Scarcity 3

The M4 is often confused with the M5A1 due to similarities in cab construction, although the M4 is larger. (U.S. Army photo)

The M4 exhaust pipe and grill for the cooling system can be seen in this photo taken in April 1944 at the Engineering Standards Research Laboratory. (U.S. Army photo)

The M4 had narrower tracks and spacing than the M4A1. (U.S. Army photo)

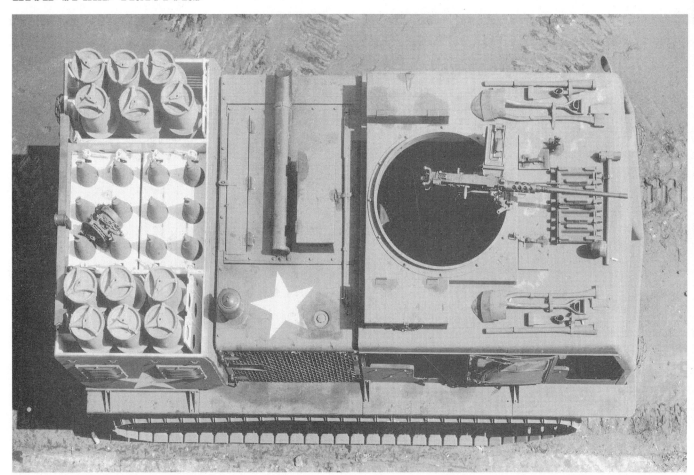

Although this M4A1 is lacking its tripod, it does have a full load of ammunition. The mud guard/fenders were added to the M4A1 variant to cover the wider track arrangement. (U.S. Army photo)

This top view of a fully equipped M4 shows the interior of the empty ammo carriers, which were painted white, the two full sets of pioneer tools mounted on the roof, and the M2 machine gun mounted on its ring. A tripod is stored just forward of the ring mount. A sledgehammer is stored just over the windshield. (U.S. Army photo)

G-162 M5 13-Ton

The M5 was intended to be the prime mover for a variety of field pieces, including the M2 105mm, M1 155mm, and the M1 4.5-in. guns. The tracks and suspension of the M5 high-speed tractor were based on those of the M3 light tank. Production began in May 1943 and ran for 24 months, with a total of 5,290 built.

This April 1944 photo of an M5 High-Speed Tractor shows the low profile of the original, open-cabbed prime mover. (U.S. Army photo)

This photo shows the central ammunition storage racks of the M5A1 tractors. Also notice the suspension system used on this and other early models. Compare this to the suspension added to later models such as the M5A3 and M5A4. (U.S. Army photo)

HIGH-SPEED TRACTORS

M5A1

The M5A1 was basically the same vehicle as the M5, but with the steel cab enclosure. It was introduced in May 1945 and only 589 were completed before production ceased in August 1945.

M5A2 & M5A3

After WWII many of the M5 and M5A1 tractors were updated with a horizontal volute suspension system, instead of the vertical volute system they were built with. This meant the M5 and M5A1 became M5A2 and M5A3, respectively.

GENERAL DATA

MODEL	M5	M5A1	M5A2	M5A3	M5A4
WEIGHT*	28,572 lbs.	30,405 lbs.	26,149 lbs.	30,350 lbs.	29,804 lbs.
MAX TOW LOAD	20,000 lbs.	20,000 lbs.	20,000 lbs.	20,000 lbs.	29,800 lbs.
LENGTH	191.125	196.375	191.125	196.375	199.125
WIDTH	100	100	114.5	114.5	115.5
HEIGHT	104	105.5	104	105.25	102.5
TRACK	83	83	83	83	90.375
TRACK WIDTH	11.625	11.625	21	21	17.125
MAX SPEED	30 mph	30 mph	30 mph	30 mph	30 mph
FUEL CAPY	100 gal	100 gal	100 gal	100 gal	100 gal
RANGE	150 mi	150 mi	150 mi	150 mi	150 mi
ELECTRICAL	12 neg	12 neg	12 neg	12 neg	12 neg
TRANSMISSION SPEEDS	4	4	4	4	4
TURNING RADIUS FT.	20	20	20	20	20

Overall dimensions listed in inches.
*Fighting weight.

ENGINE DATA

ENGINE MAKE/MODEL	Continental R6572
NUMBER OF CYLINDERS	6
CUBIC-INCH DISPLACEMENT	572
HORSEPOWER	207 @ 2900 rpm
TORQUE	455 lbs.-ft. @ 1600 rpm
GOVERNED SPEED (rpm)	Not governed

VALUES

	6	5	4	3	2	1
All models	1,000	2,000	4,000	6,000	8,500	10,000

SCARCITY

Scarcity 3

The M5A1 had substantial draft gear needed for towing artillery. (U.S. Army photo)

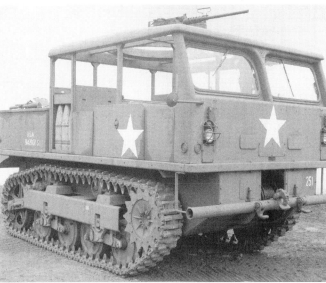

The M5 driver was centrally located, with the passengers seated on either side of the tractor. (U.S. Army photo)

The M5A1 had an enclosed cab and more streamlined look than the original M5. The antiaircraft machine gun mounting is on the roof. The pintle hook is mounted on the front bumper just ahead of the winch. (U.S. Army photo)

The M5A1 had a much-improved layout, with increased seating and cargo area compared to the earlier model. (U.S. Army photo)

RAPD 365255

The stowage boxes of the M5A4 were rearranged. (U.S. Army photo)

G-164 M39

The M39 armored utility vehicles were converted from 640 M18 Hellcat tank destroyers that had been returned to the Buick plant. The conversions were begun in 1944. Originally designated the T41, the M39 was supposed to be a high-speed fully tracked vehicle that could be used in an armored reconnaissance role, or as a high-speed tractor. With a top speed of 50 mph, the M39 certainly filled the bill for "high speed." The M39 could also be used as an armored personnel carrier, although there was only space for eight troopers in the cargo area. The U.S. Army used these vehicles until they were at last declared obsolete in 1957.

The M39 had an M2 HB .50-caliber machine gun for self-defense. Like virtually all track-laying vehicles created after the middle of WWII, it had a torsion-bar suspensioin. (Photo courtesy of the Patton Museum)

The M39 was created by removing the turret from M18 Hellcat tank destroyers and installing troop seating in the space created. (Photo courtesy of the Patton Museum)

The M39 was the ultimate of the WWII high-speed tractors, having a top speed of better than 50 mph. (U.S. Army photo)

GENERAL DATA

MODEL	M39
WEIGHT*	35,500
MAX TOWED LOAD	10,000
LENGTH	214
WIDTH	113
HEIGHT	77.5
TRACK	94.625
STD TRACK WIDTH	14.5
MAX SPEED	60
FUEL CAPY	165
RANGE	155
ELECTRICAL	24 negative
TRANSMISSION SPEEDS	3
TURNING RADIUS FT.	33

Overall dimensions listed in inches.

*Fighting weight

ENGINE DATA

ENGINE MAKE/MODEL*	Continental R975C4
NUMBER OF CYLINDERS	9 radial
CUBIC-INCH DISPLACEMENT	973
HORSEPOWER	400 @ 2400 rpm
TORQUE	940 lbs.-ft. @ 1700 rpm
GOVERNED SPEED (rpm)	2400

VALUES

	6	5	4	3	2	1
All models	7,000	13,500	20,000	26,000	30,000	35,000

SCARCITY

Scarcity 4

G-184 M6 38-Ton

The Allis-Chalmers M6 38-ton high-speed tractor was the king of the WWII high-speed tractors. Powered by two huge Waukesha 145GZ gasoline engines giving it a towing capacity up to 60,000-lbs., the M6 was intended for the toughest of the prime mover jobs. Assigned to tow 4.7-in., 240mm or 8-in. field pieces, it also transported the crews for these weapons and, depending upon the weapon, also carried 20 to 24 rounds of ammunition. The M6 was equipped with a huge 60,000-lb.-capacity drag winch in the rear.

The crew of 11 sat in two rows in the front of the vehicle, the engines were in the middle with the radiators on either side, and ammunition boxes were on the rear of the tractor. An M49C ring mount and M2 Browning

.50-caliber machine gun were mounted on the roof for defense.

Production of these huge machines didn't start until February 1944, and by August 1945 only 1,235 had been built.

GENERAL DATA

MODEL	M6
GROSS WEIGHT	76,000 lbs.
MAX TOWED LOAD	50,000 lbs.
LENGTH	257 13/16
WIDTH	120.5
HEIGHT	104 1/16
TRACK	98.5
TRACK WIDTH	22
MAX SPEED	21 mph
FUEL CAPY	250 gal
RANGE	110 mi
ELECTRICAL	12 neg
TRANSMISSION SPEEDS	2
TURNING RADIUS FT.	26.5

Overall dimensions listed in inches.

ENGINE DATA

ENGINE MAKE/MODEL	Two Waukesha 145GZ
NUMBER OF CYLINDERS	6
CUBIC-INCH DISPLACEMENT	817
HORSEPOWER	190 @ 2100 rpm
TORQUE	600 lbs.-ft. @ 1200 rpm
GOVERNED SPEED (rpm)	2100

VALUES

No reported sales

SCARCITY

Scarcity 5

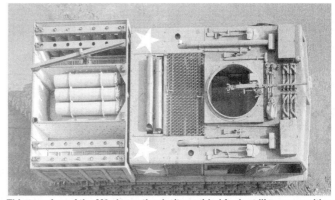

This top view of the M6 shows the davit provided for handling ammunition and the dual exhaust stacks for the twin Waukesha 145GZ gasoline engines. (U.S. Army photo)

TAlmost everything about the M6 was massive. (U.S. Army photo)

This view shows the M6's huge rear winch, the chains of the ammunition lockers, and the decontaminator and fire extinguishers mounted in the crew compartment. Notice the large backup light. (U.S. Army photo)

Like many of the Army's vehicles, the M6 could be buttoned up to protect the crew from inclement weather. This M6 has its canvas covers in place over the sides. (U.S. Army photo)

G-252 M8A1

The M8A1 was originally known as the M8E2. This high-speed tractor shares its AOS-895-3 engine and transmission with the M41 light tank. In July 1950, Allis-Chalmers was given an order for 480 of these tractors. When the engine was upgraded to the fuel-injected AOS-895-5, the vehicle's classification changed to M8A2. These vehicles were designed to tow artillery loads in the 18,000 to 32,000-lb. range.

RANGE	180	180
ELECTRICAL	24 neg	24 neg
TRANSFER		
SPEEDS	2	2
TURNING		
RADIUS FT.	pivot	pivot

Overall dimensions listed in inches.

ENGINE DATA

ENGINE MAKE/MODEL	Contin. AOS 895-3	Contin. AOS 895-5
NUMBER OF CYLINDERS	Opposed 6	Opposed 6
CU.-IN. DISPLACEMENT	895	895
HORSEPOWER	363 @ 2800 rpm	363 @ 2800 rpm
TORQUE	760 lbs.-ft. @ 2060 rpm	760 lbs.-ft. @ 2060 rpm
GOVERNED SPEED (rpm)	2800	2800

GENERAL DATA

MODEL	M8A1	M8A2
WEIGHT	37,500 lbs.	37,500 lbs.
MAX TOWED LOAD	39,000 lbs.	39,000 lbs.
LENGTH	265.125	265.125
WIDTH	130.5	130.5
HEIGHT	117.25	117.25
TRACK	102.5	102.5
TRACK WIDTH	21	21
MAX SPEED	40 mph	40 mph
FUEL CAPY	225 gal	225 gal

VALUES

	6	5	4	3	2	1
All models	2,500	4,000	5,000	7,500	9,750	12,000

SCARCITY

Scarcity 5

Although this vehicle is not so fitted, a bulldozer blade attachment was available for the G-252 M8A1 tractors. This was useful when preparing the emplacements for the weapons the tractors towed. (U.S. Army photo)

ARMORED RECOVERY VEHICLES

M31

The M31 family was an early attempt at an armored recovery vehicle based on surplus M3 series tanks. Baldwin Locomotive Works began work in October 1942 converting 509 used tanks into M31 retrievers. One hundred-fifty new diesel-powered M3A3 tanks were also converted into retrievers, being designated M31B1. These were joined later by a further 146 converted from used diesel-powered tanks.

As part of the conversion process, all the armament was removed except a .30-caliber bow machine gun. The turret was reversed and a dummy gun welded to the former turret rear. In the former front a Gar Wood 10-Y 5500 crane with a 10,000-lb. capacity was mounted in the space formerly occupied by the 37mm gun. By using boom jacks, the lifting capacity could be increased to 30,000-lbs. Inside the tank, a 60,000-lb.-capacity PTO-driven winch was mounted to the floor. The former location of the 75mm gun was occupied by a dummy gun, which was fitted to a door.

GENERAL DATA

MODEL	M31	M31B1	M31B2
WEIGHT*	65,620 lbs.	67,000 lbs.	68,000 lbs.
LENGTH	222	222	222
WIDTH	107	107	107
HEIGHT	120	123	123
TREAD	83	83	83
CREW	6	6 or 7	6 or 7
MAX SPEED	24	24	24
FUEL CAPY	175	148	175
RANGE	120	150	120
ELECTRICAL	24 neg	24 neg	24 neg
TRANSMISSION SPEEDS	5F, 1R	5F, 1R	5F, 1R
TURNING			
RADIUS FT	31	31	31
ARMAMENT	2 x .30-cal.	2 x .30-cal.	2 x .30-cal.

Fighting weight

Overall dimensions listed in inches.

ENGINE DATA

ENGINE MAKE/MODEL	Continental R975 EC2	GM 6046
NUMBER OF CYLINDERS	9	2 x 6
CUBIC-INCH DISPLACEMENT	973	850
HORSEPOWER	340 @ 2400 rpm	410 @ 2100 rpm
TORQUE	890 lbs.-ft. @ 1800 rpm	885 lbs.-ft. @ 1900

VALUES

VALUES: *Too few survivors of these type exist in private hands to establish values.*

This crewman is exiting his M31 by way of the door installed in the former location of the 75mm main gun. The M31 was a reasonably successful design, but as the M3 medium tank it was based on fell out of use it was replaced by its successor, the M4-based M32 series of recovery vehicles. (U.S. Army photo)

M32

As the M3 series vehicles were phased out, a new chassis source for recovery vehicles had to be found. With the Sherman being the standard tank, it was natural that its chassis be used. Four types of recovery vehicles were constructed: the M32, M32B1, M32B2, and M32B3. These were based on the M4, M4A1, M4A2, and M4A3 chassis, respectively. A M32B4 based upon the M4A4 was planned, but none were built.

Unlike the M31 series, the M32 series vehicles had a fixed dummy turret mounted. Instead of the M31's boom, there was an A-frame fitted to the front of the hull. This A-frame swung forward for heavy lifting, but remained to the rear for towing other vehicles. It was supported by yet another A-frame welded to the hull rear. A 60,000-lb. Gar Wood winch was mounted in the hull. It could be used in conjunction with the A-frame for lifting, or the line run through openings in the hull for direct pulls.

The M32 also had better armament than the M31. It was armed not only with .30-caliber bow weapon, but also a .50-caliber machine gun on the turret, and an 81mm mortar on the hull front. The mortar's job was to lay down smoke barrages to mask recovery operations. At the request of the Marine Corps, a recovery vehicle based on the M4A3 with horizontal volute suspension was developed. Together, Baldwin Locomotive Works and International Harvester built 80 of these vehicles in 1945.

Installation of the HVSS also brought the M32A1B1 designation to the M32B1.

Lima Locomotive Works was the first to begin construction of these new recovery vehicles, beginning production in June 1943. Production can be broken down as follows:

M32 Pressed Steel Car Co. 163
M32B1 Baldwin Locomotive 195
M32B1 Pressed Steel Car Co. 475
M32B1 Federal Machine 385
M32B2 Lima Locomotive Works 26
M32B3 Pressed Steel Car Co. 298
M32B3 Lima Locomotive Works 20

GENERAL DATA

MODEL	M32	M32B1	M32B2	M32B3
WEIGHT*	64,300 lbs.	64,200 lbs.	67,600 lbs.	64,100 lbs.
LENGTH	232	232	233	232
WIDTH	107	103	103	103
HEIGHT	116	116	116	116
TREAD	83	83	83	83
MAX SPEED	24 mph	24 mph	25 mph	26 mph
FUEL CAPCY	175 gal	175 gal	148 gal	168 gal
RANGE	120 mi	120 mi	150 mi	130 mi
ELECTRICAL	24 neg	24 neg	24 neg	24 neg
TRANSMISSION				
SPEEDS	5F, 1R	5F, 1R	5F, 1R	5F, 1R
TURNING				
RADIUS FT	31	31	31	31
ARMAMENT	1 x 81mm	1 x 81mm	1 x 81mm	1 x 81mm
	1 x .50	1 x .50	1 x .50	1 x .50
	1 x .30	1 x .30	1 x .30	1 x .30

*Fighting weight
Overall dimensions listed in inches.

The T5 was the test model for the series that became the M32. Built by Lima Locomotive Works, this T5 was photographed at Aberdeen Proving Ground in September 1943. The production M32 varied very little from the T5. (National Archives and Records Administration photo)

This M32B1 has its A-frame boom raised to the lifting position. The windlass drum attached to the right side drive sprocket was used to raise the A-frame to this position. The heavy array attached to the base of the right side A-frame member is the lifting arm, and the wire rope attached to it was used to connect it to the windlass. The vehicle was then placed in low forward gear and eased forward until the boom was erected. Then the wire rope could be removed from the windlass, restoring the vehicle's full mobility. (Photo courtesy of the Patton Museum)

The M32B1 had the flexible .50-caliber machine gun on top, a ball-mounted .30-caliber machine gun, and an 81mm mortar on the glacis plate. The M32B1's cast hull M4A1 Sherman heritage is clearly evident. (U.S. Army photo)

The M32B3 was based on the Army's standard welded-hull M4A3 Sherman tank. It carried the same equipment as the M32B1, although the difference in hull shape required that the stowage be laid out differently. (U.S. Army photo)

ARMORED RECOVERY VEHICLES

ENGINE DATA

ENGINE MAKE/MODEL	Continental R975 EC2	GM 6046
NUMBER OF CYLINDERS	9	2 x 6
CUBIC-IN. DISPLACEMENT	973	850
HORSEPOWER	340 @ 2400 rpm	410 @ 2100 rpm
TORQUE	890 lbs.-ft. @ 1800 rpm	885 lbs.-ft. @ 1900

VALUES DATA

	6	5	4	3	2	1
All models	15,000	24,000	30,000	40,000	50,000	60,000

SCARCITY

Scarcity 3

Like the Shermans upon which they were based, the M32 recovery vehicles received the improved horizontal volute suspension system, as can be seen on this M32A1B1 on display outside the Patton Museum at Ft. Knox.

The heavy-duty armored vehicle tow bar can be seen stowed on the left rear side of this M32B1's hull, and the lifting boom is in its stowed position. Virtually every inch of the recovery vehicle's outer surface is covered in tools, spares, or recovery gear. (U.S. Army photo)

The M4A3E8 was the most common tank in the postwar Army inventory, and it is not surprising that there was an M32 variant based on it.

M74

The deployment of heavier tanks like the Pershing and Patton during the Korea conflict punctuated the need for a better recovery vehicle than the M32 series. Bowen McLauglin-York (BMY) began developing such a vehicle based on surplus M4A3 chassis. Mass production of these conversions ran from February 1954 through October 1955. Rock Island Arsenal converted older M32B1 retrievers until 1958.

The M74 had several improvements over the older model, not the least of which was an increase of winch capacity from 60,000 lbs. on the predecessors to 90,000 lbs., and the introduction of separate tow and lift winches. Also, the A frame of the M74 was hydraulic elevated, and the vehicle was fitted with a front-mounted blade that could be used to anchor the retriever during heavy recovery operations, or as a light bulldozer.

Even among vehicles of the same series there was some variation in stowage. Notice the spare track blocks stored on the rear hull of this M32B1 photographed at Fort Knox, Kentucky. On one side of the hull is stowed the wheeled vehicle tow bar (the same tow bar is often seen hung on the outer side of Diamond T 969 wrecker beds), secured just above the two large pry bars. This vehicle has had its sand shields removed. (Photo courtesy of the Patton Museum)

The M74 blade was raised by attaching the rope from either the auxiliary winch (mounted on "turret" face), or the main recovery winch, whose rope played out of the opening in the glacis plate. The stowage compartments mounted along the sides of the vehicle were a welcome improvement over the stowage arrangement of the M32 series vehicles. (Photo courtesy of the Patton Museum)

The increasing size of American tanks brought about the need for a recovery vehicle with increased capabilities. The M74 was that vehicle. The spade on the front, lowered by gravity, could serve as an anchor during heavy recovery operations, or be used in light bulldozer work. (Photo courtesy of the Patton Museum)

This M74 may well be the first one. Close examination of the stenciling discloses an October, 1953 date. Bowen-McLaughlin-York finished the first one in July 1953, and mass conversion of M4A3s into M74s did not begin until February 1954. In any event, it is factory fresh, as is evidenced by the scratch-free paint on the dozer blade. (Photo courtesy of the Patton Museum)

Unlike its predecessor, the M74's large tow bar was stowed attached to the pintle hook, and swung upward around the stowed A-frame. The late-style Sherman commander's cupola was used on the M74 vehicles. (U.S. Army photo)

The M74 had a bow .30-caliber machine gun, and a .50-caliber mounted on the commander's cupola.

GENERAL DATA

MODEL	M74
WEIGHT*	93,750 lbs.
MAX TOWED LOAD	100,000 lbs.
LENGTH	313 1/16
WIDTH	121 13/16
HEIGHT	133.5
STD TRACK WIDTH	23
MAX SPEED	21 mph
FUEL CAPY	168 gal
RANGE	100 mi
ELECTRICAL	24 neg
TRANSMISSION	
SPEEDS	5
TURNING	
RADIUS FT.	pivot

Overall dimensions listed in inches. Measured with main gun facing forward, and antiaircraft machine gun mounted.

*Fighting weight

ENGINE DATA

ENGINE MAKE/MODEL	Ford GAA
NUMBER OF CYLINDERS	V-8 60-degree
CUBIC-INCH DISPLACEMENT	1,100

HORSEPOWER	450 @ 2600 rpm
TORQUE	950 lbs.-ft. @ 2100 rpm
GOVERNED SPEED (rpm)	2600

M51

The M51 was a massive recovery vehicle based on the suspension and automotive components of its contemporary, the M103 heavy tank. Although not terribly popular with the Army, which preferred the M88, the M51 was widely used by the U.S. Marine Corps, which adopted the M51 in 1958 and used it through the Vietnam War. Marine recovery vehicle crewmen went directly from the Sherman-based M32 to the massive M51, no doubt requiring a bit of orientation.

The M51 had a hydraulically driven, 45-ton-capacity recovery winch, as well as a 5-ton auxiliary winch. Hydraulically lowered anchor blades were located on both the front and rear of the M51 to stabilize the vehicle during recovery and lifting operations. A crew of four operated the vehicle.

Rather than the windlass arrangement used on the M32 to raise the A-frame, the M74 used hydraulically actuated rigging. In addition to being simpler to operate, the M74 had an A-frame that could be used as a live boom, being raised and lowered while under load. (U.S. Army photo)

ARMORED RECOVERY VEHICLES

GENERAL DATA

MODEL	M51
WEIGHT*	120,000 lbs.
LENGTH	399
WIDTH	143
HEIGHT	129
TRACK	115
TRACK WIDTH	28
MAX SPEED	30 mph
FUEL CAPY	400 gal
RANGE	200 mi
ELECTRICAL	24 neg
TORQMATIC	

TRANSMISSION		
SPEEDS		3
TURNING		
RADIUS FT		pivot

Overall dimensions listed in inches.

*Fighting weight.

ENGINE DATA

ENGINE MAKE/MODEL	**Continental AVSI-1790-6**
NUMBER OF CYLINDERS	V-12 90 degree
CUBIC-INCH DISPLACEMENT	1,790
HORSEPOWER	1,020 @ 2800 rpm
TORQUE	1,900 lbs.-ft. @ 2200 rpm
GOVERNED SPEED (rpm)	2800

Military recovery vehicles, whether wheeled or tracked, have notoriously poor off-road performance due to their great weight. Fortunately, the recovery winches make them well equipped for self-recovery. This is a pre-production M51, as is evidenced by the outriggers on the hull rear rather than an anchor spade. The ground pressure of the M51 was 12.2 psi, a full psi more than its contemporary in Vietnam, the M48. (Photo courtesy of the Patton Museum)

The M51 was a massive vehicle. The front anchor spade is visible, as is the sheave mounted on it for use in recovery operations. One advantage of its massive size was its ability to climb a 36-in. vertical wall. Just behind the fuel cans on the retriever's side is the heavy-duty tow bar. (Photo courtesy of the Patton Museum)

placed in storage and BMY even had the foresight to cast and store some extra hulls. These allowed a quick restarting of production to meet foreign orders in 1991.

The M88 is built on an armored chassis similar to a tank, and shares many components with the M48/M60 medium tanks that were its contemporaries. The lower portion of the hull is filled with two hydraulically powered winches — a hoist winch and a separate main winch. The 50,000-lb. hoist winch uses an A-frame boom and its 400 ft. of 5/8 in wire rope for heavy lifting. The main winch is of 90,000-lbs. capacity and uses 200 ft. of 1 1/4-in. rope for front recovery operations.

The crew of four includes a driver/operator, a mechanic, a rigger and a commander. The engine and final drive are located at the rear of the hull, the hoist winch in the middle, and the main winch between the hoist winch and the front of the retriever, under and between the driver and mechanic's seats.

Any addition to the two winches, other hydraulically operated equipment includes: a bow-mounted blade, boom, refueling pump, and a very powerful impact wrench. Due to the extensive use of hydraulics, the vehicle is equipped with both main and auxiliary hydraulic systems. The front bulldozer blade is used to hold and stabilize the retriever during heavy lifting and during all winching operations.

The M88A1 engine is a 750-hp, turbosupercharged Continental M12, four-cycle, air-cooled, model AVDS-1790-2DR diesel. It drives the vehicle through an Allison XT-1410-4 cross-drive transmission, which provides three forward and one reverse speed. The transmission is a combination transmission, differential, steering, and braking unit. The M88A1 is designed for power, and the 105,000-lb. vehicle has a top speed of only 26 mph. A two-cylinder, 10.8-hp diesel Auxiliary Power Unit (APU) is carried primarily to recharge vehicle batteries, and to

The rear spade used by M51 production vehicles is shown here, as is one of the gas cylinders for the torch set that all recovery vehicles carried. (Photo courtesy of the Patton Museum)

M88

The M88 was designed to replace the Sherman-based M74 recovery vehicle. The larger U.S. tanks of the 1950s, such as the M48, required a larger retriever.

Production of the M88 was approved in 1959 and Bowen-McLaughlin-York Inc., of York, Pennsylvania, was awarded a contract for 1,075 vehicles. The company's design has proven to be very well thought out and durable. The M88-type Armored Recovery Vehicle (ARV) has served many countries from the 1960s on. In keeping with the Army's goal of having an all-diesel tactical vehicle fleet, the diesel-powered M88A1 was introduced. A program to upgrade older M88s to A1 status was completed in 1982. In 1989, after 3,042 produced, M88A1 production ended, but the tooling was

The M88 was an impressive machine, large in size and recovery capabilities. The main drag winch rope can be seen protruding from the front of the hull, just below the vision slits. (Photo courtesy of the Patton Museum)

power some of the hydraulic and electrical equipment when the main engine is not running.

The M88A1 was once the heaviest armored vehicle in the U.S. inventory, but it has since been surpassed. This is the same situation that brought about the need for the M88 as a replacement of the M74 in the 1950s. While the M88A1 can easily handle an M60, it requires two M88A1s to recover one M1 Abrams main battle tank. However, the recent updating of the design to the M88A2 standard evidences the soundness of the original design. The new version has increased horsepower, a

strengthened suspension, increased armor protection, and other improvements to the now 40-year-old design.

GENERAL DATA

MODEL	M88
WEIGHT*	112,000 lbs.
LENGTH	325.5
WIDTH	135
HEIGHT	115
TRACK	135
TRACK WIDTH	28
MAX SPEED	30 mph
FUEL CAPY	445 gal

The A-frame of the M88 has been raised in this view, and the front anchor spade lowered. While sometimes used for bulldozing, it is for use such as this that the spade was installed on the vehicle. During winching operations it could be partially lowered to serve as a ground anchor, or during lifting operations it was lowered completely so the lifted load was transmitted directly through it to earth. This prevented overloading the M88s torsion-bar suspension system. (Photo courtesy of the Patton Museum)

RANGE	222 mi
ELECTRICAL	24 neg
TURNING	
RADIUS FT	pivot

Overall dimensions listed in inches.

*Fighting weight.

ENGINE DATA

ENGINE MAKE/MODEL	Continental AVSI-1790-6
NUMBER OF CYLINDERS	V-12 90 degree
CUBIC-INCH DISPLACEMENT	1,790
HORSEPOWER	1,020 @ 2800 rpm
TORQUE	1,900 lbs.-ft. @ 2200 rpm
GOVERNED SPEED (rpm)	2800

The lifting ability of the M88A1 is demonstrated here as it hoists an M109 self-propelled howitzer off the ground. Two M88A1s could be driven with an M48 medium tank suspended between them. (U.S. Army photo)

M578

This retriever has its tow bar stowed on the rear of the hull and the left side hatch is open. The A-frame is stored in its travel position. (Photo courtesy United States Army Engineer School History Office)

The M88A2 was an upgrade to the M88A1. The weight of the M1 Abrams vehicles required that the retriever be uprated. The 750-hp engine of the M88A1 was replaced with a 1,050-hp model, the brakes upgraded, and a 6,000-lb. lead winch (visible on the front of the vehicle shown) added to handle the main winch cable. The main winch capacity was increased from 90,000 lbs. to 140,000 lbs. The A-frame of the M88A2 has a rectangular cross-section, compared to the tubular cross-section used previously. (United Defense photo)

Originally designed by FMC as an air-transportable heavy lifting crane for barrel replacements of self-propelled guns of the same (M107/M110) family, the M578, primarily built by Bowen-McLaughlin-York, served more as a wrecker and a general recovery vehicle. The machine FMC conceived to meet the Army specifications on a modified M107/110 SPG chassis was originally known as the T120. The T120 developed into the T120E1 and finally the M578 Light Armored Full Tracked Recovery Vehicle.

The forward portion of the M578 hull is essentially the same as the chassis used for the M107/110 Self-Propelled Gun. The engine is mounted to the right and the driver sits on the left, separated by an insulated metal firewall. Directly behind the power plant is an auxiliary drive, which powers the generator and the hydraulic pumps when the engine main engine is shut off. The hydraulic pumps provide power for the winches, boom, cab, and rear spade.

The turret of the M578 houses the crew during recovery operations. It also has some storage for recovery equipment. There are two hydraulically powered winches in the M578 — a 30,000-lb. boom winch and a 60,000-lb. drag winch. The boom winch is a two-speed unit that uses 5/8-in. wire rope with an internal automatic brake allowing the load to remain suspended with the engine off. The boom elevation cylinders penetrate the front turret wall and are attached to the boom just forward of the cab.

Directly behind the crane operator's seat is a full-height tool locker that is accessible from outside the crane cab. While both the hull and turret cab are made of welded steel armor, the vehicle is intended to protect the crew only from small-caliber bullets and shell splinters. The M578 could not withstand a hit from any modern tank or artillery. For self-defense, an M2 .50-cal. Browning machine gun is mounted near the cupola.

The Detroit Diesel GMC 8V71T turbosupercharged, eight-cylinder, V-type, two-cycle diesel is mated to an Allison model XTG-411-2A cross-drive transmission.

ARMORED RECOVERY VEHICLES

GENERAL DATA

MODEL	M578
WEIGHT	54,000 lbs.
LENGTH	250.25
WIDTH	124
HEIGHT	130.5
TRACK WIDTH	18
MAX SPEED	37 mph
FUEL CAPY	320 gal
RANGE	450 mi
ELECTRICAL	24 neg

Overall dimensions listed in inches. Measured with boom facing forward and antiaircraft machine gun mounted.

ENGINE DATA

ENGINE MAKE/MODEL	**GM 8V71T**
NUMBER OF CYLINDERS	8
CUBIC-INCH DISPLACEMENT	567.4
HORSEPOWER	405@2300 rpm
TORQUE	980 ft.-lbs.@1700 rpm

The suspension and forward part of the hull of the M578 armored recovery vehicle was based on that of the M107/M110 self-propelled howitzer. There is a spotlight mounted near the end of the crane boom. On the left side and front of the turret are the pioneer tool rack, track jacks, fire extinguisher, and a snatch block. (U.S. Army photo)

Although the tow bar is missing from this camouflaged M578, it sports its machine gun, and a towrope can be seen stowed along the boom. The anchor spade, seen spanning the rear of the hull in the traveling position, was lowered during heavy recovery or lifting operations to stabilize and secure the vehicle. (U.S. Army photo)

The turret of the M578 would rotate 360 degrees to great flexibility in recovery, repair, and material handling operations. The vehicle in this May 1965 photograph has its boom elevated to 60 degrees. (U.S. Army photo)

LIGHT TANKS

G-103 M3 Stuart

The M3 was the standard family of light tank of the U.S. Army at the outbreak of WWII. It had entered production at American Car and Foundry during March 1941. The M3, as well as the later M5, were both listed as G-103 vehicles, but the M8 Howitzer Motor Carriage was listed as G-127.

These tanks, powered by the Continental W-670 radial engine, were produced until October 1942. In addition to these 4,526 tanks, there were 1,285 more built that had the Guiberson T-1020 engine. Rather than the usual "A" suffix, these diesel-powered tanks were designated "M3 light tank (diesel)."

Three different turrets were mounted on the M3s.

The original turret was riveted, the 279 intermediate turrets were welded face hardened armor, where the final was welded homogeneous armor. Interestingly, in addition to the turret rotation, the main gun had a + or - 20 degree traverse within its mount. Some of the later turrets did not have a cupola. The first 3,212 tanks were produced with riveted hulls, while subsequent ones were assembled by welding.

The M3A1 was introduced in May 1942 and featured power traverse, gyrostabilizer, and at last included a turret basket. None of the 4,621 M3A1 models had turret cupolas, and only 211 of them were diesel powered.

The M3A3 was the next version to reach production in September 1942, with its production run lasting a full year and totaling 3,427 tanks. The M3A3 hull resembled that of a M5 with the addition of with sloping hull sides. It also had a new turret design that included a bustle

This photograph, taken on the 24-in. wall at Aberdeen Proving Grounds, shows the suspension system of the M3 Stuart. The suspension was virtually unchanged throughout the production of these vehicle. (National Archives and Records Administration photo)

The M5 introduced the twin Cadillac V-8 power plant that was used in many later tanks. (Photo courtesy of the Patton Museum)

The M3A1 introduced a turret basket for the crew to stand on to the series. Shown here is an M3A1 belonging to the Patton Museum. This example is maintained in operating condition for historical displays. The tanks of the M3 family were reliable little vehicles, earning the nickname "Honey" by the British in Africa. (Photo courtesy of the Patton Museum)

where the radio equipment was mounted. Very few of the M3A3 tanks were used by U.S. forces. Most were supplied to foreign powers.

All versions of the basic M3 were declared obsolete in July of 1943. The diesel-powered M3A1s joined them on the obsolete list at the same time.

M5 Light Tank Family

The M5 family was developed to provide the Army with a light tank that did not use a radial aircraft-type engine, like the M3 family. Cadillac converted an M3 by installing twin Cadillac engines and Hydra-Matic transmissions that drove the tank through a two-speed

The larger turret distinguished the M5A1 from the M5. Production of the Stuart family of vehicles ceased when the last M5A1 was built in 1944. The odd-shaped box on the turret side houses the mount for the commander's machine gun when it is not in use. (Photo courtesy of the Patton Museum)

The turret of the M8 was open topped. When the M8 was used as intended, from rearward support positions, this was not a problem, but in close combat the crew was quite vulnerable. (Photo courtesy of the Patton Museum)

Though both the M3A1 and M3A3 carried 1-in. side armor, the sloping of the armor on the M3A3 greatly increased the ballistic protection of the tank. The chances of deflecting an anti-armor piercing round were improved by this new shape. In the event a shot penetrated, it would have to travel through more armor than on the older, flat-surfaced M3A1. (Photo courtesy of the Patton Museum)

automatic transfer case.

The new power plant and improved hull shape gave the M5 much more interior space than the M3. Production of the M5 began at GM Cadillac Division's Detroit plant in April 1942. In August, production was also begun in Southgate, California. Massey Harris had begun building the M5 in July. M5 production ceased at all three facilities in December 1942, with a total run of 2,074.

The M5A1 was an improvement, featuring an enlarged turret similar to the one developed for the M3A3. The M5A1 replaced the M5 on the production lines at all three of the plants mentioned above. Additional production was added by bringing American Car and Foundry into the M5A1 manufacturing group. Production was completed at all four facilities by mid 1944. A total of 6,810 of these improved light tanks were produced.

Early models had the .30-caliber antiaircraft machine gun exposed on the turret side, while later models incorporated a shield that the weapon retracted into.

Identifying early and late production of the M5A1 is difficult due to an extensive rebuilding program. Between November 1944 and June 1945 American Car and Foundry remanufactured 775 of the early models to the late model standards.

M8

The M8 was note really a tank, but rather a self-propelled 75mm howitzer built on the chassis of the M5 tank. It was built by the Cadillac Division of General Motors beginning in September of 1942. By the time production was terminated in January 1944, 1,778 vehicles had been completed. While at first glance the M8 appears to have been built aby mounting a snub-nosed cannon on an M5, that is not the case. Unlike the M5, the hull of the M8 does not have hatches for the driver and co-driver. Rather, the entire crew entered and exited through the open-topped turret. Like the M5, it could be driven by either of the drivers. Less obvious, the turret ring of the M8 was increased to 54 1/2 in. from 46 3/4 in. on the M5. For close-in and antiaircraft defese, an M2 .50-caliber machine gun was mounted on a ring on the rear of the turret.

GENERAL DATA

MODEL	M3 early	M3 late	M3A1	M3A3
WEIGHT*	28,000 lbs.	28,000 lbs.	28,500 lbs.	32,400 lbs.
LENGTH	178.4	178.4	178.4	197.9
WIDTH	88	88	88	99.4
HEIGHT	104	94	94	101
TREAD	73	73	73	73
CREW	4	4	4	4
MAX SPEED	36 mph	36 mph	36 mph	31 mph
FUEL CAPY	54 gal	54 gal	54 gal	110 gal
RANGE	70 mi	70 mi	70 mi	135 mi
ELECTRICAL	12 neg	12 neg	12 neg	12 neg
TRANSMISSION				
SPEEDS	5F, 1R	5F, 1R	5F, 1R	5F, 1R
TURNING RADIUS FT.	42	42	42	42
ARMAMENT MAIN	37mm	37mm	37mm	37mm
SECONDARY	4 x .30	2 x .30	2 x .30	2 x .30
FLEXIBLE	1 x .30	1 x .30	1 x .30	1 x .30

MODEL	M5	M5A1	M8
WEIGHT*	33,100 lbs.	34,700 lbs.	34,600 lbs.
LENGTH	174.8	190.5	196
WIDTH	88.3	90	91.5
HEIGHT	102	101	107
TREAD	88.3	73.3	73.5
CREW	4	4	4
MAX SPEED	36 mph	36 mph	36 mph
FUEL CAPY	89 gal	89 gal	89 gal
RANGE	100 mi	100 mi	100 mi
ELECTRICAL	12 neg	12 neg	12 neg
TRANSMISSION			
SPEEDS	4F, 1R	4F, 1R	4F, 1R
TURNING RADIUS FT.	42	42	42
ARMAMENT MAIN	37mm	37mm	75mm
SECONDARY	2 x .30	2 x .30	—
FLEXIBLE	1 x .30	1 x .30	1 x .50

* Fighting weight
Overall dimensions listed in inches.

ENGINE DATA

ENGINE MAKE/MODEL	Continental W-670-9A	Cadillac Series 42
NUMBER OF CYLINDERS	7	16 (8/engine)
CUBIC-INCH DISPLACEMENT	668	692
HORSEPOWER	262	296
TORQUE	590 lbs.-ft.	560 lbs.-ft.

RADIO EQUIPMENT:
— M3 vehicles were equipped with SCR 210 radios and RC61 interphones. Command vehicles had a SCR 245.

— M3A1 vehicles were provided with SCR 508 radios with integral interphone. Command tanks had the SCR 506.

— M3A3, M5, M5A1 vehicles were equipped with either SCR 508, 528 or 538, all with integral interphones. Again, the SCR 506 was fitted to command tanks.

— M8 Howitzer Motor Carriages had the SCR 510 radio set, and the RC99 interphone set.

VALUES

	6	5	4	3	2	1
All models	15,000	20,000	25,000	30,000	35,000	45,000

G-148 M22 Locust

Early in 1941, development began on an airborne light tank. Though known initially as the T9, the 830 production tanks by Marmon-Herrington were designated M22. These tanks were built between April 1943 and February 1944. The SNL number for these tanks was G-148. In an effort to keep weight to a minimum, a Lycoming O-435T aircraft engine powered the tank. The diminutive tank, armed with a 37mm gun,

The small size of the M22 is apparent in this photo of a 28th Airborne Tank Battalion crewman resting against his Locust during training. (Photo courtesy of the Patton Museum)

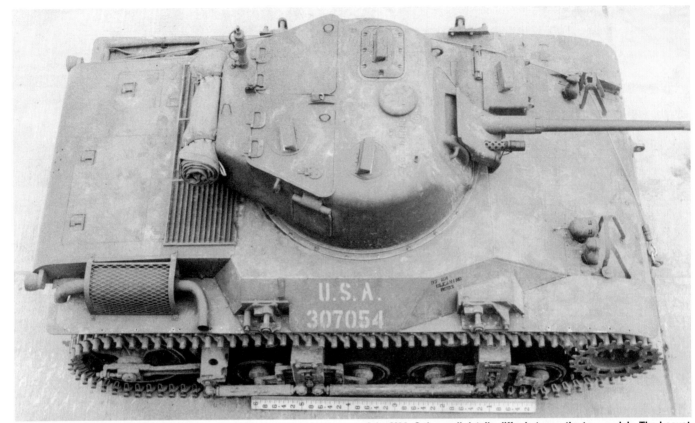

This December 1942 image is a photograph of a T9E1, immediate forerunner of the M22. Only small details differ between the two models. The Locust was intended to fly to the battlefield, albeit with the aid of an airplane. (National Archives and Records Administration photo)

was never used in combat by U.S. troops, however, some of the 260 units supplied to British forces under lend-lease were used in an airborne operation.

GENERAL DATA

MODEL	M22
WEIGHT*	16,400 lbs.
LENGTH	156
WIDTH	88.5
HEIGHT	72.5
TREAD	70.3
CREW	3
MAX SPEED	35 mph
FUEL CAPY	57 gal
RANGE	110 mi
ELECTRICAL	12 neg
TRANSMISSION	
SPEEDS	4F, 1R
TURNING	
RADIUS FT.	38
ARMAMENT	37mm
	1 x .30

*Fighting weight
Overall dimensions listed in inches.

ENGINE DATA

ENGINE MAKE/MODEL	Lycoming 0-435T
NUMBER OF CYLINDERS	6
CUBIC-INCH DISPLACEMENT	434
HORSEPOWER	192
TORQUE	360 lbs.-ft.

RADIO EQUIPMENT: *The Locust had only basic communication equipment, the radio set SCR 510 and interphone set RC99.*

VALUES

The M22 is a rare vehicle, and there is insufficient data to determine values.

G-200 M24 Light Tank

The M24 Chaffee began life as the T24. The objective of the M24 was to provide the using troops with a light tank armed with a 75mm gun, as opposed to the 37mm gun borne by the M3 and M5 series of vehicles.

The new tanks chassis utilized twin Cadillac engines and Hydra-Matic transmissions similar those used by the M5A1. However, in the T24, the automatic transfer case was replaced with a manual version. The new

The M2 .50-caliber Browning machine gun can be seen mounted in this rear three-quarter view of a Chaffee in the field. Intended for anti-aircraft use, these weapons were also used for close-in defense. The pioneer tools can also be seen in their storage rack. (Photo courtesy of Patton Museum)

In this official Armor and Engineer Board portrait of the M24, the road wheel arrangement associated with U.S. tank torsion bar suspension is illustrated. This type of suspension would be used on virtually all subsequent U.S. tanks. (Photo courtesy of Patton Museum)

transfer case had two forward speeds and a single reverse speed. Coupled with the Hydra-Matic transmissions, this provided eight forward speeds and four reverse speeds.

Suspension was via torsion bar, with five pairs of road wheels on each side. Both the driver and assistant driver had driving controls, with the assistant driver also having a ball-mount .30-caliber machine gun to operate. Production of the T24 began at Cadillac in April 1944. The designation T24 was replaced by M24 in June and production began at Massey Harris the following month. The two facilities combined to produce a total of 4,731 tanks.

This view of an M24 undergoing tests by the Armor and Engineer Board at Ft. Knox clearly shows the pivoting driver's hatch compared to the commander's vertically opening hatch. (Photo courtesy of Patton Museum)

GENERAL DATA

MODEL	M24
WEIGHT	40,500 lbs.
LENGTH	216
WIDTH*	117
HEIGHT	97.5
TREAD	96
TRACK WIDTH	16
CREW	4 or 5
MAX SPEED	34 mph
FUEL CAPY	110 gal
RANGE	100 mi
ELECTRICAL	24 neg
HYDRAMATIC	
TRANSMISSION SPEEDS	4
TRANSFER SPEEDS	2
TURNING	
RADIUS FT.	23
ARMAMENT	
MAIN	75mm
SECONDARY	2x .30-cal.
FLEXIBLE	1x .50-cal.

Overall dimensions listed in inches.

*Inside/outside width at tires.

ENGINE DATA

ENGINE MAKE/MODEL	2 x Cadillac 44T24
NUMBER OF CYLINDERS	V-8, 90 degree
CUBIC-INCH DISPLACEMENT	349
HORSEPOWER	110 @ 3400 rpm
TORQUE	240 lbs.-ft. @ 1200 rpm
GOVERNED SPEED (rpm)	Not governed

RADIO EQUIPMENT: The Chaffee was fitted with the SCR 508, 528, or 538 radio set in its turret. Command tanks also had a SCR 506 in the hull.

VALUES

	6	5	4	3	2	1
All models	15,000	25,000	35,000	48,000	60,000	68,000

G-251 M41 Walker Bulldog

The M41 began life in the late 1940s as the T41. It was to be the lightweight member of a family of three tanks. The two other tanks in this new "family" were the "medium" tank called the T42, and a "heavy" tank, the T43. The T42 would become the M47 Medium Tank, and the T43 would become the M103 Heavy Tank. The M41 was named the Walker Bulldog in honor of General W. W. Walker, who died in a jeep accident in Korea in 1951.

The doctrine of vehicle design for U.S. forces in the late 1940s and 1950s was commonality. These new tank designs were no exception. There were common components among all three, including similar range finding and sighting equipment.

The M41 was designed around the power train, which included a rear-mounted transmission and final drive. At the other end of the hull was the driver's compartment. The Bulldog had torsion-bar suspension much like the M24. The Walker had only a single driver

and, unlike its predecessors, no hull-mounted machine gun.

The gun in the Bulldog is the 76mm M32. It was the first U.S. tank gun equipped with a bore evacuator to clear the gun tube after firing. The turret had a large bustle that housed both the radio gear and a large ventilation fan. The bustle also acted as a counterweight balance for the main gun. The Bulldog was not designed as a battle tank. Its job was to be reconnaissance tank, seeking out the enemy and radioing back their strength and position. Rather than heavy armor, it relied on high speed for protection.

The primary difference between the M41 and M41A1 was in the turret. The A1s had improved gun-laying equipment in order to meet the new (at that time) Army policy of being able to open fire within 5 seconds of deciding to engage a threat. Externally, the M41 had more cast armor, including area along the lower turret side. The cast armor is only present on the front of the M41A1 turret.

There are two areas of caution what operating an M41. First, the driver could be decapitated if the turret

The Walker Bulldog's suspension had shock absorbers on the first, second, and last road wheels. One problem was the precarious position of the driver's head. (Photo courtesy of the Patton Museum)

was rotated while the driver had his hatch open and head exposed. Second, the exposed mufflers turn cherry red after a few minutes operation.

Early M41s have a plain driver's hatch that would first raise slightly, then pivot to the right. Later M41s were equipped with infrared driving lights and a mount was added to the hatch for an infrared M19 night viewing periscope. The hatch could then not be opened until the periscope was removed.

The M41's Continental gas engine was an air-cooled, six-cylinder, opposed, and supercharged model. The use of air-cooled engines in tanks was not new. At the outset of WWII many U.S. tanks were powered by air-cooled radial engines, but the advantages seemed to have been forgotten in later years.

The M41 was among the last U.S. armored vehicles to be gasoline powered. Diesel was eventually recognized as being less flammable and providing greater range and torque. The AOS-895 originally installed was carburated, but later versions were fuel injected to improve the vehicle's range. M41s and M41A1s powered with the fuel-injected engines were designated the M41A2 and M41A3, respectively.

All M41s had the Allison CD-500-3 cross-drive transmission. This type of transmission combines the transmission and steering unit into one relatively small unit. This same transmission design was also used in other vehicles that share the same general chassis as the M41, including the M44 and M52 SPG, and the M42 SPAAG (Duster).

Early models mounted a .50-caliber Browning machine gun as the coaxial weapon to the left of the main 76mm gun. Later vehicles mounted a .30-caliber instead. Over time, the .30 calibers were retrofitted to the early tanks. Initially, it was thought that the .50-caliber would save main gun rounds against targets, but it was eventually decided that the additional number of rounds that could be carried for the smaller .30-caliber outweighed the .50's hitting power.

More than 3,700 M41 series light tanks were built, and Cadillac Motors of GM was the primary manufacturer.

The simple, robust construction of the M41 has made it popular with not only collectors, but also a number of foreign militaries.

This is the Detroit Arsenal portrait of the improved M41A1 tank. The driver's hatch rotates open, and vision blocks surround his position. (Photo courtesy of the Patton Museum)

This M41A3 is shown on maneuvers in Germany. It has extra gear added to it. Four wooden chock blocks are lashed across the glacis plate, while a wire rope is looped around the eyes on the glacis. (Photo courtesy of the Patton Museum)

Although the M41 Walker Bulldog appeared too late for U.S. use in Korea and too early for Vietnam, secondary users put it to work in India-Pakistan and other locals.

GENERAL DATA

MODEL	M41	M41A1	M41A2	M41A3
WEIGHT*	51,800 lbs.	51,800 lbs.	51,800 lbs.	51,800 lbs.
MAX TOWED LOAD	10,000 lbs.	10,000 lbs.	10,000 lbs.	10,000 lbs.
LENGTH	323.375	323.375	323.375	323.375
WIDTH	125 29/32	125 29/32	125 29/32	125 29/32
HEIGHT	112 3/32	112 3/32	112 3/32	112 3/32
TRACK	102.5	102.5	102.5	102.5
TRACK WIDTH	21	21	21	21
MAX SPEED	45 mph	45 mph	45 mph	45 mph
FUEL CAPY	140 gal	140 gal	140 gal	140 gal
RANGE	100 mi	100 mi	100 mi	100 mi
ELECTRICAL	24 neg	24 neg	24 neg	24 neg
TRANSMISSION				
SPEEDS	2	2	2	2
TURNING				
RADIUS FT	pivot	pivot	pivot	pivot
AMRAMENT				
MAIN	76mm	76mm	76mm	76mm
FLEXIBLE	.50-cal.	.50-cal.	.50-cal.	.50-cal.
SECONDARY	.50-cal. or .30-cal.	.50-cal. or .30-cal.	.50-cal. or .30-cal.	.50-cal. or .30-cal.

Overall dimensions listed in inches (guns facing forward).
Fighting weight.

ENGINE DATA

VEHICLE MODEL	M41 & M41A1	M41A2 & M41A3
ENGINE MAKE/MODEL	AOS-895-3	AOS-895-5
NUMBER OF CYLINDERS	Opposed 6	Opposed 6
CUBIC-IN. DISPLACEMENT	895.9	895.9
HORSEPOWER	500 @ 2800 rpm	500 @ 2800 rpm
TORQUE	955 lbs.-ft. @ 2400 rpm	955 lbs.-ft. @ 2400 rpm
GOVERNED SPEED (rpm)	2800	2800

RADIO EQUIPMENT: *The Walker was equipped with AN/GRC-3-7 or 8; AN/ARC-3, AN/UIC, and AN/VIA-1 radio sets.*

VALUES

	6	5	4	3	2	1
All models	25,000	35,000	45,000	55,000	70,000	80,000

M551 Sheridan

The M551 Sheridan was designed to be a light reconnaissance tank with both amphibious and airborne assault abilities. The Allison Division of General Motors built 1,562 of these tanks beginning in 1966.

The 152mm Gun/Launcher could fire either conventional ammunition, or the Shillelagh anti-tank missile. The conventional rounds weren't really that conventional, they had combustible cartridge cases. These combustible cases required that there be a two-layer protective bag system to protect the ammunition from moisture and the crew from fire. One layer was an asbestos bag, and the second a rubber bag. These had to be stripped off prior to chambering a round. As the vehicle was designed primarily as a missile launcher, conventional munitions made for tremendous recoil in the big gun, even lifting the front of the lightweight vehicle off the ground.

To keep the weight down for its role in airborne and amphibious assaults, the Sheridan had a hull made of welded 7039 aluminum alloy armor plate. The turret was manufactured from steel armor. The basic hull was enclosed in high-density foam to improve floatation and a second layer of aluminum was added all around to form the exterior surfaces.

The driver was seated in the front center of the hull with the other three men in the turret. The gunner was on the turret's right, the commander behind him with the loader sat on the left. The turret crew's seats were located on the perimeter of the turret ring. The diesel engine and transmission were located at the rear of the hull. Ammo racks surrounded the driver — the

Shillelaghs to his right and conventional type rounds on his left.

Later Sheridans were fitted with a laser rangefinder. The gunner's M127 sighting telescope was replaced with the M127A1 sight on these later tanks, and the cupola could be aligned with the main gun-launcher automatically. These vehicles were classified M551A1.

The M551 saw combat in Vietnam and in Desert Storm. Some are still used at the desert training center disguised as Soviet vehicles.

GENERAL DATA

MODEL	M551
WEIGHT*	33,460 lbs.
LENGTH	248.3
WIDTH	110
HEIGHT	150
TREAD	92.5
STD TRACK WIDTH	17.5
CREW	4
MAX SPEED	45 mph
FUEL CAPY	158 gal
RANGE	350 mi
ELECTRICAL	24 neg
TRANSMISSION SPEEDS	4F, 2R
TURNING RADIUS FT.	pivot
ARMAMENT	
MAIN	1 x 152mm
SECONDARY	1 x .30-cal.
FLEXIBLE	1 x .50-cal.

Overall dimensions listed in inches. Measured with main gun facing forward and antiaircraft machine gun mounted.

**Fighting weight.*

ENGINE DATA

ENGINE MAKE/MODEL	General Motors 6V53T
NUMBER OF CYLINDERS	6
CUBIC-INCH DISPLACEMENT	318.6
HORSEPOWER	300 @ 2800
TORQUE	615 lbs.-ft. @ 2100

The M551 was amphibious, making its design a departure from the norm in U.S. tank construction. Across the glacis, just in front of the driver, the surf shield is folded down in its normal travel position. The rotary driver for the hatch, grenade launchers, and empty mount for the commander's machine gun are also visible. (U.S. Army photo)

MEDIUM TANKS

M3 Grant & Lee

The unusual (by today's standards) design of the M3 Grant and Lee tanks was the result of mounting a 75mm main gun at a time when the U.S. was not building a turret capable of handling that large of a weapon.

Production of the M3 began in June 1941 with Chrysler's Detroit Tank Arsenal and American Locomotive Company building them for U.S. forces, and Pressed Steel Car Company and Pullman Standard Car Company producing tanks for British use.

Two different 75mm weapons were mounted in the sponson during the course of production: the M2, which is distinguished by the round counterweight clamped on the end of the barrel, and the longer M3, which did not require a counterweight. A 37mm M6 gun was mounted in the turret coaxial with a .30-caliber machine gun for most of the production, but early shortages of this weapon forced the substitution of the 6-in.-shorter 37mm gun M5 on some tanks. Both the 37mm and 75mm weapons were gyrostabilized.

The turrets were steel castings, while the hulls were of riveted construction. Early production hulls had large side doors. This was a soft spot in the armor that was deleted during the course of production, as was the turret cupola and one of the hull-mounted fixed machine guns.

M3 Grants that were supplied to the British had a completely different cast turret than the vehicles built for U.S. use. The British turret design did away with commander's machine gun cupola and enlarged the turret's diameter to include a rear bustle for radio equipment. The remainder of the vehicle was basically the same as the U.S. tanks, differing only in internal and external stowage, It was the British who dubbed the M3s "General Lee," and their own the M3 "General Grant."

The M3 was designed as a stopgap. While unusual looking and of questionable combat effectiveness, it was very effective as a test bed for the chassis that would be the basis of the later Sherman. The many rivets that held the M3 together are visible in this photograph. (Photo courtesy of the Patton Museum)

MEDIUM TANKS

Production of the M3 ceased in August 1942, after 4,924 units. These tanks were declared obsolete in April 1945.

M3A1

This was basically the same tank as the M3, but featured a cast-steel hull (the M3 had a riveted hull), which was produced by American Locomotive Company from February 1942 until July of the same year. Like the M3, it eventually lost its side doors.

Twenty-eight of these 300 vehicles were powered by

a Guiberson T-1400-2 diesel engine. Today, one of these diesels today would be a great find.

M3A2

These tanks were built by Baldwin Locomotive Works beginning in January 1942. They were distinguished by their welded-hull construction. With only 12 built when production stopped in March, they are truly rare.

M3A3

Also produced by Baldwin, these tanks were driven by a model 6046 diesel engine. This power plant was a marriage of two GM 6-71 engines coupled by a collector gear. The rear of the tank hulls had to be redesigned to accommodate this installation. A total of 322 were produced during the run, which lasted from January to December of 1942. Other than the pilot models, these tanks were of welded-hull construction and their hull side doors were welded shut at the factory on the M3A3.

M3A4

The 109 tanks of this type were produced by the Detroit Tank Arsenal from June until August 1942, and are powered by the unusual 30-cylinder Chrysler A57 multi-bank engine. To accommodate this engine the hull was lengthened, and bogie spacing changed accordingly. Except for the pilot model, none of these tanks had hull side doors, and all had the track return rollers mounted on the rear of the suspension assemblies.

The M3A4 was powered by the unusual Chrysler multi-bank engine. The engine required the hull to be lengthened to accommodate it. (Photo courtesy of the Patton Museum)

The M3A1 had a much smoother-cast hull than the M3. This was also much safer for the crews, who were sometimes injured when rivet heads were sheared off by enemy fire, allowing the rivets to fly about the interior of the tank. (Photo courtesy of the Patton Museum)

M3A5

This is the same tank as the M3A3, but with riveted-hull construction, again with the side doors welded shut. All 591 were produced during the calendar year 1942.

GENERAL DATA

MODEL	M3	M3A1	M3A2	M3A3	M3A4	M3A5
WEIGHT*	61,500	63,000	60,400	63,000	64,000	64,000
LENGTH	222	222	222	222	242	222
WIDTH	107	107	107	107	104	107
HEIGHT	123	123	123	123	123	123
TREAD	83	83	83	83	83	83
CREW	6 or 7	6 or 7	6 or 7	6 or 7	6 or 7	6 or 7
MAX SPEED	24	24	24	25	20	25
FUEL CAPY	175	175	175	148	160	148
RANGE	120	120	120	150	100	150
ELECTRICAL	24 neg	24 neg	24 neg	24 neg	24 neg	24 neg
TRANSMISSION						
SPEEDS	5F, 1R	5F, 1R	5F, 1R	5F, 1R	5F, 1R	5F, 1R
TURNING						
RADIUS FEET	31	31	31	31	35	31
ARMAMENT						
MAIN	75mm	75mm	75mm	75mm	75mm	75mm
SECONDARY	37mm	37mm	37mm	37mm	37mm	37mm
FLEXIBLE	3 x .30	3 x .30	3 x .30	3 x .30	3 x .30	3 x .30

*Fighting weight

Overall dimensions listed in inches.

ENGINE DATA

ENGINE MAKE/MODEL	Chrysler A57
NUMBER OF CYLINDERS	30
CU.-IN. DISPLACEMENT	1253
HORSEPOWER	425 @ 2400 RPM
TORQUE	1060 lbs.ft.@ 1800 RPM

ENGINE MAKE/MODEL	Continental R975 EC2	GM 6046
NUMBER OF CYLINDERS	9	2 X 6
CU.-IN. DISPLACEMENT	973	850
HORSEPOWER	340 @ 2400 rpm	410 @ 2100 rpm
TORQUE	890 lbs.-ft. @ 1800 rpm	885 lbs.-ft. @ 1900 rpm

RADIO EQUIPMENT: M3 Lee vehicles were provided with SCR 508 radios with integral interphone. Command tanks had the SCR 506.

VALUES

Too few survivors of these type exist in private hands to establish values.

The pilot of what would become the M3A3 is shown in this photograph taken at Fort Knox in November of 1941. Diesel-powered tanks would not be widely accepted by the U.S. Army until 10 years later. (Photo courtesy of the Patton Museum)

Here are a variety of early WWII medium tanks. In the foreground are an early M4 (note direct vision slots and early VVSS), M3 Lee, M3A1 (notice cast hull), M4A3, M3, M4A1, M3A1, M3, and another M3, followed by eight Stuart light tanks and assorted half-track and wheeled vehicles. (Photo courtesy of the Patton Museum)

The British version of the M3 medium tank was the Grant. The two versions differed in turret shape and stowage boxes mounted on the rear deck. (National Archives and Records Administration photo)

M4 Sherman

The tank we know as the M4 Sherman was an outgrowth of the T6 Medium Tank. Designed to overcome the M3's major shortcoming of a sponson-mounted main gun, the M4 nevertheless shared many automotive components with the M3. This was done to speed and smooth the transition of production facilities to the new tank. Like their predecessors, these tanks were powered by the Wright-designed R975 radial engine.

The M4 was standardized as the Army's medium tank in September 1941, and construction of the pilot models began two months later. In December 1941, the designation M4A1 was assigned to those tanks with a cast upper hull, while M4 was used for those with a welded upper hull.

The earliest Sherman turrets had the M34 main gun mount, with the later ones having the M34A1 mount.

Early Shermans also had what is known as vertical volute suspension systems (VVSS). Later tanks had the improved horizontal volute suspension system (HVSS) which had a center-guided track (compared to the outer guided track used with the VVSS system). This change was made during the summer of 1942.

Another distinguishing characteristic on early Sherman tanks is that the glacis plate slopes at 60 degrees. This angle was changed to 47 degrees in later production.

Three different styles of transmission housings were used on these vehicles. The first was the three-piece, bolt-together unit as used on the M3 Medium Tanks. This was replaced by a less-vulnerable casting, which was later redesigned to make it thicker and come to a sharper point.

The Sherman tank was declared obsolete by the U.S. Army in 1956, but was still used by other nations for many years after that.

The Sherman leading this formation shows the early three-piece bolt-together transmission housing that was carried over from the M3 Lee. The bolt flanges made this style of transmission housing vulnerable to anti-tank fire and were soon eliminated in favor of a single-piece casting. (Photo courtesy Patton Museum)

MEDIUM TANKS

75mm Gunned Shermans

M4

Production of the welded M4 lagged behind that of the M4A1, with Pressed Steel Car Company beginning work on the M4 in July 1942. January 1943 saw production begin by Baldwin Locomotive Works, with American Locomotive Works coming on line in February, joined by Pullman Standard in May, and finally Chrysler's Detroit Arsenal in August. The run didn't last long, however. Pressed Steel stopped production in August, Pullman in September, American in December, and Chrysler and Baldwin in January 1944.

The final M4s built at Detroit Arsenal had composite hulls, with a front a single-piece casting joined to a welded rear hull.

M4A1

Lima Locomotive Works of Lima, Ohio, began producing the cast-hulled M4A1 in February 1942, and Pressed Steel Car Company began production the next month. Pacific Car and Foundry began producing the M4A1 in May 1942. Tanks built before March 1942 had

The Ford GAA-powered M4A3 was America's standard. This tank was photographed at the General Motors Proving Ground. It has an interesting mix of features. The turret retains the early M34 gun mount for the 75mm gun, and the hull still has the direct vision slots, but the suspension is the later HVSS. (U.S. Army photo)

This photo of an early diesel-powered M4A2 also shows of the two fixed machine guns installed in the hull front of the earliest vehicles. They were later found to be ineffective and were eliminated, but the adjacent ball-mounted .30-caliber Browning was retained. (Photo courtesy Patton Museum)

two fixed .30-caliber machine guns mounted in the hull front next to the .50-caliber flexible mount.

Lima built its last M4A1 with a 75mm gun in September 1943. Pacific followed suit in November, and Pressed Steel stopped in December. The three plants' production totaled 6,281 tanks.

M4A2

This tank is essentially an M4 powered by a General Motors 6046 twin diesel engine, rather than the R975 gasoline radial. Production began at both Pullman Standard Car Company and the Fisher Tank Arsenal in April 1942, American Locomotive was added in September, Baldwin in October, and Federal Machine and Welder in December. Late in the production run of these vehicles the slope of the hull front was changed from 56 degrees to 47 degrees. The last of the 8,053 of these tanks were built by Fisher in May 1944. Production was discontinued at the other facilities in the following order: Baldwin, November 1942; American, April 1943; Pullman, September 1943; Federal Machine and Welder, December 1943.

M4A3

This is the tank destined to be the U.S. standard. Powered by the Ford GAA V-8 engine, these tanks were first produced by Ford in May 1942. All M4A3s had the single-piece cast differential housing and heavy-duty

suspension components. Although the early production tanks did have the direct vision slots, that feature was soon discontinued. Ford ceased production of the tanks in September 1943 after producing 1,690 M4A3's.

This M4A1 of the First Armored Division is advancing in Italy. Although the tank is festooned by paraphernalia from its crew, the early narrow M34 main gun mount, three-piece transmission housing, and gently curved cast steel hull are still visible. (Photo courtesy Patton Museum)

After seeing some combat, the M4A3 was beefed up with additional 1-in. slabs of armor at critical spots. This U.S. Army photo shows the two pieces added to the right side. An additional single piece was affixed to the left side. (U.S. Army photo)

Production of the GAA engine by Ford continued for a number of years.

M4A3(W)

The "W" in the model number indicates wet ammunition storage. This wet stowage reduced the chance of the tanks own ammunition cooking off in the event of being hit by enemy fire. Fisher Tank Arsenal built 3,071 of these tanks between February 1944 and March 1945.

M4A4

Chrysler built the first of the M4A4 tanks in June 1942, and by the time the last was built in September 1943, 7,499 of the A57 multi-bank engine-powered tanks had been built. As was the case with the multi-bank-powered M3s, the hull of the M4A4 had to be lengthened to accommodate the engine. Most of these tanks were supplied to the British under lend-lease, although U.S. stateside training units used a few. The early M4A4 turrets had the M34 main gun mount, with the later vehicles having the M34A1 mount.

M4A6

Production of the M4A6 was began by Chrysler at the Detroit Arsenal in October 1943, but in February 1944, after only 75 of the planned 775, were built, production ceased. The M4A6 was basically an M4A4, but instead of the A57 multi-bank, the engine was the RD1820. The RD1820 was a diesel radial engine built by Caterpillar as their model D200A. The engine was based on the Wright G200 aircraft engine. All the M4A6 tanks were equipped

This is the famed "Easy Eight" Sherman, the M4A3E8, which served the U.S. military at the end of WWII and on into Korea, where this photo was taken. In addition to the 76mm gun, the tank featured new suspension with the guide teeth running between dual road wheels, rather than on either side of a single road wheel. The wider track also improved off-road performance. (Photo courtesy of the Patton Museum)

with the M34A1 main gun mount.

76mm Gunned Shermans

The 76mm-gunned Shermans used a different turret than their predecessors. This new turret, designated T23, was slightly larger and less rounded than the earlier turret.

M4(76)

This planned tank was never placed into production.

M4A1(76)

The Pressed Steel Car Company began building the M4A1(76) in January 1944. By the time the war ended they had built 3,426 of these machines. Later production vehicles in this series had an oval loader's hatch instead of the split circular hatches of earlier models. Other important variations included the muzzle brake fitted to some of the 76-mm guns, and the use of horizontal volute spring suspension and new track with center guide pins.

M4A2(76)

Most of the 2,915 M4A2(76) Shermans were supplied to Soviet Union, making it unusual to find one in this country today. Twenty-one of these tanks were built by Pressed Steel Car Company. The balance were built by Fisher between May 1944 and the summer of 1945.

M4A3(76)

In March 1944, Chrysler began producing the M4A3(76) and continued until April 1945. The 1,400 tanks produced before the end of August 1944 had vertical volute suspensions. The HVSS was introduced for the balance of 2,617 tanks. Fisher Tank Arsenal made 525 of the M4A3(76) between September and December 1944. Early in the production of the M4A3(76), the turret basket was eliminated, with the crew seats being hung from the turret ring.

105mm Gunned Shermans

M4(105)

Chrysler's Detroit Tank Arsenal began producing 105mm howitzer-armed M4s in February 1944. The first 800 had conventional suspension systems, while the balance of the 1,641 produced had the HVSS and wider tracks. Late production tanks had the vision cupola for the commander, but early vehicles had the normal split circular hatch.

M4A3(105)

Produced by Chrysler between May 1944 and June 1945, the first 500 M4A3(105) tanks had the VVSS, while the remaining 2,539 had the improved HVSS. Like the 105-armed M4, the M4A3(105) did not initially have power turret traverse, although complaints from using

A 105mm howitzer-armed M4 undergoes tests by the Armor Board at Ft. Knox. It has the old style vertical volute suspension, as used on the M3 Lee. (Photo courtesy of the Patton Museum)

troops forced its introduction near the end of production.

M4A3E2 Sherman Jumbo

Contrary to popular belief, the M4A3E2 was not built to be a tank killer. Rather it was an assault tank, built to provide close support to infantry. The armor of the M4A3 was upgraded by welding 1 1/2-in. rolled armor plate to the hull sides and front. A new final drive housing was cast that was considerably thicker, and housed the lower reduction ratio gears needed due to the tank's increased weight.

The turret was a new casting with heavier walls, and the mount used was the M62 developed for the 76mm gunned tanks, with additional armor welded to it. All the M4A3E2s were built with 75mm guns that fired superior high-explosive ammunition — critical in the role of infantry support. However, because the M62 mount was developed for the 76mm gun, the weapons were readily swapped in the field. All the M4A3E2s used the early VVSS, but with duck bill extensions on the outside of the track to reduce the formidable ground pressure. While these tanks all had wet ammunition storage, none of them had sirens or headlights.

Fisher Tank Arsenal produced 254 Sherman Jumbos between May and July 1944.

GENERAL DATA

MODEL	M4	M4A1	M4A2	M4A3	M4A3(76)	M4A4
WEIGHT*	66,900	66,800	70,200	66,700	74,200	69,700
LENGTH	232	230	233	232.5	297	238.5
WIDTH	103	103	103	103	103	103
HEIGHT	108	108	108	108	117	108
TREAD	83	83	83	83	89	83
CREW	5	5	5	5	5	5

"Gila Monster" was the name applied to this M4A1(76) undergoing tests at Aberdeen Proving Ground in May 1944.

The 76mm gun was also mounted on some of the diesel-powered M4A2 tanks, making them M4A2(76) model tanks. Most of these were supplied to the Soviet Union. Some 76mm-armed Shermans have the muzzle brake shown here, while others have none. (Photo courtesy of the Patton Museum)

This M4A3(105) named "Bang-Up" looks factory new in this overhead photo. The commander's cupola with vision ports, used on later model Shermans, is plainly visible, as is the position of the pioneer tools, and horizontal volute suspension. (U.S. Army photo)

The additional hull length and altered bogie spacing necessary to accommodate the Chrysler multi-bank engine is apparent in this Aberdeen Proving Ground photo of an M4A4. (U.S. Army photo)

This is a rare M4A6 Caterpillar-powered Sherman. Only 75 of these were built, and to find one today would be a collector's dream. (Photo courtesy of Patton Museum)

MAX SPEED	24	24	25	26	26	25
FUEL CAPY	175	175	148	168	168	160
RANGE	120	120	150	130	100	100
ELECTRICAL	24 neg	24 neg	24 neg	24 neg	24 neg	24 neg
TRANSMISSION						
SPEEDS	5F, 1R	5F, 1R	5F, 1R	5F, 1R	5F, 1R	5F, 1R
TURNING						
RADIUS FT	31	31	31	31	35	31
ARMAMENT						
MAIN	75mm	75mm	75mm	75mm	75mm	75mm
SECONDARY	1 x .50	1 x .50	1 x .50	1 x .50	1 x .50	1 x .50
FLEXIBLE	2 x .30	2 x .30	2 x .30	2 x .30	2 x .30	2 x .30

Overall dimensions listed in inches.

* Fighting weight

ENGINE DATA

ENGINE MAKE/MODEL	Continental R975 C3	GM 6046
NUMBER OF CYLINDERS	9	2 x 6
CUBIC INCH DISPLACEMENT	973	850
HORSEPOWER	400 @ 2400 RPM	410 @ 2100
TORQUE	890 lbs.-ft. @ 1800 RPM	885 lbs.-ft. @ 1900

ENGINE MAKE/MODEL	Chrysler A57	Ford GAA
NUMBER OF CYLINDERS	30	60-degree V-8
CUBIC INCH DISPLACEMENT	1,253	1,100
HORSEPOWER	425 @ 2400 rpm	450 @ 2600
TORQUE	1060 lbs.-ft. @ 1800 rpm	950 @ 2100

COMMUNICATION EQUIPMENT: *M4 Sherman vehicles were provided with SCR 508, SCR 528 or SCR 538 in the rear of the turret. Command tanks also had a sponson-mounted SCR 506. All basic radios were provided with integral interphone. Flag set M238 and panel set AP50A were also provided.*

VALUES

	6	5	4	3	2	1
All models	25,000	35,000	45,000	65,000	85,000	110,000

M26 Pershing

As early as 1942 there were plans for improvement and replacement for the M4 Sherman. A number of different models using various chassis, turret and gun combinations, were tested leading up to the "heavy" tank designs T25 and T26. The T26 was given the higher priority, and after installation of the GAF engine in 1943 it was redesignated T26E1. However, it would be 1945 before this tank finally saw combat. The two-year delay was a result of inter-service squabbling.

After a few of the new tanks were built for testing, the U.S. Army Armored Command began to show concerns about the large size of the T26 "heavy" tank design. There were reservations about transportation and bridge clearances. There was also some belief that the war would be won or lost with the M4 Sherman, period. Because of this the Ordnance Department put all its resources into improving the M4. The 76mm gun version of the Sherman is an example of this effort.

Army Ground Forces wanted 1,000 of the new T26 tanks, but they wanted the new tanks to be armed with only a 76mm gun. Armored Command was still was not interested in the new tank by the close of 1944, but it wanted the new 90mm gun from the M26E3 as an anti-tank gun.

The next hurdle in the adoption of the T26/M26 was the decision by Army Ground Forces to delay any decision on adopting new equipment until the Armored Board had tested their battle worthiness. The theory was that diverting production, supply, and training resources on untried systems could extend the war.

In the case of the new tanks, this was overcome by the Secretary of War authorizing the shipment of 20 M26E3 tanks to the European Theater of Operations in February of 1945. Sadly, the two years of indecision probably cost the lives of many U.S. tankers on the European battlefield.

The basic design of the T26/M26 would prove to be the basis of a long line of excellent tanks (M46, M47, M48 and M60) that would serve the U.S. for 40 years. The Pershing's redesigned armor, excellent 90mm gun, and improved ride was a vast improvement over everything that U.S. tankers had been provided with before. The war ended before the M26 reached full-scale production, but for two years after WWII M26s were built both at Chrysler's Detroit Tank Arsenal and at the Fisher Body Division GM Grand Blanc Tank Arsenal. Ultimately, about 2,350 M26 tanks were produced, with many of these tanks proving themselves in Korea against Soviet-built T-34s.

The engine of the Pershing was its weak link. The 500-hp Ford-built GAF simply was not up to the task of moving the 41-ton tank. To correct this deficiency, most of the M26 tanks were upgraded to M46s with an improved engine and other changes. These upgrades took place during the Korean War and for a period afterward.

The hull of the M26 was made of welded and cast steel armor. The "Heavy Tank" designation was officially changed to "Medium Tank" after the war in 1946.

The M26 had no turret basket. The turret seats were attached to the lower edge of the turret. The seats and gun equipment just hang into the hull, rotating with the turret.

While the M46 was retired from U.S. service in 1957, it laid the foundation for the series of tanks that would serve this country until 1999.

The bow machine gun can be seen on "Alice," an M26. The driver has his seat elevated so his head and shoulders are outside the hull, affording a much better view than the periscope. (U.S. Army photo)

MEDIUM TANKS

GENERAL DATA

MODEL	M26	M26A1	M45	M46
WEIGHT*	92,000 lbs.	92,000 lbs.	92,500 lbs.	97,000 lbs.
LENGTH	333.625	333.625	252	333.625
WIDTH	137	137	138	138.25
HEIGHT	109	109	109	111
TRACK	110	110	110	110
TRACK WIDTH	24	24	23	23
CREW	5	5	5	5
MAX SPEED	30 mph	30 mph	30 mph	30 mph
FUEL CAPY	191 gal	191 gal	191 gal	233 gal
RANGE	92 mi	92 mi	100 mi	70 mi
ELECTRICAL	24 neg	24 neg	24 neg	24 neg
TORQMATIC TRANSMISSION SPEEDS	3F, 1R	3R, 1R	3R, 1R	2F, 1R
TURNING RADIUS FT.	31	31	31	pivot
ARMAMENT				
MAIN	90mm	90mm	105mm	90mm
SECONDARY	2 x .30-cal	2 x .30-cal	2 x .30-cal	2 x .30-cal
FLEXIBLE	1 x .50-cal	1 x .50-cal	1 x .50-cal	1 x .50-cal

Overall dimensions listed in inches.

*Fighting weight.

ENGINE DATA

ENGINE MAKE/MODEL	Ford GAF
NUMBER OF CYLINDERS	V-8, 60-degree
CUBIC-INCH DISPLACEMENT	1,000
HORSEPOWER	500 @ 2600 rpm
TORQUE	950 lbs.-ft. @ 2100 rpm
GOVERNED SPEED (rpm)	2600

RADIO EQUIPMENT: *A variety of radio equipment was mounted in this family of tanks, including SCR 508 or SCR 608 or SCR 528, all with interphone set RC298, or AN/VRC-3 and RC99 interphone set.*

VALUES

	6	5	4	3	2	1
All models	25,000	35,000	45,000	60,000	70,000	85,000

This Armor and Engineer Board portrait of the M26 illustrates what would be the basic form of American tanks for four decades. The much-debated 90mm gun would prove itself repeatedly in battle. (Photo courtesy of the Patton Museum)

The engine exhaust outlets through the rear armor of this M26 advancing in Korea. The cooling fan exhaust is lifting an aerial recognition panel from the rear deck, showing the tremendous amount of air movement required to keep the Ford GAF engine's radiators cool. (Photo courtesy of the Patton Museum)

Here is the 105mm howitzer-armed M45. The bow and hull machine guns are both in their canvas covers, and the tripod for ground use of the commander's .50-caliber gun is stowed on the right front fender. (Photo courtesy of the Patton Museum)

The fenders of the M26, and most other American tanks, are covered with storage boxes. These are closed in most photographs, but this unusual photo shows the type of gear carried in these boxes. This type of detail is important for museum-quality restorations. (Photo courtesy of the Patton Museum)

An M46 is firing in the mountains of Korea. Notice the prominent mufflers mounted on the rear fenders compared to the rear exhaust of the M26. (Photo courtesy of the Patton Museum)

M47 Tank

The M47 was a stopgap vehicle rushed into production for the Korean War in April 1951, although it was too late to see service there. Basically, the one-piece cast turret designed for the experimental T42 was married to the M46 hull. The new turret mounted a 90mm main gun, and its armor is from 2 to 4 in. thick. Because of the M46 hull, the M47 became the last U.S. tank to have a co-driver. Like the M46, the M47 was powered by a gasoline engine — a Continental AV-1790-5B, 12-cylinder, 820-hp model. The big Continental was thirsty, and the range was meager.

Quick identifying features of the M47 are the sharply tapered turret with small gun shield, an unusually long and narrow turret bustle, and the flat upper run of track. Like most post-WWII U.S. tanks, the M47 had torsion-bar suspension.

Initially, a .50-caliber Browning machine gun was mounted co-axial with the 90mm gun. Later production had a .30-caliber Browning machine gun mounted instead. An M2 HB .50-caliber Browning machine gun was also mounted on early models via a rotating ring to the commander's hatch. This setup was eventually changed, replaced by a fixed pintle mount for the big Browning.

Production began in 1951 at the Detroit Arsenal. The M47 was issued to troops in 1952, but did not see combat during the Korean War. The Chrysler-managed Detroit Arsenal built 3,443 M47 tanks between 1952 and 1954, and American Locomotive Company built a similar number. Some of these tanks used hulls from scrapped M46 tanks, while others had new hulls fabricated for them.

As the M48 became available, the M47 was phased out of U.S. service. Many, however, were supplied to foreign nations, including many NATO allies.

In the late 1960s Bowen-McLaughlin-York, Inc., introduced an upgrade program for the M47. Using the engine and fire control system from the M60A1, the improved vehicle was dubbed the M47M. The newly installed AVDS-1790-2A turbosupercharged diesel had its exhaust routed through rear louvers rather than fender mounted mufflers as originally installed on the M47's rear fenders. The assistant driver crew position was eliminated during the rebuild, reducing crew size. Bowen-McLaughlin-York, Inc. and a tank factory in Iran produced more than 800 M47Ms.

This view of an M47 shows its fender-mounted mufflers, which are eliminated on the remanufactured diesel-powered M47M. The pioneer tool rack, turret hatches, and ventilator are also visible. (Photo courtesy of the Patton Museum)

The M47 is still in front line military service in many parts of the world, but occasionally one surfaces on the collector market.

GENERAL DATA

MODEL	M47
WEIGHT*	101,775 lbs.
MAX TOWED LOAD	10,000 lbs.
LENGTH	335
WIDTH	138.25
HEIGHT	116 5/16
TRACK	110
CREW	5
MAX SPEED	30 mph
FUEL CAPY	233 gal
RANGE	80 mi
ELECTRICAL	24 neg
TRANSMISSION	
SPEEDS	2F, 1R
TURNING	
RADIUS FT.	pivot
ARMAMENT	
MAIN	90mm

SECONDARY	2 x .30 cal
FLEXIBLE	1 x .50 cal

Overall dimensions listed in inches. Measured with main gun facing forward, and antiaircraft machine gun mounted.

*Fighting weight.

ENGINE DATA

ENGINE MAKE/MODEL	Continental AVSI-1790-5B –7 –7B
NUMBER OF CYLINDERS	V-12, 90 degree
CUBIC-INCH DISPLACEMENT	1,791.75
HORSEPOWER	810 @ 2800 rpm
TORQUE	1,560 lbs.-ft. @ 2400 rpm
GOVERNED SPEED (rpm)	2800

RADIO EQUIPMENT: *Many radio sets were used through the long life of the M47 family. Among the typical installations during U.S. were the AN/GRC-3-4-7 or 8 and AN/VIA-1 or AN/VRC-47 radio sets.*

VALUES

	6	5	4	3	2	1
All models	35,000	45,000	55,000	75,000	95,000	125,000

This M47 is shown minus its sand shields over the return track, and with the main gun in the travel position. (Photo courtesy of Patton Museum)

As the last U.S. tank with a co-driver, the M47 was also the last to have a ball-mount machine gun in the hull. (Photo courtesy of Patton Museum)

M48 Tank

The M48 was an outgrowth of M26/46 Pershing series of tanks, with the M47 serving as a stopgap until the new M48, initially called the T48, could be fully developed.

The T48 used the engine and transmission proven in the M46/47, but had a much larger turret ring, which would allow later upgunning. The turret had gently sloping sides, as opposed to the slab-sided turrets of most WWII U.S. tanks. The T48 used the 90mm T39 gun that was the main armament of the M47. There were also three secondary weapons: one .30-caliber and one .50-caliber Browning mounted coaxial to either side of the main gun, and another .50-caliber machine gun outside at the commander's cupola in a pintle mount.

From the operator's point of view, the T48 was steered like a car, with a steering wheel, rather than the wobble stick of the M47 and steering levers used during WWII. The new steering system reduced fatigue and simplified driver training, but required a more advance transmission.

Remarkably, before T48 testing was even complete, Chrysler was given an order for 548 tanks, and Ford Motor Company and Fisher Body orders for 400 each. Chrysler was the first to actually complete tanks in the spring of 1952.

Several models of M48 were produced over the years. The first M48s were similar to the prototype T48s. The only major external differences between the M48 and the M48A1 were the shape of the driver's hatch and the enclosed commander's M1 cupola with an internally operated .50-caliber machine gun. Other improvements of the M48A1 included a track tension idler wheel and a

This M48 is demonstrating its ability to bridge trenches. The top of the turret is relatively flat. Later M48A1s had a raised cupola for the commander and his machine gun. (Photo courtesy of Patton Museum)

stowage basket on the rear of the turret.

In the M48A2, the carbureted engine was replaced with a more efficient fuel-injected system that provided increased range. A stopgap fix for the limited range of the M48A1 had been the installation of a fuel rack that could be jettisoned. It held four drums of fuel on the rear of the tank. The new engine had relocated oil coolers, which increased space available in the engine compartment and allowed larger fuel tanks to either side. This also brought an improved engine deck of the M48A2 design to accommodate these changes.

The new design reduced the tank's infrared signature. The exhaust was no longer directed out the top of the louvered deck, but instead was routed through two large louvered doors at the rear of the hull. Previous models had slanted rear armor plate at this location. This rear deck and armor design remained basically unchanged through the rest of this series, as well as the

M60 Patton series. Most M48A2s have three return rollers, rather than the five per each side on earlier models. An exception appears to be Marine Corps vehicles, which evidently kept the five-roller system.

The M48A2 and its subtypes were produced in greater numbers than any of the others, and remained in production until 1959. A later variation of the M48A2 was known as the M48A2C. The M48A2C had a coincidence range finder, rather than the troublesome stereoscopic range finder of earlier models. The M48A2C did not have the small tension idler wheel introduced on the M48A1, and there were also minor changes to the fenders and lighting. Many M48A2s were exported to allied countries.

The M48A3 Patton was created by remanufacturing older M48A1s to include a diesel engine. The U.S. Army was adopting diesel fuel to increase fuel economy, reduce potential fire hazards, and ease supply. The engine used

A technician checks the telephone installation on the rear of an M48. The telephones, housed in a box on the hull rear, allowed infantryman on the ground to talk to the tank crew under combat conditions. The tank is prepared for travel, with its turret rotated to the rear and main gun in its travel lock. (Photo courtesy of the Patton Museum)

was similar to that used in the M60, whose production coincided with these conversions.

The change in power plant caused new air filter boxes to be mounted on the fenders. These filter boxes are the easiest way to tell a diesel A3 from the earlier gasoline fuel-injected A2. There were also several internal changes.

Some of the M48A3 tanks were produced with a special G305 riser package. A ring of vision blocks added under the commander's cupola improved his view. Late M48A3 tanks also had IR sights. This conversion program began in 1963, with about 600 M48A1s converted for the Army, and 419 more for the Marine Corps.

The M48A5 was the final incarnation of the M48 and it included the mounting of an M68 105mm gun (British L7) as used in the M60A1. A low-profile, Israeli-type cupola replaced the M1 Cupola/G305 Riser on the final A5 models, and the pintle-mounted .50-caliber MG that was at the commander's position was often replaced with a 7.62 M60D MG. The loader was also provided with an M60D MG. Most of the M48A5 production run was shipped to National Guard and Reserve units, but a few active U.S. Army battalions in Korea also received these tanks.

The M67 and M67A1 were flame thrower versions of these tanks. The M67 was based on the M48A1 and mounted the M7-6 flame thrower, while the M67A1 was based on the M48A2 and used the M7A1-6 flame thrower. Both tanks mounted the flame thrower in place of the main gun. The M67 was supplied to the Marine Corps, while the Army used the M67A1.

The M48A1 sported a new cupola for the commander that allowed him to fire his .50-caliber machine gun from an enclosed position. A small tension idler was added between the drive sprocket and last road wheel. (U.S. Army photo)

This view of the M48A2 shows the re-routed exhaust system adopted for the rest of this series, as well as the subsequent M60 series. (Photo courtesy of the Patton Museum)

The M48A2 had an elliptical-shaped front hull. On the rear of the turret is the stowage rack added starting with the M48A1. (Photo courtesy of the Patton Museum)

The M48A5 was the ultimate development of the M48 series. The 90mm main gun was replaced with the 105mm gun used on the M60 series. The riser with vision blocks under the commander's cupola was introduced on the late M48A3 vehicles. (U.S. Army photo)

The centered driver's hatch used on this family of vehicles is clearly seen under the main gun in this photo of an M48A3. The M48A3s were recycled M48A1s, with the major update being the installation of a new diesel engine in place of the old gasoline engine. (U.S. Army photo)

The M48 is a formidable fighting machine, still in front-line service in many parts of the world.

GENERAL DATA

MODEL	M48	M48A1	M48A2C	M48A3	M67
WEIGHT*	99,000	104,000	105,000	104,000	104,000
LENGTH	332 9/16	343 23/32	342	342	342
WIDTH	148	143	143	143	143
HEIGHT	107.5	123 5/16	121.625	121.625	121.625
TRACK	115	115	115	115	115
STD TRACK WIDTH	28	28	28	28	
CREW	—	—	—	4	—
MAX SPEED	26	26	30	30	30
FUEL CAPY	200	200	335	335	335
RANGE	70	70	160	160	160
ELECTRICAL	24 neg	24 neg	24 neg	24 neg	24 neg
TRANSMISSION					
SPEEDS	2F, 1R	2F, 1R	2F, 1R	2F, 1R	2F, 1R
TURNING					
RADIUS FT.	pivot	pivot	pivot	pivot	pivot
ARMAMENT					
MAIN	1x 90mm	1x 90mm	1x 90mm	1x 90mm	flamethrw.
SECONDARY	1 x .30 cal	1 x .30 cal	1 x .30 cal	1 x .30 cal	1 x .30 cal
FLEXIBLE	1 x .50 cal	1 x .50 cal	1 x .50 cal	1 x .50 cal	1 x .50 cal

Overall dimensions listed in inches. Measure with main gun facing forward, and anti-aircraft machine gun mounted.

*Fighting weight.

ENGINE DATA

ENGINE MAKE/MODEL	Continental AVSI-1790-5B –7 –7B –7C -8
NUMBER OF CYLINDERS	90-degree V-12
CUBIC-INCH DISPLACEMENT	1,791.75
HORSEPOWER	810 @ 2800 rpm
TORQUE	1,560 lbs.-ft. @ 2400 rpm
GOVERNED SPEED (rpm)	2800

RADIO EQUIPMENT: *Many radio sets were used through the long life of the M48 family. Among the typical installations would have been: AN/GRC-3-4-7 or 8 or AN/VRC-47, AN/ARC27 or AN/VRC-24 radio sets.*

VALUES

No reported sales.

The poor economy of the gasoline-powered versions of this series inspired the development of these auxiliary fuel racks, introduced on the M48A1. They held four drums of gasoline on the rear of the tank, and could be quickly released in a combat situation. (U.S. Army photo)

M60 Tank

Development of the M60 series of tanks began in response to the Soviet T-54. The new M60 was patterned along the lines of the very successful M48 series, with the major improvement being the adoption of an Americanized version of the British L7 105mm cannon, known as the M68 semi-automatic 105mm gun. The M1 Abrams tank used this same gun, while the later M1A1/A2 was upgunned with a new 120mm gun.

The first M60 entered production at the Chrysler-managed Detroit Tank Arsenal in 1960. Production continued until 1986, by which time over 15,000 of these reliable tanks had been built. The M60 was to remain in the U.S. Army's stable until 1999, and soldiers on around the world in the hands of our allies. The U.S. Marine Corps used the M60 even longer.

The only crewman housed in the hull of the M60, which was made from five large steel castings that have been welded together, was the driver. As with most modern U.S. tanks, the balance of the crew of four rode in the turret; a gunner to the right, the commander directly behind him, and the loader on the left of the 105mm gun. All the tanks of the M60 series used a 12-cylinder AFDS-1790 diesel engine. This engine is a fuel injected and turbosupercharged 90-degree V-12.

Production began at Detroit Arsenal after testing for the pilot M60 tanks at Aberdeen Proving Ground was completed in late 1959. Only 2,205 of the original M60s were built before they were superceded by the M60A1.

The M60A1 had an elongated turret to provide a better ballistic shape and more interior room. Changes were made in the suspension of the M60A1, with friction snubbers added on the first and sixth road wheel arms. Internally, improvements were made to the drivers controls and gun-laying systems, and the new Continental AVDS–1790–2A engine was installed, which reduced exhaust smoke and fuel consumption. This vehicle was classified standard as the 105mm Gun Full Tracked Combat Tank M60A1 on October 22, 1961.

The M60AI remained in production until 1980.

The unusual-looking M60A2 was the result of efforts to build a heavier-hitting, longer-range, tank-killing tank. The M60A2 was armed with a gun/launcher for the 152mm Shillelagh missile. The missile was developed by the Aeroneutronics Division of the Ford Motor Company, and went into production in the late 1960s.

The missile was ejected from the launcher tube at approximately 260 feet per second (fps) and then the solid rocket motor fired, which increased its velocity to 1,060 fps. The missile was guided by an infrared tracking system and flew a line of sight trajectory. As long as the gunner kept the target in his sights, the missile would home in on it. However, the tracking system was not effective at ranges less than 600 meters, so at those ranges the conventional munitions were brought into play.

Starting in 1973, Detroit Arsenal converted 526 M60A1 tanks into M60A2 variants. This work was completed in 1975, and the tanks were issued to troops starting in 1974, with European deployment in 1975. The perceived unreliability of the M60A2 made the tank unpopular, and its complexity earned it the nickname "starship."

As problems mounted with the ill-fated MBT70 program, the need to update the M60 series yet again

The M60 is easily distinguished from the rest of the series by the relatively short overhang of the turret bustle. (Photo courtesy of the Patton Museum)

became apparent. Initial upgrades included improved air cleaners, and new T142 steel track with replaceable rubber track pads. This was quickly followed by an improved suspension, a laser range finder, a more powerful -2C RISE (Reliability Improved Select Equipment) power plant, and numerous other upgrades.

The M60A3 also had British-designed M239 grenade launchers mounted externally on the turret, which were not present on the M60 and M60A1. On May 10, 1979 the improved vehicle was type classified standard as the 105mm Gun Full-tracked Combat Tank M60A3. Production began soon thereafter.

As secondary armament, the tank has a M240 coaxial machine gun on the left of the 105, and the venerable .50-caliber MG in the commander's cupola.

The M60 was not used in Vietnam, although some support variants, such as bridge launchers and engineer vehicles, were.

GENERAL DATA

MODEL	M60	M60A1	M60A2
WEIGHT*	102,000 lbs.	106,000 lbs.	102,000 lbs.
MAX TOWED LOAD	64,000 lbs.	64,000 lbs.	64,000 lbs.
LENGTH	366.5	371.5	286.85
WIDTH	143	143	143
HEIGHT	126.34	128.23	130.31
TRACK	115	115	115
STD TRACK WIDTH	28	28	28
CREW	4	4	4
MAX SPEED	30 mph	30 mph	30 mph
FUEL CAPY	375 gal	375 gal	375 gla
RANGE	250 mi	310 mi	250 mi
ELECTRICAL	24 neg	24 neg	24 neg
TRANSMISSION			
SPEEDS	2F, 1R	2F, 1R	2F, 1R
TURNING			
RADIUS FT.	pivot	pivot	pivot
ARMAMENT			
MAIN	105mm	105mm	105mm
SECONDARY	1 x .30 cal	1 x .30 cal	1 x .30 cal
FLEXIBLE	1 x .50 cal	1 x .50 cal	1 x .50 cal

Overall dimensions listed in inches. Measured with main gun facing forward, and antiaircraft machine gun mounted.

*Fighting weight.

ENGINE DATA

ENGINE MAKE/MODEL	Continental AVDS-1790-2
NUMBER OF CYLINDERS	90 degree V-12
CUBIC-INCH DISPLACEMENT	1,791
HORSEPOWER	750 @ 2400 rpm
TORQUE	1,710 lbs.-ft. @ 1800 rpm
GOVERNED SPEED (rpm)	2400

RADIO EQUIPMENT: *Many radio sets were used through the long life of the M60 family. Among the typical installations would have been: AN/GRC-3-4-7 or 8 OR AN/VRC-47, AN/ARC27 or AN/VRC-24 radio sets.*

VALUES

No reported sales.

The odd shape of the M60A2 turret presented a small target for the enemy and, as originally configured, a low profile as well. However, by the time the tank entered production the addition of a tall commander's cupola made it almost the same height as its conventionally armed siblings. (U.S. Army photo)

An M60A1 is being test driven at the Detroit Arsenal before final painting. Compare the length of the turret of this vehicle to that of the original M60. (U.S. Army photo)

The unusual shape of the M60A2 turret is apparent in this overhead view, as is the short length of the 152mm Shillelagh gun launcher. The advanced weapon, and associated sophisticated electronics, earned the M60A2 the nickname "starship." (U.S. Army photo)

MAIN BATTLE TANKS

M103 Heavy Tank

The M103 heavy tank was built to counter to the Russian JS III heavy tanks. Although only 400 were produced, the M103 was by far the heaviest tank fielded by the U.S. until the M1 Abrams many years later.

Due primarily to main gun-related problems, the development model failed its trials with the Armor Board at Ft. Knox. More than 100 changes were made, and the vehicle was placed into production as the M103. The M103 closely resembles an oversized M48. The M103 had one more road wheel than the M48 and had six return rollers per side.

One of the tank's major shortcomings was its engine, which was the same power plant that powered the M47. The massive M103 was grossly underpowered. The turret, however, was all new and huge in order to house its 120mm main gun and its tremendous recoil. Unlike most tanks, the powerful 120mm gun used tow part ammunition, with separate powder and projectile. For this reason there were two loaders in the turret, with the commander and gunner seated in the very large turret

bustle. On top of the turret was a remotely operated machine gun.

The U.S. Marine Corps was very interested in this heavy tank, and further developed it. This improved tank was classified M103A1, and 218 of the M103s were upgraded to this standard. The M103A1 had a slightly different shape to its turret than its predecessor. Internally, the most noticeable change for the crew was the addition of a turret basket. The commander's machine gun lost its remote control feature. The Army borrowed 72 of these vehicles and deployed them in Europe from 1959 until 1962. The Marine Corps used its vehicles to supply one heavy tank company to each tank battalion beginning 1958-1959.

The final upgrade to this family was the M103A1E1, later classified as M103A2. This upgrade amounted to the installation of the AVDS-1790-2AD diesel engine and CD-850 transmission, as used in the M48A3. This was a more compact power train than the original, and allowed larger fuel tanks to be installed in the engine compartment. The change in engines resulted in a reshaped rear engine deck that resembled that of the diesel-powered M48A3 and M60. The Marines converted 153 of their M103A1s into these M103A2s and used them up to 1972.

This side view of the M103A1E1, later known as the M103A2, shows the uneven spacing of both the return rollers and the road wheels. Also visible is the commander's machine gun, which had been remotely controlled on the earliest models. (Photo courtesy of the Patton Museum)

GENERAL DATA

MODEL	M103	M103A1	M103A2
WEIGHT*	125,750 lbs.	125,750 lbs.	128,000 lbs.
LENGTH	445.5	445.5	445.5
WIDTH	148	148	148
HEIGHT	113.375	113.375	113.375
TRACK	115	115	115
CREW	5	5	5
MAX SPEED	25 mph	25 mph	23 mph
FUEL CAPY	268 gal	268 gal	440 gal
RANGE	80 mi	80 mi	300 mi
ELECTRICAL	24 neg	24 neg	24 neg
CROSSDRIVE			
SPEEDS	2F, 1R	2F, 1R	2F, 1R
TURNING			
RADIUS FT	pivot	pivot	pivot
ARMAMENT			
MAIN	120mm	120mm	120mm
SECONDARY	2 x .30	1 x .30	2 x .30
FLEXIBLE	1 x .50	1 x .50	1 x .50

Overall dimensions listed in inches. Measured with main gun facing forward and antiaircraft machine gun mounted.

*Fighting weight.

ENGINE DATA

ENGINE MAKE/MODEL	Continental AV-1790-5B –7C
NUMBER OF CYLINDERS	V-12, 90-degree
CUBIC-INCH DISPLACEMENT	1,791
HORSEPOWER	810 @ 2800 rpm
TORQUE	1590 lbs.-ft. @ 2200 rpm

ENGINE MAKE/MODEL	Continental AVDS-1790 –2A
NUMBER OF CYLINDERS	V-12, 90-degree
CUBIC-INCH DISPLACEMENT	1,791
HORSEPOWER	750 @ 2400 rpm
TORQUE	1590 lbs.-ft. @ 2200 rpm

RADIO EQUIPMENT: *Many radio sets were used through the long life of the M48 family. Among the typical installations would have been: AN/GRC-3-4-7 or 8, or AN/VRC-47, AN/ARC27 or AN/VRC-24 and AN/VIA-1 radio sets.*

VALUES

No reported sales

The clean rear armor and evenly spaced return rollers of the M103 are visible in this view of the Ft. Hood M103 tank.

This M103A1E1 (M103A2) is undergoing tests at Ft. Knox.

This M103 is on display at the Fourth Infantry Division Museum at Fort Hood, Texas. The great weight of the tank has caused a failure of one of the torsion bars, resulting in the unusual road wheel position. The smaller tank beside it is its contemporary, the M48A1.

M1 Abrams

The M1 Abrams Main Battle Tank (MBT) was named in honor General Creighton W. Abrams, a former Army chief of staff and commander of the 37th Armored Battalion, and a proponent of the advanced armored crew protection. The Abrams is the current U.S. military first-line tank, and has been supplied to a few foreign nations as well.

The Abrams was designed to be able to defeat any other tank in the world, under any conditions. It's sophisticated, classified armor system not only protects the crew, but also makes the tank itself difficult to knock out.

In addition to the armor, the Abram's crew is also protected by the layout of its ammunition stowage, with the majority of the main gun ammunition in the turret bustle behind a bulkhead. In the event of an ammunition explosion, blow-off panels in the turret bustle's roof would vent the explosion out of the tank while the bulkhead doors protected the crew from danger. During operation, the ammunition is reached through fast-

closing access doors. The operation time for these doors is 250 milliseconds. This system was proven effective in the Gulf War when several Abrams were inadvertently struck with Hellfire missiles.

The first prototype of the M1, known as the XM1, underwent testing in 1976, and the tank was first issued in February 1980. Chobham spaced armor (ceramic blocks set in resin between layers of conventional armor) provides protection against most anti-tank rounds. The powerful gas turbine engine, while having high fuel consumption, makes the tank fast. The main gun is equipped with a sophisticated fire control system that makes for accurate shooting on the move. Thermal-imaging night sights allow around-the-clock accurate fire, especially when combined with the Abram's laser range finder and digital ballistic computer.

The Lima Tank Plant and the Detroit Arsenal manufactured more than 2,300 of the 62-ton M1 tanks by the start of 1985, when the new version, the M1A1, went into production. The M1A1 increased the main gun size to 120mm, had a new turret, and had improved armor.

In addition to all the M1A1 features, the M1A2 has a commander's independent thermal viewer, position

The latest generation of the Abrams, the M1A2, kicks up dust while on maneuvers. (U.S. Army photo)

navigation equipment, and a digital data bus and radio interface unit providing a common picture among M1A2s on the battlefield.

The Army is upgrading approximately 1,000 older M1 tanks to the M1A2 configuration, and the entire Abrams family is expected to remain in service at least another 20 years.

GENERAL DATA

MODEL	M1	M1A1	M1A2
WEIGHT*	120,000 lbs.	126,000 lbs.	140,000 lbs.
LENGTH	384.5	387	387
WIDTH	143.8	144	144
HEIGHT	113.6	113.6	113.6
TRACK	112	112	112
STD TRACK WIDTH	25	25	25
CREW	4	4	4
MAX SPEED	45 mph	42 mph	42 mph
FUEL CAPY	500 gal	500 gal	500 gal
RANGE	275 mi	275 mi	265 mi
ELECTRICAL	24 neg	24 neg	24 neg

TRANSMISSION			
SPEEDS	4F, 2R	4F, 2R	4F, 2R
TURNING			
RADIUS FT	pivot	pivot	pivot
ARMAMENT			
MAIN	105mm	120mm	120mm
SECONDARY	2 x 7.62mm	2 x 7.62mm	2 x 7.62mm
FLEXIBLE	1x .50 cal	1x .50 cal	1 x .50 cal

Overall dimensions listed in inches. Measured with main gun facing forward, and antiaircraft machine gun mounted.

Fighting weight.

ENGINE DATA

ENGINE MAKE/MODEL	Textron Lycoming AGT
HORSEPOWER	1,500 @ 30000 rpm
TORQUE	3,800 lbs.-ft.

VALUES

Not available to collectors

The M1 has a distinctly angular shape compared to earlier tanks. (U.S. Army photo)

The long, low look profile and the unusual road wheel spacing are trademarks of the M1. (U.S. Army photo)

The 120mm German Rheinmetall-designed smoothbore main gun was introduced on the M1A1. This version of the Abrams would see extensive use in operation Desert Storm. (U.S. Army photo)

APPENDIX 1

MACHINE GUN MOUNTS FOR U.S. TACTICAL WHEELED VEHICLES

Machine Gun Mounts For Jeeps
Pedestal Mounts

The idea of mounting an antiaircraft machine gun on the 1/4-ton reconnaissance vehicle is as old as the vehicle itself. As early as March, 1941 tests were being done at Aberdeen Proving Ground toward that end. The first reasonably successful attempt at providing a machine gun mount on 1/4-ton reconnaissance vehicle was the T47 pedestal mount. The T47 consisted of a single-braced tubular pedestal and the D38579 Pintle group.

According to the APG Report 5626/1, the mount was unstable during early test firing and two braces were added to bring the rigidity within the limits of the suspension characteristics of the 1/4-ton, 4x4 truck. It was recommended that the pedestal be modified to include braces similar to those added during the test. This triple-braced configuration of the T47 was standardized as the M31 Pedestal Mount.

James Cunningham, Sons and Company began production of the M31 mounts in 1942. This firm was the only known supplier of the M31 mount, and produced 31,653 of these mounts before it was replaced in production by the M31C.

The M31 used the same D38579 pintle and D38571 tray, as did the previously developed M24 mount used in Dodge trucks. The pintle was placed in a socket at the top of the pedestal and secured with a clamping screw. A travel lock was provided which would hold either a .30-caliber or .50-caliber machine gun level. The two supports, A303165, were to be welded to the outside of the Jeep frame to provide solid support.

When the M31 was redesigned to use the D90045 cradle and pintle assembly in March 1945, it became known as the M31C. At the same time, the ammunition box tray was changed to the D90078. The D90045 cradle and pintle, with the D90078, were together known as the E10014 cradle, pintle and ammunition box tray assembly. James Cunningham, Sons and Company was again the supplier of these mounts.

When the M38 began replacing the WWII era G-503 Jeeps, it became necessary to develop a mount for these vehicles. This mount was the M31A1. The braces were different, as were the base and under-floor components. The M38 lacked the machine gun plate that was welded to the frame of the G-503 vehicles, which caused the addition of various components to the M31A1 kit. Many of the earlier M31C mounts were converted to M31A1 standards following MWO A55-W-19.

The M31A2 pedestal mount was developed for the M38A1 vehicle. This amounted to taking a M31A1 mount and converting it back to a M31C.

As the M60 7.62mm machine gun was introduced, the mount had to be adapted to accept the new weapon. This was done by re-introducing the D38759 Y-cradle and adding a newly manufactured SK-261 platform assembly.

As the M151 series became the Army's standard 1/4-ton truck, a new mount was developed for it. The pedestal itself was the M4. There are some documented instances of the M31C mount being installed in M151 vehicles as well, although the M4 was the recommended mount.

Bracket Mounts

In addition to the pedestal mounts mentioned previously, there was another type of machine gun mounting developed for the Jeep during WWII: the M48 bracket mount. This mount would allow the fitting of a .30-caliber M1919A4 machine gun or M1918A2 BAR to the dashboard of the Jeep. The mounting could not withstand the recoil of the .50-caliber M2.

The standard pintle for use with the M48 was the D38579, although certain other pintles would fit. An E6288 adapter supported the ammunition box. Installation of the M48 bracket mount necessitated the relocation of the windshield-mounted universal rifle holder, if so equipped. Its new location was vertical on the left side of the vehicle. The shortcoming of the M48 was the limited field of fire.

Machine Gun Mounts For Dodge Trucks
The G-505 1/2-Ton Series

The first of the classic Dodge (Fargo) tactical vehicles to be armed in the WWII era were the G-505 series 1/2-ton trucks. These trucks, when armed, were fitted with the M24 pedestal mount. This mount, like the rest of the M24 family, was designed for use with the BAR, .30-caliber machine gun, .30-caliber liquid cooled machine gun, and the Browning M2HB .50-caliber machine gun.

A unique feature of the M24 mount is the inclusion of a storage point for the pintle when it is not installed in the socket. Often, the cab of the truck must be slightly notched to accommodate the installation of the gun mount.

The G-502 3/4-Ton Series

The WWII era 3/4-ton Dodge trucks, when they mounted weapons, initially used the M24A1 Pedestal Mount. The M24A1 eliminated the storage socket, and used a reshaped base to the tube that was bevel cut rather than being supported at the base.

The M24A2 pedestal mount superceded the M24A1 when it was standardized per OCM 22263 on December 2, 1943. The M24A2's improvements included additional vertical reinforcements near the outer edges and across the top of the supporting structure. These mounts were installed across the front of the bed, just behind the driver's seat. It was a fabricated steel structure, with a cast-steel socket to receive the pintle.

The installation of this mount tended to make the truck look a little awkward, and interfered not only with the easy moving from front to rear of the truck, but with the cargo canvas installation as well.

G-741 3/4-Ton Series

With the introduction of the M-37-type vehicles came a new version of the M24 mount. The additional width of the bed meant that the old mounts would no longer fit. The M24A3 mount solved this problem. The extensions on the end of the mount reached the edge of the M37 and M42 beds. This mount was intended to be installed across the front of the bed, and like its predecessors, was supported by the ends as well as bolting to the floor of the vehicle. However, these mounts were designed to be installed backwards compared to their predecessors, with the "post" on the in-bed side.

Still, operation of the weapon by the co-driver was awkward at best, requiring them to climb into the back of the truck in most instances.

G-507 (The Big Dodge)

Dodge Brothers' big tactical truck, the G-507 family of WC-62 and WC-63, had its own antiaircraft mount designed for it in the M50 ring mount. This mount was standardized 24052 on April 22, 1944.

This mount used the same heavy M49 ring, trolley and pintle as the mounts used on the GMC CCKW and a wide variety of other vehicles covered later in this section. The mounting legs were made especially for the antiaircraft application. This mount was designed to be operated by the co-driver, who was expected to stand in the center of the ring. The post-WWII M49 ring is slightly heavier constructed than its older WWII predecessor. Also, the flange that is used to bolt the ring to the mounting posts is interrupted. There are rings that have a continuous flange (M49C ring) designed for mounting on armored vehicles.

The M24A2 pedestal mount, as used on lighter Dodges, could be used on WC-62s and -63s instead of the M50 ring mount. In fact, prior to the April 1944 approval of the M50, the only authorized mount for these big Dodges was the M24A2, which was authorized for this application on December 2, 1943, by OCM 22263.

Machine Gun Mounts for 6x6 Trucks

The antiaircraft armament of 6x6 trucks is usually a .50-caliber M2 HB machine gun, traversing on a ring, supported by a structure over the truck's cab.

Rings

The ring itself could be one of several styles of the M49, or an M66, or an M66C, with the supporting structure varying widely depending on the vehicle application.

M49

The M49 ring is the most common, and allows the weapon to be elevated 80 degrees, or depressed 20 degrees. Carriage assembly D40721 was intended to be used with the M49 ring, and allowed the weapon to be traversed around the gunner, as well as being pivoted on its pintle. The pintle assembly used was the D40733, which was the weapon mount proper. Initially, the ammunition supply was supported by tray D40731, but that tray was later superceded by tray D90078.

M49C

A "C" as the suffix behind the M49 indicates that the ring has a continuous bolt flange around it. This flange is used to mount the ring on the roof of a vehicle, such as high-speed tractors and the M26 Pacific tractor.

M49A1

An "A1" suffix attached to the M49 model number denotes that that particular ring is equipped with a backrest for the gunner to lean against. This backrest rotated in conjunction with the pintle and was intended to provide a better means of tracking opposing aircraft. The ring itself and supports are identical to those used in the standard mounts.

M66

The M49A1 was recognized as a considerable improvement over the basic M49, and this idea was expanded to a bearing-equipped mount. It was initially made of steel, and in two versions. The T106 which used roller bearings, and the T106E1 used ball bearings. This mount was standardized as the M66 mount. While the mount was ballistically and operationally superior to the M49 mount, its great weight (276 lbs.) precluded its use on trucks. Keep in mind the pintle, machine gun and ammunition add another 255 lbs.

In March 1944, work began on aluminum versions of these mounts: the T108 and the T108E1. Like the T106 series, the T108 had roller bearings, and the T108E1 ball bearings.

Adding an M66 mount to a G-742 series truck, or 809 series truck, required a 2590-01-322-2694 cab reinforcement kit in addition to the 1005-01-226-4589 mounting kit. The M939 series trucks used the mounting kit 1005-01-432-3339 and the cab reinforcement kit 2590-01-436-9144.

Mounts

The most common mounting is the M36 truck mount. In its original form, the cast track support brackets were bolted to the posts. In later production these brackets were bolted to the posts. It was used with the following open-cabbed only vehicles:

— CCKW both long and short wheelbase
— AFKWX cab-over-engine truck
— DUKW amphibian truck
— Studebaker and Reo US6 cargo truck
— Diamond T 968 and 969 4-ton trucks
— Federal and Autocar 4-, 5-, and 6-ton tractors
— Corbitt and White 6-ton 6x6 prime mover
— Mack 7 1/2-ton 6x6 prime mover
— M1A1 heavy wrecker
— M20 6x4 12-ton Diamond T

The M36A1 was a later development with a new mounting ring bracket. It was designed for use on the M series 6x6 trucks. The M36A1 had a different mounting ring bracket.

The M32 mount was used on long-wheelbase, closed-cab 2 1/2-ton 6x6 trucks with conventional steel cargo bodies. This was the first mounting giving 360-degree antiaircraft coverage from a truck.

The M37 mount was designed for use with closed-cab, short-wheelbase 6x6 trucks with steel cargo bodies. The M37A1 was used on the wooden-bodied, short wheelbase deuces, and the M37A2 was used on the long-wheelbase, wood-bodied trucks.

Some of the more elusive of the WWII era mountings are:
— M37A3 mount, which was used on CCKW fuel and water tanker trucks.
— M56 mount, designed for the closed cab 4-ton Diamond T.
— M57 mount, used with closed-cab White 666 tanker trucks, as well as the 4-5-ton 4x4 tractor and 5-6-ton 4x4 tractor. The 6-ton 6x6 prime mover could use this mount as well.
— M58 was used on the Corbitt 50SD6 6-ton 6x6 prime mover, as well as the 6-ton Whites that used the M57 mounts.
— M59, which fits the closed cab G-547 Brockway and Ward La France B666 6-ton trucks.
— M60 mount, used on 4-5-ton Federal tractors, as well as 4-ton closed-cabbed 6x6 cargo and wrecker trucks.
— M61 mount, used with the 4-5- and 5-6-ton Autocar 4x4 tractors with closed cab, as well as 6-ton 6x6 prime movers.

Pintles And Cradles, But Not Hooks

The D7431 cradle is the most elaborate weapon mounting used with the pedestal mounts. It was designed for use with the M1917A1 water-cooled machine gun, but also could be used with other weapons. This would be more appropriate for an early war vehicle than for late production, and appears to not have been used with Jeeps, although it was with Dodge trucks.

The next mounting used the pintle D38579, which is a plain "fork." These were used with the M2HB .50-caliber, the Browning .30-caliber M1919A4, and the M1918A2 BAR. The obvious shortcoming of this type pintle is the total lack of a provision to hold an ammunition box when used with a belt-fed weapon. This is the type of pintle shown in figure 41.

Introduced later in WWII and used for many years, the E10014 was a combination cradle, pintle, and ammunition box tray. It was originally developed for the M24A2 and A3 pedestal mounts, and later used with the M31C series pedestal mount. It is commonly called the .30/.50-caliber cradle.

Similar to the D40733 cradle used on the M49 ring mount, the E10014 consisted of the D90078 tray, combined with either the D90045 welded and fabricated or 7068880 cast-steel cradle and pintle.

The cradle/pintle D40733, erroneously referred to in some references as a 7068880, was the type of pintle used with the M49 ring mount. A weapon mounted in this cradle assembly is capable of 85-degree elevation and 30-degree depression. It includes a provision for travel lock in either horizontal or vertical positions.

The shank of the D40733 pintle, made to be used with the ring mount, is much longer than that of the E10014, used with the pedestal mount.

The M142 pintle was developed specifically to mount the M60 7.62mm machine gun in 1/4-ton trucks. The M142 is usually used with the M4 pedestal mount, although it can also be used to affix the M60 to the M31 series mounts.

What Not To Do

The installation of weapons or mounts on vehicles carrying the red cross is forbidden by Army regulations, so its not appropriate to arm your ambulance.

While GIs in combat are ingenious and resourceful, my research thus far has not found official authorization for Jeep (M31) or half-track (M25) type post mounts in any of the Dodges, in neither bed, nor on running board.

If you are considering doing this, and entering the vehicle for judging, bring a period photograph to support this field modification.

Weapons

A variety of weapons could be used on these mounts. Which weapon you select should be guided by the era the vehicle represents, as well what usage the vehicle represents. A vehicle marked for a laundry unit at Camp Ripley, Minnesota, would not have been equipped with a weapon mount.

Live weapons, either in their fully automatic form, or modified to semi-automatic, tend to be expensive, to the point of often exceeding the cost of the truck. Dummy weapons are substantially less expensive, and are available in a variety of grades from a variety sources.

Values

The correct original pedestal mount, with all accessories, cradle and pintle, will add $600 to $1,000 to a vehicle's value.

The proper ring mount, with all accessories, carriage, cradle, and pintle, will add $800 to $1,300 to a vehicle's value.

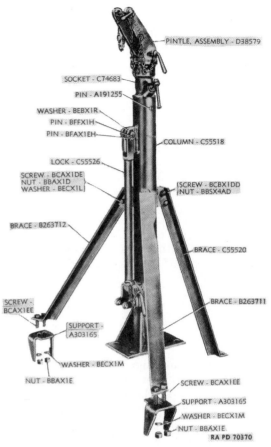

PINTLE, ASSEMBLY - D38579
SOCKET - C74683
PIN - A191255
WASHER - BEBX1R
PIN - BFFX1H
PIN - BFAX1EH
COLUMN - C55518
LOCK - C55526
SCREW - BCAX1DE
NUT - BBAX1D
WASHER - BECX1L
SCREW - BCBX1DD
NUT - BBSX4AD
BRACE - B263712
BRACE - C55520
BRACE - B263711
SCREW - BCAX1EE
SUPPORT - A303165
WASHER - BECX1M
NUT - BBAX1E
SCREW - BCAX1EE
SUPPORT - A303165
WASHER - BECX1M
NUT - BBAX1E
RA PD 70370

The M31 mount had braces, some secured to brackets added under the Jeep floor. This bracing overcame the T47's instability during firing.

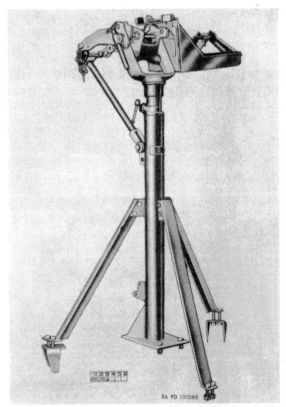

The M31C was an improvement of the M31, enabling it to use the E10014 cradle, pintle, and ammunition box assembly.

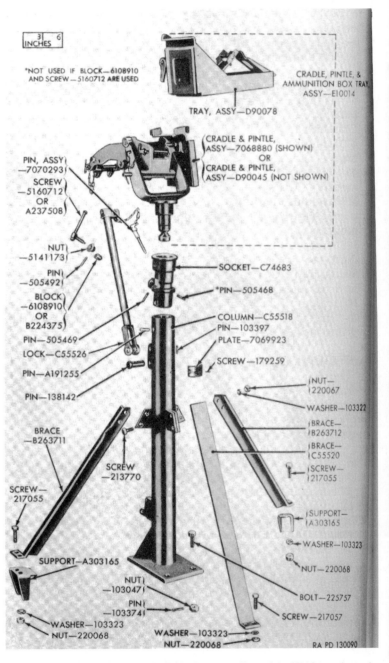

3 | 6 INCHES

*NOT USED IF BLOCK—6108910 AND SCREW—5160712 ARE USED

TRAY, ASSY—D90078

CRADLE, PINTLE, & AMMUNITION BOX TRAY, ASSY—E10014

CRADLE & PINTLE, ASSY—7068880 (SHOWN) OR CRADLE & PINTLE, ASSY—D90045 (NOT SHOWN)

PIN, ASSY —7070293
SCREW —5160712 OR A237508
NUT —5141173
PIN —505492
BLOCK —6108910 OR B224375
PIN—505469
LOCK—C55526
PIN—A191255
PIN—138142

SOCKET—C74683
*PIN—505468
COLUMN—C55518
PIN—103397
PLATE—7069923
SCREW—179259
NUT—220067
WASHER—103322
BRACE—B263712
BRACE—C55520
SCREW—217055
SUPPORT—A303165
WASHER—103323
NUT—220068
BOLT—225757
SCREW—217057

BRACE—B263711
SCREW—213770
SCREW—217055
SUPPORT—A303165
NUT—103047
PIN—103374
WASHER—103323
NUT—220068
WASHER—103323
NUT—220068

RA PD 130090

The various components and individual part numbers of the M31C are shown in this view of the mount.

Less well known and less effective than the pedestal mounts were the M48 bracket mounts. The field of fire with these units was extremely restricted

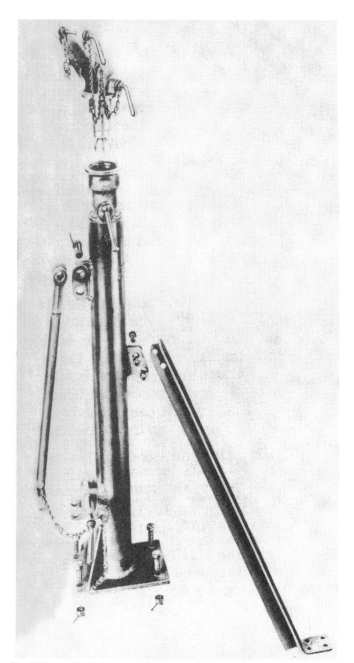

The T47 was the first reasonably successful mounting developed. It was the basis for many mounts to come.

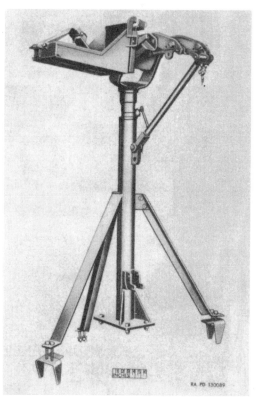

Like its predecessor, the M31C included reinforcements that were to be welded to the frame of the Jeep. The travel lock was used to hold the weapon horizontal when not in use.

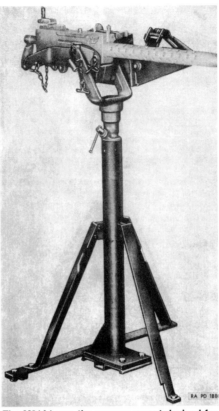

RIA 2036-43712
(1953)

The M4 mount, shown here at a flea market, was the weapon mounting designed for the M151 series of vehicles. Notice the box-like base that spanned the area between the truck's front seats.

The M31A1 was the weapon mount devised for the M38. Its under-floor brackets were completely redesigned.

The M31A1 lacked the travel lock that had been furnished with the previous mounts.

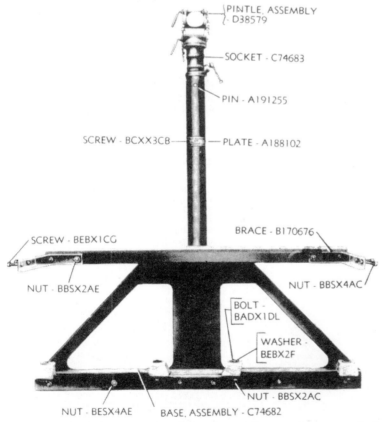

PINTLE, ASSEMBLY - D38579

SOCKET - C74683

PIN - A191255

SCREW - BCXX3CB — PLATE - A188102

SCREW - BEBX1CG

BRACE - B170676

NUT - BBSX2AE

NUT - BBSX4AC

BOLT - BADX1DL

WASHER - BEBX2F

NUT - BBSX2AC

NUT - BESX4AE   BASE, ASSEMBLY - C74682

This is the side of the of the M24 pedestal mount that was to be placed next to the bed of the truck. This mount was installed between the bed and the cab of the 1/2-ton Dodges.

This is how the M24 looked installed in a VC series Dodge. Notice the socket for storage of the pintle. (Photo courtesy of Bryce Sunderlin)

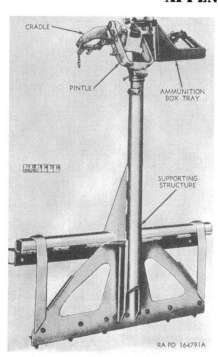

Compare this rear view of an installed M24A1 with the similar photo of an installed M24. (National Archives and Records Administration photo)

While the WWII 3/4-ton Dodge initially used the M24A1, at mid-war the M24A2 Pedestal Mount, shown here, was introduced.

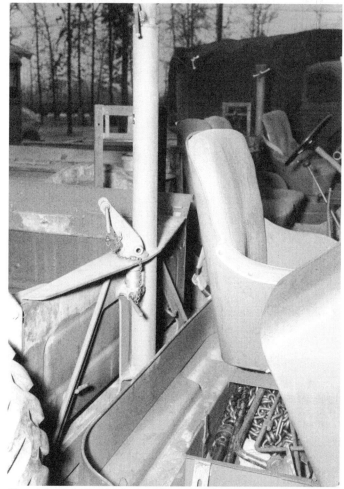

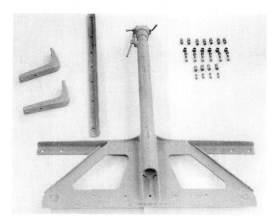

This is the front side of the M24A1 Pedestal Mount. Compare the broad tapered vertical plate in the center to the much narrower plate on the M24 mount. Also note the omission of the pintle storage socket. (National Archives and Records Administration photo)

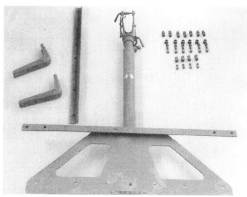

The reinforcement at the base of the post of the M24 is one of the things that caused the cabs of trucks fitted with these to be notched. (Photo courtesy of Bryce Sunderlin)

The two brackets, shown loose in this photo of the rear of a M24A1, were used to reinforce the bed. (National Archives and Records Administration photo)

This side view of an M24A1 installed in a VC Dodge gives an excellent comparison to the M24. (National Archives and Records Administration photo)

RA PD 188

The M24A3 pedestal mount was developed for the G-741 (M37) series vehicles. The mounting brackets on the ends of the upper cross-brace are more substantial than their predecessors'. The angle bracket that forms the base is also taller on the M24A3 than on the earlier mounts.

This M50 mount is installed on a WC-63. Although not shown, it is possible to install the mount and retain the liquid container. (Photo courtesy of Jimmy McCall)

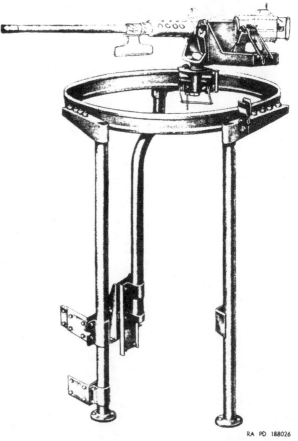

RA PD 188026

The M50 ring mount was designed for the G-507 Dodge 6x6s. While the M24A2 will fit the big Dodge, the M50 looks MUCH cooler! For 100-percent accurate installation, the bolts should have their heads marked DCPD for Dodge-Chrysler-Plymouth-Desoto. (Photo from TM 9-2016)

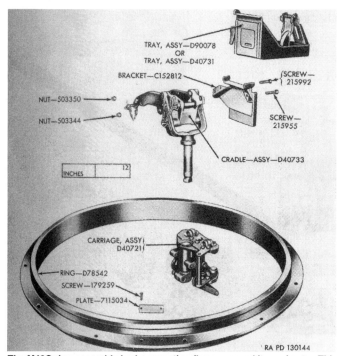

The M49C ring assembly had a mounting flange around its perimeter. This mount is not correct for a wheeled vehicle.

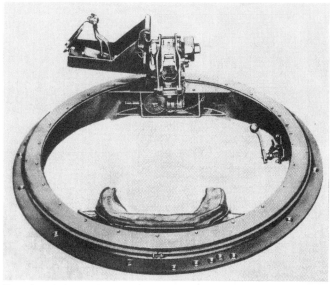

Even though it was developed late in WWII, the M66 ring mount has only recently become popular on wheeled vehicles. (U.S. Army photo)

The M49A1 introduced the idea of providing the gunner with a backrest. This has the early bolt-on track support brackets on this mount support. Later brackets were welded to the uprights. (U.S. Army photo)

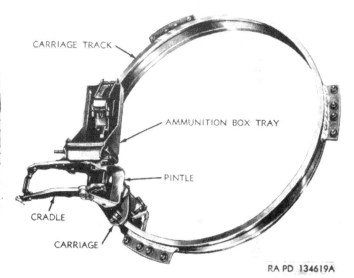

This photo of an M49 from a TM 9-2016 shows the basic components of almost all the ring mounts discussed in this appendix. Also shown are the pintle, carriage assembly, and ammo tray.

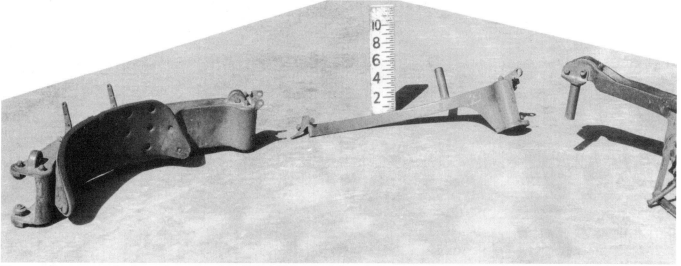

These are the components of an early version of the M49A1. Notice the linkage that connects the backrest to the weapon carriage. (U.S. Army photo)

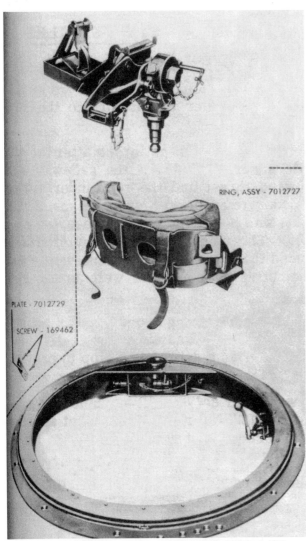

RING, ASSY - 7012727

PLATE - 7012729

SCREW - 169462

The major components of the roller-bearing equipped M66 are shown here. In addition to the two concentric cast steel rings, the mount includes a large padded backrest and a special D80030 pintle. (U.S. Army photo)

The M32's elaborate bracing was required to absorb the recoil forces of the firing weapon, and to support the weight of it in rugged off-road conditions. (U.S. Army photo)

The closed-cab CCKW-352 utilized the M37 mount to attach its antiaircraft weapon. Unlike the M32, only a small reinforcement extends to the rear of the front of the bed. Variations of this mount were used on short-wheelbase trucks with wooden beds, as well on long-wheelbase CCKW tanker trucks. (U.S. Army photo)

The M32 mount was used to install the M49 ring on a closed-cabbed CCKW. The heavy metal support appears to extend from the backside of the bed front all the way over the cab. (U.S. Army photo)

The M36 mount was the most common ring mount used during WWII. It could be installed on all the open-cab 6x6 trucks the U.S. Army fielded during WWII, including the DUKW. This November 1943 photo shows an early prototype of that mount installed on the vehicle that pioneered the military standard open cab — the rare open-cab US6 Studebaker. (U.S. Army photo)

With the adoption of the Reo G-742, there came the need for a slightly different mounting. This is an early M36A1 machine gun mount installed on M34 cargo truck. (U.S. Army photo)

Because the automatic transmission-equipped GMC G-749 trucks did not use the standard military cab, it was necessary to create a mounting kit just for them. That kit was the M36A2, shown here. (U.S. Army photo)

The Corbitt 50SD6 6-ton 6x6 prime mover had its own ring mount kit, the M58. The M58 could also be used in place of the M57. (U.S. Army photo)

The mount initially developed for the 4-ton Diamond T 6x6 trucks was the M56 mount shown here. Other mounts developed later for other trucks could also be used. The roof top ring for the trucks cab was included in all mounting kits M56-M61. (U.S. Army photo)

The M59 mounting was used to provide antiaircraft defense for B666 bridge erection trucks. Although in theory, 25 percent of U.S. 6x6 trucks were provided with weapons mounts, that percentage was not universally applied. Trucks such as bridge erection trucks, which were used in forward areas, were more frequently armed than those in rear areas. (U.S. Army photo)

This 4-5-ton Federal 94x43 tractor is equipped with the M60 mount. These trucks were widely used by transportation units moving equipment from rear areas to forward units. (U.S. Army photo)

The M57 mount was the mount of choice for White 6-ton 6x6s as well as certain truck tractors. All of the ring mount kits for closed cabbed 6x6s are hard to find now, especially those for trucks larger than 2 1/2 tons. (U.S. Army photo)

Autocar tractors used the M61 mount. The need to protect supply convoys from air strikes was great, although it was generally conceded that the vehicle would have to be stopped before there was any hope of the antiaircraft gunner hitting his target. (U.S. Army photo)

The E10014 was a combination cradle, pintle, and amunition box tray that was originally developed for the M24 pedestal mounts, but it soon found widespread use, including the M31C.

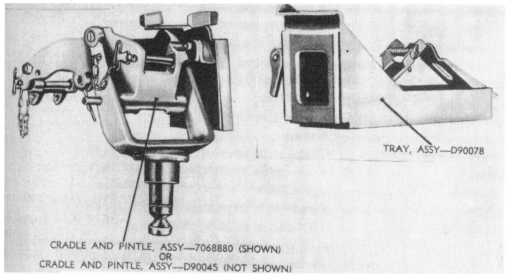

The E10014 was actually an assembly of many components, including the D90078 tray, and either the D90045 welded or 7068880 cast-steel cradle and pintle.

The almost elegant D7431 cradle was used with the water-cooled .30-caliber machine gun and other weapons at the outset of World War II. This cradle was developed for the tripod mount 1917A1 and was also used with the M24 mount.

APPENDIX 2

COLOR AND MARKINGS OF U.S. MILITARY VEHICLES

One of the biggest tasks for the military vehicle restorer is selecting and applying the appropriate paint and markings to a vehicle. The selection depends upon the time frame the vehicle was built, and the time period the restoration is to represent. An inappropriate or improperly applied paint scheme can significantly decrease a vehicle's value, especially on larger vehicles, where refinishing is a major expense. In the case of camouflaged vehicles, the paint should follow the proper camouflage pattern, and use the proper color combination for the depicted unit's area of operation.

Solid OD Color Schemes 1941-1975

Documents located by Steve Zaloga at the National Archives reveal that the Adjutant General made the Quartermaster Corps responsible for paint procurement and formulation on July 18, 1940. Four days prior to this, the Corps of Engineers had been made responsible for protective coloration. On October 12, 1940 it was specified by the Quartermaster Corps that all new material be painted in lusterless enamel. Prior to this, per OCM 14022, November 1937, vehicles had been painted in long oil (gloss) enamel. OCM 14022 specified that the long oil was a substitute standard for peacetime use only.

Although Pittsburgh Plate Glass (PPG) was the first manufacturer and supplier of OD paints to the U.S. Government in 1940, it was soon joined by others. Although all the paints were made to Quartermaster Specification ES-474 (E.S. = "engineering specification"), and were to match Specification 3-1 Color Card Supplements, slightly differing shades of Olive Drab were due to manufacturing variations among suppliers resulting from a known shortage of color cards in early 1942. Most of these paints appeared the same when first applied, but the differences began to show up as the paint weathered. Some faded towards yellow, some brown, etc. The ES-474 specification was later superceded by ES-680. It is important to note that ES-474 was not a color spec, but rather a paint and painting spec.

Olive drab was referred to on the Quartermaster Specification 3-1 Color Card Supplements as color number 22, the Corps of Engineers referring to the same color as No. 9 Olive Drab. Responsibility for paint shifted back to Ordnance October 21, 1942, and efforts were immediately begun to revise the now 22-year-old Spec. 3-1. The result of this was the March 16, 1943, issuance of Specification 3-1F/Color Card Supplement (Revision 1), which was officially adopted on April 21, 1943. For the first time, the color card actually showed a flat finish OD (prior to this, all the chips were gloss, even though the specifications stated they were to be produced in a

lusterless finish).

In January 1943, the Army Resources and Production Division wanted to replace U.S. Army Air Forces olive drab and Army Ground Forces olive drab with a new color known as AN (Army/Navy) 319 Olive Drab, which was the same color as Olive Drab number 22. However, the new paint lacked a characteristic of the Air Force paint that inhibited infrared detection, so the Army Air Force refused to adopt it.

In mid/late 1944, the paint composition was changed, becoming very slightly glossy. Instead of the rough, dead flat finish used previously, the new paint had a very slight sheen. This type of paint sealed the metal from the weather better than the flat finish, which was slightly porous, had.

Army regulation 850-15, dated August 1, 1945, introduced semigloss Olive Drab for the first time. The paint spec was 3-181, amendment 3, type V Fed. stock No. 52-E-7574 (1-gallon can). The regulation went on to say that vehicles were only to be repainted in the semigloss when repainting was otherwise required. Further, Army Motors of September 1945 stated that the semigloss would not be available through supply channels for another 60 to 90 days. Therefore, it is unlikely that any U.S. tactical vehicles painted semigloss OD saw combat during WWII.

In 1950, the flat No. 22 Olive Drab was renamed 3412 and the semigloss became number 2430 in conformance with TT-C-595, (Colors for Ready-Mixed Paint). This system was created as a result of the Federal Property and Administrative Services Act of 1949, which provided that an agency be formed that would regulate and specify standards for all types of government procurements. This number system was similar in intent to the later FS system, but used four-digit code numbers. Olive Drab No. 2430 would remain the standard color of U.S. tactical vehicles until 1956.

The standard that was created for paint was Federal Standard 595. The new system assigned a five-digit code to each color listed. This code provided differentiation between flat, semigloss, and full gloss shades.

The first digit indicated the type of finish, 1 being gloss, 2 was semigloss, and 3 was flat.

The second digit represented the color. Brown was represented by 0, 1 was Red, 2 was Orange, 3 Yellow, 4 Green, 5 Blue, 6 Gray, 7 was miscellaneous, and 8 was fluorescent.

The last three numbers were assigned in order of increasing diffuse reflectance. In theory, colors with the same last 4 numbers would be the same, only with a different sheen. Unfortunately that was not always the case, and Olive Drab was one of the exceptions.

When the colors were converted to the FS 595 five-digit code, some were essentially the same color. The numbers 2430 and 24087 were assigned to virtually the

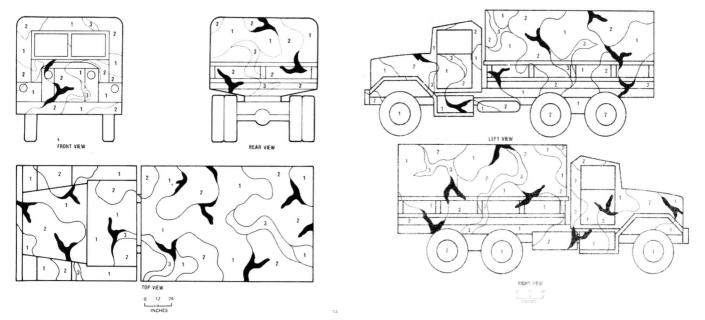

FRONT VIEW REAR VIEW LEFT VIEW

TOP VIEW RIGHT VIEW

0 12 24
INCHES

This is the painting diagram for the MERDC camouflage of G-742 series 2 1/2-ton 6x6 cargo trucks. Even though the diagram shows camouflage on the cargo canvas, the canvases were not actually painted.

same color through the various number systems. Other colors disappeared completely.

On March 1, 1956, Federal Standard 595 containing 358 colors, was issued. With the FS system, the olive drab 3412, formerly No. 22, was designated 34087.

Addendum 2 to FS 595 was issued on May 9, 1960, by U.S. Army Signal Equipment Support Agency, so it is not certain that it applied government-wide. This addendum deleted the 14087, 24087, and 34087 Olive drabs and replaced them with "interim" X-14087, X-24087, and X-34087. It is possible that the shading error was corrected at this time.

However, the Federal Color Standards are a living document, and in 1968 FS595A was issued. More colors were discontinued, and others added.

In January 1985, FS 595A was revised through change 7. With this revision the error of having three different shades as Olive Drab in one series was corrected. Prior to this time, FS-14087 was a dark, brownish-green, while lusterless FS-34087 was a light, grayish green, and FS-24087 was neither.

To fix this problem, the whole 4087 color set was deleted. In its place, two new sets were created:

The FS-4084 numbers were flat, gloss, and semigloss colors that matched the old FS-14087 dark, brownish-green.

The FS-4088 provided flat, gloss and semigloss equivalents for the old FS-34087.

Also, in the January 1985 change 7, an equivalent to the WWII flat Olive Drab made its first appearance on the Federal Standard Color List. The new number assigned to the old color was FS-33070.

To make matters even more confusing, when FS 595B was issued in 1989, the number 24087 reappeared, only it was a totally different color than the listed in FS 595A. Thus, if you are restoring a late 1950s through early '70s era vehicle, you must not only specify the color number, but the standard number as well to insure getting the correct color.

The pre-1985 FS-595A 24087 is the post-1985 FS 24084, which is not the same as the post-1989 24087.

The point of this is, it is useless and foolish to order paint by FS color number, without at the same time specifying which FS standard you are referring to: FS-595, FS-595A, or FS-595B. Without specifying, you have a 66-percent chance of getting the wrong color.

So, what color should you paint your WWII Army vehicle? Well, vehicle production information found by Jim Gilmore in the Ford Archives, Fred Coldwell in the Willys records, and myself at the National Archives and Mack archives all reveal the same thing: During WWII, all U.S. Army tactical vehicles were painted the same color. The first GPW and the last GPW; the first MA, and the last MB; the first NO, and the last NO—the same paint color was used throughout WWII production. There was no early, late, or gloss WWII shade of paint.

MERDC Four-Color Camo 1975-mid-1980s

The U.S. Army's Mobility Equipment Research & Development Command, working with the U.S. Army Project Mobile Army Sensor Systems Test, Evaluation and Review Project, developed a four-color camouflage scheme. The directive initiating this was issued on 10 December 1971. From August 1972 until March 1973 a team from MERDC was deployed to Fort Hood, Texas to carry out work on this project. By 15 January 1973, 1400 of the vehicles at Fort Hood had been experimentally painted in the new scheme. The result was what has come to be known as the MERDC scheme, or as collectors sometimes refer to it, the four-color camo scheme. This was the scheme that replaced the traditional Semi-Gloss Olive Drab #24087 "fear no evil" scheme.

As early as WWI the Army had applied camouflage to vehicles in certain theaters and certain missions, but the MERDC scheme was the first time there was an Army-wide mandate of a vehicular camouflage scheme. The earliest reference to the Army-wide application of the

NO.	ABBREVIATION	COLOR
1	W	White
2	DS	Desert sand
3	S	Sand
4	EY	Earth yellow
5	ER	Earth red
6	FD	Field drab
7	EB	Earth brown
8	OD	Olive drab
9	LG	Light green
10	DG	Dark green
11	FG	Forest green
12	BL	Black

Here is a list of colors used in the MERDC paint scheme.

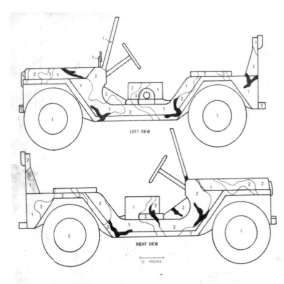

This is a MERDC painting diagram for the M151 series Jeeps. The numbers on the diagram correspond to the numbers in the left-hand columns in the chart on page 484

CONDITION	COLOR DISTRIBUTION			
	45%	45%	5%	5%
	COLOR NUMBER			
	1	2	3	
Winter US & Europe - verdant[1]	FG	FD	S[3]	BL
Snow - temperate w/trees & shrubs[2]	FG	W	S[3]	BL
Snow - temperate w/open terrain[2]	W	FD	S[3]	BL
Summer US & Europe - verdant[1]	FG	LG	S[3]	BL
Tropics - verdant	FG	DG	LG[3]	BL
Gray desert	S	FD	EY[3]	BL
Red desert	ER	EY	S[3]	BL
Winter Arctic	W	W	W	W

Notes:

[1] *Verdant means generally green—in summer due to trees, shrubs, and grass; in winter due to evergreens.*

[2] *This color combination is for use only in areas that occasionally have snow which does not completely cover the terrain, thus leaving trees or patches of soil bare.*

[3] *This 5% color should be the camouflage color that matches most closely the color of the soil in the local area. A typical color for such use is sand, but earth red, earth yellow, or one of the others may be closer to the predominant soil color and, in that case, should be used.*

With the MERDC scheme, the colors applied varied with the weather and terrain. This table was used to determine color placement and usage.

This M292 was painted following the diagram in figure 4. Although there was some slight variation, as a rule the painting diagrams were followed fairly closely.

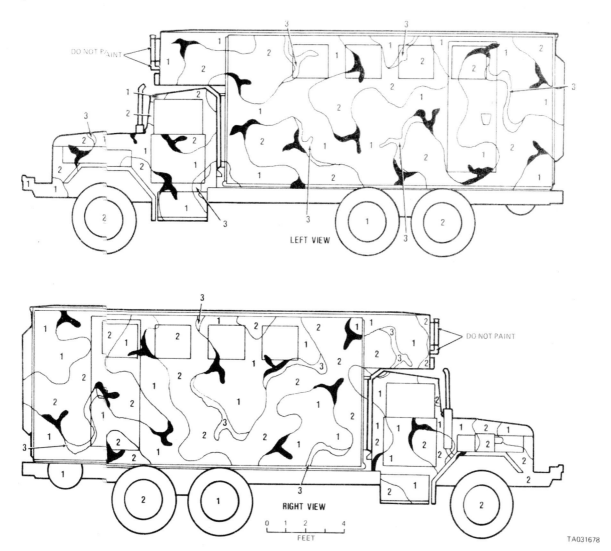

Each type of vehicle had a MERDC painting diagram designed for it. This is for expansible van trucks, such as the M291 and M292.

four-color camouflage scheme I can find a reference to is TC 5-200, dated August 28, 1975. Complete painting instructions in the four-color scheme are found in TB 43-0209, October 29, 1976. TB 43-0209 is noted on its front page as replacing TB 746-93-1, October 26, 1964 (which is the specification for the overall 24087 scheme). Since the bulk of the U.S. troops were pulled out of Vietnam in 1973, it is unlikely that any vehicles wearing four-color camouflage saw service there.

The camouflage patterns consist of wavy, irregular patches of color. The colors used for the patterns have been selected from the standard camouflage colors. The color numbers (1-12) were used in conjunction with the painting diagrams to determine the placement of these standard colors.

Color Code Conversion Used In MERDC Scheme

		FS595A	
National Stock Number			
Color	5 Gallon	1 Gallon	Color Code
Desert Sand	8010-00-111-8353	8010-00-111-8004	33637
Sand	8010-00-111-8336	8010-00-111-7988	30277
Earth Yellow	8010-00-111-8130	8010-00-111-7968	30257
Earth Red	8010-00-111-8345	8010-00-111-8003	30117
Field Drab	8010-00-111-8129	8010-00-111-7943	30118
Earth Brown	8010-00-111-8338	8010-00-111-7998	30099
Olive Drab	8010-00-111-8069	8010-00-111-7940	34087
Light Green	8010-00-111-8007	8010-00-111-7930	34151
Dark Green	8010-00-111-8042	8010-00-111-7938	34102
Forest Green	8010-00-111-8010	8010-00-111-7937	34079
Black	8010-00-111-8356	8010-00-111-8005	37038

Contemporary Army literature touted the advantages that the new paint scheme offered, including breaking up the signature characteristics of interior shadows, corners, angles, and straight lines. Considerable research was put into developing special patterns for each type of vehicle to maximize the camouflage pattern's effectiveness. Unlike both the previous primary paint colors (24087, used from 1957 until the mid-1970s, and 23070, used 1944 through 1957), which were semi-gloss paints, this new system used flat-finish paints. With the exception of the arctic region vehicles, all vehicles were painted in the same pattern, with only the colors varying according to the location and season of the year.

There was considerable emphasis placed on the theory that this four-color camouflage scheme could be adapted to virtually any climatic or geographic without repainting the entire vehicle. When changing from one geographic or climatic condition to another, the shape of the pattern itself did not change; only one or two of the colors that make up the pattern were changed. The first and second colors each covered about 45 percent of the vehicle; the third color covered 5 percent; and the fourth color, normally black, covered the remaining 5 percent. The color numbers 1, 2, and 3 identify the first three colors, and are used in the pattern designs to show what color goes where. The only exception to all of this was winter arctic, which was solid white.

In addition to the usual washing, sanding, etc., when a vehicle was to be painted in this scheme all the white markings were removed from the outside of the vehicle. If pressure-sensitive markings had been previously used,

they were first completely removed. Even though this was what the manuals declared, in actual practice many examples can be found where the old markings had been simply painted over. Alkyd enamels are the paints used in this system. Using an opaque projector, the pattern (each vehicle type has a specific pattern, none are randomly applied) was projected on the vehicle and outlined in chalk. The placement of each color "line" had a tolerance of plus or minus 2 in. Using a paint gun, these chalk outlines were then overpainted with the correct colors, with the painter taking care to wipe away the chalk as the work progressed, since paint doesn't adhere well to the chalk.

Canvas, rubber and vinyl components were not painted, even though it was originally intended that paints for canvas would be developed.

NATO Three-Color Camouflage

The current three-color "NATO" camouflage scheme was adopted in the mid-1980s. It replaced the previously used four-color scheme developed by the Army Mobility Equipment Research & Development Command. As was the case for the MERDC scheme, each type of vehicle had a pattern developed for it, and all vehicles of a given type were painted in the same pattern. The theory behind the three-color camouflage pattern is different from that of the previous MERDC patterns. The MERDC scheme attempted to match the color of an area, making the vehicle have a minimum contrast with its background.

The three-color pattern is intended to break up the lines of the vehicle into barely discernable shapes that are not readily recognized as vehicle features. The pattern and color placement are critical to disrupting those clues that would help an observer recognize a vehicle (lines, curves). To accomplish this, the camouflage pattern disrupts objects whose size exceeds one minute of arc (30 cm at 1,000 meters), yet is at least one minute of arc in size itself.

This is why, even though they are camouflaged (if done correctly), the door or hood of one truck can be installed on another and the paint lines still line up. The two exceptions to this are the overall white of the arctic winter scheme and the overall sand used during the Gulf War (which is not to be confused with the NATO "desert" scheme referred to in the tables).

For an authentic restoration using the NATO camouflage scheme, the restorer should take the time to acquire the proper camouflage pattern. Also, select the proper color combination for the area of operation of the unit you are depicting. Most importantly, follow the proper safety precautions when applying the finish.

CARC

Few things in the military vehicle hobby are surrounded by as much misinformation, mystery, and mythology as is the subject of Chemical Agent Resistant Coatings.

The paint used in this NATO scheme is generally known as "CARC." CARC was developed by the Army Research Laboratory, Aberdeen Proving Ground, Maryland, in the 1970s to provide a finish for equipment that would not absorb chemical weapon agents, and

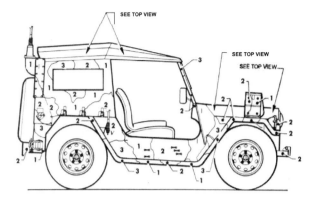

RIGHT SIDE VIEW

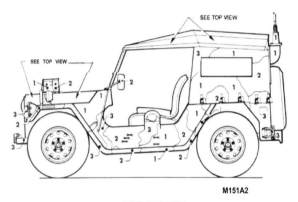

LEFT SIDE VIEW

Figure 34. Truck, utility: 1 1/4 ton M151A2. (2 of 2)

M151A2

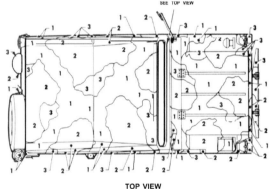

TOP VIEW

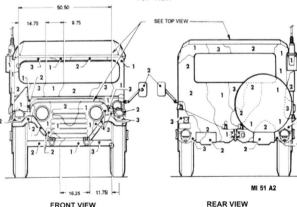

FRONT VIEW   REAR VIEW

MI 51 A2

Figure 34. Truck, utility 1-1/4ton M151A2.   of 2)

When the three-color NATO scheme replaced the MERDC scheme, new painting diagrams were developed.

would be readily cleansed of them if it were exposed. This was critical to prevent the spread of these agents and provide a quick return to mission-ready status for equipment exposed to chemical attack.

In 1983, the decision was made to adopt CARC for all combat, combat support, tactical wheeled vehicles, aircraft, and essential ground support equipment (i.e., tactical equipment). This change was supposed to be implemented in 1985. As a result of stringent health and environmental regulations, lead and hexavalent chromium were eventually removed from CARC and the levels of solvents or volatile organic compounds (VOCs) were reduced. These actions occurred before the Gulf War. To quote TM 43-0139, "A common misconception is that CARC paints present greater health/-safety/environmental hazards than do other paints. In fact, the health and safety requirements for CARC are the same as those for all paints."

The Air Force does not use CARC. Instead, it uses a polyurethane paint that has many of the same hazards as CARC, but does not have the chemical resistive properties of CARC. Mil-C-46168 is the spec for CARC that is available in the 19 different colors. The most common three colors used on vehicles are: 383 Green 34094, 383 Brown 30051, and Black 37030 or 37038.

When a unit was to be deployed to a primarily snowy area, but not arctic area, the equipment was painted in the Winter Snow (black/white/brown) scheme. As a result of tests obtained by the Saudi Arabian National Guard (SANG), desert camouflage was overall tan. Their testing indicated that in a sparse desert environment, the solid tan would be more effective than the three-color pattern.

CARC FS COLOR NUMBERS

COLOR	COLOR NUMBER
Green 383*	34094
Brown 383*	30051
Dark Green	34082
Field Drab	33105
Earth Yellow	33245
Sand*	33303
Black*	37030
Aircraft Green	34031
Olive Drab	34088
Aircraft Gray	36300
Aircraft White	37875
Aircraft Red	31136
Aircraft Black	37038
Interior Aircraft Black (with glass beads)	37031
Insignia Blue	35044
Interior Aircraft Gray	36231
Aircraft Yellow	33538
Dark Sandstone	33510
Tan	33446

Colors most often used in the three-color vehicular camouflage scheme.

Note: *Despite the word "aircraft" appearing in some color names above, remember that the US Air Force does not use CARC.*

What is CARC?

CARC is essentially a low-gloss version of automotive-grade polyurethane paint. These coatings provide the standard characteristics of any protective finish: corrosion resistance, durability, and identification marking. The resin systems used in the Army's camouflage coatings are polyureas and polyurethane-type materials. The pigments can be a variety of colors and provide the low-gloss properties and color to the paint. The solvents are generally standard hydrocarbon-based materials that assist in package viscosity and spraying properties. However, CARC formulations provide some unique properties that distinguish them from typical commercially available paints.

Chemical agent-resistant coatings all have a very matte finish, or extremely low gloss, to minimize glare or reflection from the sun or other bright light sources. Because chemical warfare agents are unable to penetrate the coating, a standard military decontaminating solution, such as decontaminating solution number two (DS2), can readily neutralize surface chemical

This truck was painted using the diagram shown below. The painting tolerance for this scheme was fairly narrow, and body components of trucks painted with these patterns can be interchanged without affecting the camouflage scheme.

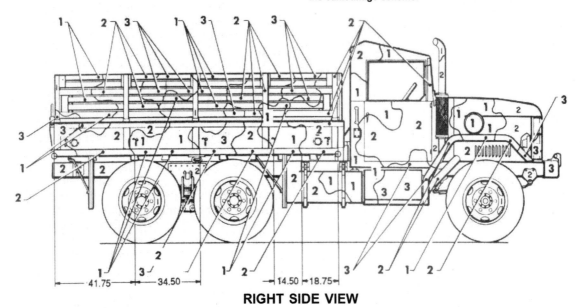

RIGHT SIDE VIEW

M35A2   M35A2C

VI8A

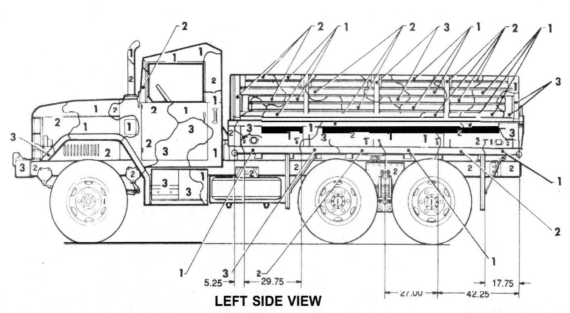

LEFT SIDE VIEW

The painting diagram for the G-742 cargo trucks was also revised. It shows the floor of the truck's bed as camouflaged, but often times it was left the base 383 color.

contaminants on CARC-painted vehicles. CARC's resistance to a variety of chemicals and solvents, and its ability to withstand weathering, has made CARC the paint of choice for outdoor use in a military-operational environment, and also benefits collectors who are forced to store their equipment outdoors.

While all colors of CARC are chemically similar, the pigmentation additives have unique properties and characteristics that make them particularly suitable for military operations. For example, the base green color — referred to as Green 383 — used in the common three-color Woodland pattern employed throughout the military, uses two types of pigments with reflectance

properties in the near-infrared region of the spectrum. The combination of these pigments mimics the reflectance properties of chlorophyll present in living foliage, such as tree leaves and grasses, and thus minimizes detection of woodland-scheme CARC-painted equipment by near-infrared detectors.

Another color, Tan 686, was reformulated with higher reflectance pigmentation to reduce the amount of solar heat vehicles would absorb (a serious concern during Operation Desert Shield). A new color, designated Tan 686A, increased the reflectance properties of the coating. Initial supplies of CARC available in the early stages of Operation Desert Shield were Tan 686. As new

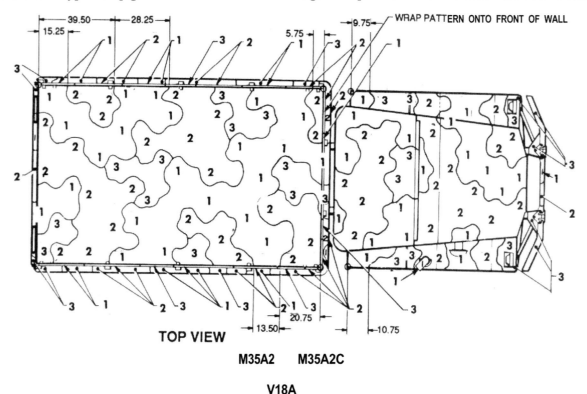

TOP VIEW

M35A2   M35A2C

V18A

FRONT VIEW

REAR VIEW

M35A2

batches of CARC were manufactured to meet the supply needs, Tan 686A became the standard. In spite of their similarities, it is not possible to mix the two components of the different tans, nor is it possible to mix components from different manufacturers, regardless of color.

There have been several different varieties of CARC, due in some cases to the need for different application techniques, and in some cases to reflect growing environmental concerns. Each of these has its specific application techniques and own hazards. CARC is a coating system that makes it easy to decontaminate surfaces that have been exposed to chemical agents.

There are three types of coatings in the CARC system: an epoxy polyamide primer, an aliphatic polyurethane paint (PUP), and an epoxy polyamide enamel. Each of the coatings is supplied as a two-component system. When the two components are combined, a terminal reaction begins that makes an impermeable coating.

The CARC system contains solvents and isocyanate (HDI).

Should I Be Concerned About CARC?

CARC, when properly applied, provides an extremely durable finish, and is absolutely hazard free when it is not disturbed. Some of the hazards involved in applying and removing CARC from historic military vehicles and equipment should be considered.

Several compounds in CARC formulations, if taken into the body in sufficiently high concentrations, may cause short- and long-term health effects. The most notable of these compounds is hexamethylene diisocyanate (HDI), which hardens, or plasticizes, the paint. Exposure to high concentrations of aerosolized HDI during spray painting will cause irritation to the skin and mucous membranes. People suffer from itching and reddening of the skin, burning sensation of the throat and nose, and watering of the eyes. These acute effects subside when the person leaves the exposure area. If the concentrations of HDI are high enough, pulmonary symptoms may occur. These would include cough, shortness of breath, pain when breathing, and chest tightness. Prompt medical attention is required in these cases.

In a small percentage of people, HDI may cause a process called "sensitization." This is an allergic-like reaction similar to what some people suffer with certain foods, medications, or bee stings. Allergic-like symptoms may include coughing, wheezing, tightness in the chest, and shortness of breath. Anyone that ever suffers any type of allergic-reaction should seek medical care immediately.

The solvents used in any painting may be inhaled or absorbed through the skin. Solvent vapors may produce eye irritation, dizziness, nausea, and headaches. Again, these acute effects subside when the person leaves the exposure area. Painters not utilizing personal protective equipment and exposed to solvents for a long period of time may suffer neurological problems such as irritability, depression, or an inability to concentrate. CARC exposure can also lead to a skin condition called dermatitis.

This G-506 series truck, owned by Dave Falk, displays the early WWII style unit markings on the door.

Long-term exposure to HDI can cause or aggravate respiratory problems, in particular, asthma. The use of personal protective equipment, such as respirators, coveralls, eye protection, gloves, and head coverings, can prevent or minimize exposures to HDI. The HDI in polyurethane paint does not present a hazard after the paint dries and cures, unless exposed to heat sufficient for thermal decomposition of the coating, such as welding.

Solvents used in CARC and other paints are flammable. Never paint near open flames or where there are sparks. Never apply CARC to surfaces that will exceed 400° F (for example, exhaust pipes and engine manifolds). Heating painted surfaces releases toxic gases, vapors, and metal fumes.

If the existing paint requires surface preparation, manual "wet" sanding is the recommended method (old paint may contain lead or chromates). Wet sanding eliminates the need for respiratory protection.

CARC can be applied by spraying, or with a brush. The overspray from one color to another cannot exceed 1 1/2 in. Roller application is not recommended. Rubber, vinyl, and canvas parts are not painted.

No Welding

Never weld or use a cutting torch on CARC-painted material. Welding or cutting painted surfaces releases toxic gases, vapors, and metal fumes.

Engines should be painted with green, heat-resistant paint that is non-CARC.

Removing CARC

Before applying any heat (such as to straighten a bent part, or cut out a piece of steel), sand or grind off the paint down to bare metal on an area 4 in. on either side of where you plan to apply heat. If the other side of the metal is painted, remove the paint from it, too.

Markings

Before discussing the specific markings applied to vehicles, first consider the level of restoration you are seeking. A truly factory-fresh vehicle would be sparsely marked, as the unit markings (bumper numbers) were applied as the vehicles were issued to using troops.

The registration number (hood number), national symbol (star) and various other markings however would

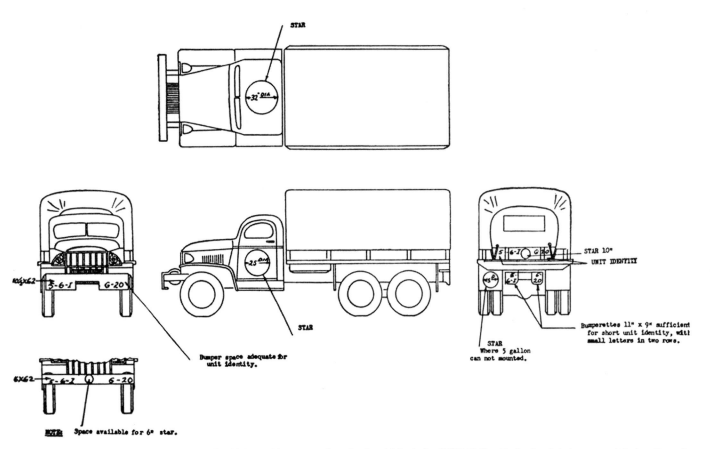

This diagram shows the proper placement of vehicle markings on a closed-cab vehicle during WWII. Notice the horizontal star was painted on the cab roof, not the hood.

have been factory applied, and neatly done. Not only does the military have very specific and strict standards for the factory application of markings, but the automobile manufacturers clearly have the expertise and equipment to apply markings without excessive overspray. Vehicles that were repainted in the field, or even at the depot level, did not have the same quality of paint and markings as those done in the factory.

Agency Identification & Registration Numbers

The registration number, sometimes called the USA Number or hood number, is permanently assigned to each vehicle, and applied at the time of vehicle manufacture. It can only be changed under very rare and unusual circumstances.

The registration number was applied 2 in. below the agency identification on vehicles with 4-in. stenciling, 1 in. below when using 2-in. stenciling. It could be in line with, and to the right of, the agency identification if that arrangement is more suitable due to space restrictions. However, the preferred placement was two lines, with the agency identification above the registration number. These markings are placed on each side of the truck at the side edges of the hood. They are also placed across the tailgate or flat body area of trucks.

The registration numbers assigned by the Army were were specific codes, as explained in the accompanying Table 6.

REGISTRATION NUMBER PREFIX CODES

The registration numbering system used during the later part of WWII incorporated a prefix to denote the vehicle's weight class. For example, in 20241146, the initial "20" signifies 1/4 ton. The prefix codes used from 1943 until 1960 are:

1943-1960

0   Trailers
00 Maintenance trucks
1   Cars and sedans
10 Kitchen trailers
2   Light trucks up to 1 ton
20 Recce trucks, buses
3   Medium trucks, 1 1/2 ton
30 Tanks and some "specials"
4   Trucks, 2 1/2 ton and up to 4-5 ton
40 Tracked and halftracked vehicles, except tanks
5   Trucks over 5 tons and prime movers
50 Fire and crash trucks
6   Motorcycles and sidecars
60 Armored cars and special technical vehicles such as command, radio, searchlight.
7   Ambulances
70 Amphibious vehicles
8   Wheeled tractors
80 Tankers
9   Full and half tracked tractors

U.S.A.
123786

This is the typeface that was to be used on US military vehicles from September 25, 1936 until April 22, 1942. The size of the registration markings was to be 1, 2, or 4 inches tall.

1960-early 1970s

From 1960, a new system was introduced, comprised of numbers and a letter, such as 2B 1234. The initial "2" signified 1/4-ton, very similar to the WWII system. When the registration number reached 2B 9999, the next letter was used, as in 2C 0001, etc. Some letters were not used because they could be confused with numbers (such as I and O).

In 1968, yet another new numbering system was introduced which incorporated a "year" into the registration number. 02 A 2168 – 12345 is an example of such a registration number.

"02" again meant 1/4-ton truck, the "A" was used as part of an alphabetical sequence, the "21" would be followed by "22" etc., but the "68" stayed the same all that year. The "12345" was the manufacturer's serial number of the vehicle, followed by 12346 etc.

Early 1970s-forward

In the early 70's, the system changed once again, and the "NB" numbering system was introduced. This is system is a little more specific than the previous systems, in that the alpha prefixes denote vehicle families rather than just weight class. NB was used on M151 vehicles instead of 20, 2, and 02, which previously indicated a 1/4-ton truck. The "NGQ" would be followed by "NGR" then "NGS" etc. This combination of three letters would, in theory, give 26x26x26 combinations.

Under this system positions 1 and 2 of the U.S. Army vehicle registration number use these code descriptions:

Tanks
JA Tank, combat, M48 series
JC Tank, combat, flamethrower
JD Tank, combat, 76 mm gun, M41 series
JF Tank, combat, 120 mm gun
JJ Tank, combat, 105 mm gun, M60 series
JK Tank, combat, 152 mm gun, M60 series
JP Combat engineer vehicle, M728
JQ Armored reconnaissance airborne assault vehicle, 152 mm, M551
JT Recovery vehicle, M51/M74/M88 series
JU Gun ft 90 mm, M56
JV Recovery vehicle, M578
JX Miscellaneous tanks
JZ Tank combat, M1 series

Combat Vehicles
KA Gun, antiaircraft, SP, 40 mm, M42 series
KB Howitzer, SP, 105 mm, M7 series

U.S.A.
123786

The type face shown here was only used a brief time, from April 22, 1942 until August 5, 1942. The size of the registration lettering changed as well, to one-inch lettering on motorcycles, and two-inch lettering on all other vehicles.

KC Howitzer, SP, 105 mm, M52 series
KD Howitzer, SP, 8-in, M110, gun, 175 mm, M107
KE Howitzer, SP, 105 mm, M108 series
KG Howitzer, SP, 155 mm, M109 series
KH Howitzer, SP, 8-in, M55 gun, 155 mm, M53 gun
KL Gun, antiaircraft, SP, 20 mm, M163 series
KZ Miscellaneous combat vehicles

Armored carriers
MB M113 Configuration
MC M113A configuration
MG M116 configuration
MH M114 configuration
MJ M571 configuration
MN M106 configuration
MP M125 configuration
MQ M548 configuration
MR M577 configuration
MS M132 configuration
MT Armored cars
MV Infantry or cavalry fighting vehicles, M2 & M3 series
MW Launcher rocket carrier, rocket launcher, SP, MLRS
MY Miscellaneous armored carriers

Tactical Vehicles
NA 1/4-ton vehicle configuration
NB 1/4-ton Vehicle configuration, M151 series
NC 1/2-ton vehicle configuration
NF 3/4-ton vehicle configuration
NG 1 1/4-ton vehicle configuration
NH 2 1/2-ton vehicle configuration, diesel
NJ 2 1/2-ton vehicle configuration, gasoline
NK 2 1/2-ton vehicle configuration, multifuel
NL 5-ton vehicle configuration, diesel
NM 5-ton vehicle configuration, gasoline
NN 5-ton vehicle configuration, multifuel
NP 6-50 ton vehicle configuration
NU Heavy equipment transporters
NW Trailers
NX Semitrailers
NY Miscellaneous tactical vehicles

Other automotive categories
PA Semitrailer, van, stake configuration
PB Trailer, bed configuration
PC Trailer, utility, and cargo configuration
PE Trailer, special-purpose, bakery, and kitchen
PF Trailer, special-purpose, electronics
PG Trailer, special-purpose, radar
PH Trailer, special-purpose, water

PJ Trailer, special-purpose, fuel
PK Trailer, special-purpose, other
PL Dolly and miscellaneous trailer configuration

Prototype Equipment
TE Prototype equipment (all configurations)

Construction equipment (self-propelled or towed)
UA Construction support equipment
UB Paving equipment
UC Tractors (tracked, wheeled industrial and agricultural)
UD Cranes
UE Graders and loaders

Power Generation equipment (vehicle mounted)
VA Generators-high power 60 Hz, 30, 45, and 60 KW
VB Generators-400 Hz, all KW sizes
VC Generators-low power, 60 HZ, 10 KW and under
VD Generator-medium power, 60 HZ, 15 KW
VE Generator-super power, 60 HZ, 100 KW and over
VF Generators-direct current, all KW sizes

The truck on the left has been camouflaged for desert warfare with a coat of overall Tan 686. The truck on the right is painted in the standard NATO woodland scheme. The cab and cargo covers of both trucks are the new-style camouflaged vinyl type.

Other ground forces support equipment (vehicle mounted or floating equipment)
WE Welding and gas generating equipment
WF Bridging equipment
WG Marine equipment
WJ Materials handling equipment, electric
WK Amphibious equipment (See note)
WL Materials handling equipment, diesel or gasoline
WR Food preparation equipment
WS Compressors
WT Miscellaneous support equipment (not otherwise classified)

Note: *Non-tactical wheeled vehicles C_ All commercial non-tactical vehicles (second position will be alpha, except I,O,Q,X, and Z). Also, the assignment of U.S. Army registration numbers to marine and amphibious equipment is limited to tactical river-crossing equipment and equipment used by recreational activities.*

This number system is still in use today, but once a piece of equipment is assigned a registration number, it is not changed. This is why even today trucks built in the 1950s are being surplused still baring registration numbers three systems back.

Agency Identification & Registration Numbers 1940-1955
Prior to late 1940, the registration numbers were painted in white, but at that time the prescribed color was changed to blue-drab. Thus, most WWII-era vehicles had their registration numbers applied in blue-drab. This color was selected because in black and white photography, the blue-drab blends almost perfectly into the base color of the vehicle. This characteristic was very valuable in the days before color photography was commonplace, as it hindered enemy intelligence-gathering abilities. This blue-drab was originally known as Quartermaster Corps ES-810, but a close match from FS-595B is FS-34158. This was to have changed to flat white in February 1945, however, it was stipulated that existing stocks of the blue-drab were to be exhausted. For that reason, some vehicles still appeared with blue-drab registration numbers in the later 1940s. After that

"Eve of Destruction," the sole remaining authentic Vietnam-era gun truck, is displayed at the Army Transportation Museum with the distinctive yellow band of the 8th Transportation Group.

Ralph Doubeck's CCKW displays the proper WWII-era markings.

ABCDE
FGHIJK
LMNOP
QRSTU
VWXYZ
1 2 3 4 5
6 7 8 9 0
& ? - .

In the post-WWII era, the style of lettering had another slight change, then using the pattern shown here. The introduction of the MERDC scheme brought about yet another slight change in lettering style, to a Vertical Gothic style, as seen here. With this scheme, the registration markings moved to inside the vehicle, and were to be marked in solid black

The introduction of the MERDC scheme brought about yet another slight change in lettering style, to a Vertical Gothic style, as seen here. With this scheme, the registration markings moved to inside the vehicle, and were to be marked in solid black.

time, the registration numbers, like most of the rest of the markings applied to solid green vehicles, were done in lusterless white, equivalent to today's No. 37875.

AR 850 specified that beginning in January 1942, the "W" prefix was no longer to be assigned as part of the registration number for new vehicles. However, on vehicles with the W already assigned it was NOT to be deleted, but the W was to remain as part of the registration number.

According to AR 850-5, September 25, 1936, the markings were "U.S.A." (note periods) followed by the registration number. During this time period this information could appear in 1-,2-, or 4-in. lettering. One-inch was used on motorcycles, 2-in. on trailers, and 4-in. on all other vehicles.

The lettering was to be applied with stencils, and were to be of a gothic, sans-serif style.

The stencil pattern for these letters was very specific. When restoring a vehicle, be sure to carefully match the lettering style for an authentic looking restoration. Shown above is the stencil pattern used by the U.S. Army from August 1942 until well into the post-WWII era.

Change number 2 to these regulations, April 22, 1942, changed the type style to a serif type.

On August 5, 1942, these regulations were again changed, with the type style reverting to the previously used sans-serif lettering and with the size now specified as 1-in. for motorcycles, and 2-in. for all other vehicles. Although actually introduced in 1942, the suffix "S" was not mentioned in AR-850-5 until Change 9, January 27, 1944. The "S" suffix was to be applied to the registration numbers of those vehicles that passed the radio interference suppression test, which was a large percentage of the vehicles. This "S" was to be made as conspicuous as possible by leaving a letter size space between it and the preceding numeral.

Agency Identification and Registration numbers 1955-1975

When AR 746-2300-1 "Marking and Packing of Supplies and Equipment, Color and Marking of Vehicles and Equipment" was issued December 29, 1955, the type style changed slightly. The shapes of the B, G, M, Q, S, W, 2, 3, 4, 5, 6, and 9 were different from those previously used. These markings were to be applied in 1-, 2-, 3-, or 4-in. letters and numbers, using the largest that would fit in the available space. Lusterless White 3715 was used on vehicles painted semi-gloss or lusterless olive drab.

By the time Army regulations AR 746-2300-1 was published on December 29, 1955, "U.S. Army" had replaced "U.S.A." as the agency identification. And by October of 1964 it was specified that the registration number and agency identification (U S Army) were always to be applied in 3-in. numbers and letters, unless there physically was not enough space, in which case smaller letters and numbers could be used.

While the text of TB 746-93-1 specifies periods after the "U S" in U S Army, the painting diagrams in the same technical bulletin omit them. An examination of photographs taken at the Mack and Kaiser factories and at Aberdeen Proving Grounds shows no periods, while those taken in country show some vehicles with and others without the periods. NOS pressure-sensitive markings do NOT include the periods.

In all cases, when traditional stencils were used, the "webs" were to be filled in by hand such that each letter or number is unbroken. However, this policy was not always adhered to on field-repainted vehicles.

Paint Or Decals?

TB 746-93-1, October 1964 authorized the use of permanent, pressure-sensitive vinyl markings on vehicles as an alternative to painting. Prior to that, the only accepted method of marking U.S. Army vehicles was with paint. The only stipulation attached to the application of vinyl markings was that adjacent markings be applied with the same method, as well as all markings of the same type on a given vehicle were to use the same method. That is, if the registration number was vinyl in one place on a vehicle, then all that vehicle's registration numbers were to be vinyl. The exception to this is the National Symbol, which was specifically permitted to be applied with different methods in different locations.

It has been my experience that when exposed to the weather, these markings last about three years. As an aside, the Marine Corps authorized the use of self-adhesive decals in about the same time period, although

These markings can be interpreted as 18th Brigade, 35th Group, 553rd Engineer Company, Float Bridge, 97th vehicle.

The post WWII-era continued to use the same basic unit marking style introduced in August of 1942.

The more familiar, later-style WWII markings are shown on the rear of an M3A1 scout car.

they used yellow as the marking color rather than white. Also, according to USAF T.O. 36-1-3, 15 (September 1958), the only approved method of marking Air Force blue vehicles was with yellow reflectorized decals. The Air Force did not use reflectorized markings on olive-drab vehicles.

Agency Identification & Registration Numbers 1975-mid 1980s

The lettering style used in the MERDC scheme is similar to the one used in the overall 24087 scheme, with only the shapes of some of the characters changing. When comparing the 24087 style with the MERDC style, note the slightly different shapes of the C, D, G, 3, 6, and 9. Also, this typeface is slightly different from the one used with the later three-color NATO scheme. Unless otherwise specified, all lettering described below should be done in No. 37078 Black when applied as part of the MERDC scheme.

According to AR750-58, with the MERDC paint scheme the agency identification and registration number were no longer to be applied to the exterior of the equipment, but rather marked on the interior. Normally this is just the registration number, and it is applied to the interior of the doors in 4-in. numbers. The registration number is permanently assigned when the vehicle is delivered and is not changed, regardless of the number of times a vehicle is painted or reassigned.

Agency Identification & Registration Numbers Mid-1980s To Present

The lettering style used with the NATO or CARC scheme was the same vertical Gothic style that had been used with the MERDC scheme. Again, this style varies only slightly from its predecessor. The color of lettering also changed, and is now dependent on the background, sometimes with two colors being used in a single number or letter. Unless otherwise specified, all lettering to vehicles in the NATO scheme should be applied in this manner. Strangely, pressure- sensitive lettering is still authorized, but I am not real sure how they could be configured into the multicolor format.

The CARC scheme also brought about the return of the agency identification "U S Army", missing from the MERDC scheme. According to TM 43-0139 (July 27, 1988), with this paint scheme the registration number AND agency identification are to be applied to the interior of vehicles. Usually, it is applied to the interior of the doors using lettering not exceeding 4 in. in height. The registration number and agency identification should be placed so that they are visible without opening the door. There are no periods used in the agency identification U S Army.

When purchasing stencils or lettering, compare what is being sold to what is shown in these figures letter by letter to insure you get the correct letters for your era. The military used an interlocking brass stencil set in many cases, which not only insured the right shape letters, but also the correct spacing.

National Symbol

On August 5, 1942, the national symbol (five-point

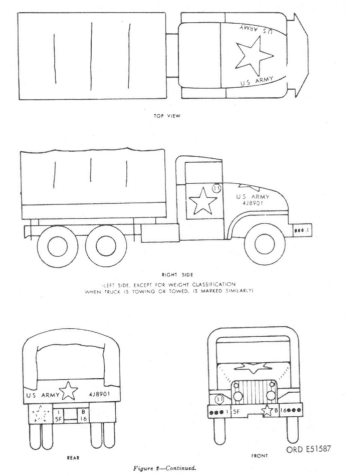

TOP VIEW

RIGHT SIDE
(LEFT SIDE, EXCEPT FOR WEIGHT CLASSIFICATION WHEN TRUCK IS TOWING OR TOWED, IS MARKED SIMILARLY)

REAR

FRONT

ORD E51587

Figure 2—Continued.

In the postwar era, the star has been rotated 180 degrees from its WWII orientation, with one point now facing forward. Invasion stars were not used after WWII.

star) became mandatory on soft-skin vehicles assigned to tactical units. On February 15, 1945, this was amended to include vehicles assigned to Army Ground Forces installations.

The familiar five-pointed star was centered in the largest area of the top, both sides, front, and rear of each vehicle. It was not applied to canvas or vinyl, nor where canvas, windshields, spares, etc. will obscure it. The circle surrounding the star (the "invasion star") was introduced in about November 1942 to aid aerial identification. This surround was specified to have a thickness equal to 1/7 of the diameter of the star. Although originally intended only for the horizontal (hood) star, soon all the stars on European theater vehicles seemed to have surrounds. Initially, these surrounds were painted on in lusterless chrome yellow, but the yellow soon gave way to the more common white. Some early vehicles, usually with yellow surrounds, had the fields of the horizontal stars painted blue. The field is the area inside the circle that is not taken up by the star. Later, it was fairly common for the horizontal star's field to be painted with a gas-detecting paint, Liquid Vesicant Detector, M-5. This was a pea green paint that would change colors to a deep red if exposed to poisonous gases. Unfortunately, it would also change colors when exposed to heat. The hood exposed the paint not only to engine heat, but heat from the sun as well, causing it to turn red.

The surrounded star (invasion star) was not normally found on vehicles in the Pacific Theater. The invasion star is not appropriate for any vehicle in the post-WWII era. Ambulances did not carry the national symbol in any form.

The normal locations for these stars are the: hood, both doors, the front bumper, and centered on the tailgate. For open-cab vehicles the placement was slightly different. The size of these stars varies depending upon the vehicle.

During the WWII era, the star was oriented such that on horizontal surfaces the single point was toward the rear of the vehicle. In the post-WWII era, the orientation of the star was changed so that one point was directly toward the vehicle front. USAF vehicles in the postwar era continued to orient the single point to the rear. The sizes for the most commonly collected postwar vehicles are listed below.

Vehicle	Size in inches	Location
1/4-Ton Utility Trucks	6	Right, left sides
	6	Front fenders or cowl
	20	Top of hood
3/4-Ton Cargo Trucks	6	Tailgate, front bumper
	16	Right, left doors
	20	Top of hood
2 1/4-Ton Cargo Trucks	6	Tailgate, front bumper
	16	Right, left doors
	20	Top of hood
2 1/2-Ton Van Trucks	2	Front bumper
	6	Right, left van sides
	20	Rear of van body
	20	Top of hood
2 1/2-Ton Fuel Tankers	6	Front bumper
	16	Right, left doors
	20	Top of hood
	20	Rear doors, centered
5-Ton Cargo Trucks	6	Tailgate, front bumper
	16	Right, left doors
	20	Top of hood
5-Ton Truck Tractors	6	Front bumper
	16	Right, left doors
	20	Top of hood
5-Ton Wreckers	6	Front bumper
	6	Rear of hood box
	16	Right, left doors
	20	Top of hood
10-Ton Truck Tractors	6	Front bumper
	16	Right, left doors
	20	Top of hood
1/4-Ton Two-Wheel Trailers	6	Front, rear
	6	Right, left sides
1 1/2-ton Tank Trailers	0	Right, left sides
	12	Front, rear top
6-Ton Van Semi-Trailers	20	Front, rear
	20	Right, left sides
12-Ton Cargo Semi-Trailers	20	front, rear
	20	Right, left sides
12-ton Van Semi-Trailers	20	Front, rear
	20	Right, left side
	32	Top of van roof
12-Ton Fuel Tank Semi-Trailers	20	Front, rear
		Right, left side
	20	Top of tank

The star with the circle around it, known as the invasion star, was originally intended to only be applied to horizontal surfaces, such as the hood of this CCKW. Notice that one point of the star points directly to the rear of the vehicle.

Flat-Bed Trailers	6	Right, left sides
	6	Rear
Road Graders	10	Right, left sides
	20	Top of cab roof
Truck-Mounted Cranes	16	Front
	16	Right, left sides
	20	Top
Self-Propelled Cranes (Track)	20	Right, left sides
	20	Right, rear, top
Tractors	12	Right, left sides
	20	Top of hood
	20	Rear
Road Rollers	6	Rear
	12	Side
	20	Top
Fork Lifts	6	Right, left sides
	10	Top, rear
Warehouse Trucks	6	Rear
	10	Front
	12	Top
Tanks	12	Rear (2)
	16	Top of turret
	20	Right, left sides of turret
	20	Front of bull (top)
Armored Personnel Carriers	10	Front, rear
	16	Right, left sides
	20	Top

On vertical surfaces one point was oriented squarely upwards regardless of service or era.

With the introduction of the MERDC scheme, the large white star so proudly worn by U.S. vehicles gave way to two, small (fitting inside a 3-in. circle) black stars centered one each on the front and rear of the vehicles. These were usually placed on the front bumper and tailgates of wheeled vehicles. This was carried over into the NATO scheme as well.

Other Hood Markings

During WWII, vehicles that had been winterized or prepared for desert use with glycol coolant were specially marked on the leading edge of the hood or radiator shell. Because this data was to be changed if the coolant was, the markings were done with gasoline-soluble paint. The format for these markings was:

WINTERIZED -30   **PRESTONE 44**
ANTIFREEZE 1943   **ETHYLENE-GLYCOL**

These markings were usually applied with 1/2- to 1-in. stenciled lettering.

Anyone who has raised the hood of a military vehicle can appreciate the weight of them, and the hazard that one falling would be. That is why Uncle Sam, in AR 746-2300-1, dated December 29, 1955 specified that 1-in. letters with the legend:

WARNING: SECURE HOOD
IN RAISED POSITION WITH
SAFETY HOOK BEFORE
SERVICING ENGINE

These should be applied to the rear underside area of

each vehicle's hood using white paint. These markings are applied with black paint to MERDC and NATO camouflaged vehicles.

During WWII there were no such markings applied to the underside of the hood.

Lube Markings

The legend "LUBE ORDER" was often stenciled on the holder for a vehicle's lube card during WWII.

The application of 3/4-in. red dots around grease fittings came about in 1943. It was discontinued per TB 9-265 (December 5, 1958), although this discontinuance was also mentioned as early as October 1952 in TM 5-505. Many vehicles had an undercoating applied at the factory, and the black was left visible underneath until the vehicles were repainted in the field years later.

Tire Pressure & Speed Markings

The familiar tire pressure stenciling — TP-40, for example —, above each wheel position is strictly a post-WWII innovation, dating back to 1946. Prior to that the only such stenciling found was on the dashboard.

In the post-WWII era, the tire pressure markings were in 1-in. letters directly above each wheel, except on tandem-axle vehicles, where the marking is centered above and between the axles. These are marked with the letters "TP" preceding the numerals for the correct tire pressure (i.e. "TP 50"). TB 746-93-1 also states that the tire pressure should be marked on the dashboard of the vehicle, and implies that this should also be done in the 1-in. letters, though in most instances the vehicle's data plate lists the tire pressure.

When the first MERDC and NATO paint schemes were introduced, the tire pressure markings were retained, although they were applied in black.

During WWII, vehicles passing through the British Isles were marked with their convoy speed restriction. This was done in 2-in. black or white Gothic lettering applied to the left side of the tailgate or body. The format used was:

MAX SPEED
25 MPH

The number assigned as the maximum speed varied. In the case of vehicles in the post-war period, AR 746-2300-1 dated 29 DEC 1955 specified that "MAX SPEED" and the vehicles maximum high gear speed are to be stenciled on the dash in one-inch letters if that information is not included on the vehicle operation data plate.

Left Hand Drive

Again, only on vehicles passing through the British Isles during WWII was it required that the following marking be applied on the right side rear of the vehicle.

CAUTION
LEFT HAND DRIVE
NO SIGNALS

Excessive Fuel Tank Pressure

On fuel tanks where the marking would be readily visible (such as 6x6 trucks), it is correct to measure 2 in. down from the top of the tank and mark the following in 1-in. letters, with a 1/4 x 8 in. line:

CAUTION ——————
DO NOT FILL ABOVE THIS LINE

On vehicles where the fuel tank is not readily visible (such as the M-37), as near as possible to the filler pipe should be the following marking in 1-in. letters:

CAUTION DO NOT OVERFILL-ALLOW FOR EXPANSION

These markings, introduced after WWII, were to be done in black on camouflage painted vehicles, and in white on vehicles painted in the earlier schemes.

Maximum Safe Fuel Acceptance Rates
The maximum safe fuel-filling rate was to be marked on each fuel tank near the filler cap. When the tank is enclosed, this marking was to be as near as possible to the filler cap. It could be arranged like either of the two examples below, depending on space. These markings were also in 1-in. letters.

MAX. SAFE
FUEL ACCEPT
28 GPM (or)
MAX. SAFE FUEL
ACCEPT 28 GPM

Deuces and 10-ton trucks had a 28-gpm acceptance rate like shown in the example, 5 tonners a 31-gpm rate, and M37 variants 23 gpm. For smaller vehicles, the M38A1 rate is 17 gpm, while the M170 and MUTTs have a 20-gpm rate.

These markings, introduced after WWII, were to be done in black on camouflage-painted vehicles, and in white on vehicles painted in the earlier schemes.

Air Tanks
While the following marking was quite commonly found in 1-in. letters on trucks equipped with air, or air/hydraulic brakes, there was no Army-wide directive for this. While the vehicle TM required this draining to be done daily, the marking of such was strictly a local command Standard Operating Procedure. Nevertheless, for both realism and safety's sake this marking is not a bad idea. This is done as near as possible to the air tanks.

Drain Air Tanks Daily
These markings, introduced after WWII, were to be done in black on camouflage-painted vehicles, and in white on vehicles painted in the earlier schemes.

Batteries
Another common local SOP was the following legend usually applied to the battery box door in 1-in. letters.

CHECK BATTERIES
DAILY

While on the subject of batteries, there is an additional marking that gets judging points. TM 9-6140-200-15 requires that batteries in the tropics have the specific gravity of their electrolyte dropped from the normal 1.280 into the 1.200-1.225 range. Batteries with this tropical electrolyte are required to be marked with a 1-in. white dot near the positive terminal.

These markings, introduced after WWII, were to be done in black on camouflage painted vehicles, and in white on vehicles painted in the earlier schemes.

Unit Markings
The infamous "bumper numbers" are a source of much confusion. The Army has used two basic styles of unit markings. The first was in use from the 1930s until mid 1941, when the second was introduced. The second system, with some slight changes remains in use today. The first system, unlike the other markings described in this appendix, was not applied with stencils. Rather, these markings were applied by sign painters, using both upper- and lower-case letters. Initially, these markings were done in white, but the marking color was changed to blue-drab in late 1940.

With this system, the marking consisted of merely of an abbreviation of the unit's regimental code (division and company, troop, regiment, or battery). These markings were centered on the front doors of vehicles so equipped. On vehicles without doors, the markings were on the body sill beneath the doorway, or applied as two lines on both sides of the cowl. The words "company," "battery," "battalion," etc. were abbreviated in these markings.

In 1940, the marking concept was expanded to include the vehicle's order of march number. The order of march number amounted to the vehicle's convoy position when the company was to move as a unit. Normally, the commander's vehicle was No. 1, and the rest numbered sequentially from there.

The order of march numbers were not painted on the sides of the vehicles, but rather were the beginnings of the bumper markings. The order of march number was painted on the far right side of the front bumper (looking from the front). Preceding it were the regimental markings, as on the doors, LESS the abbreviations for the words "company", "battery," "battalion," etc. Placement of the markings on the rear of the vehicles was not as consistent as it was on the front, and some vehicles had no rear unit markings whatsoever.

The capital letters were approximately 3 in. tall, and the entire marking was both over and under scored with lines about 1/2-in. wide. In August 1942, the system of unit markings was changed to the system that is still in use, and the markings reverted to being painted in white.

There are four pieces of information given in these bumper markings. Using a front bumper as an example, reading left to right, the information contained is:

Major command (Army/Corps/Division)
Intermediate command (regiment/battalion)

APPENDIX 2

Unit or activity (company)
Vehicle number (order of march)

When applied to bumperettes, the same information is arranged as follows

Left
Major Command (Army/Corps/Division)
Intermediate Command (regiment/battalion)

Right
Unit or activity (company)
Vehicle number (order of march)

Abbreviations normally found in the unit identification markings are found below.

Abbreviations normally found in the unit identification markings are found below.

The first group of numbers desginated the smallest appropriate unit listed below, using the codes listed.

Division (infantry): Arabic numeral.
Division (armored) Arabic numeral followed by triangle 3 inches high with 1/4-inch stroke.
Division (cavalry): Arabic numeral followed by letter C.
Corps (army): Roman numeral.
Corps (cavalry): Roman numeral followed by letter C.
Corps (armored): Roman numeral followed by triangle 3 inches high with 1/4-inch stroke.

Army: Arabic numeral followed by letter A.
Air force: Arabic numeral followed by a star 3 inches high.
Zone of communications: ZC.
Army Ground Forces: AGF
Services of Supply: SOS.
General Headquarters: GHQ.
Zone of interior: ZI.
Reception center: RC
Replacement training center: RTC preceded by arm or service symbol.
Training center: TC preceded by arm or service symbol.
Firing center: FC preceded by arm or service symbol.
All others non-conflicting letters.

The second group designates separate regiments, brigades, groups, etc by appropriate number or symbol, followed by arm or service in accordance with the abbreviations listed below.

Airborne: AB
Army Air Forces units: Star 3 inches high.
Antiaircraft: AA
Amphibious: AM
Armored regiment: Triangle 3 inches high with 1/4-mch stroke.
Cavalry: C
Chemical Warfare Service: G
Coast Artillery Corps: CA
Corps of Engineers: E
Field Artillery : F
Infantry:I (preceded by dash 1/2-inch square)
Medical Department: M
Military police: P
Ordnance Department: letter O (preceded by dash 1/2-inch square)

Quartermaster Corps: Q
Signal Corps: S
Tank Destroyer: TD
Tank group: TG

The third group will designate companies and similar organizations by letters in accordance with the following code:

Organization: Designation
Headquarters and headquarters company (or headquarters and headquarters and service company) of lowest unit identification in previous groups: HQ
Service company of lowest unit identified in service groups: SV
Headquarters and headquarters company of battalion not previously identified: Numerical designation of battalion followed by letters HQ.
Service company of battalion not previously identified: Battalion number followed by letters SV
Lettered company: Letter designation.
Separate company identified in second group: X or abbreviation of company.
Antitank: AT
Maintenance: MT
Heavy weapons: HW
Cannon: CN
Reconnaissance:R
Train: TN
Weapons: W

"Name" company (other than headquarters company, headquarters and service company or service company): Non-conflicting letters assigned for identification purposes, preceded by the battalion number, when necessary.

Fourth group designates the order of march. This number will designate the position of the vehicle in the normal order of march. Vehicles assigned to any headquarters will be combined for purposes of numbering with those of the appropriate headquarters company or similar organization, and will be given the smaller serial numbers therein.

Major Command, Organization, or Activity:
(1) Army. The Arabic numeral as assigned, followed by the letter A.
(2) Corps. The Roman numeral as assigned, followed by the following applicable symbol:
  (a) Airborne. Letters AB.
  (b) Armored. Equilateral triangle with base down.
(3) Division. Arabic numeral is assigned, followed by the following applicable symbol:
  (a) Airborne. Letters AB.
  (b) Armored. Equilateral triangle with base down.
(4) Brigade. Arabic numeral as assigned, followed by letters BG.\
(5) Group. Arabic numeral as assigned, followed by letters GP.
(6) Continental Army Command. Letters CARC.
(7) Army Air Defense Command. Letters AADC.

(8) Military District of Washington. Letters MDW.
(9) Reception Center. Letters RC.
(10) Replacement Training Center. Letters RTC, preceded by the applicable branch of service symbol.
(11) Training Center. Letters TC, preceded by the applicable branch of service symbol.
(12) U.S. Army Materiel Command. Letters AMC.
(13) U.S. Army Supply and Maintenance Command. Letters SMC.
(14) U.S. Army Mobility Command. Letters MOCOM.
(15) U.S. Army Missile Command. Letters MICOM.
(16) U.S. Army Electronics Command. Letters ELC.
(17) U.S. Army Munitions Command. Letters MUCOM.
(18) U.S. Army Weapons Command. Letters WCOM.
(19) U.S. Army Test and Evaluation Command. Letters TEC.
(20) U.S. Army Combat Development Command. Letters CDC.
(21) Major Overseas Commands. Appropriate and non-conflicting letters to properly identify the command.
(22) Other Major Commands, Organizations, or Activities. Appropriate and non-conflicting letters and where applicable, numerals to properly identify the command, organization, or activity.

Intermediate Organization or Activity

(1) Regiment, Battalion, Separate Company or Detachment, or Similar Unit. Arabic numeral as assigned, followed by the applicable branch of service symbol.
(a) Airborne. Letters AB.
(b) Antiaircraft. Letters AA.
(c) Amphibious. Letters APH.
(d) Armored. Equilateral triangle with base down.
(e) Chemical. Letter C.
(f) Engineer. Letter E.
(g) Field Artillery. Letter F.
(h) Infantry. Letter I, to be separated from the numeral by a dash 1/2 inch long.
(i) Medical. Letter M.
(j) Military Police. Letter P.
(k) Ordnance. Letter O, to be separated from the numeral by a dash 1/2 inch long.
(1) Quartermaster. Letter Q.
(m) Signal. Letter S.
(n) Transportation. Letter T.
(2) Organizations under the Combat Arms Regimental System (DA Pam 220-1).
(a) Battle Group (attached). Arabic numeral as assigned, followed by the letter B and basic identification of the infantry unit.
(b) Reconnaissance Squadron. Arabic numeral assigned, followed by the letter R and basic identification of the cavalry unit.
(c) Tank Battalion. Arabic numeral as assigned, followed by the armored symbol and basic identification of the armored unit.
(d) Field Artillery Battalion. Arabic numeral as assigned, followed by the letter F and basic identification of the field artillery unit.

(3) Installation. Appropriate non-conflicting letters, normally not to exceed 3, to identify the installation.
(4) Other Intermediate organization or activity. Appropriate non-conflicting letters and where applicable, numerals, to properly identify the organization or activity.
(5) No intermediate organization or activity. Letter X.
(i) Unit or Activity is as follows:
(1) Company, Battery, or Other Company Type Unit. Letters as assigned, or one of the following symbols where applicable.
(a) Headquarters and headquarters unit, or headquarters and headquarters service unit. Letters HQ. If the unit is of a battalion not previously identified, the numerical designation of the battalion will precede the letters HQ.
(b) Service Unit. Letters SV. When the unit is of a battalion not previously identified, the numerical designation of the battalion will precede the letters SV.
(2) Separate company or detachment identified in h above. One of the following symbols, as applicable:
(a) Ammunition. Letters AM.
(b) Automatic Weapons. Letters AW.
(c) Construction. Letters CON.
(d) Depot. Letters DP.
(e) Guided Missile. Letters GM.
(f) General Support. Letters GS.
(g) General Automotive Maintenance. Letters GAS.
(h) Heavy Weapons. Letters HW.
(i) Maintenance. Letters MT.
(j) Direct Support. Letters DS.
(k) Missile. Letters MSL.
(1) Mortar. Letters MR.
(m) Parachute Maintenance. Letters PM.
(n) Reconnaissance. Letter R.
(o) Repair. Letters RP.
(p) Rocket. Letters RT.
(q) Other Name Units. Appropriate and non-conflicting letters, normally not to exceed three, to properly identify the name of the unit. When necessary, the numerical designation of the battalion will precede the applicable symbol.
(3) Transportation Motor Pools at installation. Letters TMP.
(4) Organization or activity fully identified in h above. Letter X.

The vehicles will be numbered as indicated below.
(1) This marking is the sequence number of the vehicle in the normal order to march within the unit to which it is assigned.
(2) Vehicles assigned to any headquarters will be numbered with the vehicles of the appropriate headquarters unit, and will be given the lower sequence numbers used therein.

When used in bumper markings, the letters I and O

were preceded by a dash or a dot. This was to differentiate them from the numerals 1 and 0. The exception to this policy is when the letter I is used in a Roman numeral designating a Corps.

Division was the least of the high command levels used in bumper markings, and they were designated by an Arabic number followed by branch symbol. Division numbers were one or two digits. Between the division and intermediate designation there would sometimes be another Arabic number with a suffix of GP or BG, representing group or brigade.

Army numbers were designated by Arabic numerals followed by the letter A, and were usually only applied to Corps or Army headquarters level vehicles.

An intermediate unit was assigned similar numbers. They were three or four digits, and immediately followed the major command, but were separated by a dash from the major command numbers.

As a rule, only the three lowest level of assignment, including company, was marked on the bumpers. In some exceptional cases, four levels of assignment were shown.

At levels below battalion, headquarters units were company level functions, and as such HQ was used as the company designator, and an X placed in the intermediate level position.

However, at the division level, there were several headquarters companies. These were special detached activities, and used a slightly different marking scheme. Instead of a company letter, the unit number and branch service code was stenciled on the bumper.

These numbers are to be applied in the largest practical size, and not to exceed 4 in. tall. Any symbols used will be of "about the same size" and have the same stroke width as the letters and numbers used. It was originally specified that these markings be applied with gasoline-soluble paint.

A star, usually 3 to 6 in. in size, was placed on the center of the front bumper. On vehicles where the front winch interfered with this placement, the star was moved to whichever side of the front bumper had the most space. In some cases, there was a star placed on either side of the winch opening.
TB 746-93-1, October 1964, revised the specification to allow these markings in removable vinyl lettering or the previously specified gasoline-soluble paint.

During the Vietnam War, certain units had there own distinctive insignia applied. Some units painted logos on

the vehicle doors, others used various colored bands on the hoods. If you are considering painting your vehicle to represent a truck assigned to one of these units, it is essential to obtain period photographs in order to properly replicate these markings.

When the MERDC scheme was adopted, the unit markings remained the same, but were then applied in lusterless black, and the size of the national symbol was greatly reduced 3 in.

Good Driver

Vehicles built after August 1962 had DA Label 76, a good driver, applied to them. This water transfer decal has a yellow background with a black border and text printed on it. On trucks other than Jeeps, this was applied to the inside of the left door, near the top front corner. M-38s had them applied directly under the windshield wiper motor, M38A1s had them on the map compartment door, and MUTTs had them on the windshield frame to the left of the steering column. Also, on M-series vehicles, each instrument's function was labeled in white lettering on the instrument panel beneath the gauge.

Bridge Weight Classification Markings

The bridge weight classification plate has its origins with the British during WWII and in 1943 was adopted by U.S. forces.

Often, collectors and others mistakenly believe that the bridge weight classification number is simply the vehicle's weight, rounded up to the nearest ton. The vehicle classification number represents the effects of the vehicle on a bridge while crossing it. The effect is a combination of gross weight, weight distribution of the vehicle, speed at which the vehicle crosses the bridge, and the impact loading of the vehicle on the bridge.

The weight classification of a given vehicle is assigned based upon a complicated formula taking in to

The post-WWII bridge plate featured a single line of moveable numbers, allowing it to be changed for different loads. The C was to be displayed when towing a load, indicating combination weight. When the NATO camouflage scheme came into use, the yellow bridge plates were discontinued in favor of green plates.

The basic bridge weight classification of vehicles was also marked on the passenger's door in the post-WWII era.

M715	4
V17A/MTQ	11
V18A/MTQ	11
XM706 Commando	8

consideration many factors. The military recommendation for determining the weight classification number of a vehicle is to look it up in FM 5-36. Failing that, the recommendation is to use the gross weight of tracked vehicles, and 85 percent of the gross weight in tons of wheeled vehicles.

The weight classifications of many commonly collected military vehicles are shown in the following table.

BRIDGE WEIGHT CLASSIFICATION OF COMMONLY COLLECTED WWII VEHICLES

Vehicle	Unladen Class	Loaded Class
M1,A1 Wrecker	13	
M4 Sherman		30
M5 tractor		14
M8A1 tractor		30
M8,20 Armored car	7	9
M26,A1	28	
M29C	2	3
WC51	3	
WC52,56,57	4	
G7107 Chevy	5	6
U7144 Autocar	5	14
B666 Brockway	17	
T980 Diamond T	18	70

Note: Unlike the postwar system which assigns a different "M number" to virtually each body style, during WWII the designation CCKW was applied to virtually every configuration of the GMC chassis. This causes confusion when it comes to military load classification, with unladen classes known to vary between 6 and 8, while loaded swung from 9 to 10. Though there are some exceptions, as a rule specialist bodies are at the lower end of the range, while cargos and tippers tend to have higher classification numbers.

WEIGHT CLASSIFICATION OF POST WWII WHEELED VEHICLES

M34	5	10
M35	5	10
M35A1		10
M36	5	10
M37	3	4
M41		18
M47		10
M48		6
M49,49C,A1C,A2C	6	10
M50,A1		11
M51,A1,A2		21
M52,A1,A2		8
M54,A1,A2		20
M55,A1,A2	10	21
M59		10
M60		13
M62		24
M108		11
M109,A1,A2,A3	7	10
M123,C,D,A1C	15	15
M125	12	34
M135	6	11
M211	6	11
M215		11
M217,217C		10
M220		10
M221		5
M222		10
M246,A1,A2		23
M275		5
M292,A1,A2,A3,A4,A5	11	19
M342		12
M543,A1,A2		17
M656		11

WEIGHT CLASSIFICATION OF TOWED WHEELED VEHICLES

M10 Ammo	5
M15A1	59
M15A2	78
M21 Ammo	9
M23 Ammo	11
M271,A1 Pole	7
M100	4
M101,A1	6
M104,A1,A2	6
M105,A1,A2	6
M106,A1,A2	4
M107,A1,A2	4
M127,A1,A1C	30
M127A2C	29
M149,A1	4
M172	19
M172A1	36
M269,A1	24
M270,A1	24
M332 Ammo	4
M345	20
M416	4

COMBINATION VEHICLES

M35 W/M105	7	12
M54 W/M105	9	20
M52 W/M131A1C	13	30
M123 W/M15A2	25	78

Sources for this chart are TB-746-93-1 and a military manual, whose cover is missing, thus the name, number and date of publication are unknown.

Vehicle Applications

As a rule, weight classification numbers are not appropriate on Jeeps and other smaller vehicles. Regulations do not require classification numbers displayed on vehicles having a gross weight of 3 tons or less (even though in most cases these classification numbers have been calculated and are tabulated). However, during WWII some Jeeps had them applied as a local SOP. They are not required on vehicles having rated payloads of 3/4 to 1 and 1 1/2 tons. This later policy does NOT apply to vehicles authorized for towing loads. Thus, an M-37 should display a classification plate (it's authorized to tow a load), while the similar M-43 would not (even though built on similar chassis, it has no pintle hook, and thus couldn't tow a load). Local commanders have wide authority, and may have authorized or required some Jeeps to display classification numbers in the post-WWII era as well.

WWII

In its earliest incarnation, the US Army used a 7-in. square plate, but its later design became a disk. The British had used a simple 9-inch diameter yellow disk, which found use by US units as well. Regardless of shape, the weight classification permanently marked on it in black. For combination vehicles (trucks pulling trailers, etc), there were two numbers on the plate. The lower number is the single vehicle weight, while the upper number is the combination weight classification. If the design of the vehicle was such that the right front corner of the vehicle had a suitable surface, this information (including the yellow circle) was painted directly onto the vehicle. In some instances of the weight classification was marked directly on the bumper in a yellow rectangle as wide as the bumper is tall.

Post-WWII Semi-Gloss OD Scheme

After WWII, just as vehicles became more complicated, so did the weight classification plate. Gone were the simple painted disk or rectangle, replaced with a sophisticated assembly with changeable numbers for different vehicles and loads, and a reversible top plate with a red "C" on it. This "C" was also destined to confuse collectors and public alike.

There were two types of vehicle signs: front and side. Front signs, used on most vehicles, show the classification of the laden vehicle. Trailers do not use front signs. Side signs on towing vehicles and trailers were used to show the classification of the laden towing vehicles or trailers only by themselves.

In the postwar era, the familiar moveable number plate became the standard, and it was also painted yellow. This continued through the mid-1960s (semi-gloss vehicles were to use lusterless yellow, color chip 33538 was specified in TB 746-93-1, October 1964). The front sign was mounted on the front of the vehicle, above or on the bumper, and below the driver's line of vision. In most instances it was bolted to the grill of the vehicle, although it could be mounted directly to the vehicle when a suitable surface existed (the front fender of 5- and 10-to trucks for example). When possible, it was placed on the right side of the vehicle, facing forward. The side sign was on the vehicle's right side facing outward, typically in the upper right corner of the passenger door. It is a 6-in. yellow circle with the vehicle's basic vehicle weight classification marked on it in black. The yellow used for this is Lusterless Yellow 33538, and the black of the number is Gloss Black 17038. The inscription on the side sign was as large as the sign allowed.

The front sign indicates the vehicle's laden solo class, except on towing vehicles and tank transporters.

Bridge Weight Markings On Trailers & Other Towed Loads

For WWII-era combination weights, an approximation can be made by adding the towing vehicle's classification to 1/2 of the towed vehicle's classification.

In the postwar era, to quote FM5-170:

"When a single vehicle tows another vehicle at a distance less than 30.5 meters and the vehicles are not designed to operate as one unit, the temporary vehicle MLC number may be assigned to this combination. The classification number assigned is nine-tenths the sum of the normal vehicle classification numbers if the total of both classifications is less than 60. If the sum of the two military classification numbers is 60 or over, then the total becomes the MLC number for the nonstandard combination."

In other words, if you are towing a trailer or another vehicle with your historic military vehicle, then you get to display the nifty red letter "C" above the weight classification number on the front of your towing vehicle. This "C" denotes combination weight classification.

On towing vehicles, the front sign indicates the train's combined load class. Above this number, write the letter C to distinguish the vehicle as a towing vehicle. The side sign (used only by prime movers of combination vehicles and trailers) indicates the laden solo class of the prime mover or trailer. Single vehicles carry only the front sign, towing vehicles carry both front and side signs, and trailers carry side signs only.

MERDC Scheme Bridge Classification Markings

Lusterless Yellow No. 33538 continued to be the color with the introduction of the four-color camouflage era of the 70s (as specified in TB 43-0209, October 1976). The complete kit through this era was NSN 9905-00-565-6267, if you are lucky enough to find one.

NATO Scheme Bridge Classification Marking

With the change to the three-color "NATO" camo scheme, the yellow weight classification plate was done, replaced with the now familiar 383 Green classification plate (TM 43-0139). The yellow door marking was also done away with, replaced by a black number with black circle around it. Equipment prepared for deployment overseas during Desert Shield/Desert Storm had their classification plates (like the rest of the vehicle) repainted in the sand color No. 30277.

Other Markings

Wreckers, fuel tankers, ordnance disposal, and other specialized vehicles used a variety of special markings. The appropriate manuals should be consulted for more information on these.

When authorized by the responsible commander, vehicles used in non-tactical areas, which could present a hazard due to size or function, could have yellow stripes painted on the bumper. These stripes were to be 4 in. wide and inclined at 45-degree angles from the centerline to form an inverted V pattern. This type of marking was most commonly found on wreckers and 10-ton tractors. This yellow was Gloss Yellow 13538.

Further, the service brake glad hands, covers, and chains on the rear of 6x6s, and on 5- and 10-tons, were painted yellow (as opposed to the blue now used). Similarly, the glad hands, covers, and chains on the emergency side were to be painted red.

Final Thoughts

No accessory, piece of gear, or sign will be as visible to the public as the paint and markings of a vehicle. It is therefore extremely important that the finish and markings be applied properly, and researched properly. Improper color or inappropriate markings could necessitate an expensive repaint and depreciate the value of a vehicle.

Must-Have References for Militaria Collectors

Standard Catalog of Military Firearms
The Collector's Price and Reference Guide • 6th Edition
by Phillip Peterson

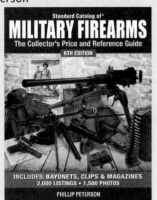

If you collect military firearms, your best insurance policy is to know what you're collecting and how much it's worth. There's no better source of this knowledge than the updated, revised 6th edition. From handguns to rifles to shotguns and fully-automatic machine guns and submachine guns, this book provides a remarkable complete guide to the world's military firearms and their accessories.

Softcover • 8 ¼ x 10 7/8 • 528 pages • 1,500 b&w photos

Item#Y0772 $32.99

Mauser Military Rifles of the World
4th Edition
by Robert W.D. Hall

The ultimate Mauser military rifle reference, this superior guide is packed with more models, all-color photos and Mauser history tailored to meet your needs and collecting interests. With *more than 50 countries represented*, 75 years of Mauser military rifle production is meticulously cataloged with descriptions, historical details, model specifications and markings, making for easy and accurate identification of arms.

Hardcover • 8 ¼ x 10 7/8 • 448 pages • 1,300+ color photos

Item#Z0322 $49.99

Old Gunsights & Rifle Scopes
Identification and Price Guide
by Nick Stroebel

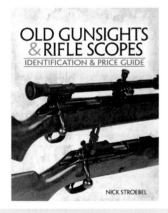

The first and only collecting and price guide for scopes and sights! Whether you're a shooting buff, collector, historian, antique dealer, or military aficionado, this book helps you identify, research, and determine market pricing for old gunsights and rifle scopes—all in one easy-to-use volume. Inside this book, you'll find over 750 photos, along with market values for collectible scopes and sights from the mid-1800's through 1985.

Softcover • 8 ¼ x 10 7/8 • 584 pages • 100 color photos, 650 b&w photos

Item#Z2346 $34.99

Flayderman's Guide to Antique American Firearms and Their Values
9th Edition
by Norm Flayderman

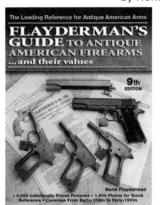

Flayderman's is where it's at for checking updated collector values of all your antique arms, while you brush up on the characteristics of vintage firearms manufactured between the colonial era and 1900. Meticulously researched data, descriptions of stampings and markings for more than 4,000 antique American firearms make Flayderman's the ultimate guide. This book is a must own for any serious collector.

Softcover • 8 ¼ x 10 7/8 • 752 pages • 1,900 b&w photos 16 page color section

Item#Z0620 $39.99

Military Small Arms of the 20th Century
7th Edition
Ian V. Hogg & John S. Weeks

This is the complete and ultimate small arms reference by Ian Hogg, international military arms authority. This book includes every arm in service from 1900-2000; complete with specifications, history and insightful commentary on performance and effectiveness. This is no comparable book.

Softcover • 8 ½ x 11 • 416 pages • 800+ b&w photos

Item# MSA7 $24.95

Standard Catalog of Civil War Firearms
by John F. Graf

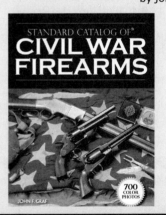

Americans are as fascinated as ever with the weapons carried by soldiers during the Civil War. With both sides struggling to keep up with the demand for guns, many manufactured models and variants exist. Because of the market for reproductions and fakes, Civil War collectors need accurate, up-to-the-minute values and this book delivers; with meticulously researched descriptions, color photographs and a rarity scale from one to five for each weapon.

Softcover • 8 ¼ x 10 7/8 • 256 pages • 650 color photos

Item# Z1784 $27.99

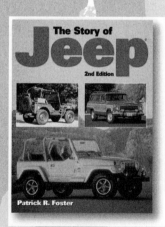